FEMINIST INTERPRETATIONS OF THOMAS HOBBES

RE-READING THE CANON

NANCY TUANA, GENERAL EDITOR

This series consists of edited collections of essays, some original and some previously published, offering feminist re-interpretations of the writings of major figures in the Western philosophical tradition. Devoted to the work of a single philosopher, each volume contains essays covering the full range of the philosopher's thought and representing the diversity of approaches now being used by feminist critics.

Already published:

Nancy Tuana, ed., *Feminist Interpretations of Plato* (1994)
Margaret Simons, ed., *Feminist Interpretations of Simone de Beauvoir* (1995)
Bonnie Honig, ed., *Feminist Interpretations of Hannah Arendt* (1995)
Patricia Jagentowicz Mills, ed., *Feminist Interpretations of G. W. F. Hegel* (1996)
Maria J. Falco, ed., *Feminist Interpretations of Mary Wollstonecraft* (1996)
Susan Hekman, ed., *Feminist Interpretations of Michel Foucault* (1996)
Nancy Holland, ed., *Feminist Interpretations of Jacques Derrida* (1997)
Robin May Schott, ed., *Feminist Interpretations of Immanuel Kant* (1997)
Céline Léon and Sylvia Walsh, eds., *Feminist Interpretations of Soren Kierkegaard* (1997)
Cynthia Freeland, ed., *Feminist Interpretations of Aristotle* (1998)
Kelly Oliver and Marilyn Pearsall, eds., *Feminist Interpretations of Friedrich Nietzsche* (1998)
Mimi Reisel Gladstein and Chris Matthew Sciabarra, eds., *Feminist Interpretations of Ayn Rand* (1999)
Susan Bordo, ed., *Feminist Interpretations of René Descartes* (1999)
Julien S. Murphy, ed., *Feminist Interpretations of Jean-Paul Sartre* (1999)
Anne Jaap Jacobson, ed., *Feminist Interpretations of David Hume* (2000)
Sarah Lucia Hoagland and Marilyn Frye, eds., *Feminist Interpretations of Mary Daly* (2000)
Tina Chanter, ed., *Feminist Interpretations of Emmanuel Levinas* (2001)
Nancy J. Holland and Patricia Huntington, eds., *Feminist Interpretations of Martin Heidegger* (2001)
Charlene Haddock Seigfried, ed., *Feminist Interpretations of John Dewey* (2001)
Naomi Scheman and Peg O'Connor, eds., *Feminist Interpretations of Ludwig Wittgenstein* (2002)
Lynda Lange, ed., *Feminist Interpretations of Jean-Jacques Rousseau* (2002)
Lorraine Code, ed., *Feminist Interpretations of Hans-Georg Gadamer* (2002)
Lynn Hankinson Nelson and Jack Nelson, eds., *Feminist Interpretations of W.V. Quine* (2003)
Maria J. Falco, ed., *Feminist Interpretations of Niccolò Machiavelli* (2004)
Renée J. Heberle, ed., *Feminist Interpretations of Theodor Adorno* (2006)
Dorothea Olkowski and Gail Weiss, eds., *Feminist Interpretations of Maurice Merleau-Ponty* (2006)
Nancy J. Hirschmann and Kirstie M. McClure, eds., *Feminist Interpretations of John Locke* (2007)
Penny A. Weiss and Loretta Kensinger, eds., *Feminist Interpretations of Emma Goldman* (2007)
Judith Chelius Stark, ed., *Feminist Interpretations of Augustine* (2007)
Jill Locke and Eileen Hunt Botting, eds., *Feminist Interpretations of Alexis de Tocqueville* (2008)
Moira Gatens, ed., *Feminist Interpretations of Benedict Spinoza* (2009)
Marianne Janack, ed., *Feminist Interpretations of Richard Rorty* (2010)
Maurice Hamington, ed., *Feminist Interpretations of Jane Addams* (2010)

FEMINIST INTERPRETATIONS OF THOMAS HOBBES

EDITED BY
NANCY J. HIRSCHMANN
AND
JOANNE H. WRIGHT

THE PENNSYLVANIA STATE UNIVERSITY PRESS
UNIVERSITY PARK, PENNSYLVANIA

Chapter 5 was previously published as Gordon J. Schochet, "Thomas Hobbes on the Family and the State of Nature," *Political Science Quarterly* 82 (September 1967): 427–45. Reprinted by permission from the Academy of Political Science.

An earlier version of chapter 9 was previously published as Wendy Gunther-Canada, "Catharine Macaulay on the Paradox of Paternal Authority in Hobbesian Politics," *Hypatia* 21 (May 2006): 150–73. © Wendy Gunther-Canada. Material used with permission from John Wiley and Sons.

Library of Congress Cataloging-in-Publication Data

Feminist interpretations of Thomas Hobbes / edited by Nancy J. Hirschmann and Joanne H. Wright.
   p.   cm.—(Re-reading the canon)
Summary: "A collection of essays analyzing the seventeenth-century British political theorist Thomas Hobbes from a feminist perspective"—Provided by publisher.
Includes bibliographical references and index.
ISBN 978-0-271-05635-7 (cloth : alk. paper)
ISBN 978-0-271-05636-4 (pbk. : alk. paper)
1. Hobbes, Thomas, 1588–1679.
2. Feminist theory.
I. Hirschmann, Nancy J.
II. Wright, Joanne H. (Joanne Harriet), 1966–

B1247.F46   2012
192—dc23
2012028428

Copyright © 2012 The Pennsylvania State University
All rights reserved
Printed in the United States of America
Published by The Pennsylvania State University Press,
University Park, PA 16802-1003

The Pennsylvania State University Press is a member of the Association of American University Presses.

It is the policy of The Pennsylvania State University Press to use acid-free paper. Publications on uncoated stock satisfy the minimum requirements of American National Standard for Information Sciences—Permanence of Paper for Printed Library Material, ANSI Z39.48-1992.

To Ross Rudolph, who first cultivated my interest in Hobbes and his world.—J.W.

To Dick Flathman, who taught me about Hobbes as much by example as by exegesis.—N.H.

Contents

Preface   ix
Nancy Tuana

Acknowledgments   xiii

Introduction: The Many Faces of "Mr. Hobs"   1
Joanne H. Wright and Nancy J. Hirschmann

1 Hobbes, History, Politics, and Gender: A Conversation with
Carole Pateman and Quentin Skinner   18
Conducted by Nancy J. Hirschmann and Joanne H. Wright

Part One: Classic Questions, New Approaches

2 Power and Sexual Subordination in Hobbes's Political Theory   47
S. A. Lloyd

3 Defending Liberal Feminism: Insights from Hobbes   63
Jane S. Jaquette

4 Hobbes and the Bestial Body of Sovereignty   83
Su Fang Ng

Part Two: The Gendered Politics of Gratitude, Contract, and the Family

5 Thomas Hobbes on the Family and the State of Nature (1967)   105
Gordon J. Schochet

6 Gordon Schochet on Hobbes, Gratitude, and Women 125
   Nancy J. Hirschmann

Part Three: Hobbes and His(torical) Women

7 Margaret Cavendish and Thomas Hobbes on Freedom,
   Education, and Women 149
   Karen Detlefsen

8 When Is a Contract Theorist Not a Contract Theorist?
   Mary Astell and Catharine Macaulay as Critics of
   Thomas Hobbes 169
   Karen Green

9 Catharine Macaulay's "Loose Remarks" on Hobbesian
   Politics 190
   Wendy Gunther-Canada

Part Four: Hobbes in the Twenty-First Century, or What Has Hobbes Done for You Lately?

10 Thomas Hobbes and the Problem of Fetal Personhood 219
   Joanne Boucher

11 Choice Talk, Breast Implants, and Feminist Consent
   Theory: Hobbes's Legacy in Choice Feminism 240
   Joanne H. Wright

12 Toward a Hobbesian Theory of Sexuality 260
   Susanne Sreedhar

   Notes on Contributors 281

   Index 285

Preface

Nancy Tuana

Take into your hands any history of philosophy text. You will find compiled therein the "classics" of modern philosophy. Since these texts are often designed for use in undergraduate classes, the editor is likely to offer an introduction in which the reader is informed that these selections represent the perennial questions of philosophy. The student is to assume that she or he is about to explore the timeless wisdom of the greatest minds of Western philosophy. No one calls attention to the fact that the philosophers are all men.

Though women are omitted from the canons of philosophy, these texts inscribe the nature of woman. Sometimes the philosopher speaks directly about woman, delineating her proper role, her abilities and inabilities, her desires. Other times the message is indirect—a passing remark hinting at women's emotionality, irrationality, unreliability.

This process of definition occurs in far more subtle ways when the central concepts of philosophy—reason and justice, those characteristics that are taken to define us as human—are associated with traits historically identified with masculinity. If the "man" of reason must learn to control or overcome traits identified as feminine—the body, the emotions, the passions—then the realm of rationality will be one reserved primarily for men,[1] with grudging entrance to those few women who are capable of transcending their femininity.

Feminist philosophers have begun to look critically at the canonized texts of philosophy and have concluded that the discourses of philosophy are not gender-neutral. Philosophical narratives do not offer a universal perspective, but rather privilege some experiences and beliefs over others. These experiences and beliefs permeate all philosophical theories whether they be aesthetic or epistemological, moral or metaphysical. Yet this fact has often been neglected by those studying the traditions of philosophy. Given the history of canon formation in Western philosophy, the perspective most likely to be privileged is that of upper-class white males. Thus, to be fully aware of the impact of gender biases, it is imperative that we re-read the canon with attention to the ways in which philosophers' assumptions concerning gender are embedded within their theories.

This series, Re-reading the Canon, is designed to foster this process of reevaluation. Each volume will offer feminist analyses of the theories of a selected philosopher. Since feminist philosophy is not monolithic in method or content, the essays are also selected to illustrate the variety of perspectives within feminist criticism and highlight some of the controversies within feminist scholarship.

In this series, feminist lenses focus on the canonical texts of Western philosophy, both those authors who have been part of the traditional canon, and those philosophers whose writings have more recently gained attention within the philosophical community. A glance at the list of volumes in the series reveals an immediate gender bias of the canon: Arendt, Aristotle, Beauvoir, Derrida, Descartes, Foucault, Hegel, Hume, Kant, Locke, Marx, Mill, Nietzsche, Plato, Rousseau, Wittgenstein, Wollstonecraft. There are all too few women included, and those few who do appear have been added only recently. In creating this series, it is not my intention to rectify the current canon of philosophical thought. What is and is not included within the canon during a particular historical period is a result of many factors. Although no canonization of texts will include all philosophers, no canonization of texts that excludes all but a few women can offer an accurate representation of the history of the discipline, as women have been philosophers since the ancient period.[2]

I share with many feminist philosophers and other philosophers writing from the margins of philosophy the concern that the current canonization of philosophy be transformed. Although I do not accept the position that the current canon has been formed exclusively by power relations, I do believe that this canon represents only a selective history of the tradition. I share the view of Michael Bérubé that "canons are at once the location, the index, and the record of the struggle for cultural representation; like any other hegemonic formation, they must be continually reproduced anew and are continually contested."[3]

The process of canon transformation will require the recovery of "lost" texts and a careful examination of the reasons such voices have been silenced. Along with the process of uncovering women's philosophical history, we must also begin to analyze the impact of gender ideologies upon the process of canonization. This process of recovery and examination must occur in conjunction with careful attention to the concept of a canon of authorized texts. Are we to dispense with the notion of a tradition of excellence embodied in a canon of authorized texts? Or, rather than abandon the whole idea of a canon, do we instead encourage a reconstruction of a canon of those texts that inform a common culture?

This series is designed to contribute to this process of canon transformation by offering a re-reading of the current philosophical canon. Such a re-reading shifts our attention to the ways in which woman and the role of the feminine are constructed within the texts of philosophy. A question we must keep in front of us during this process of re-reading is whether a philosopher's socially inherited prejudices concerning woman's nature and role are independent of her or his larger philosophical framework. In asking this question attention must be paid to the ways in which the definitions of central philosophical concepts implicitly include or exclude gendered traits.

This type of reading strategy is not limited to the canon, but can be applied to all texts. It is my desire that this series reveal the importance of this type of critical reading. Paying attention to the workings of gender within the texts of philosophy will make visible the complexities of the inscription of gender ideologies.

Notes

1. More properly, it is a realm reserved for a group of privileged males, since the texts also inscribe race and class biases that thereby omit certain males from participation.

2. Mary Ellen Waithe's multivolume series, *A History of Women Philosophers* (Boston: M. Nijoff, 1987), attests to this presence of women.

3. Michael Bérubé, *Marginal Forces/Cultural Centers: Tolson, Pynchon, and the Politics of the Canon* (Ithaca, N.Y.: Cornell University Press, 1992), 4–5.

Acknowledgments

For research and travel funds that supported various aspects of this project, Joanne Wright wishes to thank the University of New Brunswick Research Fund and the Harrison McCain Foundation Scholars Award, and Nancy Hirschmann wishes to thank the R. Jean Brownlee Endowed Term Chair and The University of Pennsylvania. We are both grateful to Sandy Thatcher, whose visionary leadership brought this important Rereading the Canon series into being and kept it going, and to Kendra Boileau for taking it up. Thanks to Julie Schoelles for her patience, skill, and flexibility in the copyediting, and to Carol Smith for transcribing the interview. Thanks also to our contributors for their patience and persistence.

Introduction

The Many Faces of "Mr. Hobs"

Joanne H. Wright and Nancy J. Hirschmann

The very idea of a volume of feminist essays on Hobbes may seem at first glance to be puzzling, if not futile.[1] As a theorist whose trademark is a relentlessly logical argument for absolute sovereignty, Hobbes may seem initially to have little to offer twenty-first-century feminist thought. Hobbes makes few references to women throughout his corpus, being explicitly concerned with political power, which—in seventeenth-century England, a period in which Elizabeth's recent reign was fodder for a burgeoning literature on patriarchal theories of politics—for the most part excluded women from its concerns. Unlike Locke, who explicitly recognized women's entitlement to authority and respect in the bourgeois family (and explicitly recognized their need to work in poor families), Hobbes's comments on women, sex, and the family are scant.

Readers of Hobbes might interpret his remarks on gender as offhand, made in passing as he moves through "larger" arguments about power, freedom, and order.

Further, Hobbes is often cast as the founding figure of a rationalist hyperindividualistic political vision that is inimical to a twentieth- and twenty-first-century feminism committed to democracy, participation, and mutual relations of care and community. Consider, for example, Jean Bethke Elshtain's early characterization in *Public Man, Private Woman* in 1981: "If Hobbes's epistemology is methodological individualism, his ontology is abstract individualism."[2] This understanding of Hobbes dominated feminist interpretations; as Christine Di Stefano noted in her influential *Configurations of Masculinity*, Hobbes's ontology demonstrated a "distinctively modern masculinist orientation to the realm of social life."[3]

Yet despite Hobbes's stark language and unsentimental portrayal of the social and political world—or possibly because of it—he has held a fascination for feminists since the early days of feminist political thought. This is especially evident in Teresa Brennan and Carole Pateman's "'Mere Auxiliaries to the Commonwealth': Women and the Origins of Liberalism" (1979) and in Pateman's later work *The Sexual Contract* (1988), both of which pay particular attention to Hobbes as a figure relevant to unpacking the politics of gender, sex, and the family.[4] At the same time, however, Hobbes has been undertreated in the history of feminist thought. None of the other early feminist classics treat Hobbes as significant enough to warrant a separate chapter. From Susan Moller Okin's *Women in Western Political Thought* and Lorenne Clark and Lynda Lange's *The Sexism of Social and Political Theory*, to Elshtain's *Public Man, Private Woman* and Zillah Eisenstein's *The Radical Future of Liberal Feminism*, Hobbes's work only merits a few pages.[5]

Did early feminists not deem his thought patriarchal enough to require deeper investigation? Or did they perhaps think that he was so far beyond rescue for feminism that a deeper investigation would be fruitless? Our contributors show that the exercise of unpacking Hobbes's assumptions about gender is worth the trouble. But the dearth of feminist analysis of Hobbes is also a product of his larger reception in political thought. In his book *Hobbes: A Very Short Introduction*, Richard Tuck suggests that Hobbes is the most undertreated of great Western thinkers—not just by feminists, but by historians of political thought of all stripes.[6] As unbelievable as this might seem, especially in light of his frequent designation as the greatest philosopher in the English language, it may be that

Hobbes's status as a theorist of absolute power writing at the outset of more liberal and, later, democratic ideas about politics has contributed to this eclipse.

As we endeavor to give Hobbes his due, as well as to acknowledge a huge debt to some of the important ground broken by the early feminist interpretations, this volume of feminist interpretations seeks to investigate more deeply what his significance for feminism might be. Ranging from an argument that the right to self-preservation may leave room for a defense of modern abortion rights, to a radical and libertarian theory of sexuality, to an understanding of the will and consent that choice feminism can deploy, to a portrayal of the powerful mother in the state of nature who becomes an outcast in civil society like the she-wolf displaced by the swineherd, feminists in this volume have plumbed a rich trove of possibility from the brilliant writings of the man from Malmesbury. This is a Hobbes who will excite some readers, horrify others, but hopefully challenge all.

Most emphatically, there is no "straw Hobbes" here, no caricatured picture of Hobbes as theorizing the "atomistic individualism," "possessive individualism," or "abstract individualism" of which feminists were enamored in the 1970s and 1980s; there is no reductionist Hobbesian man incapable of relationship, peace, or love. Rather, emerging from this collection is a picture of Hobbes that is, on the one hand, nuanced and complex, and, on the other, potentially surprising for readers, feminist and nonfeminist alike. Each one of these essays plumbs the depths of Hobbes's political thought and legacy, and each reveals a dimension or aspect of the man and his thought that broadens and renders more nuanced our overall image. As a result, we present a collection of essays, almost all original to this volume, that we hope will be of interest to a wide audience, from political theorists to specialists in early modern intellectual history and philosophy, and from feminist political theorists and philosophers, some of whom have been interested in Hobbes and others not, to Hobbes specialists, some of whom have been interested in questions of gender and others perhaps not. And like the diversity of these essays, the authors included here represent a range of disciplines, including philosophy, political science, English literature, and history—an interdisciplinarity needed to obtain the complex portrait of Hobbes that we sought.

Indeed, the diverse contributors to this volume demonstrate that Hobbesian political thought provides fertile ground for feminist inquiry.

It is fertile in that, in engaging Hobbes, feminist theory engages with what is perhaps the clearest and most influential articulation of the foundational concepts and ideas of modernity: freedom, equality, human nature, authority, consent, coercion, political obligation, gratitude, and citizenship. Hobbes's rigorous and provocative interpretation and analysis of these concepts are distinctive in the modern canon, demanding the attention not only of his contemporaries but of twenty-first-century scholars as well. Certainly, other political theorists have had more to say on the subject of women. For example, Aristotle's theory of the household in *Politics* offered considerable material for feminists to chew on, as unpalatable as it may taste to feminists today. Rousseau devoted entire chapters, such as "Sophie, or the Woman" in *Emile,* and even entire books, such as *Julie, or The New Heloise,* to commentary on women, sexuality, and the family—but again, putting forth views that arguably make him the figure whom feminists most love to hate. This certainly could explain why volumes on these figures appeared much sooner in the Rereading the Canon series than the present Hobbes volume.

At the same time, however, Hobbes stands with Plato as one of the relatively few thinkers in the canon of Western political philosophy who entertained the idea that women's subordinate position might be the result of convention rather than nature. While we would be overstating the case if we concluded that Hobbes was a feminist any more than was Plato, Hobbes's ability to consider the issue of human equality in a non-gender-specific way is a significant starting point for feminist analysis.

Hobbes's political writing is fertile ground for another reason as well. Hobbes is not only a foundational thinker but also an immensely creative and rhetorically skillful one. Since the work of Quentin Skinner, David Johnston, Richard Tuck, and others, gone is the acceptance of the earlier commonplace view of Hobbes as only interested in rational argumentation or a science of politics. Why do we still read and debate chapter 13 of *Leviathan* if not for Hobbes's ability to create a lasting image of the state of nature as "solitary, poore, nasty, brutish, and short"? In the passages in which he recounts Amazons entering sexual contracts with men of neighboring countries, who would keep the male issue, and in those in which he writes of queens and describes powerful mothers as the "lords" of their children, are many possible references, meanings, and intentions, all ripe for feminist assessment and evaluation. Thus, we believe that Hobbes does have something quite valuable to offer twenty-first-century feminism, even if it is not a progressive theory in support of women's liberation: at his best, he offers a vision of strong, powerful women who can contract with men, raise children independently (maternity being the first political right), and protect their own interests in the state of nature. At the very least, he offers an opportunity to engage and analyze some of the most provocative, problematic, and challenging arguments of Western modernity concerning the place of women in the family—which, admittedly, are highly ambiguous—and the meaning of gender itself.

As the first collection of essays dedicated exclusively to feminist interpretation of Hobbes, this volume is meant to redress his frequent absence from feminist interpretation. The book is a testament to how far the enterprise of feminist political theory has come, from posing the initial questions about women's absence from political texts, and mining the brief references to women in those texts, to querying a whole range of other issues, such as: What are the gendered implications and legacies of Hobbes's political thought, especially his ideas of the citizen, the commonwealth, freedom, equality, and the social contract? What women did Hobbes have in mind when he wrote about Amazons and queens, and what powerful women did he encounter who might have influenced his thinking? Also, were there women writers and thinkers whom Hobbes might have seen as interlocutors but whom we have written out of intellectual history and especially the history of political thought? By asking different questions of Hobbes, feminist political theory shows its maturity and generates a range of different answers, not all of which can be fully reconciled.

Thus, we make no claims to presenting a unified image of Hobbes in the way that Hobbes sought a unified sovereign. Indeed, we are not sure that Hobbes can be all of the things our contributors say he is at one and the same time: Can he be a political theorist interested in forging bonds of community, as some contributors suggest, while also seeking to close opportunities for resistance, as others assert? Can his arguments open avenues for libertarian sexuality, as some provocatively demonstrate, while also using the concept of gratitude to suggest that subjects owe the sovereign their obedience because they owe him or her their lives, as others argue? Yet what we are sure of is that each of these authors stakes out a strong theoretical position that is worthy of exploration and that leads us down fruitful paths of interpretation.

The volume opens with a conversation between two centrally important interpreters: Carole Pateman and Quentin Skinner. Among feminist interpretations of Hobbes and other canonical "fathers," Pateman's is the most influential in drawing attention to the ellipses in Hobbes's thought with respect to gender. Hobbes is notorious for his rather unconventional suggestion of women's and men's equality in the state of nature, a line of argument that is quickly left behind once he makes his case for the necessity of the social contract. In *The Sexual Contract*, as well as in her article "'God Hath Ordained to Man a Helper,'" Pateman argued that Hobbes retained some aspects of patriarchalism in his political thought while eschewing others, and that the social contract was preceded by a hidden sexual contract that subordinated all women to all men.[7] Pateman's reading of Hobbes exposed the ways in which political theorists' arguments about vital concepts, such as freedom and citizenship, are embedded with assumptions about gender and women's status—assumptions that will remain invisible unless they are deliberately drawn out. *The Sexual Contract* also opened the door for broader feminist inquiry into social contract theory itself (as well as influencing critical race theory, such as Charles Mills's *The Racial Contract*) and led feminists to take notice of this important device as a mechanism of patriarchal thinking.[8] Indeed, virtually all contemporary feminist interpretations of social contract theory and of Hobbes—even those that question her approach or conclusions—build upon the important foundation laid by Pateman, expanding its parameters and bringing a variety of disciplinary and theoretical perspectives to bear on Hobbes's texts.[9]

Approaching Hobbes's texts from a different angle and with a different set of interests and questions is Quentin Skinner, the leading thinker of what can loosely be called the "Cambridge school." If we are to truly understand Hobbes, according to Skinner, we must see him as a writer engaged in a political conversation with his mid-seventeenth-century Civil War contemporaries, using the terms and language available to him in the period. For Skinner and other historical interpreters of Hobbes, what matters most is understanding how Hobbes saw his own enterprise, uncovering, to the extent possible, what his own intentions and motivations might have been. It is this approach that has guided Skinner's most important works on Hobbes, and the results of this approach have fundamentally changed the dominant reading of Hobbes.[10] Far from being a straightforward apologist for bourgeois property relations, or a cold rationalist or international realist, Hobbes was a writer equipped with the tools of a Renaissance humanist—tools he found to be as important as rational argumentation, if not more so, in the effort to persuade his contemporaries about his theory of politics. Just as Pateman initiated new discoveries with regard to the political significance of social contract theory, Skinner has given us a new sense of Hobbes the man and the writer, one far more nuanced and interesting than was evident previously.

Although these two illustrious scholars of political thought engaged in a critical exchange on democratic theory in the journal *Political Theory* in 1973 and 1974, they have never dialogued in this manner about Hobbes.[11] In their conversation here, Pateman and Skinner highlight what are, from their perspectives, the central problems to be addressed. For Pateman, it is most important to shine a bright light on "aspects of [Hobbes's] argument that are typically glossed over" in traditional analysis, while for Skinner the central goal is to "treat individual texts essentially as contributions" to "some preexisting tradition of discussion and debate." One of the reasons we proposed this conversation was that the two schools—feminist approaches to political theory, and the so-called Cambridge school—have not generally intersected.[12] Indeed, the approach to reading historical texts that has most influenced Pateman—a combination of the analytical and neo-Marxist approach evidenced by C. B. Macpherson—is the very approach with which Skinner's earliest work on Hobbes took issue. Like other historians of political thought, Skinner was concerned about anachronistic readings of Hobbes that had him responding to and thinking about things well outside his field of vision. Pateman's forward-looking conclusions, that Hobbes remained committed to a modern form of fraternal patriarchy even as he did away with the older, paternal variant, are bound to be in tension with Skinner's, since the historical sensitivity associated with the Cambridge school prevents consideration of a seventeenth-century theorist through twenty-first-century lenses.

This conversation is one we find valuable and remarkable on several levels. The differences not only between the two schools represented, but also between our respondents' respective disciplines of political science and history, mark various productive tensions about the roles, place, and even possibility of feminism in the history of political thought. Is scholarship in the history of political thought becoming more attuned to gender, as Skinner claims, and is there more of an accepted background assumption that gender matters? Or are the majority of scholars still tone-deaf to feminist arguments about the centrality of gender, as Pateman claims? How do answers to those questions differ by disciplinary norms of history, political science, philosophy, and literature—all represented in this volume? What are the best approaches to take for those interested in questions of gender in canonical figures? How should we combine the attention to context that Skinner urges with the attention to the logic of the argument that Pateman insists on, when it seems that these different approaches reveal different interpretations of the place of gender in canonical texts?

In terms of Hobbes interpretation specifically, the dialogue leads to additional challenging questions: Is all feminist interpretation of Hobbes historically anachronistic because it considers the role of gender, a concept unfamiliar to seventeenth-century writers? Does adherence to a historical reading risk overlooking important power dynamics at work, dynamics that may remain invisible unless we locate ourselves in our own time and political context? How are Hobbes's patriarchalist aspects to be measured against his gender-egalitarian ones? Are these two approaches represented by Pateman's and Skinner's work immiscible, or the source of some productive tensions? We ourselves found the interaction to offer fascinating insights into possibilities for both feminist and historical interpretation, Hobbesian analysis, and political theory more generally. In discussing these different approaches explicitly, we gain greater insight into each of them and have opportunities to see areas of overlapping interest, including a consideration of how Hobbes viewed the gender of sovereignty, the significance of his concept of the family, the impact of our increasing awareness of seventeenth-century women political writers on the enterprise of Hobbes interpretation, and, finally, the future of Hobbesian interpretation and his ongoing relevance to the politics of the twenty-first century. We think this exchange makes a vital contribution to the field. As the interviewers and editors, we have tried to preserve the freshness of the conversation, leaving provocative openings that invite further thinking. We hope that the reader will enjoy seeing firsthand what these two important intellectuals had to say to each other.

The essays that follow this interview explore a wide range of approaches and substantive topics that reflect the changes that have taken place in feminist re-readings of the canon and particularly of Hobbes. Building upon this conversation and especially upon the classic questions posed by both Pateman's and Skinner's work, the first section of essays focuses on some of the key concepts of political theory, such as sovereignty and the meaning of commonwealth, as well as women's absence from civil society, but with some significant differences. Sharon Lloyd's essay begins by posing the question that confronts all feminists reading Hobbes: Did women freely consent to their own subordination and, if so, why? This question was, of course, the animating source of Pateman's (and before that, Brennan and Pateman's) earlier work, but Lloyd's essay will give the reader who is unfamiliar with feminism a good introduction to many of the central issues that feminists have highlighted over the past several decades and will set the stage for the articles that follow. Lloyd runs through the textual evidence of Hobbes's use of gender but, in contrast to many earlier feminist analyses of Hobbes, posits that there is nothing inherently misogynistic about his concepts or thought—although she does find evidence of a stowaway sexism. What Lloyd calls her "just so" analysis centers on the working of power in Hobbes's thought; she argues that there may be enough small differences of power and strength between the sexes, which, when added up, create an even larger gulf and cause women to enter into pre-civil contracts to ensure their own survival. Yet Lloyd's conclusion is not Pateman's, and she is clear that there is nothing in Hobbes that necessitates that things move in favor of institutionalized patriarchy—it might have gone the other way, maybe even toward matriarchy.

Jane Jaquette takes up similar themes of exploring the degree to which patriarchy is inevitable for Hobbes, or just happenstance, and she writes in a similar, if more provocative, vein of trying to recuperate a more sympathetic reading of Hobbes out of the standard observations and criticisms that feminists tend to emphasize. Most theorists, intellectual historians, and philosophers would not consider Hobbes a liberal, given his advocacy of absolute authority, and many feminists reject both Hobbes and liberalism as not adequately serving the interests of women. In contrast to Elshtain and others, however, Jaquette positions Hobbes as an important contributor to liberalism and thereby to contemporary liberal feminism. Jaquette wishes "to defend the core liberal values present in Hobbes" and urges feminism to come to terms with the debt it owes him, to discover how it depends on liberal political values. Critiquing "radical" feminist interpretations of Hobbes—readings that throw out the baby of freedom, equality, and individual choice with the bathwater of abstract individualism, authoritarian patriarchalism, and the natural subordination of women—she seeks to develop a reading of Hobbes that can be useful for feminists of the twenty-first century.

By contrast, drawing on Skinner's discussion of the gender neutrality of sovereignty, a topic that surfaces in the conversation between Pateman and Skinner, Su Fang Ng considers what she calls its "bestial nature" and comes to a somewhat less favorable conclusion than either Lloyd or Jaquette. Hobbes's portrayal of the original sovereignty of mothers in the state of nature, she suggests, is influenced by the myth of the suckling she-wolf who becomes an important marker of the boundary between the natural and civil states. In a parallel move, she argues, the state itself becomes ungendered and women are excluded from it. This creates more than just an ambiguity about women's place in Hobbes's theory; it shows that gender both underwrites and threatens incoherence for the Hobbesian state—which may be why Hobbes's consideration of women is not explicitly elaborated in his text but is instead buried inside other stories, leaving today's feminist scholars to unearth and decipher it. Yet, Ng's conclusions nevertheless leave spaces for an optimistic reading; specifically, she suggests that Hobbes finds gendered forms of sovereignty to be primitive, and that in degendering political right, Hobbes "leaves room for new forms of civil engagement by men or women."

The second section of the volume in many ways contributes to the project of the first, but with a specific thematic focus. As influential for feminist scholarship on Hobbes as was *The Sexual Contract* is the early work of Gordon Schochet, whose groundbreaking essay on Hobbes, patriarchalism, and the family is included here. "Thomas Hobbes on the Family and the State of Nature" appeared in *Political Science Quarterly* in 1967—before "feminist theory" was even a bona fide subfield in the academy. It was subsequently included as a chapter in his equally groundbreaking book *Patriarchalism in Political Thought*. Schochet himself, of course, did not write this piece as a work in feminist theory; as Nancy Hirschmann points out in her commentary on the essay, Schochet did not have specifically feminist questions in mind when he first plumbed Hobbes's thought on the family. But his work nevertheless led feminists down the important road of investigating what Hobbes was trying to do with his familial analogy. Influenced by, but not wedded to, the methodologies of historical interpretation, he is cited in many early feminist interpretations of Hobbes, including Pateman's *The Problem of Political Obligation* and Christine Di Stefano's *Configurations of Masculinity*, as well as significant journal articles by feminist scholars such as Elizabeth Fox Genovese, Mary Shanley, Virginia Sapiro, Ruth Bloch, and Ruth Perry.[13] Acting as a bridge between these different approaches within political thought, Schochet's essay is also important for having raised the issue of patriarchalism and the role of the family among a generation of Hobbes scholars who paid these issues little attention. In later work, Schochet went on to address more explicitly the gendered dimensions of Filmer's and Locke's thought and the "significant sounds of silence" surrounding the gender question—sounds that get replicated in the work of historians of political thought as well. For all these reasons, it is fitting to include this original essay that influenced and indeed arguably motivated decades of feminist analysis.[14]

In her chapter, Hirschmann links Schochet's earlier essay with his more recent work through the concept of gratitude. Gratitude is Hobbes's fourth law of nature, but as such it has received much less attention than Schochet and Hirschmann believe it deserves. Hirschmann takes Schochet's original essay and teases out its various claims and inconsistencies, pushing it to answer to more explicitly feminist interests, including the question of what happens to women once the civil contract is in place and why. Hirschmann and Schochet agree that gratitude is the "linchpin of Hobbes's theory" and that the family serves as a foundation for the state, but Hirschmann argues, against both Schochet and Pateman, that marriage does not precede but rather follows the social contract. If Schochet and thereby Pateman are correct that marriage does precede the social contract, then the only possible explanation for women's ultimate subordination in civil society must stem from their gratitude toward men who spared their lives in the state of nature. Hirschmann finds this possibility useful for its explanatory ability, but ultimately problematic for a feminist recuperation of Hobbes.

Taking up the current scholarly interest in women's political thought, the third section of the book includes three essays dealing with Hobbes and the historical women who read and responded to him. Signaling an important development in feminist political theory, this scholarly trajectory is guided by the recognition that for too long we have read male thinkers as the only authoritative sources on key political issues facing all human beings. Although feminists have long understood women to be active political subjects, and have demonstrated how women have exercised political agency throughout history and into the present, the move to integrate women's writings on politics into the history of ideas has been slow to follow. The essays in this section survey three women whose critiques of and responses to Hobbes resonate nicely with later feminist analysis: Margaret Cavendish (1623–1673), Mary Astell (1666–1731), and Catharine Macaulay (1731–1791).

In the first of these chapters, Karen Detlefsen considers the one woman philosopher and writer who knew and conversed with Hobbes, even if it was only because of her marriage to one of Hobbes's patrons, William Cavendish, Duke of Newcastle. Margaret Cavendish had direct access to the most learned circle of individuals in the seventeenth century, which included figures such as Descartes, Gassendi, and Hobbes. There is immense scholarly interest in Cavendish today, primarily among literary historians but also increasingly among philosophers interested in the early modern period. Thus, an examination of Cavendish's and Hobbes's mutual intellectual influence and relationship has potential to yield a different kind of feminist interpretation of Hobbes.[15] As William's friend, employee, and interlocutor, Hobbes spent time in the Cavendish household but likely exchanged little in the way of conversation with Margaret. As she put it, "I never spake with Master Hobbes twenty words in my life."[16] This is in no way surprising since women in the seventeenth century were not supposed to be the intellectual equals of men and were often limited by their inability to understand or read Latin; and Cavendish, by her own account, was reserved and shy around people outside her immediate family.[17] Cavendish might have caught more of the male conversations than she let on, however, for according to Detlefsen, Cavendish's thoughts on freedom were in direct response to Hobbes, and they offer a "proto-feminist" conception of freedom and the individual. Detlefsen treats Cavendish's plays as relevant texts of political philosophy, particularly revealing Cavendish's theory of freedom, and draws on her more overtly philosophical writings to justify her interpretation. She thereby shows that whereas Hobbes's theory takes a strong individualist view, as has been argued and documented by many scholars of Hobbes, Cavendish assumes a more social individual, one who "freely chooses to pursue actions conceived of in terms of how the agent relates to others, close and distant," in keeping with twentieth- and twenty-first-century feminist accounts of "relational autonomy." Yet her account of free will is much more robust than that of Hobbes, who reduced will to desire and saw it paradoxically entwined with necessity. Detlefsen maintains that Cavendish "provides a view of women's freedom that escapes some of the less advantageous aspects of Hobbes's own view."

Drawing on the ideas of both Mary Astell and Catharine Macaulay as early and cogent critics of Hobbes's social contract theory, Karen Green, like Jane Jaquette, questions the tendency of contemporary feminists to dismiss liberalism as having no value for the feminist project. But in contrast to Jaquette, Green's intent is not to defend Hobbes and liberalism but rather to drive a bigger wedge between the two. Green posits the need to look beyond Hobbes to a broader tradition of women intellectuals who contributed vitally to the foundation of liberal democracy. For example, neither an advocate of rights nor an easy figure for feminists to celebrate, Astell anticipated later feminist critiques of Hobbes by questioning his portrayal of human beings as perfectly autonomous in the state of nature as well as his equation of consent and coercion. In looking back to women's political thought, Green makes a case for a more complex understanding of the roots of liberalism as lying especially in the eighteenth-century republican ideas of Macaulay. In her little-known *Treatise on the Immutability of Moral Truth*, Macaulay offers a non-Hobbesian argument for a social contract between the people and their rulers based not on consent but on trust. Keeping alive a negative reading of Hobbes for his "egoistic, instrumental rationality," Green's chapter encourages feminist readers to like Hobbes less while perhaps liking liberalism a little bit more.

Wendy Gunther-Canada's chapter continues the conversation on Hobbes with both Pateman and Schochet, centering on Macaulay as an early Hobbesian interpreter who offers her own "challenge to the metanarrative of patriarchy in early modern political thought." Gunther-Canada draws our attention to the historical antecedents to Pateman's critique of Hobbes: in her *Loose Remarks* on Hobbes, Macaulay had also noted the convoluted dimensions to Hobbes's patriarchalism. Cleaving more to the view of Hobbes as a rational individualist thinker, this chapter develops a contrast between what Gunther-Canada calls the calculus of force, which lies behind Hobbes's social contract, and the calculation of care, which she sees lying behind Macaulay's contractual vision. The contrast between force and care that Gunther-Canada identifies is, indeed, evident in a number of the chapters in the present volume.

In the final section of the book, we move some distance away from questions that could have been of interest to Hobbes and more directly into the territory of feminism's current preoccupations. Of course, it can be a challenge bordering on anachronism to theorize about canonical thinkers in terms of issues that press on our contemporary political consciousness. Our students often ask what Hobbes, or Plato, or Hegel, would have thought about the invasion of Iraq, or gay marriage, or other issues of twenty-first-century significance, and we often caution them about making conjectures on a theorist's position on a problem he or she could never have even imagined, much less ever actually addressed. Yet feminist analysis is always concerned with issues facing the women of today, and the project of drawing lessons from the canonical thinkers in ways that may help us think through those issues is a valid and important one. Joanne Boucher and Joanne Wright are less concerned with what Hobbes would think about abortion or breast implants, but rather more with how feminist thinking about Hobbesian concepts and categories of analysis can help us, as twenty-first-century feminists, think about those issues.

Boucher locates Hobbes's argument about self-defense as a potential source of support for abortion rights, noting that even though the sovereign has absolute authority, derived from his or her subjects' consent, to make whatever laws he or she wants—including laws to outlaw abortion—Hobbes also allows that if such laws endanger citizens' lives, they revert to a state of nature. Since it is never in the sovereign's interest to create such conditions, the sovereign would likely permit abortion. Such a position has particular resonance for contemporary thinking about the Supreme Court's decision in *Gonzales v. Carhart,* which outlaws certain kinds of late-term abortions—specifically, the "intact" D&C, or "partial-birth" abortion—even though it is notably safer for the woman than the "standard" D&C, which the court let stand and which requires the repeated insertion of sharp instruments into the woman's vagina to dismember the fetus in utero, thus greatly increasing the chances of perforation, infection, and death. The court's romanticized concern with the potential well-being of a fetus at the expense of the actual well-being of the female citizen is one that Hobbes would have likely decried on grounds of consistency, if nothing else, since in either procedure the fetus is being killed. What seems more important to the court is the "gruesomeness" of what the male observer is obliged to see.[18] Hobbesian thinking about the sovereign's responsibilities to subjects is well worth consideration by feminists today as they engage with women's status as citizens denied the rights of protection that the liberal state is supposed to provide.

Joanne Wright similarly takes up issues of immediate political concern for feminism: the rise of choice feminism and its defense of elective cosmetic surgery. In particular, she is interested in the legacy left to contemporary liberal society by Hobbes's analysis of consent and the will. For his own political reasons, Hobbes was interested in decentering the problem of coercion and demonstrating through his materialist understanding of the will and freedom that all of our actions are voluntary and a direct reflection of our own will. Yet, from the beginning, feminism has sought to problematize such a collapse of consent and coercion and to show that, although women may appear to be consenting to the dictates of patriarchal society, their consent is underwritten by relations of power and oppression, and so should not necessarily be understood to be an accurate reflection of their abstract "free will." To draw a line between legitimate and illegitimate consent, while nonsensical to Hobbes, is essential to the project of feminism. Yet this distinction has been all but abandoned in this new era of choice feminism, a feminism that is both liberal and Hobbesian in its celebration of choice as the benchmark of freedom, and which is used to justify women's participation in a pernicious "makeover culture."

Susanne Sreedhar returns us to more traditional terrain of exegetical analysis of Hobbes's texts, but by focusing on a topic that is central to twenty-first-century feminism, namely sex and sexuality. She mines Hobbes's various remarks about sexuality, particularly his references to the Amazons, finding no normative basis for a specific sexual practice and no indication of his moral judgment on sex. Sreedhar uncovers evidence for a more positive vision of Hobbes than we might expect, as potentially sexually progressive and, reminiscent of Lloyd's essay, as "neither irredeemably nor even consistently misogynistic." Indeed, this is perhaps the most positive light cast on Hobbes in this volume. Yet Sreedhar is also mindful of the countervailing evidence for such a portrayal, especially the fact that, once the sovereign is in place, Hobbes would have no quarrel with any positive law that severely limits sexual freedom—a fear linking Sreedhar's and Boucher's chapters and echoed in Hirschmann's suggestion about how patriarchy comes to be. Nor does Hobbes have any moral objection to sexual coercion, for, as we have seen, he strategically blurs the distinction between consent and coercion. Thus, once again, a nuanced understanding is called for, one that sees Hobbes's writings—at least in this respect—as potentially but not necessarily an ally to feminism.

Indeed, a multilayered reading is what we hope to have achieved in this volume. If readers come away from these essays with a more complicated vision of what Hobbes has to offer, on the one hand, and the multiple ways in which feminists can read, interpret, and use Hobbes's texts and ideas, on the other, we will consider the exercise of *Feminist Interpretations of Thomas Hobbes* a success. Of course, there may be no clear answer to the question of what exactly Hobbes offers to feminism, as the opinions here are divided and in some cases the feminist critique of his system of thought is deepened. But what is clear is that there is something to be gained in engaging with Hobbes, on his own terms as well as on ours, as we continue the process of clarifying and analyzing feminist priorities.

Notes

1. With regard to the title of this chapter, in an era of nonstandardized spelling Hobbes's contemporaries referred to him variously as Mr. Hobbes, Mr. Hobbs, or even Mr. Hobs. See, for example, Sir Robert Filmer, *Observations Concerning the Original and Various Forms of Government* (London, 1696), in which he addresses "Mr. Hobbs's Laviathan," and *Observations Concerning the Originall of Government, upon Mr Hobs 'Leviathan,' Mr Milton Against Salmasius, H Grotius 'De Jure Belli,'* in *Filmer: 'Patriarcha' and Other Writings*, ed. Johann P. Sommerville (New York: Cambridge University Press, 1991), 184–234.

2. Jean Bethke Elshtain, *Public Man, Private Woman: Women in Social and Political Thought*, 2nd ed. (Princeton, N.J.: Princeton University Press, 1993), 109.

3. Christine Di Stefano, *Configurations of Masculinity: A Feminist Perspective on Modern Political Theory* (Ithaca, N.Y.: Cornell University Press, 1991).

4. Teresa Brennan and Carole Pateman, "'Mere Auxiliaries to the Commonwealth': Women and the Origins of Liberalism," *Political Studies* 27, no. 2 (1979): 183–200; Carole Pateman, *The Sexual Contract* (Stanford: Stanford University Press, 1988). See Brennan and Pateman's twenty-first-century reflections on their article in "Afterword: Mere Auxiliaries to the Commonwealth in an Age of Globalization," in *Feminist Interpretations of John Locke*, ed. Nancy J. Hirschmann and Kirstie M. McClure (University Park: Pennsylvania State University Press, 2007), 75–90.

5. Susan Moller Okin, *Women in Western Political Thought* (Princeton, N.J.: Princeton University Press, 1979); Lorenne Clark and Lynda Lange, eds., *The Sexism of Social and Political Theory: Women and Reproduction from Plato to Nietzsche* (Toronto: University of Toronto Press, 1979); Zillah Eisenstein, *The Radical Future of Liberal Feminism* (New York: Longman, 1981).

6. Richard Tuck, *Hobbes: A Very Short Introduction* (Oxford: Oxford University Press, 2002), xi.

7. Pateman, *Sexual Contract*; Carole Pateman, "'God Hath Ordained to Man a Helper': Hobbes, Patriarchy, and Conjugal Right," *British Journal of Political Science* 19, no. 4 (1989): 445–64.

8. Charles W. Mills, *The Racial Contract* (Ithaca, N.Y.: Cornell University Press, 1999). See also Nancy J. Hirschmann, *Rethinking Obligation: A Feminist Method for Political Theory* (Ithaca, N.Y.: Cornell University Press, 1992), and Nancy Hirschmann and Carole Pateman, "Political Obligation, Freedom, and Feminism," *American Political Science Review* 86, no. 1 (1992): 179–88.

9. See, for instance, Joanne H. Wright, *Origin Stories in Political Thought: Discourses on Gender, Power, and Citizenship* (Toronto: University of Toronto Press, 2004); Joanne Boucher, "Male Power and Contract Theory: Hobbes and Locke in Carole Pateman's *The Sexual Contract*," *Canadian Journal of Political Science* 36, no. 1 (2003): 23–38; and Jane S. Jaquette, "Contract and Coercion: Power and Gender in *Leviathan*," in *Women Writers and the Early Modern British Political Tradition*, ed. Hilda L. Smith (Cambridge: Cambridge University Press, 1998), 200–219.

10. See particularly Quentin Skinner's *Hobbes and Republican Liberty* (Cambridge: Cambridge University Press, 2008) and *Reason and Rhetoric in the Philosophy of Hobbes* (New York: Cambridge University Press, 1997).

11. Quentin Skinner, "The Empirical Theorists of Democracy and Their Critics: A Plague on Both Their Houses," *Political Theory* 1, no. 3 (1973): 287–306; Carole Pateman, "Criticising Empirical Theorists of Democracy: A Comment on Skinner," *Political Theory* 2, no. 2 (1974): 215–18.

12. And some would deny that there is such a thing as the Cambridge school at all. However, for our purposes, it makes sense to group historical interpreters together as guided by the principles Skinner outlines.

13. Elizabeth Fox Genovese, "Property and Patriarchy in Classical Bourgeois Political Theory," *Radical History Review* 4, nos. 2–3 (1977): 36–59; Mary Lyndon Shanley, "Marriage Contract and Social Contract in Seventeenth Century Political Thought," *Western Political Quarterly* 32, no. 1 (1979): 79–91; Virginia Sapiro, "Research Frontier Essay: When Are Interests Interesting? The Problem of Political Representation of Women," *American Political Science Review* 75, no. 3 (1981): 701–16; Ruth H. Bloch, "The Gendered Meanings of Virtue in Revolutionary America," *Signs* 13, no. 1 (1987): 37–58; Ruth Perry, "Mary Astell and the Feminist Critique of Possessive Individualism," *Eighteenth-Century Studies* 23, no. 4 (1990): 444–57.

14. Gordon Schochet, "The Significant Sounds of Silence: The Absence of Women from the Political Thought of Sir Robert Filmer and John Locke (or, 'Why Can't a Woman Be More Like a Man?')," in Smith, *Women Writers and the Early Modern British Political Tradition*, 220–42.

15. See Lisa Sarasohn, "*Leviathan* and the Lady: Cavendish's Critique of Hobbes in the *Philosophical Letters*," in *Authorial Conquests: Essays on Genre in the Writings of Margaret Cavendish*, ed. Line Cottegnies and Nancy Weitz (Madison, N.J.: Fairleigh Dickinson University Press, 2003), 40–58; Sara Hutton, "In Dialogue with Thomas Hobbes: Margaret Cavendish's Natural Philosophy," *Women's Writing* 4, no. 3 (1997): 421–32; and Anna Battigelli, *Margaret Cavendish and the Exiles of the Mind* (Lexington: University Press of Kentucky, 1998).

16. Quoted in Katie Whitaker, *Mad Madge: The Extraordinary Life of Margaret Cavendish* (New York: Basic Books, 2002), 94.

17. Ibid., 26.

18. *Gonzales v. Carhart*, 127 S. Ct. 1610, 1626 (2007). Justice Ruth Bader Ginsberg's dissent on the sexist hypocrisy of the court is blistering. See also Nancy J. Hirschmann, "Stem Cells, Disability, and Abortion: A Feminist Approach to Equal Citizenship," in *Gender Equality: Dimensions of Women's Equal Citizenship*, ed. Linda C. McClain and Joanna L. Grossman (Cambridge: Cambridge University Press, 2009), 154–73.

1

Hobbes, History, Politics, and Gender

A Conversation with Carole Pateman and Quentin Skinner

Conducted by Nancy J. Hirschmann and Joanne H. Wright

Nancy J. Hirschmann and Joanne H. Wright asked Carole Pateman and Quentin Skinner to meet with them to talk about Hobbes and feminism. They kindly agreed. This text is the result.

NH: Each of you is a leading representative, perhaps even the founding figure, of a different school of Hobbes scholarship and criticism: the Cambridge school and feminism. So it might be a helpful place to start if each of you could talk about your respective orientation, your view of the school, as well as your own individual approach within that larger framework. What is its and your primary orientation in thinking about Hobbes, what kinds of questions do you think the approach helps uncover, what sorts of puzzles does it help resolve? How, in your opinion, have your respective approaches helped us understand Hobbes better and in what ways?

CP: The very first feminist paper that I published about Hobbes was in 1979, "Mere Auxiliaries to the Commonwealth." I did not do it alone; I wrote the piece with Teresa Brennan, and as I recall (though it was a long time ago and sadly I cannot ask her now), one of the important contributions that Teresa made was to notice how odd Hobbes's accounts of the family were. In only one definition does he actually mention the mother; otherwise it is an entirely male entity, which obviously is very peculiar.

Apart from the article with Teresa (which was about Locke as well as Hobbes), I wrote a chapter on Hobbes in my book on political obligation, also first published in 1979. Some of my work on the book and the paper with Teresa was going on at roughly the same time. In 1988, my argument on Hobbes in *The Sexual Contract* drew on them both. *The Problem of Political Obligation* only has scattered references to women and feminist arguments, but in the afterword to the second edition (1985) I had more to say about how feminist insights challenge and can change conventional interpretations of one basic problem, political obligation, in political theory. By the mid-1980s, I had begun to see more clearly—it took me a long time—how feminist arguments (and in the early days most of them were from outside academia) made a difference to the work I was doing in political theory. In 1989, I published "'God Hath Ordained to Man a Helper': Hobbes, Patriarchy, and Conjugal Right," a feminist interpretation of Hobbes in which I considered why it was that Hobbes, a thoroughgoing conventionalist, could be seen as a Filmerian patriarchalist, yet his transformation of naturally free and equal women into subordinated wives in civil society could be completely overlooked. That is to say, I raised the question of why commentators on Hobbes and political theorists more generally invariably ignored conjugal right— men's power as husbands over wives—as a political problem.

What kind of questions do I think that my approach helps resolve? It helps to understand Hobbes much better if you have a feminist perspective, which highlights aspects of his argument that are typically glossed over. For instance, something that hardly anyone had noticed, or if they had noticed they quickly moved along and didn't mention it, was that Hobbes is the only theorist of an original contract who begins with men and women as equals in the state of nature. Feminists take Hobbes seriously on this point, and this was the basis for our argument in "Mere Auxiliaries" about how and why wives posed an embarrassing problem in political theory. To begin from the premise of natural freedom and equality and assume that the sexes are naturally equal poses a major problem about how wives become subordinate to their husbands in civil society. Neither Hobbes nor his commentators provided an explanation; no one had treated it as a problem and obviously did not want to.

Another feminist insight into Hobbes is that—given that in his state of nature there are no matrimonial laws, no marriage—marriage, along with everything else, is conventional; it is created as a political construct along with civil society. And that is something else that political theorists have been, and many still are, very loath to acknowledge; marriage and the family are so often treated as natural, not conventional, institutions. So these are two problems that a feminist approach raises.

QS: The first article I published was on Hobbes's *Leviathan*—it was even called "Hobbes's *Leviathan*." That was in 1964, and then I published a series of articles on Hobbes over the next five years. During that period, I also began to worry about the idea of interpretation, especially because at that time Marxist assumptions about historical explanation rather held the field in Hobbes scholarship, particularly through the work of Christopher Hill and C. B. Macpherson. There seemed to me something deeply wrong with their approach, and my efforts to think out my own position caused me to devote myself for a period in the late 1960s to mid-1970s exclusively to the study of philosophical questions about interpretation, which I eventually published as a book called *Regarding Method*.

My general approach stems from a desire to make a strong distinction between the attempt to recover meanings and the attempt to recover speech acts. I am interested, that is, not just in the meaning of what is said, but in what is meant by what is said. I make a kind of Wittgensteinian move in which the emphasis is placed on the use of concepts rather than on attempts to recover the alleged meanings of the terms used to express them.

I still want to cleave to that fundamental distinction. It has never troubled me that the first pole—the attempt to recover meanings and especially intended meanings—ran into (and deservedly ran into) serious criticism from postmodernist critics in the course of the late 1960s, especially after the publication of Derrida's *Grammatologie* in 1967 and everything that flowed from that. Derrida's critique of the project of recovering intended meaning always seemed to me basically right. I am not interested so much in that pole of interpretation as in the other—that is to say, in the understanding of the underlying purposes for the sake of which particular concepts are used. This approach has pointed me in a strongly "death of the author" direction. I have wanted to say that most of the works of moral and political theory that we study historically need to be construed as interventions in some preexisting tradition of discussion and debate, so I have wanted to treat individual texts essentially as contributions to those broader discourses. A major part of the act of interpretation, I have proposed, consists of recovering the precise nature of the intervention constituted by any given text: How far did it support or question or develop or ignore or satirize (or whatever) existing conventions and traditions of discourse? This was the approach I tried first to apply to Hobbes, but then in the 1970s I wrote a more general book, *The Foundations of Modern Political Thought*, which was organized according to these ideas.

The way in which I have tried to apply my approach to Hobbes has been reflected in two books. The first, which I called *Reason and Rhetoric in the Philosophy of Hobbes*, was published in 1996, and the second, *Hobbes and Republican Liberty*, appeared in 2008. What I tried to do, especially in the first of these studies, was to show something that I thought hadn't been properly recognized in the secondary literature. To make my point, I tried to situate Hobbes in the intellectual and cultural and, above all, educational context in which he was formed. What I tried to show was that his formation was recognizably that of a rhetorically educated student of the humanities, that he was a late Renaissance humanist intellectual.

Hobbes presented himself in later life, especially in his autobiography, as a man who went to Oxford and was taught a lot of scholastic nonsense, which he then threw away, finally arriving at his distinctive and purely materialist ontology by way of his discussions with the leading lights of the scientific revolution in France. This is a complete fabrication. Hobbes was initially educated at a grammar school where he was brought to an extraordinary level of proficiency in the classical languages—so that, for example, his parting gift to his schoolteacher was a translation of the *Medea* from Greek into Latin verse. His basic education was in the classical languages. Moreover, if you read the statutes of the University of Oxford in force during the time when Hobbes was an undergraduate, you find that what he studied at university included a great deal of classical rhetoric, especially Quintilian and Cicero, as well as ancient literature, including Homer and Horace. These were all prescribed texts in the university ordinances. Finally, Hobbes's first publication fully reflected this formation as a humanist intellectual, for it took the form of the earliest translation of Thucydides's history ever made directly from Greek into English.

I wanted to say that Hobbes's basic formation always remained with him. In particular, I wanted to highlight the extent to which *Leviathan* is a humanist text. Not only is it one of the great works of seventeenth-century prose, but it's also a Renaissance satire. I could summarize the sort of thing I was trying to show by saying that, while we associate Hobbes with writers like Descartes, we could equally well associate him with Rabelais. The *Leviathan* is a text in which the weapons of ridicule that Hobbes had learned from his rhetorical training are constantly and devastatingly deployed. They are used to denounce the role of the church in relation to the state, to mock and scorn the theology associated with the Catholic Church, to express utter contempt for the parliamentarian and Leveller writers of the 1640s. All these enemies are subjected to an endless stream of very funny and violently rhetorical castigation. There's an instance, then, of my claim that we can hope to see the texts we study in new and perhaps more fruitful ways if we situate them within the precise educational and intellectual contexts in which they were formed.

CP: Since you have talked about your methodology, let me say that I always find it difficult to answer questions about methodology. I have never sat down and thought about methodology as such. My approach is, and always has been, that I am interested in problems and I worry away at them until I think I have written something that looks reasonably satisfactory. So it is a very eclectic approach. It has been influenced by the Oxford philosophy that I was, so to speak, brought up in—the analytical tradition—and, of course, by the leftist analysis (the wrongheaded approach!) that Quentin just mentioned, particularly that of C. B. Macpherson on Hobbes, Locke, and radical individualism, and then by a large array of different aspects of feminist work. By the time I wrote *The Sexual Contract*, there was a good deal of work in postmodernism and poststructuralism, and, despite what a lot of people maintain, I was actually influenced by that when I wrote the book. So I would say that, insofar as I have a methodology, it is that you get your teeth into the problem and you worry it to death.

QS: I should say that I'm not interested in methodology either. I'm interested in questions about what it is to interpret, and those are philosophical questions, not methodological ones. What's been important to my practice as a historian is a view that became central to the philosophy of language in the mid-twentieth century through the work of Quine and Wittgenstein. Both in effect asked us to stop talking about meanings and take a holistic view of language, trying to see how different webs of belief and forms of life are mapped in language. The implications of that approach for historians, it's always seemed to me, are extremely important. What Quine's holism asks of you is that you try to recover what may at first sight look like a very alien point of view. So I suppose that, by strong contrast with the Marxism so prevalent in the 1960s, what I really wanted to say was this: don't think of the texts we study as in some way reflections of something more real—of a socioeconomic base, for example, as Macpherson did. Ask yourself instead why each text exists at all. Why do we have them? What were they for? What are they doing? What are their underlying purposes?

NH: I think that brings us to some of the fundamental differences between historical and feminist approaches. Many historians of political thought, following Quentin's important work, have made a case for the need to avoid "reading history backward"—bringing our present concerns and politics into our readings of historical thinkers. The concern, from this perspective, is that there are no perennial political problems and therefore that we must read Hobbes's political thought with the goal of understanding his intentions. Feminists, by contrast, tend to take a more analytical approach—for instance, the argument, led by Carole's important interpretation, that women's subjugation to men occurs in the state of nature and founds the social contract. Such an argument cannot, of course, be historically validated, yet many feminists consider it vital to understanding what Hobbes is and is not saying. Does this pose a fundamental impasse between the two approaches?

CP: In my reading of Hobbes, it is logic rather than history that is crucial. Hobbes portrays a radically individualist state of nature; it follows from his own logic and method. He begins with atomized entities in perpetual motion, which he then reconstitutes as human beings, but as they have no natural relations with one another they must then necessarily look at the world in a purely subjective fashion. This means that there is a major problem about forming any kind of association in the state of nature. It is never in your interest to act second, as he puts it, if you have been foolish enough to enter into an agreement with another. And if you have entered an agreement and it then seems to be to your advantage to break it, you will do so. So the first problem is this intractable coordination problem.

Another difficulty is over women's equality—indeed, it is actually more than equality because mothers are lords in the state of nature. Again, Hobbes is very logical. If a woman gives birth, she has absolute power over her child; she can kill her infant or not as she pleases. If it pleases her to keep the infant, according to Hobbes, that is tantamount to a contract or agreement between the child and mother. The child has agreed to be brought up by the mother and so owes obedience in exchange for protection. Mothers are lords in the state of nature because they have the power of life and death by virtue of giving birth. There is no analogous power for men. If men are to exercise power over someone else, then they always have to arrange for that to happen, perhaps through a coercive preemptive strike, or, alternatively, another individual has to think that it is to their advantage to consent to an exercise of power over them.

As I have emphasized, Hobbes's premise of sexual equality in the natural condition poses a major problem about why it is that women are subordinate as wives in civil society. Why should naturally free and equal women always agree that men should, as husbands, exercise power over them? This is not a problem for the other theorists of an original contract because, one way or another, they build women's subordination into the state of nature. There are a few places where Hobbes offers a conjectural history that parallels the claims of the other theorists, but it runs against the logic of his arguments. Thus, there is a very big logical gap in Hobbes's theory; how do free and equal women in the natural condition always agree to become subordinates as wives after civil society has been created through the original contract? I offered my own little conjectural history to show how the problem of the transition from women's natural freedom to their civil subordination as wives might be explained. Of course, my story was never meant as history, although rather curiously some critics have thought that is what I intended, or that somehow you could find evidence for my story in Hobbes's text. If there was evidence, I would not have needed to offer my conjecture. Logically, it seemed to me, the only way to account for the transition was that all or a large enough number of women had already come under the power of men before the original contract was concluded. It followed that men made the contract and dictated the terms.

QS: I should like to say something about the incursion, as it were, of feminist thinking into the discussion of Hobbes's philosophy. This was a development that happened some time after people of my generation started to think about Hobbes. As I said, my earliest work was published in the 1960s. But it wasn't until the early 1970s that a lot of serious feminist thinking began to be done about the canon of philosophy. I feel that we shouldn't think of this development as simply another contribution to the debate: it was something more than that. Compare it with some of the other changes that took place at around the same time in the historiography of Hobbes's philosophy. It was at around the same time that scholars began seriously to reopen questions about Hobbes's theological and religious beliefs. This was an important development, and it made a great difference in how we now think about Hobbes. But the feminists contributed something much more. They made us see that there was a whole dimension missing from the interpretations we had hitherto been offering of texts such as Hobbes's *Leviathan*. What they produced was not so much an addition to our knowledge as a reorientation. And it has been permanent. Nobody would now address any of the major historical texts of political theory without issues of gender at the back of their minds.

I felt myself very much affected by these changes when I returned to working on Hobbes in the 1990s, and in two ways. One of these I haven't much written about, but it seems to me important and interesting—and I hope we shall say a word about it today—which is the role of women in Hobbes's life. If you're my sort of historian, biography is in a certain way important, because you always want to know answers to questions like: where did these people go to school, who were their teachers, what did they study, which university (if any) did they go to, what was the curriculum, who subsequently employed them? These are all questions, in effect, about where the writers we study fit into intellectual traditions and structures of discourse, but of course they're traditional biographical questions as well.

I hope we can come back to these questions, but for the moment I want to stress that what mattered to me in the 1990s, when I was writing the essays I eventually collected in my book *Hobbes and Civil Science*, was the fact that Hobbes seemed, in the construction of his theory of the state, to want to get away from gender. This may seem a backhanded way of paying tribute to the importance of what I have called the feminist incursion, but my point is that I'm certain I wouldn't have had that insight if feminists had not pleaded with us to think about gender in the first place.

Hobbes himself points to this avoidance when he says in the "Epistle Dedicatory" to *Leviathan*, "I speak not of the men but in the abstract of the seat of power." Yet more strikingly, in replying to Wallis in his *Considerations* in 1662, when Wallis had raised questions about the sacerdotal standing of monarchs, Hobbes retorts that "though man"—here, of course, he means "mankind"—"be male and female, authority is not." These remarks set me thinking again about Hobbes's conception of the political covenant. He tells us in *Leviathan* that it is a covenant performed by each and every member of the multitude. The question as to whether this is a multitude of men *and women* is a crucial one, and we should come back to that. But anyway, the members of the multitude covenant, each with each, to authorize a representative to speak and act in their name. The name of this representative is the sovereign, whose will now counts as the will of all. Notice that Hobbes thinks that the sovereign representative can just as well be a woman as a man. He agrees that most commonwealths have been erected by men, but in chapter 20 of *Leviathan* he explicitly notes that it would be a misreckoning to suppose that men necessarily possess greater prudence or even strength.

The outcome of the covenant is thus the creation of a representative. But a representative of whom? It's very important that the answer is *not* that the sovereign is the representative of the members of the multitude. As we have seen, when the members of the multitude covenant together, they acquire a single will, namely, the will of their representative. But if they have a single will, then there's a sense in which they are now, as Hobbes says, One Person. And, as Hobbes is careful to state, the sovereign is the representative of that Person—not the representative of the members of the multitude, but rather of the Person that the multitude creates out of itself by the act of agreeing to be represented.

Now, the central question in Hobbes's theory of the state is, what is the name of that person? And the answer is that Leviathan is the name of that person, because that is the person generated (notice the sexual metaphor) out of the covenant. But that person has no gender. Leviathan is the name of the state, and the state is neither a man nor a woman. As

Hobbes expresses it, the state is a person "by fiction." This, then, is what I think I was helped to see by being made to recognize the importance of asking about gender: that although, for Hobbes, the sovereign can be a man or a woman, what matters most is the state, which has no gender at all.

CP: Since the figure of the representative is a unity, it is a fictional unified person, and I have my doubts whether it could be a female figure. This was the argument in my essay "'God Hath Ordained to Man a Helper.'" I argued that women are neither parties to the original contract nor—because, as wives, they are subject to their husbands—rulers in the family. Thus it seems very implausible that the figure would be female. Hobbes is very insistent that no one can have two masters, and he writes in chapter 22 of *Leviathan* that "Private Bodies Regular, and Lawfull" are united through "one Person Representative." In the family, one such "regular body," the father or master, "ordereth the whole Family"; he is an absolute familial sovereign (and Hobbes, in conjectural history mode, states that fathers had this power before a commonwealth was instituted). Moreover, as Teresa and I emphasized, Hobbes usually portrays the family as an entirely male association, so I find it very hard to see how a female fictional person can arise out of this background. If the fictional person, the "Person Representative," is going to bear any resemblance to a real person, the figure will be a male person, not a female.

QS: But I think we must be careful not to suppose that the person of the state is male *or* female. The *sovereign* will be male or female, but the state is neither.

CP: Yes, I take your point that Hobbes is speaking in the abstract of the state as the seat of power. The state, or civil society, is conventional or artificial; it is generated through the original contract. But I am not entirely convinced by your argument that the sovereign is the representative of the "Person" that the multitude creates out of itself when it agrees to be represented. The original contract is, in Hobbes's terms, a "contract," not a covenant. Because of the severe coordination problem, the agreement cannot be one in which anyone is to perform second—that is, a covenant. To leave the state of nature, each individual must simultaneously contract with every other individual. In making such a contract, the collection of natural individuals transform themselves into civil members of a commonwealth, which seen in the abstract is the state. They are transformed into a social order of households, economic activities, and subjects of an absolute ruler. The logic of Hobbes's argument seems to me to be that the ruling representative, who is simultaneously created through the words that generate the original contract, represents the members of the commonwealth—members of a civil society, not a collection of individuals. But who exactly are the individuals in the state of nature who make the original contract? There is a major problem with forming associations in the natural condition, but it can be done. The masters of those associations, including families, will usually be men, and it is thus men (masters) who conclude the original pact. Why would the figure of the "Representative Person" be female, and why would they choose a woman as their sovereign in the state?

QS: Hobbes admits in chapter 20 of *Leviathan* that commonwealths have usually been set up by men, and in the famous frontispiece it's true that the head of the sovereign is shown as male. Actually, Hobbes can't quite represent his own theory because his theory is not that the sovereign is the *head* of the commonwealth, but rather that the sovereign is the *soul* of the commonwealth—as he twice says, most emphatically at the end of chapter 21. But he can't represent the idea of the soul, so he goes back to the traditional idea of the sovereign as head of state. My point is that there's no difficulty with *that* person being a woman. Although Hobbes says that usually commonwealths are set up by men, he explicitly mentions the Amazons, saying that they formed a commonwealth of women. Furthermore, he is a very strong believer in hereditary succession. As he says in his discussion of sovereignty in chapter 19, King Charles I held the succession from a descent of six hundred years. There was no Salic law in England, so there was no reason why such a succession shouldn't bring a woman in place of a man. And of course it sometimes did, and Hobbes was born in 1588, when there was a queen regnant. So for Hobbes there's no difficulty with having a woman as our sovereign representative. But that has nothing to do with the person of the state.

CP: Well, this does bring out the tricky question of the relation of Hobbes's logic to his (conjectural) historical passages, which is connected to my question of who makes the original contract to create civil society. The Amazons, of course, were all women, so there was no problem of subordination to men. There were many arguments about queens and husbands in this period, and Mary Astell was very good on this point. She sarcastically says that if all women are governed by men and husbands, then queens would be ruled by their footmen.

QS: Hobbes does, of course, mention that point in chapter 20. It's in relation to the point you made earlier as to the question of who has dominion over a child. Dominion over a child in the state of nature must be in the mother, because the grounds of obedience are protection and it's the mother who protects. But Hobbes also asks in chapter 20 about the position of the child of a couple in which the woman is the queen regnant. He says that's no problem at all because her husband is her subject. So once again the child is subject to the mother, not the father.

CP: Then that makes queens an anomaly (and often seen as such) because every other wife is subject to her husband.

QS: Well, I'm not sure about that. When Hobbes talks about what he calls families, he has two kinds of families in mind. There are the families he discusses in chapter 13, which, as he says, are based on a mere concord of natural lust. He thinks that's the situation among Native Americans, who, he believes, have no government at all; and if there's no government, then everything that Carole said earlier is right, which is that women have dominion in the state of nature over children. But in civil associations there are laws of matrimony, and that makes a big difference. However, Hobbes's view of these families is rather a peculiar one, which is that they are associations within the overarching civil association. He talks about the various types of these associations in chapter 22, where he makes it clear that he doesn't much like them. He doesn't like churches and he doesn't like corporations, because they both tend to make claims against the state. But, of course, he has to accept the family. However, his view of the family is that it is a unit with a representative who has the right to speak and act in the name of its members. But this representative can be a man or a woman, and in the case of a widow with children it *is* of course a woman. It's true that wives are subject to their husbands. But Hobbes leaves open the possibility of families within civil associations that have women as their heads. Hobbes was used to that situation, because he was employed by the widow of the second Earl of Devonshire for many years. In fact, she sacked him at a certain point.

CP: I am still not entirely happy with that. It is true that exceptions are often made for widows, but Hobbes's "families" are very peculiar. As I have already said, this is precisely what Teresa and I pointed out in "Mere Auxiliaries"; it is the problem of the disappearing wife and mother. The issue of the concord of lust and Native Americans is a very different discussion, about which I say something in my chapter "The Settler Contract" in my book with Charles Mills, *Contract and Domination*. In the case of America, the state of nature is portrayed as a real, historical condition. We have arrived in the New World, and what have we found? A veritable state of nature: people are still living as they were in the first ages of the world. Are we looking at history or are we looking at logic? This question always has to be considered when reading theorists of an original contract, but particularly when reading Hobbes.

QS: Well, in Hobbes it's quite clear. Hobbes's view of the state of nature is that it figures as a terrible warning.

CP: Exactly. I agree that Hobbes provides an awful warning of what happens if you start to disobey the state or start to think that you could possibly live without it. But the warning is most stark in the state of nature as a theoretical, heuristic, or logical device, not as a real historical condition as in America.

QS: I would say that Hobbes's account of the state of nature is essentially an anthropology. It is important to remember that Hobbes was a member of the Virginia Company and that his employers were deeply involved financially in the act of colonizing. Hobbes is very interested in America and thinks of Native Americans as living in a state of nature. So it's a mistake to suppose that we can place Hobbes in some story about the social contract seen in Rawlsian terms as a fiction through which we can produce moral imperatives about justice. That's not how it figures in Hobbes at all. As I've suggested, for Hobbes it's an anthropology, and what it tells you is what it would be like to live without law. His answer, contrary to what was generally agreed, is that it would be terrible to live without law. So the story about the Native Americans is a warning not to try it. You may be prone to try it because you think that the state takes away your freedom. But, as he says, even if it took away all your freedom, the alternative would always be worse.

CP: I think this is where we really do start disagreeing. Your response raises a whole range of questions. First, the point of the exercise for the theorists of an original contract was to justify the basic institutions of the modern state. Most political theorists today assume that there is no fundamental problem about justifying those institutions. One aspect of much of my work since *The Problem of Political Obligation* has been to show that this assumption is mistaken. The early modern theorists knew that there was a problem because they were right at the beginning, as it were. Their premises undercut all the familiar solutions to the question of why one person should be governed by another, and Hobbes reveals this brilliantly. The only solution left is free agreement; hence the stories of original contracts and arguments about consent. But contemporary theorists typically proceed as if the early modern theorists had solved the problem and it can now be forgotten, except for working out which is the best justification.

Second, I do not see Hobbes's state of nature as an anthropology. It has elements of that, especially in the passages of conjectural history, but it is largely a logical exercise. Certainly he sometimes talks about America. The early modern theorists were fascinated by America because here were people running around in the wild woods, living in an example of the first stage of the world. (Locke, of course, has a great deal more to say about that.) My approach is one that Quentin really rather disapproves of. I do not think of myself as a historian of political thought in the way that Quentin is. I don't have his erudition about the theorists, their times, the context, and so forth. I have never been in the archives. Of course, I am interested in them intrinsically, and I love reading them, particularly Hobbes; he is a wonderful stylist. But my major interest is and always has been in contemporary problems, and I have long thought that you will not get much grasp of whatever problem you are interested in or ways to resolve it if you do not have some inkling of how we got where we are and how the problem came into being. That is largely how I approach the texts.

Third, I certainly do *not* think that the early modern theorists of an original contract were in any way the same as Rawls. Rawls is doing something very different from theorists like Hobbes or Locke. The idea of an original contract does real work in their theories, which were political theories about the modern state and its power structures (including sexual and racial structures of power). Rawlsian theory is about moral reasoning in the choice of principles of justice; contract operates merely as a metaphor. I have always taken seriously Hobbes's procedure in starting with entities in perpetual motion and building them back up into recognizable human figures. The entities are sexless, but if they are to resemble human individuals, then Hobbes has to make them male and female and acknowledge that there is at least one difference between the male and female individuals. Women give birth and men do not, and mothers become lords. As I have already discussed, individuals in the (logical) state of nature have no natural connections, so that each looks at the world from their own personal perspective and everything is a matter of private judgment—hence the coordination problem.

QS: Could I say something about that? I'm very interested in the fact that Hobbes is deeply concerned with the visual representation of his political ideas. I've already mentioned the frontispiece of *Leviathan*, but there's an equally complex and iconographically contrasting frontispiece to *De Cive*. The picture includes a representation of a woman on a pedestal, and the pedestal is marked *Libertas*. What that reminds us is that the state of nature is a state of complete liberty, as Hobbes calls it—that is to say, it's a state in which you have the right to do anything you wish. As Carole rightly says, the way in which the concept of the state of nature features in these theories is that it figures life without law. So now we have a picture of liberty.

So what is life without law? Well, if you look closely at Hobbes's visual representation of the answer, what you see in the background is an adaptation of one of de Bry's engravings of the Virginia pictures painted by John White in the 1580s. De Bry had shown men hunting a stag with bows and arrows, but Hobbes shows men hunting another *man* with the same weapons, and in the background there are people roasting what appears to be a human limb over a fire. Moreover, the figure of liberty is shown holding a bow and arrow. The point is that, in the state of nature, no one is going to defend you as the law does; you are going to have to defend yourself. And what do you have to be armed against? Nothing less than instant death at the hands of your fellow man. This is life without law, but it is presented as if you were trying to live it, and that's how it would be.

I also want to say a word about the *Leviathan* frontispiece. Looking at the many small figures who make up the body of the people, I am struck by two things. One is that this is an artificial body: obviously no sovereign's body is made up of lots of little people. The sovereign is the name of a natural person—that's to say a man or a woman or a body of men or women—but this natural person also takes on, as Hobbes says, the artificial person of being a representative. The other point that strikes me is that the little figures we see appear to constitute the whole of civil society. How closely Hobbes was involved in this element of the design is not clear, but it's very striking that what's shown are soldiers as well as civilians, children as well as adults, and, crucially, women as well as men. The men wear hats; the women wear shawls and have bonnets. That's the body of the people. So that appears to be the covenant embodied.

CP: Again we get the problem of abstraction and the context. We agree that Hobbes wants to show the awful condition that exists in the absence of law; it is the famous war of all against all. The lines between the logic and the anthropology and history get blurred. Hobbes's radically individualist state of nature is a logical picture, not reality. A real state of nature is some form of society; if America is an actual state of nature, then of course there are societies, law, and lawmakers (though not in the form that the original settlers understood as "law"). But Hobbes maintained that in America, native societies were held together by the concord of lust, and Locke further held that their governments were little more than generals with their armies and their sovereignty very moderate. Moreover, the state of nature, whether a real historical or logical condition, always has to be transformed—that is, left behind—and developed into a civil society, a modern state.

But Hobbes's individualist logic abstracts from the society of his time and from real human beings. That is why in the state of nature individuals have no natural connections and there are no social institutions, such as marriage. What happens is that the social and law-governed background is implicitly presupposed. This is where the laws of nature come in. If there is going to be an original contract, there has to be an understanding of the practice of contracting. Individuals have to know what it means to make a contract or a covenant. That is not possible if there is merely a collection of individuals with no natural relations to one another, each locked into their own private judgment. So all the social and intersubjective understandings fundamental to human social life are tacitly presupposed. They surface in the laws of nature, particularly those about keeping covenants and endeavoring peace (I forget the numbering).

QS: The first and fundamental law of nature is to seek peace.

CP: That's right, but then that entails that all the individuals in the state of nature act on an understanding of what it means to keep peace and an understanding of the practice of making contracts. They understand all the social practices that help constitute civil society (or it could not be brought into being) but that have been abstracted away to portray the original condition. This is quite different from America seen as a real natural condition, a historical stage of the world that justifies journeying across the oceans, taking other people's lands, and turning them into a civil society. This is discussed in my chapter on the settler contract, although I mention Hobbes only in passing; perhaps I should write another chapter!

JW: It strikes us both that there's been relatively little interaction in the field of Hobbes scholarship between the two subfield specialties that you represent. It seems to us that a lot of the young PhDs coming out who are interested in the history of political thought are no longer interested in questions of gender, and that gender analysis remains marginal within the history of political thought and the history of philosophy. Is it because gender analysis has been "done," or is something else going on?

QS: What I'm struck by is that those colleagues of mine who are interested in questions about gender in history would never think of concentrating on Hobbes. And those who are interested in Hobbes want to address themselves to what they see as the larger historiographical issues. It's also true that, if I think of the most brilliant women I have supervised as PhD students in recent years—scholars such as Annabel Brett, Hannah Dawson, Felicity Green—they have not worked on feminist themes. Annabel is currently writing about Hobbes, Hannah about Locke, and Felicity about Montaigne. It is my firm impression, however, that all these scholars have completely internalized the kind of feminist thinking I mentioned earlier. Having absorbed its lessons, they look with new eyes at some of the central figures and issues in early modern thought.

CP: I will leave Quentin to speak for history, but I think that the picture in political science and perhaps philosophy too is rather different. In the 1970s, when feminist scholarship first started seriously in political theory, many of us in political science thought that what we were dealing with *were* the big questions. Feminism was showing the deficiencies in the way in which texts had been read, or the partial and one-sided way in which central concepts of political theory and political science had been interpreted, with so much left out. We liked to think that what we were doing was going to transform the discipline. That hasn't happened. There are now many more feminist political theorists than there were forty years ago, many books and panels at conferences on women and politics, and new subfields, such as feminist international relations, but we now seem back to the position—rather like two steps forward and one step back—where the general view seems to be that feminism has its place in questions about women or "women's issues" but that the *big* questions do not require feminist insights—or it might even be a handicap in a career in political science for a young scholar to take a feminist approach to discuss mainstream questions.

QS: It seems to me that among intellectual historians the situation is perhaps less dismal. Take the case of a historian interested in the emergence of the theory of natural rights. Surely it would be impossible nowadays—in a way that it would not have been impossible at the time when I was first studying such issues—to address that question without asking whether rights are gender differentiated. It seems to me, in other words, that feminist history produced what looks like a permanent change. Feminism *has* transformed my discipline, and it isn't just a "contribution" like other contributions. Everybody now, whatever question they're asking, finds themselves thinking about gender, and how it is confronted—or ignored or evaded—in the works they read.

CP: Actually, Quentin, I disagree. I don't think that it is always so in the case of rights, for example. There are many examples where feminist questions are entirely absent and the question of sexual power is never addressed. One of the topics I have been interested in for a while now is basic income for all citizens. There are some academics involved, including some very enthusiastic young men. Many, though, contrive to shove the discussion of basic income into the narrow parameters dominated by Rawlsian theory, liberalism, communitarianism, and republicanism, without any feminist argument. And most of Rawlsian contract theory is untouched by feminism, albeit that they might use "she" or perhaps refer to Susan Okin's critique of Rawls, but for the most part the Rawls industry trundles on, neglecting feminist scholarship. We have not had the impact that thirty years of original scholarship deserves. One explanation is that political science, particularly in the United States, has become so big and professionalized that there is a little niche for everybody. You can do your work and no one else takes any notice of it. That is not the whole story, but I think it is an important part.

NH: But, of course, feminist philosophers still have similar struggles with the "mainstream" of their profession as well. And I should note that Ruth Abbey is producing *Feminist Interpretations of John Rawls* for the Rereading the Canon series, of which this Hobbes volume is part.

QS: I still want to say that among historians an insensitivity to questions about gender would be much less common than it was thirty years ago and much less common, as I see it, than you are describing in political science.

However, if we're talking about the history of political theory, then I do see one way in which the kind of insights that feminism brought to bear on historical questions may be getting sidelined or underestimated. The feminist critique of the 1970s was largely directed at showing us insensitivities, and in consequence lacunae, in our understanding and awareness of what was going on in the texts we analyzed. That, I felt, was its major achievement in that generation. However, it sometimes involved an approach to these texts that was absolute anathema to many historians, since it seemed not to take the historical texts on their own terms, seemed to judge them by anachronistic standards.

I think there may really be a tension here. What we now try to do as historians of philosophy, historians of any kind of discourse, is to *listen*. What we *don't* do is say: well, here are the issues they failed to raise, the things they should have talked about but didn't, and it's an outrage that they didn't. We just say: let's try and hear what they're saying. The point is to try to get at their underlying assumptions and premises. This takes me back to what I said at the very beginning. Historians like me want to see texts as interventions, as elements in ideologies, and to recover if possible the underlying purposes for the sake of which they were written. But as I say, there may well be a tension between approaching the historical material in this way and paying proper attention to the sort of issues that Carole is talking about.

CP: I think Quentin is quite right; we are largely talking about the difference between the discipline of history and the very large amount of feminist work in history, and the discipline of political science, and philosophy, where there is less.

JW: To return to matters of interpretation, Quentin, in your article "Hobbes on Representation," you articulate the need to embed Hobbes within a larger conversation on representation and that in doing this you are not merely providing background. It's not just background; he was participating in a public conversation. In another vein, Carole, you have written on Wollstonecraft's political thought, and you have also written the conclusion to Hilda Smith's *Women Writers and the Early Modern British Political Tradition*. We now know that there was a vast number of women writing on politics in Hobbes's period—not just the Leveller women but others, including people like Margaret Cavendish. They may not have written political treatises per se, but their writing was political in intent nevertheless. How does our increased knowledge of women's presence in the literary and public discourse change our sense of what Hobbes was doing, in terms of not just being background but part of this larger conversation? Does it affect the way we think about Hobbes and his ideas about gender?

QS: That's a very good question. Hobbes undoubtedly saw himself as taking part in a conversation. *Leviathan* can be read as a defense of the possibility that you can be obliged to a regime that was not lawfully established, because you shouldn't think of political obligation in terms of right; you should think of it in terms of protection. If the question is—as it was in the England of his time—who is protecting you, then the answer is Oliver Cromwell, not Charles I. So Hobbes certainly saw himself as taking part in a debate about the English commonwealth. Moreover, I can't but feel that he would have wished to privilege himself as a particular kind of voice. He always refers to *Leviathan* as a treatise. He's writing a treatise, something completely systematic. It's a very male sort of notion.

As you say, however, there were other ways of writing about politics. For example, Hobbes was obliged to take note of the fact that Margaret Cavendish wrote political plays. She wrote, among other things, about the conflict of virtue and vice in the political sphere. But Hobbes, in *Leviathan*, tells us that he too is writing about what he calls the science of virtue and vice. So you could say that they were writing about the same thing in different ways. Moreover, Hobbes cannot fail to take note of Cavendish, for she is, after all, a duchess, as well as being the wife of one of his most important patrons, the Duke of Newcastle. But, on the other hand, Hobbes does seem to me to be trying to discount Cavendish's work. I find his response to Cavendish, when she sends him her plays, quite a defensive one. He can't fail to reply, but what he says is that Cavendish is not in a position to know about virtue and vice because she is such a noble and wonderful person that she knows nothing about vice. This is presented as a flowery compliment, but you can read the letter as an attempt to sweep Cavendish off the board. Cavendish also tells us that, although Hobbes was always at her husband's table, he would never speak to her. She does add that she was bashful. But she wasn't so very bashful, for she made a celebrated appearance at the Royal Society. I see a subterranean debate here about how to present yourself as a writer, and whether women can do so at all.

There are several other fascinating biographical questions raised by Hobbes's relations with women. Yet more interesting is his relationship with Christian Bruce, the widow of the second Earl of Devonshire, whom Hobbes had tutored. They appear to have had two serious arguments, in the first of which Hobbes was fired and was out of a job with the Devonshire family for at least two years. In the second argument, he took sides against her with the third earl, her son, whom Hobbes had tutored in the 1630s. When the earl attained legal age in 1638, he planned legal proceedings against his mother over her management of his estates during his minority. Hobbes claims that he restrained the earl from going to law, but he certainly signed and probably helped write a long document of protest against her, drawn up by her son. There are some Gothic depths here that we need to think about in considering the place of gender in Hobbes's life and thought.

CP: Many years ago, I read a biography of Hobbes and learned that he was brought up by women—that is an intriguing area.

QS: The most important woman was, I'm sure, his mother. We know from the biography of Hobbes written by his friend John Aubrey that Hobbes's father was an alcoholic who couldn't cope with his job and was repeatedly in trouble for violent behavior. And we know that in 1604—Noel Malcolm discovered the date—the father abandoned his family and went to London, where he was never heard of again. Hobbes was only fifteen at the time, and during the period when his father was incapable, somebody must have been keeping the young Hobbes at his books, and somebody must have been trying to get together the money to send him to Oxford. Surely this can only have been his mother. The Oxford education was paid for by a prosperous uncle, but someone had to persuade the uncle. And Hobbes was a younger son, so that no special effort would have been made on his behalf unless someone decided that he was a boy worth encouraging. I sense that his mother must have been of great importance.

CP: To get back to Joanne's question, it is important to emphasize that it is only relatively recently in political theory that writers such as Margaret Cavendish, Mary Astell, or Mary Wollstonecraft have been mentioned at all, let alone their less well-known contemporaries. It did not matter how well known women who engaged in political argument and wrote political theory were in their own day (and some of them were very well known); they were very quickly forgotten and in the twentieth century did not enter into the conventional canon of the "history of political thought." This meant that the standard history included only male writers and usually paid little attention to what they had to say about the characteristics of and relations between the sexes, or about the embarrassing feminism of John Stuart Mill. It also meant that the male writers are presented as standing only in relation to one another; feminist arguments are not acknowledged as having existed at the time at which they were writing. So once again a partial "history" was presented as if it was all that there was to be said. This gradually began to change when, in the 1990s, some feminist political theorists started to take an interest in Mary Wollstonecraft. But even now it is possible to find histories of political thought that have very little or nothing to say about the place of feminist political thought, or political argument by women more generally, in that history. Similarly, all the work that historians have done on women's arguments, lives, and activities does not necessarily find its way into political theory. When I wrote the conclusion to Hilda Smith's *Women Writers and the Early Modern British Political Tradition*, it was absolutely fascinating to discover from the chapters in the volume how much women were doing. According to Susan Staves's chapter, for example, women were even busily investing in the new stock exchange. Nobody ever told us about women's activities when I was learning about political theory.

QS: Some women even seem to have voted. Keith Thomas did some fascinating work on what could happen if you were an independent widow. The great thing was to be a well-to-do widow, because you got control of your property again. But because voting was based on property qualifications, it would have been hard to exclude an independently propertied woman who wanted to vote. The question that had to be answered was "Are you a 40 shilling freeholder?" The answer might well be, if you were a widow, "Yes."

CP: That was something that women in the suffrage movement took up in the nineteenth century. They appealed to their old liberties, and they actually did quite a bit of research on instances where women had voted.

NH: Another question about that topic derives from Hobbes's definition of a family. As Carole points out, in both *De Cive* and *Leviathan*, the family is defined as a father, children, and servants. But in *The Elements of Law* he defines the family as a father *or* mother *or* both, with children and servants. Is there a conscious change, do you know? Or is that just happenstance of style that the mother drops out?

QS: I think that this shift between *The Elements of Law* and *Leviathan* relates to one of the largest changes in the evolution of Hobbes's civil philosophy, which is the introduction of the concepts of authorization and representation. These two concepts are completely absent from *The Elements of Law*. So, for example, in *The Elements of Law* the political covenant is a covenant of submission, whereas in *Leviathan* it's a covenant of authorization, and what this granting of authority produces is an authorized representative. As we were saying earlier, in *Leviathan* the family is modeled on the state. The state is instituted when individuals authorize a representative to speak and act in their common name. If you now think of families in that way, then the figure who will most naturally be treated as the authorized representative will be the father, and that's how the issue is presented in chapter 22 of *Leviathan*, where Hobbes speaks of families as an example of "systems" within the state. In *The Elements of Law* Hobbes operates entirely without this apparatus, so the question of who is head of the family cannot be posed in terms of who is to be regarded as the family's representative. It's for this reason, I think, that fathers are privileged in *Leviathan* more than in Hobbes's earlier texts.

NH: And in *Leviathan* he does include mothers in the chapter on paternal power. He refers to them under the rubric of "the paternal."

QS: He does, that's right, in chapter 20. But in that discussion he is talking about what Carole was talking about much earlier. If we consider the condition of mere nature, he is asking, who has dominion over children? He's perfectly clear that it's the mother. That connects with his general views about obligation and the divorce between obligation and right, which is so characteristic of his civil philosophy. If you tie obligation to protection instead—and Carole has already made this point—then the mother has dominion.

JW: Perhaps we could close our conversation with your reflections on the future of Hobbes interpretation; how is Hobbes relevant, useful, or important to the twenty-first century, or is relevance even an important consideration for scholarly interest in Hobbes? Why should twenty-first-century feminists be interested in him, and why should historically oriented Hobbes scholars care about feminist concerns?

QS: Shall I say something about relevance? Because that's a big issue for historians. I'm unfashionable, I think, among my colleagues in thinking that we should be willing to pose the question of relevance in a fairly philistine way. We should be asking: Why are we bothering to find out about the past? What's the *point*? As Clifford Geertz once excellently remarked, aren't these people supposed to be working for us? I like that phrase. The trick of being a useful historian, it seems to me, is to approach the past in such a way that you don't *make* our forebears work for us, but the outcome is that they nevertheless do. It's rather like cultural anthropology, Geertz's discipline. The motivation for studying the past, on this account, is the hope that, by examining a culture very different from our own, we may be able to cast light on our own. The relevance of our studies stems not from thinking of our forebears as sufficiently similar for us to be able to draw direct lessons from studying their societies; it stems from their not being at all like us in many respects. That is my own motivation as a historian, and I wouldn't feel comfortable writing about the past if I didn't have it.

Let me give an example of this view of relevance taken from my study of Hobbes's philosophy. I've already mentioned my book about Hobbes's theory of liberty. Hobbes's understanding of this concept is a very familiar one. He thinks of liberty as consisting in essence in not being impeded in the exercise of your powers. But what I tried to show in my book was that, at the time when he put forward this claim, it was an intensely polemical one. He was trying—very successfully, as things turned out—to discredit a rival view, according to which liberty is the name of a status, the status of citizens by contrast with slaves, and consists essentially in not being dependent on the goodwill or arbitrary power of anyone else. It seems to me well worth thinking about this different understanding of liberty as, so to speak, an option for us here and now. Is freedom better understood as absence of interference or as absence of dependence? I came upon that question as a historian, but it seems to me a deeply important question in current democratic politics. The best way to approach the question is to study the historical moment at which the two understandings were in contestation with each other. That's the history I have tried to write, but my underlying purpose in writing it was to raise a question that, it seems to me, we ourselves need to reconsider here and now.

CP: Certainly I think there are many lessons you can learn from Hobbes. In general, the premises of the theories of original contract are revolutionary premises. The ramifications of the notion that by nature individuals are free and equal are still being played out. And Hobbes is the most radical of all the theorists of an original contract because he insists that men and women are naturally equal, which none of the others do. The others make sure that women are subordinated in the state of nature, and, in general, they try to head off the more radical and startling implications of their premises. Apart from the feminist questions we have talked about, Hobbes is extremely interesting because of his radical individualism and its link with current arguments about contract and what I call contractarianism in *The Sexual Contract* (but is usually called libertarianism). I think Marx would be very surprised to see how dominated the world is by freedom of contract. Long before Durkheim and Parsons, Hobbes showed the importance of the noncontractual bases of contract and the unfortunate social consequences and breakdowns if you do not take that lesson to heart. That is another relevant area. I also drew attention in *The Sexual Contract* to the curious ambivalence about whether women are free or not. The contract theorists all agree that individuals are free and equal, and Hobbes says that women are equal to men. Women certainly have the freedom to make at least one contract, the marriage contract, but then their freedom disappears. I also argue in *The Problem of Political Obligation* that if you start with radical individualism you end up with Leviathan, and these days he is armed with a great deal more than a sword. That is another relevant area.

QS: Could I just round off by saying a word about the future of Hobbes scholarship, because that was the other question you raised? I've come to feel, though this may be a private fantasy, that there is a future for the study of all these major works of philosophy. They turn out to be bottomless and endless. The horizons always shift, we always ask new questions, we always find something new to say about them. So I'm optimistic that it's a story without end.

Part One

Classic Questions, New Approaches

2

Power and Sexual Subordination in Hobbes's Political Theory

S. A. Lloyd

Hobbes famously describes the individuals inhabiting the state of nature as sufficiently equal in bodily strength and mental intelligence that every one of them is vulnerable to aggression by others. Within this normal range of adult human capabilities, the weaker can kill the stronger while the latter sleeps, or through stealth methods like poisoning, or in concert with others. Although Hobbes uses the term "men" to refer to individuals, women also fall under the term, as Hobbes writes of the sexes that "the inequality of their naturall forces is not so great, that the man could

My thanks for helpful discussion of the arguments of this paper are owed to the members of the Southern California Law and Philosophy Group, to Jerry Gaus and Zlatan Damnjanovic, and to the editors of this volume, Nancy Hirschmann and Joanne Wright.

get the Dominion over the woman without warre."[1] This degree of natural equality does not imply that no individuals are subordinated in the state of nature, for sometimes by war some are able to conquer others and extract promises of obedience from them. But the degree of natural inequality between the sexes is not so great that we should expect women as a class to find themselves under the dominion of men as a class.

How, then, feminist scholars have asked, does it come to be that women's independence and equality all but disappear in Hobbes's political society, with women absorbed into the households of their husbands along with children and servants? If the assumption of natural equality that Hobbes and the later social contract theorists posit is true, as it certainly seems to be, how is it that women are systematically, institutionally subordinated in most societies?

Philosophers, who seek to assess alleged justifications of women's subordination rather than to pursue an empirical investigation into the actual historical genesis of women's de facto subjugation, have tended to assume that men value women for their sexual and reproductive qualities, and collaborate to forcefully conquer them and distribute rights to them among themselves. Whole armies treat women as spoils, killing or threatening their existing children and forcing new children on them. Philosophers have not found it terribly surprising that women have had relatively little success in organizing effective resistance once social systems of subordination are in place.[2] The question asked by feminist Hobbes scholars, however, raises a real puzzle from a philosopher's point of view: What in Hobbes's theory accounts for the *legitimacy* of the subordination of women Hobbes unquestioningly assumes in his own society? Social contract theories aim to justify, rather than to explain, social arrangements. If women's subordination is the result of free contract, why on earth would women make such a contract?

Carole Pateman argued that this incorporation of women into civil society as subordinates is an endemic feature of all social contract theories, because such theories must assume a limitless freedom of contract that threatens to undermine substantive autonomy; and further, that this feature exposes an inherent flaw in the social contract approach.[3] I have my doubts that evolved social contract theories such as that of John Rawls share this defect. Here I will merely sketch an outline of Hobbes's social contract theory that neither assumes limitless freedom of contract against women's fundamental interests nor embraces the sort of radically individual, aggressively masculine, atomistic, mother-free picture of the human psyche advanced by Christine Di Stefano as an interpretation of Hobbes's agents.[4]

Our interpretive problem arises because Hobbes's theory assumes that the parties entering into the social contract are free and equal and do so on equal terms.[5] His Law of Nature expressly requires that "at the entrance into conditions of Peace, no man require to reserve to himself *any* Right, which he is not content should be reserved to *every one* of the rest,"[6] and in making the original contract, every man is to "be contented with so much liberty against other men, as he would allow other men against himself."[7] For women in civil society to find themselves systematically subordinated to private men and not just like every other subject to their civil sovereign, they must either have agreed as contracting parties to the original contract to subequal terms,[8] or the civil sovereign must have deprived them of their equal status as subjects after the contract was instituted,[9] or they must never have been parties to the original contract in the first place. On the last of these possibilities, women would *already* have been absorbed as subordinates into the households of men, with their interests only indirectly represented (if at all) by the men who make the original contract on equal terms *only with one another*.[10] Such a possibility would retain the formal equality of the original contractors and of the terms of contract, while provisionally carrying over a covert sexism into civil society.

Of course, such stowaway sexism could only be provisional in Hobbes's scheme, because the sovereign may remake the relative status and entitlements of any subject or class of subjects in whatever manner it conscientiously judges best for the common good. But were the generality of men to have entered civil society in this way—with subordinate women in tow—it would surely be imprudent for a sovereign to release those women from their prior obligations. If men have seen fit to seek dominion over women, particularly at the cost of risking war, they must value that dominion enough that to deprive them of it might invite the sort of "discontent" that Hobbes identifies as one of three necessary conditions of sedition or rebellion.[11]

In the section "Theoretical Equality," I argue that there is nothing *inherently misogynistic* in Hobbes's theory, no element that requires women's subordination to fellow subject men—husbands or fathers or brothers. Women are relevantly equal for all normative purposes in the state of nature. Natural law *does not* impose gender inequality by requirements that differentially advantage the sexes. Civil law *need not* impose gender inequality. The content of civil law may be as the sovereign—queen or king or assembly, as the case may be—makes it to be. Revealed religion *need not be interpreted* by the sovereign to impose gender inequality. So sexism is no formal feature of Hobbes's system. His system provides no *guarantee* against sexist regimes, but then, it provides no *guarantee* against *anything*. It is an absolutist system, one that provides no guarantee of rights for anyone, nor guarantee against abridgement or denial of rights to anyone on any basis whatsoever. Fortunately, something stronger than this can be said in Hobbes's favor: Hobbes *never suggests* that proper civil legislation or interpretation of Christian religion should include discriminatory norms against women. Hobbes may not have thought much of women (I'm pretty sure he wouldn't have liked me!), but he made absolutely no effort in his political theory to subordinate them.[12]

These sorts of formal consideration establish that Hobbes's system neither requires nor rules out the subordination of women. But this weak showing is insufficient either to exonerate or to sustain the charge that Hobbes's theory is sexist. How does Hobbes's theory fare when we take into account plausible empirical assumptions about the dynamics of social interaction in the state of nature? If Hobbes knew, or should have known, that these dynamics were likely to result in the systematic subordination of women prior to the social contract, then we should judge his theory to be discriminatory despite its formal neutrality.

In the section "Practical Inequality," I argue that the social fact of women's subordination in Hobbes's civil society can be explained in terms of Hobbes's account of power. Power, in Hobbes's view, is essentially comparative. Small differences in power can easily snowball into large differences in power. Because people seek as much power as they can get, those who have more may be expected to use it to disempower those who have less, increasing the power gap. Differences in bargaining power rooted in differences in power will affect the terms of lesser civil contracts such as marriage contracts, with enduringly detrimental consequences for women. The equality of Hobbes's formal system is compatible with the inequalities we see in his own civil society. This argument constitutes a charitable case for the criticism that Hobbes's theory does indeed allow the subordination of women.

In the section "The Road Not Taken," I offer a Hobbesian reply to the criticism. This reply depends upon showing that the outcome of conflict in Hobbes's state of nature could easily have been radically different, and in fact could have led to the subordination of men as well. I conclude in the section "All Roads Lead to Home" that closer consideration of the dynamics of power in a state of nature shows that we cannot expect to find the systematic subordination of any group to any other, and that it is precisely for this reason that Hobbes insists a sovereign political authority is needed. What makes possible a willing submission to political authority on the part of all is a seldom-noted moral motivation of all Hobbesian agents, namely, the desire to have our actions and our characters affirmed as justified in the eyes of others.[13]

Theoretical Equality

Men and women are sufficiently equal in the state of nature that disputes between them cannot be decided without war. That means the claims of women count, and count equally, with those of men. When it comes to sexual relations or to the disposition of children, these, like every other question in the state of nature, must be settled by war or by contract. Hobbes holds that a child owes its life to and hence ought to obey the person by whom it is preserved, and this is always, initially, the mother. If she carries it and nurses it once born, she has dominion over it for as long as she continues to preserve it. Hobbes notes, "Originall Dominion over children belongs to the Mother, and among men no lesse than other creatures: The birth followes the belly."[14] He is here calling on both the natural duty of gratitude to benefactors under the fourth Law of Nature, and the (tacit or presumed) contractual obligation underwritten by the natural duty articulated by the third Law of Nature to keep covenants once made.

Any change of dominion must pass by contract. Hobbes tells, in every version of his political philosophy, of the Amazons, who contracted with their neighbors for intercourse, with the female offspring to remain under their dominion while the male offspring went to their contract partners. Hobbes recognizes contracts of copulation alone, as the Amazons had;[15] of cohabitation and society of bed ("concubinate" contracts), where again children pass according to their parents' covenant; and marriage contracts, which Hobbes terms covenants of cohabitation for "society of all things." These last require a sovereign partner to settle all disagreements. Hobbes observes that although in most societies women have passed the right of government over themselves and their children to their husbands, "sometimes the government may belong to the wife only, sometimes also the dominion over the children shall be in her only; as in the case of a sovereign queen, there is no reason that her marriage should take from her the dominion over her children."[16]

Does the Law of Nature take from women their natural equality? Does it impose on them different requirements than it does on men? The Law of Nature contains no sex-differentiating provisions. The laws concerning property, for instance, require that disputed goods should be enjoyed in common, or else enjoyed alternately, or, if that is impossible, assigned by some random decision mechanism, such as a fair lottery, or first possession or first birth, all without regard to gender. Hobbes is emphatic in his insistence that the Law of Nature, which is "eternal and immutable," requires the same thing of everyone: *"Do not to another, which thou wouldest not have done to thyself."*[17] Hobbes acknowledges women as equal others, and so, on entrance into a contract for civil society, the Law of Nature requires that *"whatsoever right any man requireth to retain, he allow every other man to retain the same."*[18] This entails that the terms of the social contract establishing submission to a civil sovereign must be the same for every individual, male or female.

The natural law directs individuals to submit to a sovereign upon equal terms, but does not dictate the content of the civil laws the sovereign is to legislate. It does suggest areas for legislation—concerning property, distinctions of honor, and indeed reproduction—but is barely schematic in the outline of the needed laws. Hobbes holds that sovereigns have, under the Law of Nature, a duty to secure the good and the safety of the people, which he specifies as a duty to try to establish the welfare "of the most part."[19] Women being fully half of the population, women will have to be counted in any calculation of the welfare "of the most part." This sovereign duty entails a duty to try to increase the healthy population, God having declared that he wants humans to multiply. And that duty requires ordinances concerning copulation that will tend to increase procreation of healthy subjects. According to Hobbes, such ordinances should include laws forbidding "such copulations as are against the use of nature" (homosexual and bestial copulations); incest between close relatives, such relations being "prejudicial to the improvement of mankind" (presumably on grounds of the chance of mental disability in the inbred offspring); and polyandry and "the promiscuous use of women."[20] Such restrictions may be unnecessary, but they are not sex-discriminatory. Hobbes never insists upon nor even suggests any sex-discriminatory civil laws among his recommendations to sovereigns.

Revealed religion would seem to be a fertile possible source of civil constraints on women in a Christian commonwealth, but Hobbes never argues for such an interpretation of Christian religion. He faults Adam and Eve equally for their prideful self-assertion in trying to judge good and evil for themselves. Crucially, he deems the civil sovereign the authorized interpreter of religious doctrine. Doctrine can be as misogynistic or as man-hating or as misanthropic or as philanthropic as the sovereign sees fit to interpret it. That is left to the conscientious judgment of the queen or king or sovereign assembly that is authorized to interpret the state's religion. Nothing in Hobbes's theory requires that revealed religion be interpreted by the sovereign to impose gender inequality on subjects.

The fair conclusion, then, is that Hobbes's formal theory neither assumes nor entails the subordination of women. They are equal enough (sufficiently equal) by nature that they must be offered equal terms for submission. The natural law does not demote them; the civil laws and revealed religion need not demote them.

Practical Inequality

To understand how, in Hobbes's system, anyone comes to be subordinate to another, we need to understand relations of *power*.[21] Hobbes defines power as one's present means to obtain some future apparent good. By this definition, power does not depend on the capacity to obtain what really is good, but only what seems to the agent to be good. Power is temporal in nature, as it is geared toward prospective satisfaction. Most significantly, power is comparative and relative; it doesn't matter how much power I have in absolute terms unless I have more power than you do. The reason for this is that your plans may cross mine, and the measure of my power can only be my ability to carry out my plans against your contrary design. Any power is only an excess of power.

Hobbes categorizes powers into "natural," those eminent capabilities one is born with, and "instrumental," those acquired by natural power or by luck. Original or natural powers include *eminent* (1) strength, (2) "forme," that is, beauty, (3) prudence, (4) arts, that is, skills, (5) eloquence (to persuade others), (6) liberality, (7) nobility, and (8) natural wit. Although Hobbes doesn't say so, some of these natural sources of power will obtain in a state of nature, and others will not. Nobility is an obvious case. Distinctions of noble birth obtain only inside of commonwealths. They are conferred by convention, and so, while persons within civil society may be born with rank distinctions, persons in a state of nature cannot be.[22] Prudence, as Nancy Hirschmann points out, serves more as a power to defend against harms from others than to gain advantages. While beauty and eloquence may help you gain an advantage over me, my natural prudence may serve to keep me from being swayed by the siren song of your charms. This seems quite right, and in no way diminishes the value of the power of prudence; for my present means to avoid some future undesired outcome is no less a power than my present means to achieve some future desired outcome.[23]

Hobbes asserts that people in the state of nature are sufficiently equal in strength and natural wit that none can count on securing their ends without war, but that does not mean that there are no smaller differences of strength or intelligence among them. The two basic means of mastering others, which Hobbes terms "force" and "wiles," may be possessed to differing degrees by different people, as can beauty to attract, eloquence to persuade, and liberality to win friends and influence people.[24] Hobbes maintains that a state of nature discourages the development of arts, although perhaps there could be differences among individuals in untrained talents such as a good natural singing voice. Prudence, Hobbes argues, is developed over time and with experience, and comes pretty much equally to all in the same age cohort, with older people enjoying greater prudence than younger people.

None of these natural powers is the possession of one sex rather than the other, but there may be small differences between the groups in the degree to which the average member possesses the trait and the way in which traits are valued that affect gender differences in power. For instance, if men as a group tend to be somewhat stronger than women and so are better at forcibly taking goods from others, women may value strength and liberality in men more than men value those traits in women. If so, possession of strength and liberality would confer greater power on men than on women. If women enjoy a shorter amount of time to spend securing food and have a narrower geographical range within which to do it (either because they are carrying children or are reluctant to travel too far away from children), then they may regard the greater efficiency of men in securing food an advantage of power.

Any such small differences in natural powers may be magnified by resulting differences in what Hobbes terms "instrumental" powers. Instrumental are those powers acquired either by natural powers or by luck that enable one to acquire more powers. These include *eminent* (9) wealth, (10) reputation, (11) friends, (12) good luck (notice that this appears twice in Hobbes's account), (13) any qualities that make one widely loved or feared, and (14) success. Although Hobbes speaks of instrumental powers as those that enable one to acquire further powers, they should also be understood to be powers themselves—that is, present means to obtain some future apparent good. So eminent wealth (which may have been acquired by strength or wit or merely good luck) serves both as a means for obtaining what one wants and as an instrument for obtaining more such means—for instance, success, or friends, or reputation for liberality.

Hobbes's account of instrumental powers makes it possible to see how even a tiny, average sex-based difference in natural powers might snowball into a substantial difference in power between men and women. Even slightly greater natural strength may enable men to better amass goods, hence wealth and reputation of success, making them feared and enabling them to buy friends, in turn expanding their ability to amass goods, and so on. Because power is necessarily comparative, and people must desire power in order to secure their ends, those who have power are only rational to use it to diminish the power of their competitors.[25] Individual men can be expected to use their power against one another, while men as a class can be expected to use whatever power advantage they have over women to increase their power differential. Even though the Law of Nature requires submission to a civil sovereign on equal terms, many men will already have used their superior power as bargaining power to strike bargains with women that bring those women under their authority, and so remove them (as well as their children) as independent parties to the social contract. One of the many uses of male power would likely be to control access to the most desirable sexual partners and ownership rights over their offspring.

This idea of the cascading of small power inequalities between the sexes as groups is not inconsistent with Hobbes's insistence on sufficient natural equality among individuals, such that their disputes cannot be settled without the prospect of war. This, and even his express declaration that men as a class are not sufficiently naturally superior to obtain dominion over women as a class without war, is compatible with the possibility that tiny advantages to men in strength and (because they have more to share [and if women supporting children need more]) liberality might differentially facilitate their acquisition of instrumental powers to such a degree that many women might be induced to forego government of themselves and their children in exchange for such an increase in their chance of protecting their families.

Hobbes observes, when answering the charge that no state of nature has ever really existed as a historical reality, that "the savages of America" lived in his own time in a state of nature, being (as he thought) governed only by *families* drawn together originally by "the concord of natural lust."[26] He maintains that "a great Family, if it be not part of some Common-wealth, is of it selfe, as to the Rights of Soverainty, a little Monarchy"[27] and that in feudal times the German people lived in this way. All historical states of nature have in fact been comprised not solely of individuals, but also of ordered families. That is why, to conceive of a pure "condition of mere nature" for Hobbes's theoretical purpose—a condition in which no political obligations exist—he resorts to the fiction of a condition in which "men are sprung up like mushrooms" with no prior obligations of obedience to parents or benefactors.[28]

If this explanation for women's subordination as arising from the escalation of marginal group differences in natural powers to significant group differences in instrumental powers is plausible in the case of gender, shouldn't it also explain all sorts of relations of subordination—of the stupid to the smart, or of the ugly to the beautiful, the older to the younger, say—that would cut across gender lines? It might. But notice this would not bear on gender subordination, which is what our account seeks to explain, *unless* patterns of power from possession of natural powers (including intelligence and beauty) and the instrumental powers they attract crisscross gender lines *robustly enough to counteract* the average gendered difference in strength and its consequent increase in ability to afford liberality. For any account of women's subordination of the sort I am proposing to be decisive, we would need to assure ourselves that no competing group differences in natural powers would attract instrumental powers that would suffice to reshuffle the deck toward women's parity.

I won't undertake the ambitious project of trying to show that. Remaining with my "just so" story of how small average differences in natural sex-based powers might have resulted in large enough differences of instrumental power that many women might have willingly entered pre-civil contracts of subordination with men, Hobbes could explain how the parties to the social contract come to be male heads of household, concerned to maintain their state-of-nature sovereignty over those households within the civil law. Of course, all such prior contracts could be undone with a wave of the sovereign's hand, if it so wished. But as Hobbes flatly notes, marriage contracts and civil laws advantage men because, usually, men rule.[29] Notice, though, something very important. Whether husbands enforce the terms of their legal entitlements within their marriage contracts may well depend on their wives' "extralegal" powers inside the house. A man may prefer to live with a wife who chooses to make a happy home with him, creating for him a world in which his (or whoever's) children would rather play with their father than avenge his beatings of their mother and sisters whenever the boys grow big enough to fight back. If Hobbes's observation that all are sufficiently vulnerable was ever worth taking seriously, the little boy's natural desire to live in harmony with the women he loves will surely move him to pull his punches with his "extralegal" powers against them, and direct those powers instead toward securing their good and avenging any wrong a nasty patriarch might perpetrate.

That's a subjective response, but let's continue with the objective fact of the matter of human value, as defined by Hobbes. He defines a person's value or worth as the price others would pay for the use of his or her powers. So if women as a class possess less power in a commonwealth than do men as a class, they will have diminished worth or value. If so, it would not be surprising for women themselves to share with men this view of their inferior value. That would be the clear-eyed response to their objective position.

What Hobbes calls a person's "public worth" or "dignity" is the value set on him or her by the sovereign and is expressed by appointment to offices of command, judicature, or public employment, or the conferral of titles. So we can look to the distribution of such things to see how a society values women. In Hobbes's society, offices of command, judicature, and public employment fell almost exclusively to men, and women's titles were generally parasitic on those of the men in their families. In fact, Hobbes shows how all titles are derivative from male command offices: "Titles of Honour, such as are Duke, Count, Marquis, and Baron, are Honourable; as signifying the value set upon them by the Soveraigne Power of the Common-wealth: Which titles, were in old time titles of Office, and Command, derived some from the Romans, some from the Germans, and French. Dukes, in Latine *Duces,* being Generalls in War: Counts, *Comites,* such as bare the Generall company out of friendship; and were left to govern places conquered, and pacified: Marquises, *Marchiones,* were Counts that governed the Marches, or bounds of the Empire."[30] This suggests that if women haven't occupied positions of military command, whatever titles they carry will depend on the titles of their husbands or fathers.

Much of women's power depends on the specifics of civil law. The law can empower them, or disempower them. If women are not permitted to hold or dispose of property, or to divorce, or to retain custody of their children when separated, or are barred from higher education or honorable employments, or from political or military office, their power is limited. But sovereigns make civil law, and Hobbes does not dictate the content of what sovereigns may legislate. Indeed he could not do so, without seeming to limit sovereign power. So if a sovereign desired to write positive laws that empowered women, or disempowered men, Hobbes's theory would pose no barrier to doing so. Hobbes does have some recommendations for sovereigns about what to legislate—those laws he takes to operationalize the requirements of the laws of nature—but he nowhere suggests legislating any of the sorts of discriminatory laws just mentioned. So his theory is, with respect to civil law, gender neutral.

The Road Not Taken

As we've seen, nothing in Hobbes's theory necessitates the subjection of women. And while we can tell one story about how slight gender-based differentials in strength could have snowballed into systemic institutional disempowerment of women, other stories are compatible with Hobbes's conceptual framework. The Amazons, who form a separate society of women, reserving all positions of political and military command and titles of honor for themselves, constitute one such alternate story. A mixed-gender but matriarchal society would, in fact, be the more natural story for Hobbes to have told. Women who bear and nourish children have dominion over them, and those children are under both a natural duty of gratitude and an obligation of obedience to them in perpetuity. This is a striking relation of natural domination that would put all men under the obligation of obedience to their caretaking mothers. Those men, and their sisters, would be required to defend their mothers against any aggression by other men, including their own fathers. The power Hobbes assigns to the caregiving parent outside of civil society is staggering:

> Children therefore, whether they be brought up and preserved by the father, or by the mother, or by whomsoever, are in most absolute

subjection to him or her, that so bringeth them up, or preserveth them. And that person may alienate them, that is, assign his or her dominion, by selling or giving them in adoption or servitude to others; or may pawn them for hostages, kill them for rebellion, or sacrifice them for peace, by the law of nature, when he or she, in his or her conscience, thinks it to be necessary.[31]

This expansive power, usually held by the mother, is also a lasting one: "And though the child thus preserved, do in time acquire strength, whereby he might pretend equality with him or her that hath preserved him, yet shall that pretence be thought unreasonable, both because his strength was the gift of him, against whom he pretendeth; and also because it is to be presumed, that he which giveth sustenance to another, whereby to strengthen him, hath received a promise of obedience in consideration thereof."[32]

If most children are under obligations of obedience to their mothers in this way, we should expect the contracting heads of household in the original contract of submission to government to be mostly women. Men whose mothers had died might be free agents, unless their mother had willed to their sisters or to some other woman dominion over them. And since, according to Hobbes, those who have power will seek to preserve and expand it, we would expect that any institutional discrimination in the resulting civil society carried over from the state of nature would favor women over men.

All Roads Lead to Home

What is really interesting about Hobbes's system is that even if the state of nature were matriarchal, the logic of conflict in the state of nature would make that fact irrelevant. Neither natural matriarchy nor patriarchy makes any difference to the terms of civil life. This is so not just because civil authority levels all previous hierarchical relations and treats each individual as a subject whose primary obligation is of obedience to the sovereign. It is because the logic of conflict in the state of nature exempts no gender alliances. Although men are the subjects of their mothers, they are under no obligation not to attack other people's mothers; indeed, the mother's competition with others for resources, or her diffidence, or her pursuit of glory may induce her to require such efforts at conquest. Mothers may incentivize men by offering to allow them dominion over any household they conquer. We have no reason to suppose that a Hobbesian state of nature populated by female heads of household would be any less warlike than one populated by male heads of household. This situation is made even more unpredictable by rebellious teenagers, friendships, and religious alliances.[33] Disagreement abounds as to what actions count as violations of obligations and natural duties. Idiosyncratic private judgment yields what Hobbes terms irresoluble perpetual contention. There are no effective enforcement mechanisms to ensure that people perform their obligations and duties, even if it were possible to agree on what those obligations and duties are. Obligations and natural duties are unenforceable in the state of nature. The problem remains the same; only the names have changed.

And Hobbes's solution remains the same. The Laws of Nature make one set of demands on all contractors: seek peace with willing others, on terms of equality. No contractor is to reserve to herself any right she is not content to have reserved to all the rest.

This means that prior social relations, whether matriarchal or patriarchal, or age-based or religion-based, are irrelevant to setting the terms of Hobbes's social contract. Nothing enforceable is carried over, no matter who tries to carry it over; for if it were, the sovereign's authority would not be absolute.

Locke crafts a social contract theory suited for "property-owning" men only. Rawls finally makes social contract theory take its egalitarian commitments seriously. But Hobbes, properly understood, has as sturdy and sound a philosophical basis as did Rawls to establish the political equality of women. It's time that Hobbes should receive the credit for the important feminist work he did.

Notes

1. Thomas Hobbes, *Philosophical Rudiments Concerning Government and Society* [*De Cive*], in *The English Works of Thomas Hobbes of Malmesbury*, ed. Sir William Molesworth, vol. 2 (London: John Bohn, 1841), 9.3. References to *De Cive* are to chapter and paragraph in this edition.

2. John Stuart Mill offers a thoughtful explanation of this in "The Subjection of Women," in *On Liberty and Other Essays*, ed. John Grey (Oxford: Oxford University Press, 1991), 471–582.

3. See Carole Pateman, *The Sexual Contract* (Stanford: Stanford University Press, 1988). I won't speak here to the larger question of whether social contract theories must assume a limitless freedom of contract that threatens to undermine substantive autonomy—that "a free social order cannot be a contractual order. . . . Taken to a conclusion, contract undermines the conditions of its own

existence" (ibid., 232)—or to whether the fact that contract theories, at least prior to Rawls's, seemed to incorporate women as subordinates exposes an inherent flaw.

4. Christine Di Stefano, *Configurations of Masculinity: A Feminist Perspective on Modern Political Theory* (Ithaca, N.Y.: Cornell University Press, 1991).

5. In contrast to rational bargaining theories, which allow the superior bargaining position of some contractors to impose differentially disadvantageous terms of agreement on others.

6. Thomas Hobbes, *Leviathan*, ed. Edwin Curley (New York: Hackett, 1994), 15.22, emphasis added. References are to chapter and paragraph.

7. Ibid., 14.5.

8. Karen Green may hold such a view, although I am not entirely sure about this. She seems to hold that women may have willingly accepted subequal terms of political subjection out of a non-egoistic interest in rearing children and encouraging other adults to encourage in citizens a love of virtue and honor and fidelity to the moral law. See her "Christine De Pisan and Thomas Hobbes," *Philosophical Quarterly* 44, no. 177 (1994): 473–74.

9. This is the argument made by Nancy Hirschmann in chapter 6 of this volume and in her *Gender, Class, and Freedom in Modern Political Theory* (Princeton, N.J.: Princeton University Press, 2008).

10. Gordon Schochet advanced such a view in "Thomas Hobbes on the Family and the State of Nature," *Political Science Quarterly* 82 (September 1967): 427–45; reprinted as chapter 5 of this volume. Jane S. Jaquette argues that "reading the social contract as excluding women categorically is not consistent with Hobbes's position" and that "contract theory demands attention to the power relations within which contracts are made." See her "Contract and Coercion: Power and Gender in *Leviathan*," in *Women Writers and the Early Modern British Political Tradition*, ed. Hilda L. Smith (Cambridge: Cambridge University Press, 1998), 101–2.

11. Thomas Hobbes, *The Elements of Law, Natural and Politic*, ed. Ferdinand Tönnies (London: Frank Cass, 1969), 2.8.1. References are to part, chapter, and paragraph. Machiavelli also noted the sort of hostility a prince engenders when he threatens men's domestic sovereignty, stoking hatred by taking their women or other property; and Mill observes that men of lower social classes (who feel that much of their lives are in the control of their social superiors) are particularly keen to have mastery over someone, making it politically destabilizing to seek to abridge their authority over their wives and children. Mill writes in "The Subjection of Women," "And how many thousands are there among the lowest classes in every country, who, without being in a legal sense malefactors in any other respect, because in every other quarter their aggressions meet with resistance, indulge the utmost habitual excesses of bodily violence towards the unhappy wife, who alone, at least of all grown persons, can neither repel nor escape from their brutality . . ." (508).

12. At one point in *Behemoth* he does seem to belittle them, when he writes disapprovingly of the translation of the Bible into vulgar languages so that "every man, nay, every boy and wench, that could read English, thought they spoke with God Almighty, and understood what he said"; see Thomas Hobbes, *Behemoth, or The Long Parliament*, ed. Ferdinand Tönnies (Chicago: University of Chicago Press, 1990), 21. But this remark, differentiating those literate in Latin from those literate only in English, seems more a class slight than a gender slight. Joanne Wright has argued that Hobbes exhibited none of what she calls "anxious masculinity," and may even have had some degree of respect for Margaret Cavendish, Bess of Hardwick, or Elizabeth I.

13. I offer an extended defense of this desire for self-justification as the primary psychological feature of humans that impels them to adhere to Hobbes's laws of nature in *Morality in the Philosophy of Thomas Hobbes: Cases in the Law of Nature* (New York: Cambridge University Press, 2009), 88–94 and 248–52. In this I am rejecting all standard interpretations of Hobbes as holding an egoist or "preservation-dominant" conception of human nature, including the more nuanced interpretation of Karen Green and others that "the achievement of all aims, whether they are egoistic or altruistic, almost always depends on one's own survival" (ibid., 464). I had already argued that Hobbes was

concerned to address "transcendent" interests in such things as salvation, justice, liberty, and the welfare of loved ones that trump individuals' interests in their own temporal bodily preservation and everything that depends on that preservation. See S. A. Lloyd, *Ideals as Interests in Hobbes's "Leviathan": The Power of Mind over Matter* (Cambridge: Cambridge University Press, 1992).

14. Hobbes, *De Cive* 9.3.
15. On the Amazons, see Hobbes, *Leviathan* 20.4; Hobbes, *De Cive* 9.3–5.
16. Hobbes, *Elements of Law* 1.4.7. On sovereign queens, see also Hobbes, *Leviathan* 20.6 and 20.7; Hobbes, *De Cive* 9.5.
17. Hobbes, *Leviathan* 15.35.
18. Hobbes, *Elements of Law* 1.17.2.
19. Hobbes, *De Cive* 13.2–4.
20. Hobbes, *Elements of Law* 2.9.3.
21. Hobbes offers an account of power in chapter 10 of *Leviathan*.
22. Hobbes writes that "nobility is power, not in all places, but onely in those Common-wealths, where it has Privileges: for in such privileges consisteth their power" (*Leviathan* 10.11). However, although nobility proper has no place in the state of nature, "to be descended from conspicuous parents, is Honourable; because they the more easily attain the aids, and friends of their Ancestors" (10.45).
23. This also suggests the possibility within a Hobbesian view of a "charm offensive" by which one uses his or her powers of persuasion to preempt resistance and lock in confederates. Nothing in Hobbes rules this out as a source of power.
24. Wiles and eloquence are the primary means by which religious leaders gather followings in the state of nature. See chapter 12 of *Leviathan*.
25. Nor does the Law of Nature disapprove of such use. Because we would see such use of power as rational were we to possess power, we cannot fault others for so using their power.
26. Hobbes, *Leviathan* 13.11.
27. Ibid., 20.15. Of course, to be a real commonwealth, it would have to have sufficient power to deter attacks on itself.
28. Hobbes, *De Cive* 8.1. Some Hobbes interpreters have imagined that Hobbes spoke of persons as "sprung up like mushrooms" in order to emphasize what these interpreters have taken to be his individualism. Rather, because Hobbes consistently acknowledges that no person could have been born motherless, he counterfactually and hypothetically asks us to imagine ourselves "sprung up like mushrooms" without any obligations to our mothers, precisely so that we can imagine an anomic, "obligation-free" world. You already owe your mom more than you can possibly repay, and strict matriarchy would be the default position throughout all political theory.
29. There is an open question about whether someone's private dominion over another person can actually survive the social contract. We might hold that all such pre-civil contracts are voided in the original act but can be immediately reinstated by the civil sovereign; alternatively, we might hold that all such contracts survive the original contract unless and until the sovereign voids them. To my mind, this is a distinction without a difference: six of one, half a dozen of another. Hobbesian sovereigns may be morally faulted but cannot be legally resisted for any decisions about authority or changes in relative authority they impose on their subjects.
30. Hobbes, *Leviathan* 10.52.
31. Hobbes, *Elements of Law* 2.4.8.
32. Ibid., 2.4.3.
33. In chapter 12 of *Leviathan*, Hobbes grants that religious factions may have a powerful influence on people even in a state of nature. A vulnerability toward religious belief is natural to humans, and people can be expected to try to gain power over others by exploiting that vulnerability.

3

Defending Liberal Feminism

Insights from Hobbes

Jane S. Jaquette

Conventional interpretations of Hobbes—that his pessimistic view of men as selfish and violent required an absolute sovereign to keep them in line—make him an ideal foil for feminist critics. Although Hobbes is the one canonical political theorist who asserts that women are equal to men in strength and faculties of mind, Hobbes has been used by influential feminist theorists to argue that liberalism based on social contract theory is fundamentally patriarchal.[1] They see in Hobbes a host of masculine biases, including his view of human nature as violent and competitive, his "abstract individualism," his depiction of the state of nature as a war of all against all, and his insistence that the power of sovereignty must be "absolute."

I am grateful to Nancy Hirschmann and Abe Lowenthal for their persistence, constructive criticism, and support, without which this essay could never have been written.

This chapter argues for a more positive assessment of Hobbes's contributions, both to liberalism and to feminism.[2] I argue that Hobbes's individualism is not abstract but embodied, and that Hobbes's individuals are not isolates but embedded in social and normative networks. Hobbes's "state of nature" is an imaginative fiction that shows the strategic causes of conflict; Hobbes uses it to illustrate why civil association is not natural but must be constructed based on consent. His view of sovereignty may be absolute, but he is not an absolutist. In contesting Hobbes's feminist critics, I am concerned to defend the core liberal values present in Hobbes that have made it possible for women to demand citizenship, challenge male dominance, and become moral and political agents in their own right.

Early Feminist Critiques: Elshtain, Pateman, and Jones

Jean Elshtain's critique of Hobbes is brief but telling, for it states in telegraphic form key points that others develop more fully. Elshtain maintains that there is a close correspondence between what she calls Hobbes's "methodological individualism" and his absolutism. In Elshtain's view, Hobbes's "method, his theory of human nature, and his creation of a polity in which each consents to be ruled absolutely, entail and reinforce each other."[3] To live in peace, Hobbes requires his subjects to "quell the inner voices of passion." He achieves this by imposing "a new vocabulary . . . that is dispassionate, neutral, 'scientific.'"[4] Hobbes's individuals are "guided by an instrumentalism shorn of sentiment";[5] his nominalism denies them "the capacity to think, to judge, to question, and to act."[6] Anticipating Carole Pateman's argument in *The Sexual Contract*, Elshtain writes that Hobbes "tak[es] patriarchalism for granted and insert[s] the act of consent."[7]

Carolyn Merchant's ecofeminist critique also attributes what she sees as Hobbes's dehumanizing portrayal of humans to his method. She describes Hobbes as a "mechanist," referring to a scientific approach that brought "a new concept of the self as a rational master of the passions housed in a machine-like body." Mechanism displaced the medieval view of the self as "an integral part of a close-knit harmony of organic parts united to the cosmos and society."[8] To Hobbes, Merchant argues, the mind was simply a "calculating machine,"[9] his egalitarianism nothing more than a by-product of his "atomistic" view of human relations, lacking any normative content.[10]

Carol Pateman's critique of the social contract is widely cited as providing convincing evidence that liberalism is foundationally patriarchal.[11] Hobbes states that "every woman that bears children, becomes both a *mother* and a *lord*,"[12] but Pateman sees an ellipsis in Hobbes's account that reveals his hidden patriarchal assumptions. If Hobbes makes men and women equal in the state of nature, she asks, why are women absent when "the fathers of families" enter into the social contract?[13] In the state of nature, there is "no reason why a woman should contract of her own free will to enter into a long-term sexual relationship" or become the "servant (slave) of a man." But because women in the state of nature are weakened by pregnancy and caring for young children, they are soon forcibly subjected by men. "The original political dominion of maternal lordship is quickly ... replaced by masculine right," as each man obtains "a 'family' of a woman servant and her child."[14] Thus, the social contract is "a *sexual* contract that institutes political right in the form of patriarchal power."[15] Liberalism must hide its subjection of women by separating the public and private spheres, making civil freedom a "masculine attribute" that "depends upon patriarchal right."[16]

Further, the marriage contract is nothing but a sham: women become "citizens for a day" to "consent" to their subjection. By extension, all contracts are suspect. Far from being Hobbes's reciprocal "promises mutual," contracts are alienating. Pateman cites Rousseau: if a man "attempts to separate his capacities ... from himself by alienating them through contract, ... his freedom is turned into mastery or subjection."[17] Because contracts disguise coercion as consent, Pateman concludes, "a free social order cannot be a contractual order." The "feminist dream is subverted by entanglement with contract."[18]

Kathleen Jones challenges Hobbes's concept of sovereignty. In *Compassionate Authority*, which reflects the pluralist turn in feminist thought, she asks why we still accept a largely Hobbesian concept of sovereignty in which the authority of the state is "absolute." A feminist conception of political life would "move away from authority as domination to authority as meaningful, mutually constructed communal bonds."[19] Hobbes's insistence on the unity of the sovereign "negate[s] the possibility of including divisible bodies—women's bodies—in the scheme." The "divided" female body gives women the ability to put themselves imaginatively in the place of the other.[20] The demand for political representation of women is inadequate; having women rather than men rule in families or in states "does not make a difference" if authority is understood to mean "a final, unimpeachable command."[21] Jones would replace the modern concept of "rational-legal" authority, based on sovereignty, with a "compassionate" authority that "cuts through this orderly universe with feelings that connect us to the specificity and particularity of actors and actions."[22]

I take up each of these arguments in turn: that Hobbes's individuals are atomized by his scientific method; that their violent and competitive behavior is justified by the inevitability of conflict in the state of nature; that he imagines a society based on conflict among asocial, calculating individuals lacking human bonds of connection; and that absolute sovereignty is the extreme example of Hobbes's use of contract to legitimize coercion as consent.

Hobbes's Individuals

Ann Tickner shows that the way we think about Hobbes is still used to contest the relevance of liberalism to feminist concerns. In *Gendering World Politics*, she writes that the contemporary use of "empiricist" methods reflects a recognizably Hobbesian interpretation of the liberal tradition, in which human beings are "conceived of as isolated individuals with no necessary connection with each other." In the 1960s and 1970s, Tickner maintains, "feminists began to question [the] liberal belief in the possibility of women's equality, empiricist methodologies . . . [and] liberal feminists' prescriptions" for addressing gender inequalities. The problem with liberal feminism is liberalism's emphasis on individualism and rationality, which "promoted masculine values" and privileged "mind over body and individualism over relationships."[23] She suggests an alternative, a "feminist standpoint" methodology, which is "rooted in concrete 'reality' that is the opposite of the abstract, conceptual world inhabited by men, particularly elite men," and asserts that "in this reality lies the truth of the human condition."[24]

Characterizing empirical political science as "Hobbesian" is one way to decry the trend in international relations toward quantitative and rational choice methodologies, but it is not a fair portrayal of Hobbes's method. Although Hobbes must be included among the new natural philosophers of the seventeenth century, he took a rationalist, not an empiricist—that is, experimental or inductive—approach to science. Unlike

Francis Bacon and the luminaries of England's Royal Society, Hobbes argued that experiments could never prove anything beyond doubt and therefore never produce true science.[25] Instead, his method was based on the logic of geometry. Reading Euclid convinced him that it was possible, by starting from clear definitions, to develop an internally consistent theory of political obligation that would be straightforward and uncontestable, just as geometric theorems were beyond debate.

The first several chapters of *Leviathan* reflect Hobbes's attempt, drawing on his own experiences and introspection, to establish clear definitions on topics ranging from power to a broad spectrum of human emotions. These chapters show that Hobbes was an acute observer of social relations in seventeenth-century England, but they do not constitute an experimental approach. Although he rejected Aristotle and the authority of the ancients, Hobbes's method was closer to classical thought than to modern science. Rationalism posits a discoverable, underlying order to physical and biological phenomena; Hobbes saw himself as supplying a rationalist and material understanding of human behavior in order to construct political authority on a more reliable basis than had yet been possible.[26]

There are important distinctions to be made here. Hobbes's materialism is not mechanism, and his view that humans are "Rationall" does not mean that they are lacking in passion or are selfish and instrumental. We can compare Hobbes to Descartes, who was also a rationalist, and who shared Hobbes's "plenist" view that the universe is filled with matter and that all cause and effect can theoretically be explained by "local motion" transmitted directly from one body to the next. His effort to make room for God in his materialist model of the world led Descartes to adopt a dualist view of the relation between mind and body.[27] By contrast, Hobbes conceived of the mind and even of God in materialist terms.[28] Cartesian dualism privileged the mind over the body, as classical theory had privileged reason over the passions. But Hobbes praises desire: "All Stedinesse of the minds motion, and all quickness of same, proceeding from thence. For to have no Desire, is to be Dead." Hobbes reverses the classical relationship: reason does not discipline but rather serves desire: "For the Thoughts, are to the Desires, as Scouts, and Spies, to range abroad, and find the way to the things desired."[29] Daniela Coli sees reason in Hobbes not as an abstract quality but as one that depends on language, memory, and imagination. Without imagination, she writes,

Hobbes thought "men would be devoid of passions, but also of any talent or intelligence."[30]

Hobbes's individuals are not atoms; they are fully embodied. As he seeks to formulate clear definitions that will serve as the basis for reasoning about civil association, Hobbes describes in corporeal, even visceral, terms how people perceive, understand, and act in the world. He accepts (and does not judge) the body. At one point he suggests that, like humans, animals are also capable of cause-and-effect reasoning and understand signs.[31] These comparisons shocked his contemporaries, who believed that man's unique ability to reason was the basis on which humans could be expected to act according to moral rules.[32] Today we take Hobbes's ability to see similarities between men and animals as an indication of his capacity to "put himself imaginatively in the place of" the other. By contrast, Descartes, having decided that animals could not have souls, thought of them as mere animated machines.

Elshtain asserts that Hobbes's method replaced a discourse rooted "in the living reality of singularities, differences, and individualities" with one that produced a "human mass as objects of control or manipulation."[33] Hobbes argues emphatically, however, that people are not alike. Humans may have similar *passions* ("desire, fear, hope, &c"), but they differ markedly from one another in the *objects* of their passions and in the mix and intensity of their desires.[34] These differences arise "partly from the different Constitution of the body," Hobbes says, but also "partly from different Education,"[35] that is, from experience. Richard Flathman concludes that Hobbes thinks that humans are so different from one another that that they are often mutually unintelligible.[36] Without differences, we would not need the social contract, and, as Nancy Hirschmann points out, without difference, we would not need a concept of agency.[37]

An important source for feminist interpretations of Hobbes's thought is his characterization of individuals in the "state of nature." Hobbes does not begin his chapter on the state of nature with an account of human nature, however. Instead, he asks us to imagine the consequences of *equality* in the absence of political authority: "Nature hath made men so equall, in the faculties of body and mind; as that though there bee found one man sometimes manifestly stronger in body or quicker in mind then another; yet when all is reckoned together, the difference between man and man, is not so considerable, as that one man can thereupon claim to himselfe any benefit, to which another may not pretend, as well as he."[38]

Equality makes everyone equally hopeful of achieving their ends and equally able to attack one another; both can lead to violent confrontation. But equality is not an aspect of man's *nature*; it describes a structural condition, one claimed as an objective by both liberalism and Marxism. In Hobbes's imagined state of nature, where there is no common power, equality leads to violence as people fight to protect the resources they think they need to survive in accordance with their natural right of self-preservation.

Hobbes then lists three causes of "quarrel" among men: scarcity, diffidence, and glory. He writes, "The first maketh man invade for Gain; the second for Safety; and the third, for Reputation."[39] As Kathleen Jones puts it, "Greed drove everyone to want everything," but the lack of anyone's having adequate "power and means to live well made everyone . . . vulnerable."[40] At least two of Hobbes's three causes of war are structural or "strategic," however—not the product of flaws in man's nature. For example, scarcity is often portrayed (as Jones does, for example) as a consequence of human greed. This interpretation seems justified by Hobbes's famous declaration that "I put for a generall inclination of all mankind, a perpetuall and restlesse desire of Power after power, that ceaseth only in Death."[41] But, Hobbes tells us, the reason for this is not greed but *uncertainty*. Humans have a much more profound capacity than animals to think in terms of cause and effect, and to imagine how these might play out in the future.[42] Because we do not know when we will die, and as our temporal imaginations are infinite,[43] our desires also have no limit. As Hobbes explains, this "perpetuall and restlesse desire" is not always because "a man hopes for a more intense delight, than he has already attained to" but because "*he cannot assure the power and means to live well, which he hath present, without the acquisition of more.*"[44]

Conflict over what each person deems legitimately necessary now and in the future is intensified by the insecurity that results when there is no political authority—when there is, as Hobbes says, "no Mine and Thine," nor just or unjust, because there is no common power to make and enforce laws.[45] When people are insecure and life is unpredictable, they are highly motivated to hoard and defend what they have. It follows that, in the state of nature, no one can hold "a convenient Seat" because others will come, armed, to take it from him, along with "the fruit of his labour . . . [and] his life, or liberty," as well.[46] Uncertainty is a *strategic* problem that inevitably arises when people seek their self-preservation under conditions of equality and anarchy.[47] Civil association addresses scarcity by ensuring security.

Diffidence is also a strategic source of violence. The contemporary definition of diffidence is timidity, and it has been suggested that in the state of nature, diffidence tempts the strong to attack the weak. But the "archaic" definition of diffidence is based on the Latin, *di + fidere*, meaning lack of trust. Under conditions of anarchy, diffidence causes *the weak to arm themselves* to ensure their safety against real or perceived threats from others. This does not require that all men be naturally aggressive. As Hobbes says in *De Cive*, "though the wicked were fewer than the righteous, yet because we cannot distinguish them, there is a necessity of suspecting, heeding, anticipating, subjugating, self-defending, ever incident to the most honest and fairest conditioned." This puts everyone in a condition of readiness for war, which is as detrimental to peace as actually being at war.[48] Francois Tricaud concludes that in *Leviathan* Hobbes makes it clear that "whatever evil may ensue" does not come "from men's inner nature, but from the external (and disastrous) circumstances of their precontractual encounter," or, in Hobbes's own words, "the ill condition, which man by meer nature is actually placed in."[49]

Of the three causes of quarrel, *glory* is a human flaw, and it arouses Hobbes's ire. Although glory can be analyzed in strategic terms (as a "zero-sum" good that can only be achieved by some at the expense of others), Hobbes sees the competition for glory as inimical rather than necessary to self-preservation. Leo Strauss reminds us that the biblical Leviathan is the "King of the Proud," lamenting that Hobbes has broken with classical tradition by substituting fear for honor as the basis for political authority.[50] But in *Leviathan* and even more clearly in *Behemoth*, Hobbes's concern about glory is more contextual than abstract. The sin of pride that so disturbed Hobbes is "vainglory." "The vainglorious thinke themselves wiser, and abler to govern the Publique, better than the rest," Hobbes warns, "and these strive to reforme and innovate, one this way, another that way; and thereby bring it into Distraction and Civill War."[51] They are the "Presbyterians and sectarians" who justify their attacks on the king by claiming "conscience" or loyalty to a "higher law." They are "driven to rebellion not only by ambition and love of gain, but by *malice* and *envy*."[52] Victoria Kahn, describing the "common lawyers, natural rights theorists, Presbyterians, Independents and radical sectarians" as "the crown's chief competitors in producing ideological fictions," argues that they drew on romantic notions of heroism and honor to incite men to rebel.[53] In the context of the Civil War, the social contract was a creative act of political imagination. "Instead of presupposing a rational and autonomous individual who consents to the political contract," however, "17th century contract theorists were compelled to create a new political subject *ex nihilo*."[54]

The Social Contract

A second focus of feminist critiques is the social contract itself. Carole Pateman's critique is gendered: women are excluded from the social contract, which legitimates male sex-right. What Hobbes says, however, is that "for the most part (but not alwayes) . . . Commonwealths have been erected by the Fathers, not by the Mothers of families."[55] Hobbes, born during the reign of Elizabeth I, does not contest women's right or capacity to rule.

Kathleen Jones and others object that Pateman's narrative makes women the "hapless victims of sexual exploitation."[56] By subjecting women, Pateman says, men "obtain a family of a woman servant and her child." But in *Leviathan* Hobbes usually refers to "families" in a larger sense, as, for example, "a man, and his children, and servants together."[57] It might be more accurate to judge Hobbes's social contract as exclusionary on the grounds of class rather than gender. Hobbes's concept of "family" appears to describe the powerful elite families of seventeenth-century England, composed of children, servants, and retainers as well as wives.[58] Most women, but also most men, were not family heads in this sense, and the term "servants" described a substantial proportion of England's population, including the peasants who worked the land. Those who were without property or obligation to a "lord" were not attached to families; these "masterlesse men" were also excluded from Hobbes's social contract at its founding. That exclusion did not bar their later inclusion, however, as liberal egalitarian arguments have often been marshalled to expand the number of enfranchised citizens.

Elshtain maintains that Hobbes goes against both classical and medieval traditions to portray human relations as "contractual and artificial" rather than "essential and intrinsic." Although Hobbes sees the ability to make and keep promises as essential to a healthy society, he does not suggest that human relations can be understood in terms of contract alone. And if we look beyond his state of nature to his laws of nature, it is clear that Hobbes is engaged in constructing a form of civil association that makes it possible for people to act both prudently and morally.

Hobbes begins the discussion by positing a "Right of Nature": "the Liberty man hath, to use his own power, as he will himselfe, for the preservation of his own Nature; that is to say, of his own Life."[59] In the state of nature, everyone has the right to everything, but it is an empty right because, absent enforceable laws, individuals cannot be assured of keeping anything they gain and cannot protect themselves against servitude or violent death.

Hobbes's laws of nature identify a set of virtues and their opposing vices. The fourth law of nature, for example, calls for gratitude, "without which there will be no beginning of benevolence, or trust; nor consequently of mutual help, nor reconciliation of one man to another."[60] The fifth law is "compleasance": "*That every man strive to accommodate himselfe to the rest.*" Those who strive toward this virtue are "sociable," and those who do not are "stubborn" and "intractable." Given that Hobbes has been characterized as a prescient apologist for capitalism, it is striking that he uses greed as his example of a breach of the fifth law, and he suggests a harsh remedy. When a stone is too hard for masons to work, Hobbes writes, and is "by the builders cast away as unprofitable, and troublesome, so also, *a man that by asperity of Nature, will strive to retain those things which to himself are superfluous, and to others necessary*; and for the stubbornness of his Passions, cannot be corrected, is to be left, or cast out of Society, as cumbersome thereto."[61]

In the state of nature, as we have seen, equality can lead to violence. In civil society, however, equality, defined as equal respect, is a requirement for peace. Opposing Aristotle, who maintained that some are naturally more fit to rule others, Hobbes declares that "the question of who is the better man has no place in meer nature." Whatever inequality "that now is, has bin introduced by the Lawes civill,"[62] that is, by human convention. In the end, "men that think themselves equall, will not enter into conditions of Peace, but upon Equall termes. . . . And therefore the ninth law of Nature I put thus, *That every man acknowledge other for his Equall by Nature*. The breach of this Precept is Pride."[63]

Hobbes understood that fear or force alone could not sustain long-term allegiance to a regime, Mary Dietz argues. Civil association required a "more richly constituted" subject.[64] Although Hobbes was very aware of the importance of the Bible as the source of moral guidance, many

Christian virtues—including "love, hope, and faith; meekness, compassion and humility"—are absent from Hobbes's laws of nature. Instead, Dietz suggests, Hobbes was "promoting private virtue for public ends." The laws of nature concerning justice, gratitude, modesty, equity, and mercy are "civic attributes that reveal the kind of person the Hobbesian citizen is, or should be."[65] Hobbes's laws of nature are not intended to "contain" subjects, "but to *reconstitute* them as citizens."[66]

Hobbes thought that the only true laws are those made by the sovereign and backed by the sword. In what sense are the laws of nature obligatory? The answer is ambiguous. Hobbes combines an instrumental understanding of obligation with something approaching a natural-law interpretation. "Injustice, Ingratitude, Arrogance, Pride, Iniquity and Acceptance of persons [i.e., favoritism] . . . can never be made lawfull," Hobbes declares. "For it can never be that Warre shall preserve life, and Peace destroy it."[67] Therefore, we should act according to the laws of nature for instrumental reasons, for the laws of nature promote peace, and peace is everyone's highest interest. On the other hand, Hobbes asserts, no one can escape the moral obligations of the laws of nature, because they can be put into "one easie sum: Do not that to another, which thou wouldest not have done to thy selfe."[68] Here he seems to be claiming that there are shared ethical rules that are not inconsistent with, but not reducible to, individuals' short or even long-term self-interest.[69]

Hobbes's own explanation of how the laws of nature bind individuals again emphasizes the importance of security to trust, and suggests that he thinks people are both guided by and capable of acting in accordance with shared moral rules. But they cannot be expected to do so in the absence of effective political authority: "The Lawes of Nature oblige *in foro interno*; that is to say, they bind to a desire they should take place; but *in foro externo*; that is, to the putting them in act, not always. For he that should be modest, and tractable, and performe all he promises, in such time, and place, when no man els should do so, should but make himself a prey to others, and secure his own ruine, contrary to the ground of all Lawes of Nature, which tend to Nature's preservation." Even without that security, however, the laws of nature oblige "to a desire, and endeavor," and by that, he says, "I mean an unfeigned and constant endeavor."[70]

Absolute Sovereignty

Hobbes does declare that sovereignty is all-powerful. It is the "Common Power" that keeps men "in awe," "the *Mortall God*, to which wee owe under the *Immortal God*, our peace and defence. For by this Authoritie, given him by every particular man in the Common-Wealth, he hath the use of so much Power and Strength conferred on him, that by terror thereof, he is inabled to forme the wills of them all, to Peace and home, and mutuall ayd against their enemies abroad."[71] Several scholars are convinced, however, that Hobbes's view of sovereignty is not as absolute as he declares it to be. Michael Oakeshott believes Hobbes limits the power of the sovereign by limiting the scope of the state, noting that Hobbes declares that "the 'greatest liberty' of subjects derives from the silences of the law."[72] Deborah Baumgold points out that Hobbes embeds the sovereign in a complex social network, and concludes that Hobbes has a "weak theory of rights" but a "strong theory of excuses."[73] Richard Flathman believes that subjects "cannot have reliable legal protections against the excesses of their rulers" and "certainly cannot rule themselves."[74] What limits the sovereign is Hobbes's commitment to "individuality and individual self-making."[75]

The laws of nature describe the social contract as an irrevocable covenant, yet they also grant individuals the right of self-preservation, and each individual judges "*as he* [or she] *will himselfe*" whether the sovereign is exercising "rightful dominion." That is, the sovereign must deliver "protection" on the subject's terms, or the latter can rightfully cease to obey.[76] Jones provides a feminist reading, noting that, in *De Cive*, Hobbes argues that women have dominion over children not only because they bear them but also because they raise them. Should a mother "expose" the child "and another find it and nourish it, the domination is in him [sic] that nourisheth it."[77] Unless a mother's biological claim was "matched by actions to preserve the life of the child, mothers could not justify their continued rule over children. Nor could rulers of states."[78]

The argument that "absolute sovereignty" simply means that in any state there must be a final arbiter seems tautological, but it should not be dismissed. Hobbes favored absolute monarchy, but he defined sovereignty as *effective political authority*—that is, as a concept, not as a particular ruler or even a particular form of government. Hobbes repeatedly insists that sovereignty must be absolute to prevent conflicts from sliding into civil war. Effective political authority is also desirable, however, because it makes it possible for the commonwealth to act as a whole. As Jane Mansbridge points out, any decision rule that defines consent as consensus will always favor the status quo.[79] Further, on any given issue, some will disagree.

If the group is all *talk*, there is no need for an enforceable decision rule. But when groups or states must *act* and there is no consensus, there must be some means of arriving at a final decision, and some must yield. In a democracy, this kind of "power over" to enable "power to" is justified when there is a fair procedure for making decisions that does not systematically exclude some and favor others. It is obvious, however, that Hobbes does not make participation in public debate his goal; indeed, he sees the sphere of public discourse as an arena in which the vainglorious all too easily mislead the credulous. He criticized the opportunities for corruption and demagoguery that democracy would provide[80] and saw the Civil War as a consequence of ideas run amok. Hobbes gives the sovereign the power to limit debate and censor doctrines, which, to the degree it is exercised, bars *both* men *and* women from the public sphere.

Nonetheless, Hobbes is deeply concerned about fair procedures, and his laws of nature counsel several ways of achieving justice: individuals should not be judges in their own case, rehabilitation is better than revenge, and arbiters should be acceptable to both sides of a dispute, for example.[81] Yet, when "a common policy is needed" and there is no natural unanimity of wills . . . we must have an artificial will, and this is the will that the sovereign provides."[82] From this standpoint, it seems to me that Jones's call for a "multivocal" sovereign misreads the meaning of sovereignty. A state can be "multivocal" in its procedures; it can be tolerant or recognize difference to ensure more equal participation and representation. But multivocality cannot substitute for the sovereign capacity of a political community to decide for the whole.

Sharon Lloyd approaches the issue of what Hobbes means by "absolute" from an entirely different angle. She suggests that we should think of the term as applying to the way subjects think about obligation, rather than as applying to the sovereign's power to punish. The English Civil War was fought over "competing transcendent . . . religious interests," Lloyd points out, and most of Hobbes's readers were believers for whom obedience to God was an "absolute command." Therefore, the conditions of the Civil War "both allowed for, and required, an absolutist solution"—the Leviathan as a "Mortall God." What is absolute about

Hobbes's sovereign is in his requirement that subjects *"adhere to a principle of unconditional* [that is, absolute] *obedience."*[83]

Transcendent issues do make compromise very difficult, which is precisely what makes sectarian battles so deadly. But, although Hobbes tries throughout *Leviathan* to show that his ideas are consistent with biblical injunctions, he did not think that citizens should literally see the sovereign as a "Mortall God." There is nothing godlike about Hobbes's sovereign, whose powers come from the office, not from charisma, nobility, or divine right.

Lloyd's proposition that the adjective "absolute" applies to the *beliefs of citizens* is intriguing, however, and suggests a positive, even utopian, reading of Hobbes. When citizens create civil association by adhering "absolutely" to the will of the sovereign (as expressed in positive law based on the laws of nature), sovereignty becomes a *projection of citizens' wills* rather than a defense of the dictatorial power of the state over citizens as subjects. A society that is governed consistently, under enforceable laws, creates the security that makes it possible for people to keep their promises, follow decision procedures that are fair, address scarcity, and pursue the "individual self-making" that Flathman finds at the heart of Hobbes's thought.

Viewed from this perspective, what is absolute about sovereignty is *the attitude subjects take toward it*, not the freedom a monarch or assembly has to abuse it. In this construction, the capacity of the state to guarantee the security of citizens depends first on *how citizens treat one another*. If people are obliged, as Hobbes suggests, to "unfeigned and constant endeavor" to act toward one another according to the laws of nature, and are bound by the social contract even when it is not in their immediate self-interest, the state will only rarely need to use its power of the sword to ensure peace—against those who are intractable and whose passions cause them to pursue vices rather than virtues. Hobbes believed that they would be few, as most people desire peace. Under these conditions, sovereignty then becomes "more than Consent or Concord."[84] It is the power of "wills united" that Hobbes claimed for it.

Hobbes and Feminist Liberalism

Two questions raised at the outset remain: Was Hobbes patriarchal? And are contracts coercive? Joanne Wright is probably correct that Hobbes's declaration of women's equality in the state of nature did not reflect any deep commitment to women's rights on his part, but rather constituted an effective argument to upend his patriarchalist opponents.[85] I also think Joanne Boucher is right to argue that when Hobbes says, "For there is not always that difference of strength, or prudence between the man and the woman, as that the right can be determined without War," he leaves the decision of "right" (that is, whose will shall prevail) to a contest of strength, and over time this contest is likely to go to men, whom Hobbes describes as "naturally fitter than women for actions of labor and danger."[86] When Hobbes identifies weaknesses in women, however, he attributes them to women's dependency, not to their defective natures. Contrary to Pateman, there is no evidence that Hobbes drew a line between the public and private spheres.[87]

Women's rights and marriage did receive attention in the "world turned upside down" of the seventeenth century,[88] but the overall trend was in the opposite direction. As Boucher notes, the radicalism of the Levellers fell far short of granting women equality,[89] and Hirschmann shows that women's economic and political status declined throughout the period.[90] But in contrast to all the (male) theorists before him and to most who came after, Hobbes explicitly included women as equals, not because he experienced or championed a world in which women were equal to men, but because his geometry of politics was—not just mathematically but also morally—a fundamentally egalitarian one. Locke retreats from Hobbes's position that marriage is conventional, reverting to the idea that natural differences between men and women determine their social and political roles. Rousseau idealized women as the mothers of citizens but denied that they could be citizens themselves. By contrast, as Gordon Schochet maintains, Hobbes's portrayal of women as equal to men in the state of nature imagines the possibility that women might demand political equality.[91]

Feminist, postmodern, and postcolonial debates have greatly enriched our understanding of how liberal institutions can oppress and exclude, and how liberal states can act like empires. But without liberalism's ideals of equality and universality, and its claim that all individuals have a right to the resources that make citizenship possible, there would be no consistent basis on which to assert the demand that we must not demean, exclude, or exploit "the other," and no effective basis for women (or slaves, or other marginalized groups or individuals) to demand their voice and their rights. Liberalism may coexist with various forms of oppression, but its fundamental assumptions provide the moral and practical bases for challenging them, and for designing or reforming institutions to address them. Liberalism provides the space in which different communities can live together and cooperate, although respect for both group and individual differences means that liberal societies will primarily be based on tolerance and negotiation, that is, on promise- and contract-making, not on solidarity alone.

We owe much of this liberal egalitarian tradition to Hobbes, who argued that political authority must ultimately be based on the wills of citizens who acknowledge one another as equals while recognizing difference, and who believed that the private conscience of the individual should be protected, even as he made a strong case for the necessity of a capable state. The concept of a social contract forces us to think about the *terms* under which people consent to be ruled. Hobbes's laws of nature make it the responsibility of citizens to develop attitudes that promote civility and justice.

Feminist hostility to liberalism is misplaced, in my view, and has contributed to the feminist movement's loss of social conscience and political momentum. By rejecting liberalism and its institutions rather than pressing for their reform, and by holding out a feminist utopian vision that is ultimately homogenizing rather than respectful of difference, many feminists have lost sight of the movement's liberal origins and agenda, for which we owe an often overlooked debt to Hobbes.

Notes

1. "And whereas some have attributed the Dominion to the Man onely, as being of the more excellent Sex; they misreckon it. For there is not always that difference of strength, or prudence between the man and the woman, as that the right can be determined without War." Thomas Hobbes, *Leviathan: Authoritative Text, Backgrounds, Interpretations*, ed. Richard E. Flathman and David Johnston (New York: W. W. Norton, 1997), ch. 20, 111. Unless otherwise indicated, references are to chapter number from part 1 and page number from the Flathman and Johnson text.

2. On feminism and liberalism, see Lisa H. Schwartzman, *Challenging Liberalism: Feminism as Political Critique* (University Park: Pennsylvania State University Press, 2006), and Ruth Abbey, *The Return of Feminist Liberalism* (Durham, UK: Acumen, 2011).

3. Jean Bethke Elshtain, *Public Man, Private Woman: Women in Social and Political Thought* (Princeton, N.J.: Princeton University Press, 1981), 109. She borrows the term "methodological individualism" from Steven Lukes, commenting that "Hobbes's mechanistic cosmology—matter in motion—turned mind to matter" (109n13).

4. Ibid., 113.

5. Ibid., 108–9. But see David Johnston, *The Rhetoric of "Leviathan": Thomas Hobbes and the Politics of Cultural Transformation* (Princeton, N.J.: Princeton University Press, 1986), chs. 1–2.

6. Elshtain, *Public Man*, 112. Cf. Philip Pettit, *Made with Words: Hobbes on Language, Mind, and Politics* (Princeton, N.J.: Princeton University Press, 2008). Pettit contends that Hobbes was the first to argue that speech makes thought possible.

7. Elshtain, *Public Man*, 112.

8. Carolyn Merchant, *The Death of Nature: Women, Ecology, and the Scientific Revolution* (Stanford: Stanford University Press, 1988), 214.

9. Ibid., 232–33. Cf. Terrell Carver, *Men in Political Theory* (Manchester: Manchester University Press, 2004).

10. Merchant, *Death of Nature*, 211.

11. See Carole Pateman's *The Sexual Contract* (Stanford: Stanford University Press, 1988) and "'God Hath Ordained to Man a Helper': Hobbes, Patriarchy, and Conjugal Right," in *Feminist Interpretations and Political Theory*, ed. Mary Lyndon Shanley and Carole Pateman (University Park: Pennsylvania State University Press, 1991), 53–73. For a similar argument that exchange theories hide structural inequalities and therefore obscure relations of dominance, see Nancy Hartsock, *Money, Sex, and Power: Toward a Feminist Historical Materialism* (New York: Longman, 1983).

12. Thomas Hobbes, *De Cive*, in *Man and Citizen: Thomas Hobbes's "De Homine" and "De Cive,"* ed. Bernard Gert (New York: Anchor Books, 1972), 9.3. References are to chapter and section number.

13. Pateman, "'God Hath Ordained to Man a Helper,'" 64–65.

14. Ibid. Of course, men are also "subjected," both in the state of nature and, in civil association, to the "absolute" sovereign, and virtually all societies separate public and private and/or "male" and "female" spheres. Liberal egalitarianism provides one of the most effective arguments against that separation, a split that is reinforced in the Western secular tradition by Rousseau and in most other traditions by religious sanction.

15. Ibid., 67.

16. Ibid., 2. Combining arguments that can be seen in Elshtain and Merchant, Pateman asserts that men see "[w]omen, their bodies and bodily passions" as representing "the 'nature' that must be controlled and transcended if social order is to be created and sustained" (100). This is at odds with Hobbes's positive view of the body and its desires. In *Hobbes and the Making of Modern Political Thought* (London: Continuum, 2009), Gordon Hall compares Hobbes and Aristotle, and argues that Hobbes anticipates Foucault as "a theorist of biopolitics" (14).

17. Pateman, *Sexual Contract*, 76.

18. Ibid., 232.

19. Kathleen B. Jones, *Compassionate Authority: Democracy and the Representation of Women* (New York: Routledge, 1993), 166.

20. Ibid., 83.

21. Ibid., 67 and 70.

22. Ibid., 149.

23. J. Ann Tickner, *Gendering World Politics: Issues and Approaches in the Post–Cold War Era* (New York: Columbia University Press, 2001), 12–13.

24. Ibid., 17. "Feminist standpoint" is an approach developed by Nancy Hartsock.

25. See R. E. Ewin, *Virtues and Rights: The Moral Philosophy of Thomas Hobbes* (Boulder, Colo.: Westview Press, 1991), and Noel Malcolm, *Aspects of Hobbes* (Oxford: Oxford University Press, 2002), chs. 5 and 10. Cf. Steven Shapin and Simon Schaffer, *Leviathan and the Air-Pump: Hobbes, Boyle, and the Experimental Life* (Princeton, N.J.: Princeton University Press, 1985).

26. "The skill of making, and maintaining Common-wealths, consisteth in certain Rules, as doth Arithmetique and Geometry; not (as Tennis-play) on Practise onely: which Rules, neither poor men have the leisure, nor men that have had the leisure, have hitherto had the curiosity, or the method to find out." Hobbes, *Leviathan*, ch. 21, 115.

27. See Susan R. Bordo, *The Flight to Objectivity: Essays on Cartesianism and Culture* (Albany: State University of New York Press, 1987).

28. Hobbes's assertion that God was material, not "Spirit" (in his Latin text, *Deus es corpus*), although not original, was taken as tantamount to atheism in seventeenth-century England. See the discussion in George MacDonald Ross, *Starting with Hobbes* (London: Continuum, 2009), 148–54.

29. Hobbes, *Leviathan*, ch. 8, 43.

30. Daniela Coli, "Hobbes's Revolution," in *Politics and the Passions, 1500–1850*, ed. Victoria Ann Kahn, Neil Saccamano, and Daniela Coli (Princeton, N.J.: Princeton University Press, 2006), 75.

31. Hobbes, *Leviathan*, ch. 3, 17.

32. See, for example, Edward Hyde, "A Brief View and Survey of the Dangerous and Pernicious Errors to Church and State in Mr. Hobbes's Book, Entitled *Leviathan*," in Hobbes, *Leviathan*, 287.

33. Elshtain, *Public Man*, 50, 53, quoted in Jones, *Compassionate Authority*, 240.

34. Hobbes, *Leviathan*, introduction, 10.

35. Ibid., ch. 8, 42.

36. Richard Flathman, *Thomas Hobbes: Skepticism, Individuality, and Chastened Politics* (Newbury Park, Calif.: Sage, 1993), 2.

37. Nancy J. Hirschmann, *The Subject of Liberty: Toward a Feminist Theory of Freedom* (Princeton, N.J.: Princeton University Press, 2003), 230.

38. Hobbes, *Leviathan*, ch. 13, 68.

39. Ibid., ch. 13, 69–70.

40. Jones, *Compassionate Authority*, 44–45.

41. Hobbes, *Leviathan*, ch. 10, 54.

42. Ibid., ch. 5, 27; and ch. 6, 34.

43. On temporality in Hobbes, see Samantha Frost, *Lessons from a Materialist Thinker: Hobbesian Reflections on Ethics and Politics* (Stanford: Stanford University Press, 2008).

44. Hobbes, *Leviathan*, ch. 11, 55–56; italics mine.

45. Ibid., ch. 13, 71.

46. Ibid., ch. 13, 69.

47. On uncertainty in Hobbes's thought, see Loralea Michaelis, "Hobbes's Modern Prometheus: A Political Philosophy for an Uncertain Future," *Canadian Journal of Political Science* 40, no. 1 (2007), 101–27.

48. Hobbes, *Leviathan*, ch. 13, 70.

49. Quoted in Francois Tricaud, "Hobbes's Conception of the State of Nature," in *Perspectives on Thomas Hobbes*, ed. G. A. J. Rogers and Alan Ryan (Oxford: Oxford University Press, 1989), 120.

50. Leo Strauss, *The Political Philosophy of Hobbes: Its Basis and Genesis* (Chicago: University of Chicago Press, 1963), 128. Quentin Skinner, citing Noel Malcolm, points out that in one tradition of biblical interpretation, the word "Leviathan" "is used for the name of the many made one." Skinner, *Hobbes and Republican Liberty* (Cambridge: Cambridge University Press, 2008), 190n42.

51. Hobbes, *Leviathan*, ch. 17, 95. And of the scholastics, who have perpetuated absurd notions such as "incorporeal substances," thereby confusing the gullible, Hobbes writes, "When men write whole volumes of such stuffe; are they not Mad, or intend to make others so?" (ch. 9, 47).

52. Steven Holmes, "Political Psychology in Hobbes's *Behemoth*," in *Thomas Hobbes and Political Theory*, ed. Mary G. Dietz (Lawrence: University Press of Kansas, 1990), 132.

53. Victoria Kahn, *Wayward Contracts: The Crisis of Political Obligation in England, 1640–1674* (Princeton, N.J.: Princeton University Press, 2004), 136. She argues that Hobbes intends his "scientific" and measured rhetoric to be an antidote to romantic "mimesis."

54. Ibid., 1.

55. Hobbes, *Leviathan*, as quoted by Joanne Boucher, "Male Power and Contract Theory: Hobbes and Locke in Carole Pateman's *The Sexual Contract*," *Canadian Journal of Political Science* 36, no. 1 (2003): 28. Boucher observes that the ellipsis in Hobbes can be filled in by several different narratives. For a critique of Pateman, see Jane S. Jaquette, "Contract and Coercion: Power and Gender in

Leviathan," in *Women Writers and the Early Modern British Political Tradition*, ed. Hilda L. Smith (Cambridge: Cambridge University Press, 1998), 200–219.

56. Jones, *Compassionate Authority*, 44.
57. Hobbes, *Leviathan*, ch. 20, 113.
58. See especially chapter 10 of *Leviathan*, which identifies the sources of an individual's power.
59. Ibid., ch. 14, 72.
60. Ibid., ch. 15, 83.
61. Ibid., ch. 15, 8; italics mine. Sheldon Wolin uses the analogy of the masons to argue that Hobbes's civil association is in fact a "culture of despotism," a Foucauldian analysis that contradicts the conventional view that Hobbesian men are social isolates, but put to the same critical end: Hobbes creates individuals only to subject them to despotic rule. See Wolin, "Hobbes and the Culture of Despotism," in Dietz, *Thomas Hobbes and Political Theory*, 9–36.
62. Hobbes, *Leviathan*, ch. 15, 84–85.
63. Ibid., ch. 15, 85.
64. Mary Dietz, "Hobbes's Subject as Citizen," in Dietz, *Thomas Hobbes and Political Theory*, 92.
65. Ibid., 103.
66. Ibid., 107.
67. Hobbes, *Leviathan*, ch. 15, 89. See Richard Tuck, *Hobbes: A Very Short Introduction* (Oxford: Oxford University Press, 1989), 56.
68. Hobbes, *Leviathan*, ch. 15, 87.
69. Karen Green defends Hobbes's laws of nature as having moral validity beyond prudence: "Hobbes recognizes an equality of natural right which exists independently of our power to enforce it. . . . It is our moral intuitions grounded in this notion that enable us to recognize that there are situations in which individuals may be forced to consent to unjust pacts, and that consent of itself does not entail justice." Green, *The Woman of Reason: Feminism, Humanism, and Political Thought* (New York: Continuum, 1995), 57. Cf. Ross Harrison, *Hobbes, Locke, and Confusion's Masterpiece* (Cambridge: Cambridge University Press, 2003).
70. Hobbes, *Leviathan*, ch. 15, 87.
71. Ibid., ch. 17, 95–96.
72. Michael Oakeshott, *Hobbes on Civil Association* (Indianapolis: Liberty Fund, 1975), 47–48.
73. Deborah Baumgold, *Hobbes's Political Theory* (Cambridge: Cambridge University Press, 1988), 80.
74. Flathman, *Thomas Hobbes*, 99–100.
75. Ibid., 72; see also 87.
76. Hobbes is contradictory on whether and under what circumstances subjects have a right to rebel. For two views, see Flathman, *Thomas Hobbes*, 119; and Richard Tuck, "Hobbes and Locke on Toleration," in Dietz, *Thomas Hobbes and Political Theory*, 165–70.
77. Hobbes, *De Cive* 9.4, quoted in Jones, *Compassionate Authority*, 56.
78. Jones, *Compassionate Authority*, 56.
79. Jane Mansbridge, "Feminism and Democracy," in *Feminism and Politics*, ed. Anne Phillips (Oxford: Oxford University Press, 1998), 142–60. R. E. Ewin makes this argument in reference to Hobbes in *Virtues and Rights*, 167 and 200–205.
80. See, for example, Hobbes, *Leviathan*, ch. 29.
81. Ibid., ch. 15, 32.
82. Ewin, *Virtues and Rights*, 28.
83. S. A. Lloyd, *Ideals as Interests in Hobbes's "Leviathan": The Power of Mind over Matter* (Cambridge: Cambridge University Press, 2003), 308.
84. Hobbes, *Leviathan*, ch. 17, 95.
85. Joanne H. Wright, "Going Against the Grain: Hobbes's Case for Original Maternal Domination," *Journal of Women's History* 14, no. 1 (2002): 123.

86. Hobbes, *Leviathan*, ch. 20, quoted in Boucher, "Male Power," 28.
87. Wright, "Going Against the Grain," 2.
88. See Christopher Hill, *The World Turned Upside Down: Radical Ideas During the English Revolution* (New York: Penguin, 1972), ch. 15.
89. Boucher, "Male Power."
90. Nancy J. Hirschmann, *Gender, Class, and Freedom in Modern Political Theory* (Princeton, N.J.: Princeton University Press, 2008), 46.
91. Gordon Schochet, "The Significant Sounds of Silence: The Absence of Women from the Political Thought of Sir Robert Filmer and John Locke (or, 'Why Can't a Woman Be More Like a Man?')," in Smith, *Women Writers and the Early Modern British Political Tradition*, 221.

4

Hobbes and the Bestial Body of Sovereignty

Su Fang Ng

Leviathan opens with an unforgettable image of the body of the commonwealth. But instead of picturing the natural body from the familiar body-state analogy, Hobbes offers a body that he terms "an Artificiall Man," that is, a machine; and for Hobbes, machines are "*Automata* (Engines that move themselves by springs and wheels as doth a watch)." This body is artificial in that it is artful, a man-made thing (introduction, 9).[1] In *De Cive*, Hobbes compares the workings of a state to "an automatic Clock or other fairly complex device" (preface, 10).[2] As mechanical clockwork, Hobbes's state resists gendering. On the one hand, in presenting the human body as a machine without sex, Hobbes apparently leaves sovereignty ungendered. On the other hand, by calling the Leviathan an artificial *man*, Hobbes seems to adhere to traditional categories of gender.

Hobbes's gender politics have been much debated. His inclusion of the paternal state suggests residual patriarchalism, but at the same time, he evidently derives sovereignty from consent.[3] Feminist scholars particularly puzzle over what happens in the transition from the state of nature, where mother-right prevails, to civil society, where men are dominant. This troubling gap prompted Carole Pateman to offer a conjectural history positing that the marriage contract came before the social contract, and that it follows from men's conquest of the mother, who is put at a disadvantage by childbirth: "A man is then able to defeat the woman he had initially to treat with as an equal (so he obtains a 'family')."[4] Wives become servants and the family is acquired, like a kingdom might be, through conquest. However, Pateman's account has itself sparked controversy among other feminist scholars.[5] As Quentin Skinner notes in the dialogue that opens this volume, Hobbes's inclusion of queens and other sovereign women suggests that he does not gender sovereignty as exclusively male, opening a space for reconceptualizing gender relations.[6]

The body of Hobbes's sovereign has thus proven difficult to gender. The iconic frontispiece to *Leviathan* depicting a gigantic crowned man composed of multitudes seems an unarguably masculinist representation. Yet, as Skinner argues, "the features of the multitude requiring to be pictured or represented are common to everyone, men and women alike," and so "the multitude can equally well be represented by a queen regnant as by a king."[7] That the visibly male image of the body of Leviathan represents both male and female monarchs might suggest another instance of the "false universal,"[8] but a close examination shows Hobbes implicitly including mothers in his definition of paternal power. Skinner detects women and children among the multitude: "The sovereign is thus shown to owe his position entirely to the support of his subjects, and . . . he is being upheld by the whole of civil society: women appear to be present as well as men, children as well as adults, soldiers as well as civilians."[9] Even so, the pictorial representation shows women as only subjects and not sovereigns. Thus, following Pateman's emphasis on the priority of the marriage contract, some scholars see Hobbes's citizen as feminized. Comparing the Hobbesian subject to "the female subject of romance or of seventeenth-century domestic manuals, the wife who consents to be bound by her own passions to a hierarchical, inequitable, irrevocable marriage contract," Victoria Kahn argues, "the ideal Hobbesian subject is the docile, effeminized political subject of an absolute sovereign, [and] the fear of the sovereign may be construed as a gendered fear—what seventeenth-century manuals called the 'fear' of one's husband that leads to appropriate subordination and reverence rather than insubordination and emulation."[10] But even if the body of the subject is so gendered, the body of the sovereign remains difficult to gender, as Hobbes's writings insist on sovereignty's gender neutrality: responding to concern regarding "his Attributing to the Civil Soverign all Power Sacerdotal," Hobbes acknowledges, "But this perhaps may seem hard, when the Sovereignty is in a Queen: But it is because you are not subtle enough to perceive, that although Man may be male and female, Authority is not."[11]

More often than not, Hobbes tries to degender bodies—of sovereigns as well as the constituent parts of the sovereign body. An examination of the ways in which Hobbes conceives of bodies, in particular the body of sovereignty, reveals the unusual lengths to which he would go to degender authority. This degendering may be part of Hobbes's attempt to create an immortal body of the state, but his reformation of the trope of the body politic is not simply in making the body politic a mechanical body.[12] Rather, if we look beyond the body-state analogy, we find that Hobbes's body devolves into other objects.

Hobbes's embodiment of sovereignty takes two forms. The first is a mechanization and abstraction of the body. The clearest expression of this is the Hobbesian state as mechanical clockwork, which has been much discussed. The second embodiment of the state is the animalization of the body. It occurs most prominently in the characterization of man as bestial in the state of nature, but it is not confined to the state of nature. There is a fragmentary form of sovereignty in the state of nature, which forms the basis of the Hobbesian state. Moreover, the bestial nature of Hobbesian sovereignty can be discovered from a close reading of his scattered references to the wolf. I argue that Hobbes rejects the story of Lucretia's rape as the foundational myth of Rome in favor of the earlier fable of the wolf suckling Remus and Romulus, which represents a more monarchical aetiological myth of state formation.

Both embodiments of the state degender the body by making it unhuman. In representing the state as nonhuman entities—the machine and the animal—Hobbes takes gender out of the equation. However, in the case of the second embodiment, the focus of my essay, Hobbes has still to contend with the female gender of the Roman wolf, the surrogate mother of Remus and Romulus. I suggest that Hobbes's initial formulation of sovereignty in the state of nature as mother-right may be inspired by this myth of the suckling she-wolf. At the same time, as critics have pointed out, mother-right is quickly superseded by a sovereignty apparently wielded by men or, alternatively (the argument I favor), by ungendered sovereignty. Even as Hobbes tries to exorcise gender from sovereignty to formulate an ungendered state, the she-wolf's female gender is nonetheless the originary marker of boundaries between civil and uncivil, human and animal. This gender, though strangely, unhumanly embodied in a savage wolf, functions as a kind of remainder of the state of nature, which has to be contained through abstractions of the corporate state. Ultimately, the degendering of the state means the exclusion of women *qua* women.

Although mother-right in the state of nature has dominated the discussion of gender in Hobbes, this feminization of power is anomalous. Rather, with each iteration of his theory, Hobbes increasingly excludes women from the civil state. Although he does not succeed in completely excluding gender as he struggles to refute the highly gendered patriarchalist conception of political power, he tries to construct a gender-neutral system to the extent possible. The animalization of the state is the more problematic aspect of Hobbes's strategy, in which the female term returns to haunt his conception of sovereignty, thus necessitating its suppression. That he ultimately does not succeed may be because he continues to be trapped in gendered discourses of his period. But it is also because Hobbes uses the female gender to represent the raw power of force in the state of nature.

The mechanization of Hobbes's civil society contrasts sharply with his emphasis on the barbaric conditions of the state of nature. The incorporated Leviathan state dehumanizes by excluding human bodies and human relations. But his state of nature is equally dehumanizing in that bodies are animalized. In *Leviathan*, Hobbes famously describes the life of man in the state of nature as "solitary, poore, nasty, brutish, and short" (ch. 13, 89). The state of nature is the condition of perpetual warfare, without rule of law, where one has to kill or be killed. Without security, the state of nature is also a condition of primitiveness. Hobbes describes it as without culture in the primary sense of lacking agriculture as well as in the secondary sense of lacking crafts and the higher arts. The bestial aspects of the state of nature were widely recognized as such by his contemporaries, who reacted strongly against what they saw as a debasement of human dignity. A typical critical response was Bishop John Bramhall's rejection of the idea that humans were comparable to animals: "If God would have had men live like wild beasts, as lions, bears, or tigers, he would have armed them with horns, or tusks, or talons, or pricks; but of all creatures man is born most naked, without any weapon to defend himself, because God had provided a better means of security for him, that is, the magistrate."[13]

Modern critics, post-Darwin, have been far more amenable to fuzzier distinctions between animal and human; nonetheless, they too look for points of difference between the two.[14] Consequently, modern critics emphasize the unbridgeable divide between the state of nature and civil society. Largely confining the animal nature of man to the state of nature, they assume that civil society has subdued man's bestial nature. Richard Ashcraft upholds the division even when he says that Hobbes rejects the distinction between civilized Christians and beastly Others so as to see animality as the natural human condition outside the law.[15] Some critics who consider the animal self in civil society view it as a manifestation of madness and thus maintain the human/animal binary.[16]

The sharp distinction between the state of nature and civil society, a prominent feature of Hobbes's political philosophy, is seemingly secured by the human-animal opposition. In chapter 17 of *Leviathan*, Hobbes considers the natural sociability of bees and ants only to explain why humans are not similarly sociable: he argues that these creatures do not compete for honor, lacking private property, the use of reason, and language.[17] His description of man in *Leviathan* underlines this opposition of human and animal through the importance ascribed to language. Without speech, which he names the greatest invention, he says, "there had been amongst men, neither Common-wealth, nor Society, nor Contract, nor Peace, no more than amongst Lyons, Bears, and Wolves" (ch. 4, 24). By corollary, the condition in the state of nature of perpetual war without contract and without society suggests the animal nature of man. The wolf has a special significance for Hobbes, who references it in his revision of Plautus's line in *Asinaria*: "Lupus est homo homini, non homo, quom qualis sit non novit" (Man is no man, but a wolf, to a stranger).[18] I argue that the wolf's part in the foundational myth of Rome—Rome as a city built by Romulus, who with his twin brother Remus was suckled by a wolf—is important to Hobbes's reimagining of originary dominion. This myth constitutes the framework for Hobbes's state of nature. Preferring it to the republican myth in which the rape of Lucretia gave rise to the Roman republic, Hobbes revises the myth of Romulus and the wolf to make it the basis of sovereign power.

In *De Cive*'s dedicatory letter to William Cavendish, the Earl of Devonshire, Hobbes argues that even as they accused kings of being rapacious beasts, the Roman people themselves acted like savage wolves:

> *The Roman People had a saying* (Most Honoured Lord) *which came from the mouth of* Marcus Cato, the Censor, *and expressed the prejudice against Kings which they had conceived from their memory of the Tarquins and the principles of their commonwealth; the saying was that Kings should be classed as predatory animals* [bestiarum rapacium]. *But what sort of animal was the Roman People? By the agency of citizens who took the names* Africanus, Asiaticus, Macedonicus, Achaicus, *and so on from the nations they had robbed, that people plundered nearly all the world. So the words of* Pontius Telesinus *are no less wise than* Cato's . . . *that Rome itself must be demolished and destroyed, remarking that there would never be an end to* Wolves *preying upon the liberty of* Italy, *unless the forest in which they took refuge was cut down. There are two maxims which are surely both true:* Man is a God to man, *and* Man is a wolf to Man [Homo homini Deus, & Homo homini Lupus]. (dedication, 3)[19]

Hobbes's fear and loathing of populist government is unsurprising. Taking Cato's republican formulation of kings as animals preying on their people and reversing it to call the people wolves, he notes that the Roman people were themselves plunderers of other nations. Thus, the accusation of predatory wolfishness leveled at kings can be seen as a kind of displacement. But Hobbes goes further, positing that acts appearing to be savage animality can be understood as positive traits: "The wickedness of bad men compels the good too to have recourse, for their own protection, to the virtues of war, which are violence and fraud, i.e. to the predatory nature of beasts" (dedication, 4). Attempting to escape the undesirable and insecure state of war through a social contract commanding submission to sovereign authority that will ensure perpetual peace, he allows for self-preservation by violent means. Rereading Cato to reverse the valence of predatory behavior, Hobbes argues that warfare is a legitimate means of self-preservation. If warfare is sometimes necessary, then by arguing that going to war is akin to behaving as predatory animals, he erases the distinction between good and bad acts of violence, moving seamlessly from the king's violence to the people's and thus chiding Cato for censuring "in Kings what he thought reasonable in his own people" (dedication, 4). For Hobbes, predatory acts are acceptable in both people and kings, except that in civil society the people would have transferred their right to warfare to the sovereign.

Critics treating the question of animality in Hobbes tend to pay attention only to his second maxim on the wolfish character of man.[20] In fact, Hobbes calls attention to two maxims, that "Man is a God to man" and that "Man is a wolf to Man." The first is Seneca's response to Plautus: "Homo, sacra res homini" (Man is a sacred thing to man).[21] While this defines the relations among citizens, the second applies to relations among commonwealths. By the first maxim, Hobbes refers to the godliness that he believes citizens approach when they practice the "virtues of peace," while by the second, he means to suggest the recourse to "virtues of war, which are violence and fraud, i.e. to the predatory nature of beasts," in relations of conflict, as between two sovereign powers (dedication, 4). While some contemporaries were disturbed by the comparison to animals, Hobbes neutralizes it by reinterpreting Cato's denunciation of monarchs. The practices of war, like those of predatory beasts, are not vices when needed for self-preservation, and they lack the moral valence Cato ascribes to them. War is a necessity when two sovereign powers, who do not have a relation defined by contract, come into contact—whether in the case of relations between two sovereign commonwealths or relations among people in the state of nature. So-called predatory relations are necessary when social contracts are absent.

Hobbes's Leviathan monarch is thus a sovereign wolf, whose predatory behavior is not a negative trait. His account is not one of transition from wildness to civilization, as described by Donna Haraway: "Man took the (free) wolf and made the (servant) dog and so made civilization possible."[22] Rather, civilization is made when the wolf becomes sovereign. Hobbes's sovereign wolf resembles instead Giorgio Agamben's sovereign, the correlative figure to the *homo sacer* characterized as the banned Germanic outlaw, the *wargus*, or wolf-man: for Agamben, "in the person of the sovereign, the werewolf, the wolf-man of man, dwells permanently in the city."[23] Although Hobbes deflects Cato's criticism of wolfishness onto the Roman people, he takes care to defend predatory behavior, redefined as the Machiavellian virtues of violence and fraud suited to occasion.[24] *Leviathan* makes it clear that the people authorize the actions of their representative, the sovereign, and cannot oppose him. In the reading I offer, the sovereign as wolf is too provocative a subject for Hobbes to approach straightforwardly outside of a dedicatory letter written in Latin.

Nonetheless, there are hints that a wolf story may lie behind his theory of sovereignty and, indeed, that it may be a she-wolf.[25]

In the quotation above from the "Epistle Dedicatory" to the Earl of Devonshire, Hobbes makes reference to the Tarquins, whose tyrannical rule of Rome led finally to a revolt during the reign of Lucius Tarquinius (cognomen Superbus) when his son Sextus Tarquinius raped Lucretia. The revolt led by her kinsman Lucius Junius Brutus and her husband Lucius Tarquinius Collatinus (also a Tarquin) overthrew the monarchy to establish the Roman republic. Lucretia herself became immortalized as the faithful wife who committed suicide after the rape. This was a powerful myth of the founding of republican Rome, with a sacrificial woman thrown in. Hobbes's dislike of the story is evident from his discussion of Tacitus in his early work *Horae Subsecivae*:

> Every one that has read the Roman Histories, can tell how much this act of Lucius Brutus has been magnified, insomuch as they instituted in the honor of it, an holiday, by the name of *Regifugium* [flight]: and how the imitation of it drew another of the same race, and name, into such another action, who came not off with the like applause, though otherwise with the like fate. But I shall never think otherwise of it than thus: "*Prosperum et felix scelus virtus vocatur.*" [Prosperous and fortunate evil is called virtue.] For it was but a private wrong, and the fact not of the king, but the King's Son, that Lucretia was ravished. However, this, together with the pride, and tyranny of the King, gave color to his expulsion, and to the alteration of government.[26]

Rejecting Lucretia as a symbol of Roman republican liberty, Hobbes contains the story's affective power by terming it a private quarrel. If we examine his narrative of the origins of civilization in the state of nature, we get a very different tale.

I argue that Hobbes replaces the story of the rape of Lucretia with the myth of Romulus's founding of Rome to frame his state of nature. In implying that by defending the honor of one's kinswoman one also defends the liberty of one's country, the avenging of Lucretia's rape is an aetiological myth of Rome wherein *patria* encompasses not only country but also the lineal family, with the woman serving as a symbol of the motherland. However, Hobbes is not sympathetic to the figuration of state as family, as I have argued elsewhere.[27] The story of Remus and

Romulus, on the other hand, encapsulates a number of aspects of Hobbes's political philosophy: sibling rivalry as representative of the state of nature before the creation of the civil commonwealth, as well as the arbitrary nature of sovereign power in which the nonhuman nurturer of the child/subject utterly defamiliarizes—in the sense of making unfamiliar and de-familied—the concept of paternal power to decouple it from biological generation. Moreover, if we consider that the wolf suckling Remus and Romulus must be a she-wolf, we also get a female figure very different from Lucretia. A passive figure, acted upon rather than an acting subject, Lucretia's one deed is to commit suicide, itself a work of negation. In contrast, by suckling the twins, the she-wolf becomes an active shaper of what will emerge as Rome. Reading that alternative myth of the origins of Roman sovereignty illuminates the relation between the state of nature and civil society.

There are reasons to think that Hobbes would prefer the myth of Romulus to the story of the rape of Lucretia. The latter marks the beginning of the Roman republic, whose authors and their republican influence on his countrymen he critiqued. In *Behemoth*, Hobbes describes how the English ruling class, which was reading books "by famous men of the ancient Grecian and Roman commonwealths concerning their polity and great actions; in which books the popular government was extolled by the glorious name of liberty, and monarchy disgraced by the name of tyranny," imbibed through their classical education repugnant republican principles.[28] The former myth, on the contrary, is about the origins of monarchy in Rome. When Hobbes wrote to elevate self-preservation above all else, the myth of Romulus suckled by a wolf might have offered a few lessons. Several versions of the myth can be found in Plutarch's *Life of Romulus*. Hobbes would have been able to read the original, having himself translated Thucydides, though Plutarch was widely available in Sir Thomas North's translation, *The Lives of the Noble Grecians and Romaines, Compared Together*, the first edition of which appeared in 1579. Of the several possible stories of Romulus's birth and life, at least two involve the abandonment of Romulus and his twin, Remus, by a riverbank, where their lives were preserved by a she-wolf who "gave them suck"; they were later discovered by a swineherd who took them into his household.[29] However, in another version of the story, the wolf is a metaphorical wolf. In this alternate version, the name signified not the wild animal but a whore. The story goes that the nurse who gave the twins suck was a former prostitute named Acca Laurentia: "For the Latins do call with one self name she-wolves *Lupas,* and women that give their bodies to all comers, as this nurse, the wife of Faustulus (that brought these children home to her house) did use to do."[30]

The myth of Romulus suckled by a wolf presents an apt outline for Hobbes's analysis of perpetual war in the state of nature in service of self-preservation. He certainly knew the myth. In *Horae Subsecivae,* Hobbes recounts his visit to the Capitoline Hill in Rome, where he viewed the ruins of the ancient Capitol and numerous statues both inside and outside buildings in the area, among which was the statue of Romulus and Remus suckled by a wolf; he probably saw it while accompanying his charge, William Cavendish of Devonshire, on the continental tour. This particular subject was so popular that he notes it twice in a paragraph on Roman statuary:

> In the buildings there [on the Capitoline Hill] be also many principal Statues, as one of a Scolding Woman, so well done, as it would almost fear one to look on it. A Hercules in Brass. Julius and Augustus Caesar in Marble. Romulus and Remus sucking a Wolf, in Brass. Quintus Curtius on horseback, in brass, and Jupiter in Marble. Of Romulus and Remus sucking a Wolf there be many in Rome, and not defaced, being ever left by them that sacked it, to put the people in mind of their base beginning. But it seems in this respect, they never thought the worse of themselves, seeing they have in so many public places made representation of this.[31]

The brass statue of Remus and Romulus suckled by a wolf that Hobbes witnessed may well be the famous Capitoline wolf displayed on the Capitoline from around 1438. Long thought to be of Etruscan origin, with the twins added in the late fifteenth century, possibly by Antonio Pollaiuolo, it has recently been argued that the sculpture may be medieval.[32] Nonetheless, it and others like it were displayed in Rome when Hobbes visited the city. Whether the actual Capitoline wolf or a version of it, the statue Hobbes saw would have been that of a lean wolf with obvious dugs hanging from her torso, from which the twins sucked. Curiously, in *Horae Subsecivae,* Hobbes does not mention the wolf's gender, but the Capitoline wolf's dugs make its feminine gender quite plain, in keeping with the legend of the she-wolf, even as its lean and hungry aspect belies stereotypes of nursing mothers.

Although little attention has been paid to Hobbes's "A Discourse of Rome," which seems simply a guide to Rome—A. P. Martinich characterizes it as "adolescent"—Roman self-fashioning in the display of the city's history through the monuments and statuary recorded in this text may provide an insight into Hobbes's early responses to ideas about the origins and foundations of states.[33] Todd Butler argues that in his description of "the multitude of statues, temples, triumphant arches, and other impressive monuments scattered across the city," Hobbes evinces political awareness: he is "alternately fascinated by and hostile toward the power of images," drawing on the rhetorical device of "vivid description (*enargeia*), of setting forth images to an audience's eyes not just to illustrate a scene but to move listeners to agreement, if not action."[34] While he does not comment on particular antiquities, Hobbes discusses more generally the sort of "singular use and profit that may be gathered from the knowledge of them": first, they illustrate history; second, "the ancient Statues of the Romans, do strangely immortalize their fame"; third, the richness of the antiquities publicizes the magnificence of ancient times; and fourth, the architecture demonstrates unequalled "singularity, especially of the Statues, which are so done, that never any could come near the original for exquisiteness in taking the Copy: so that a man cannot but gather, that in this place, and those times, there were conjoined all singularities together, best workmen, best wits, best Soldiers, and so in every kind Superlative."[35] The Capitoline wolf would have been one such statue conveying the magnificence and greatness of ancient Rome; moreover, the popularity of its subject, seen in numerous examples around the city, might have impressed upon Hobbes the significance of the story of Romulus to the Romans and their city.

Hobbes's mother-right in his state of nature may indeed originate from this story of Rome's founding, even if he neglects the wolf's gender in his account—perhaps due to its telegraphic nature. Just as in the state of nature the child comes under the mother's dominion because she preserves his life, so too in both versions of Plutarch's life of Romulus, a female *lupa*, whether a wild she-wolf or a prostitute, is instrumental in preserving the twins' lives. This story of abandonment becomes the story of Rome's foundation. The question is in what ways it is also the story of Hobbes's civil sovereignty. Does Hobbes's initial gendering of dominion as female in the state of nature suggest that the sovereign wolf is in fact the Roman she-wolf? For there is indeed a brief window in Hobbes's state of nature when sovereignty is conceptualized as female. At the same time, however, nowhere in *Horae Subsecivae* does Hobbes note the gender of the Capitoline wolf.

Hobbes's state of nature is the only sphere in which power is explicitly gendered, albeit briefly: "Seeing the Infant is first in the power of the Mother, so as she may either nourish, or expose it; if she nourish it, it oweth its life to the Mother; and is therefore obliged to obey her, rather than any other; and by consequence the Dominion over it is hers." Hobbes quickly moves away from a maternal conception of power to one available to both genders: "If she [the mother] expose it [the child], and another find, and nourish it, the Dominion is in him that nourisheth it" (*Leviathan,* ch. 20, 140). The gender of parent shifts from female to male. The brief, originary gendering of power as maternal is best understood in relation to patriarchalism. By gendering dominion as female, Hobbes opposes patriarchalists' narratives of the origin of society, as they strongly gender sovereignty as male, deriving monarchical power from paternal power. Hobbes's strong revisionist reading of patriarchalism extends beyond gender to a revision of the chronological development of society. While modern critics are content to accept not just an animal aspect but also an animal phase in human civilizational development, Hobbes's patriarchalist opponents were not. Richard Ashcraft interprets Hobbes's description of small families as living in continual warfare thus: "Hobbes simply incorporated the theory of patriarchalism into his description of the state of nature."[36] This depiction of the origins of mankind and of the paternal state would have been anathema to many of Hobbes's contemporaries. Rejecting the state of nature, Bishop Bramhall insists, "Paternal government was in the world from the beginning, and the law of nature."[37]

In addition to reversing the patriarchal gendering of originary dominion, Hobbes also strikes at Sir Robert Filmer's argument from historical antiquity. Hobbes's reference to Native Americans as an example of people living in the state of nature is nothing less than a rebuttal of Filmer's argument that takes West Indians (Hobbes's Americans) and other pagans as evidence of the ubiquity of the exercise of the power of life and death by fathers: "The judicial law of Moses giveth full power to the father to stone his disobedient son, so it be done in the presence of a magistrate. . . . Also, by the laws of the Persians and of the people of the Upper Asia, and of the Gauls, and by the laws of all the West Indies, the parents have power of life and death over their children."[38] In *Leviathan,* Native Americans are notable as a society organized in families: "The savage people in many places of *America*, except the government of small Families, the concord whereof dependeth on naturall lust, have no government at all; and live at this day in that brutish manner" (ch. 13, 89). What is for Filmer the basis of monarchy—families—is for Hobbes no basis for government but rather a state of perpetual war from which his system provides escape.

Hobbes's position on women has been so difficult to parse because he systematically rejects the role of families in commonwealths. His mother-right in the state of nature is ambiguous, lending itself to both feminist and antifeminist arguments. The *domina*, the lordly mistress, of the state of nature either disappears or is reconstituted as the subjected citizen of the Leviathan state. But beyond sovereign queens, it is difficult to discern female presence in Hobbes's civil state. Mary Nyquist suggests it is rather the child-slave who is the quintessential Hobbesian subject, with "despotism or slave mastery" as Hobbes's model for sovereignty.[39] From this premise she contends, "Wives and mothers, not being subject to absolute dominion, cannot properly illustrate the structure and significance of sovereign power. Adult women have no place in Hobbes's theorization of sovereignty . . . because they do not submit to anyone's dominion."[40] Nyquist reframes the issue to argue that Hobbes leaves women out of his account of the formation of civil society, thus highlighting the lacuna in his account. This reading of the relation between gender and sovereignty stems from her observation that Hobbes collapses categories to erase the difference between children or subjects and *servi*, "provocatively trivializing differences between *liberi* and enslaved."[41] She rightly sees Hobbes restructuring citizenship not in the binary of male/female but rather in the different terms of sovereign/slave. In the process, instead of deploying gendered subjecthood, *Leviathan* writes gender out. While individual women may be either sovereigns or slaves, the gendered subject is not to be found in Hobbes. The woman is excluded and incorporated into other ungendered identities.

I suggest that the exclusion Nyquist identifies can also be understood in terms of the figure of the wolf. Embedded in Hobbes's account of the state of nature is a fragmentary pre-civil sovereignty: the relation of mother and child is the relation of sovereign and subject. The mother is in fact the sovereign *avant la lettre*. While undermining the assumed primacy of paternal power, mother-right connects women with the she-wolf of Romulus and Remus. Hobbes links the woman with the wolf by characterizing sovereignty, or dominion, in the state of nature as both female (in terms of mother-right) and, I argue, lupine. In so doing, he "others" the woman, turning her body into the site of the bestial. Like the Germanic outlaw who is *wargus*, or wolf, the woman is excluded from society and becomes an exilic *lupa*. As outlaws, neither women nor wolves come under the jurisdiction of the city. Although the woman occupies the position of sovereign in the state of nature, she becomes Agamben's *homo sacer* in civil society, an outcast, not worthy to be sacrificed but whose death does not really matter. The she-wolf's displacement by the swineherd, who actually raises the twins, figures also the mother's own displacement when the state of nature transitions into civil society. Hobbes moves exceedingly quickly from mother-right to the situation wherein the mother abandons the child: "But if she expose it, and another find, and nourish it, the Dominion is in him that nourisheth it. For it ought to obey him by whom it is preserved" (*Leviathan*, ch. 20, 140). The lupine heart of Hobbes's mother-right belies the argument that the woman is the ideal Hobbesian subject. Rather, the woman is the displaced sovereign wolf.

Hobbes's failure to mention the gender of the Capitoline wolf may suggest a mind that tends not to categorize by gender or one that is intent on suppressing gender. The gendering of the wolf is approached obliquely: while the she-wolf must be female in order to suckle the twins, its character as a savage animal can be emphasized so as to transcend gender. After all, the sovereign's defining attribute is the absolute power to kill. Although women were at the originary moment of state formation—for the relation between the child and the nurturing mother is, for Hobbes, a relation of contract—they are then excluded, first through the characterization of the state of nature as bestial and then through the disappearance of women *qua* women in civil society. This female/lupine pre-civil sovereignty is superseded by a social contract, which Hobbes describes as mainly the creation of men: "For the most part Commonwealths have been erected by the Fathers, not by the Mothers of families" (*Leviathan*, ch. 20, 140). The difference between pre-civil sovereignty and the social contract is their reach and extent: the one operates between two persons while the other involves a multitude yielding their wills to a single sovereign. But Hobbes also emphasizes the difference between the two by his differing characterizations of the one as animal and the other as mechanical. The lupization of power is the counterpart to Hobbes's mechanization of power. Both involve the displacement of human bodies or human bonds for animals or machines so as to degender bodies.

If in the state of nature *homo homini lupus est*—man is a wolf to man—then at the most fundamental level the gender of the parent does not matter to Hobbes even if the mother has sovereignty in the state of nature. What ultimately matters is whether the child encounters the wolf who suckles or the one who devours. Rather than a feminized citizen, we have a degendering of sovereigns through lupization. Yet, gender does play a part: just as the wolf must be female to suckle, Hobbes retains mother-right as the initial, originary form of sovereignty in the state of nature. However, in separating his two states—the state of nature and commonwealths—Hobbes renders them as unlike each other as possible. The difference stems from his displacing bare life onto the woman so that she can be the marked one, the one banned from the city. Unlike Agamben, who thinks separation impossible, by this displacement Hobbes tries to keep sovereignty free from the taint of bare life (or in his terminology, the state of nature), thus maintaining the vast gulf between the machine and the wolf.

Hobbes's embodiment of sovereignty takes two so very different forms that they seem almost contradictory. Despite apparent dissimilarities, in both cases Hobbes attempts to degender state and sovereign, each time breaking with the gendered, familial forms of the state. Mechanization renders the sovereign artificial, genderless, and immortal while animalization aligns the sovereign with savagery. While initially the beast, a she-wolf, is gendered, that gender is ultimately done away with. Just so is mother-right in the state of nature the initial, originary form of sovereignty that disappears in the transformation to the civil commonwealth. Eschewing familial bonds, Hobbes imagines new forms of associations through metaphors of the body independent of biological ties or dynastic lineages. The figure of the wolf makes Hobbes's rejection of family ties even starker, for the wolf is expected to devour the helpless child on the presupposition that it lacks any affective bonds with it, whether familial or humane. In this way, Hobbes valorizes bonds forged through the power of the sovereign to preserve life (or alternatively, the power to kill) over familial ones.

In confining gendered sovereignty to a brief period in the state of nature, Hobbes suggests that gendered forms are primitive. His revisions of patriarchalism show him opposed to the gendered constructions of the family as foundational for the state. But rather than hypothesizing an artificial commonwealth from the start, Hobbes begins from the condition of the she-wolf's sovereignty, which allows him to explore more thoroughly the abandonment of the conventional familial forms of patriarchalism. In particular, the story of Remus and Romulus is, at its heart, a story of child abandonment, used by Hobbes as a complex fable to discard familial bonds completely and to clear a conceptual space for imagining a wholly different structure for society free from kinship bonds.

Mortal bodies are vulnerable to decay and cannot be the basis for an immortal state. Hobbes's concern with fashioning an immortal state is the reason why he sees the king as a god, quoting from the favorite scripture of King James I: "For there God sayes, *Non habebis Deos alienos*; Thou shalt not have the Gods of other Nations; and in another place concerning *Kings*, that they are *Gods*" (*Leviathan*, ch. 30, 234). To describe the effect of disobedience to the laws, Hobbes turns to the myth of Peleus's daughters, who, "desiring to renew the youth of their decrepit Father, did by the Counsell of *Medea*, cut him in pieces, and boyle him, together with strange herbs, but made not of him a new man" (ch. 30, 234). When his daughters listen not to their father's sovereign will, but to their own (or worse, to a foreigner like Medea), they end up committing patricide and regicide. The Leviathan sovereign, who is essentially the same as the state, cannot be divided. The fragmentation of Peleus's body is the terrifying consequence of wrongheaded attempts to remake the state. Change is undesirable because it leads to fragmentation and decay. The mortal aspects of the body—its individuality, its gender—all threaten eventual death. In order to immortalize the body of sovereignty, Hobbes makes it other than human.

The absence of human gender in Hobbes ironically invites feminist readings, for it severs the patriarchal link between the gendered roles of family and ideal forms of government, putting each in new contexts and allowing both family and government more room for innovation than when they were yoked together. The gendered she-wolf represents not only a primitive form of government, but also an elective one that is not reliant on precedent or on the supposedly natural bonds of family (or even of species). Hobbes's emphasis on the mechanical and corporate (or incorporated) body of civil society favors voluntary design and association rather than individual roles predefined by gender. By not making gender fundamental to his theory of political power, Hobbes clears away a number of patriarchal presumptions and leaves room for new forms of civil engagement by men or women.

Notes

1. Thomas Hobbes, *Leviathan*, ed. Richard Tuck (Cambridge: Cambridge University Press, 1991). Citations to *Leviathan* are from this edition and given parenthetically by chapter and page number.
2. Thomas Hobbes, *On the Citizen [De Cive]*, ed. and trans. Richard Tuck and Michael Silverthorne (Cambridge: Cambridge University Press, 1998). Citations to *De Cive* are from this edition and given parenthetically by chapter and page number.
3. Gordon Schochet resolves the dilemma by suggesting that Hobbes's families are patriarchal, but he derives patriarchal power from consent rather than from generation. See Schochet, *Patriarchalism in Political Thought: The Authoritarian Family and Political Speculation and Attitudes Especially in Seventeenth-Century England* (New York: Basic Books, 1975), 241.
4. Carole Pateman, *The Sexual Contract* (Stanford: Stanford University Press, 1988), 50.
5. Pateman's feminist critics include Susan Moller Okin, "Feminism, the Individual, and Contract Theory," *Ethics* 100, no. 3 (1990): 658–69; Karen Green, "Christine De Pisan and Thomas Hobbes," *Philosophical Quarterly* 44, no. 177 (1994): 456–75; Nancy Fraser, *Justice Interruptus: Critical Reflections on the "Postsocialist" Condition* (New York: Routledge, 1997); Donna Dickenson, *Property, Women, and Politics: Subjects or Objects?* (New Brunswick: Rutgers University Press, 1997); Joanne H. Wright, *Origin Stories in Political Thought: Discourses on Gender, Power, and Citizenship* (Toronto: University of Toronto Press, 2004); and Nancy J. Hirschmann, *Gender, Class, and Freedom in Modern Political Theory* (Princeton, N.J.: Princeton University Press, 2008). Pateman herself acknowledges the logical difficulties in both *The Sexual Contract* and a later essay, which nonetheless reiterates her conjectural history, "'God Hath Ordained to Man a Helper': Hobbes, Patriarchy, and Conjugal Right," in *Feminist Interpretations and Political Theory*, ed. Mary Lyndon Shanley and Carole Pateman (University Park: Pennsylvania State University Press, 1991), 53–73.
6. See Joanne H. Wright, "Going Against the Grain: Hobbes's Case for Original Maternal Dominion," *Journal of Women's History* 14, no. 1 (2002): 123–48.
7. Quentin Skinner, "Hobbes on Representation," *European Journal of Philosophy* 13, no. 2 (2005): 175.
8. See Hilda L. Smith, *All Men and Both Sexes: Gender, Politics, and the False Universal in England, 1640–1832* (University Park: Pennsylvania State University Press, 2002).
9. Quentin Skinner, *Hobbes and Republican Liberty* (Cambridge: Cambridge University Press, 2008), 191.
10. Victoria Kahn, *Wayward Contracts: The Crisis of Political Obligation in England, 1640–1674* (Princeton, N.J.: Princeton University Press, 2004), 170.
11. Thomas Hobbes, *Considerations upon the Reputation, Loyalty, Manners & Religion, of Thomas Hobbes of Malmesbury, Written by Himself, by Way of Letter to a Learned Person* (London: William Crooke, 1680), 40.
12. For Hobbes's mechanical body, see Katherine Bootle Attie, "Re-membering the Body Politic: Hobbes and the Construction of Civil Immortality," *ELH* 75, no. 3 (2008): 497–530. Unlike Attie, I find Hobbes's comparisons highly unconventional in leaving out the major body parts of heart and head. See Su Fang Ng, *Literature and the Politics of Family in Seventeenth-Century England* (Cambridge: Cambridge University Press, 2007), 90–95.
13. Quoted in Sir William Molesworth, ed., *The English Works of Thomas Hobbes of Malmesbury*, 11 vols. (London: J. Bohn, 1839–45), 5:165. For contemporary responses to Hobbes's state of nature, see Richard Ashcraft, "Hobbes's Natural Man: A Study in Ideological Formation," *Journal of Politics* 33, no. 4 (1971): 1075–1117; and Steven Mintz, *The Hunting of Leviathan: Seventeenth-Century Reactions to Materialism* (Cambridge: Cambridge University Press, 1962), 80–109.
14. David Gauthier argues, "Men are like those beasts which are naturally wild, but capable of being tamed"; Gauthier, *The Logic of Leviathan: The Moral and Political Theory of Thomas Hobbes*

(Oxford: Clarendon Press, 1969), 30. Philip Pettit finds Hobbes distinguishing between the animal mind common to both humans and animals and the mind of language and reason separating human civilization from animal life; Pettit, *Made with Words: Hobbes on Language, Mind, and Politics* (Princeton, N.J.: Princeton University Press, 2008), 4.

15. Richard Ashcraft, "Leviathan Triumphant: Thomas Hobbes and the Politics of Wild Men," in *The Wild Man Within: An Image in Western Thought from the Renaissance to Romanticism*, ed. Edward Dudley and Maximillian E. Novak (Pittsburgh: University of Pittsburgh, 1973), 141–81.

16. In a working paper, Diego Hernán Rossello puts Hobbes in the context of early modern melancholia, and in particular lycanthropy, the disease causing the delusion of believing oneself to be a wolf, arguing, "The fact that the melancholic is at the verge of becoming an animal might mean that, by doing so, it interrupts the subjection imposed by man, reason, and the civil state." Rossello, "Hobbes and the Wolf-Man: Animality and Melancholy in Modern Sovereignty," Northwestern University, August 18, 2009, 7; available at http://ssrn.com/abstract=1456923 (accessed March 2, 2010).

17. See Ross Harrison, *Hobbes, Locke, and Confusion's Masterpiece: An Examination of Seventeenth-Century Political Philosophy* (Cambridge: Cambridge University Press, 2003), 97–99.

18. Titus Maccius Plautus, *Asinaria, or The Comedy of Asses*, in *Plautus*, trans. Paul Nixon, vol. 1 (Cambridge, Mass.: Harvard University Press, 1966), act 2, line 495.

19. The Latin original is quoted from Thomas Hobbes, *De Cive: The Latin Version Entitled in the First Edition "Elementorum Philosophiae Sectio Tertia De Cive" and in Later Editions "Elementa Philosophica de Cive,"* ed. Howard Warrender (Oxford: Clarendon Press, 1983), 73.

20. See Paul J. Johnson, "Hobbes and the Wolf-Man," in *Thomas Hobbes: His View of Man: Proceedings of the Hobbes Symposium at the International School of Philosophy in the Netherlands (Leusden, September 1979)*, ed. J. G. van der Bend (Amsterdam: Rodopi, 1982), 31–44. Johnson suggests that Hobbes conceives of human nature not as bestial but as radically individualistic. For Hobbes's radical individualism, see C. B. Macpherson, *The Political Theory of Possessive Individualism: Hobbes to Locke* (Oxford: Clarendon Press, 1962).

21. Lucius Annaeus Seneca, *Ad Lucilium Epistulae Morales*, trans. Richard M. Grummere, vol. 3 (Cambridge, Mass.: Harvard University Press, 1961), epistle 95, sect. 33. The full quotation is as follows: "Homo, sacra res homini, iam per lusum ac iocum occiditur et quem erudiri ad inferenda accipiendaque vulnera nefas erat, is iam nudus inermisque producitur satisque spectaculi ex homine mors est" (Man, an object of reverence in the eyes of man, is now slaughtered for jest and sport; and those whom it used to be unholy to train for the purpose of inflicting and enduring wounds, are thrust forth exposed and defenceless; and it is a satisfying spectacle to see a man made a corpse).

22. Donna Haraway, *Companion Species Manifesto: Dogs, People, and Significant Otherness* (Chicago: Prickly Paradigm Press, 2003), 28.

23. Giorgio Agamben, *Homo Sacer: Sovereign Power and Bare Life*, trans. Daniel Heller-Roazen (Stanford: Stanford University Press, 1998), 107. Jacques Derrida also correlates bestiality with sovereignty; see Derrida, *The Beast and the Sovereign*, The Seminars of Jacques Derrida, vol. 1, ed. Michel Lisse, Marie-Louise Mallet, and Ginette Michaud, trans. Geoffrey Bennington (Chicago: University of Chicago Press, 2009).

24. For Hobbes and Machiavelli, see Vickie B. Sullivan, *Machiavelli, Hobbes, and the Formation of a Liberal Republicanism in England* (Cambridge: Cambridge University Press, 2004).

25. For Agamben on Hobbes, see Luc Foisneau, "Souveraineté et animalité: Agamben lecteur de Hobbes," in *Animal et animalité dans la philosophie de la Renaissance et de l'Âge Classique*, ed. Thierry Gontier (Louvain-la-Neuve: L'Institut Superieur de Philosophie/Peeters, 2005), 231–44.

26. Thomas Hobbes, "A Discourse upon the Beginning of Tacitus," in *Three Discourses: A Critical Modern Edition of Newly Identified Work of the Young Hobbes*, ed. Noel B. Reynolds and Arlene W. Saxonhouse (Chicago: University of Chicago Press, 1995), 33.

27. Ng, *Literature and the Politics of Family*, 76–102 passim.

28. Thomas Hobbes, *Behemoth, or The Long Parliament*, ed. Ferdinand Tönnies (Chicago: University of Chicago Press, 1990), 3.

29. Plutarch, *Plutarch's Lives*, trans. Sir Thomas North, ed. Roland Baughman, 2 vols. (New York: Heritage Press, 1941), 1:57–58.

30. Ibid., 59.

31. Hobbes, "A Discourse of Rome," in *Three Discourses*, 77.

32. R. Ross Holloway, *The Archaeology of Early Rome and Latium* (New York: Routledge, 1994), 172; and Lawrence Richardson, *A New Topographical Dictionary of Ancient Rome* (Baltimore: Johns Hopkins University Press, 1992), 150–51. For the new dating of the Capitoline wolf, based on the work of art historian Anna Maria Carruba, see "Famed Roman Statue 'Not Ancient,'" *BBC News*, July 10, 2008, available at http://news.bbc.co.uk/2/hi/europe/7499469.stm (accessed March 4, 2010).

33. A. P. Martinich, *Hobbes: A Biography* (Cambridge: Cambridge University Press, 1999), 30.

34. Todd Butler, "Image, Rhetoric, and Politics in the early Thomas Hobbes," *Journal of the History of Ideas* 67, no. 3 (2006): 472. See also Quentin Skinner, *Reason and Rhetoric in the Philosophy of Hobbes* (Cambridge: Cambridge University Press, 1996).

35. Hobbes, "A Discourse of Rome," 80, 81, 82.

36. Ashcraft, "Leviathan Triumphant," 161.

37. Molesworth, *English Works*, 5:165. See also Nicholas D. Jackson, *Hobbes, Bramhall, and the Politics of Liberty and Necessity: A Quarrel of the Civil Wars and Interregnum* (Cambridge: Cambridge University Press, 2007).

38. Sir Robert Filmer, *Patriarcha and Other Writings*, ed. Johann P. Sommerville (Cambridge: Cambridge University Press, 1991), 18.

39. Mary Nyquist, "Hobbes, Slavery, and Despotical Rule," *Representations* 106, no. 1 (2009): 4.

40. Ibid., 19.

41. Ibid., 9. For my discussion of how Hobbes collapses the categories of paternal and despotic kingdoms, see Ng, *Literature and the Politics of Family*, 83–84.

Part Two

The Gendered Politics of Gratitude, Contract, and the Family

5
Thomas Hobbes on the Family and the State of Nature (1967)

Gordon J. Schochet

Author's Note

I am pleased that the editors find this essay, which I wrote over forty-five years ago, worthy of republication. And while I remain committed to its general claims, I would reframe my arguments today. When I wrote, women and the family on the one hand and gratitude on the other were relatively unexplored subjects in the Hobbes literature, and they had not previously been seen as related. With the benefit of others' now extensive work and my own continued attention to these two increasingly popular themes, I am

---

This article has been prepared with the assistance of a grant from the Research Council of Rutgers, The State University. I wish to thank Professor Benjamin E. Lippincott of the University of Minnesota and Mr. Peter Laslett of Trinity College, Cambridge, for commenting on earlier versions.

even more strongly persuaded that the association of gratitude with the state-of-nature household resolves many puzzles and difficulties in Hobbes's political thought.

I have extended my argument in two subsequently published papers— "Intending (Political) Obligation: Hobbes and the Voluntary Basis of Society," in Thomas Hobbes and Political Theory, *ed. Mary G. Dietz (Lawrence: University Press of Kansas, 1990), 55–73, and "De l'idée de sujétion naturelle à l'indifférenciation par convention: Les femmes dans la pensée politique de Sir Robert Filmer, Thomas Hobbes, et John Locke," in* Encyclopédie politique et historique des femmes: Europe, Amérique du Nord, *ed. Christine Fauré (Paris: Presses Universitaires de France, 1997), 73–93—which Nancy Hirschmann discusses in her chapter that follows.*

I am more fully aware of a large, gratitude-based context for Hobbes's writings than I was in 1967. Gratitude has long been a concern of moral philosophers and theologians, evident as far back as the Hebrew Bible and the New Testament, Aristotle's Ethics, *Cicero's* De officiis, *and Seneca's* De benificiis. *It was prominent in the writings of Renaissance and early modern philosophers and casuists and an important notion in the Scottish Enlightenment. The familiar adage "One good turn deserves another" can be traced back at least to the mid-seventeenth century; it is precisely this workaday wisdom that Hobbes turned on its head in the admonition to be grateful so that one's benefactor "have no reasonable cause to repent him of his good will" (*Leviathan, *116). Replacing what appears to have been the prevailing conception of gratitude as affect and morality with one based in self-interest and rational calculation, Hobbes was doing something far more radical and individualistic than I recognized in my analysis of his fourth law of nature. His appropriation and transformation of the well-worn concept of gratitude are thus an integral part of his empiricist and "behavioral" moral psychology. Even more than "consent" and "agreement," gratitude cushions the burdens of force, compulsion, and fear that hold all social institutions together for him by reserving at least the patina of affective-based duties.*

Among the most celebrated passages in the literature of political philosophy is Thomas Hobbes' classic description of the incommodious, barren, and uncertain life in the state of nature: "no Arts; no Letters; no Society; and which is worst of all, continuall feare, and danger of violent death; And the life of man, solitary, poore, nasty, brutish, and short."

Seventeenth-century critics, assuming that even the most rudimentary social unit, the family, was excluded from the Hobbesian state of nature, often opposed this view of "*the* naturall condition *of Mankind*" with the patriarchally governed household and insisted that the natural "warre of every man against every man"[1] never existed. The reaction of Bishop John Bramhall was typical:

> there never was any such time when mankind was without Governors and Lawes, and Societies. Paternall Government was in the world from the beginning, and [by] the Law of Nature. There might be sometimes a root of such Barbarous Theevish Brigants, in some rocks, or desarts, or odd corners of the world, but it was an abuse and a degeneration from the nature of man, who is a politicall creature.[2]

Manifesting the same attitude, Sir Henry Sumner Maine wrote in the last century:

> It is some shifting sandbank in which the grains are Individual men, that according to the theory of Hobbes is hardened into the social rock by the wholesome discipline of force. . . . But Ancient Law, it must be repeated, knows next to nothing of Individuals. It is concerned not with Individuals, but with Families, not with single human beings, but groups.[3]

And G. P. Gooch has said against Hobbes' conception, "The unit of primitive society was not, as [Hobbes] imagined, the individual, but the family or some other group."[4]

All three of these statements suggest the more familiar complaints of Sir Robert Filmer, who wrote in opposition to the Hobbesian theory of original and natural freedom and equality:

> I cannot understand how this right of nature can be conceived without imagining a company of men at the very first to have been all created together without any dependency one of another, or as mushrooms (*fungorum more*) they all on a sudden were sprung out of the earth without any obligation one to another, as Mr. Hobbes's words are in his book *De Cive*, chapter 8, section 3; the scripture teacheth us otherwise, that all men came by succession, and generation from one man: we must not deny the truth of the history of the creation.[5]

These anti-individualist interpretations rely, in large measure, upon the presumption that the Hobbesian state of nature was intended as an actual historical account of man's prepolitical condition. It is generally argued today, however, that Hobbes designed his state of nature as a logical and reductionist device that was to demonstrate the necessity of absolute government.[6] I suggest that this is an oversimplified notion that should be modified in view of Hobbes' failure to maintain a consistent distinction between the logical and historical aspects of his political theories; the point here is that any such differentiation was wasted on Hobbes' contemporaries. Many seventeenth-century thinkers shared with Filmer the belief that it was only necessary to show that familial status had been established by God at the Creation to prove that natural equality and liberty and a state of nature constituted an absurd and irrelevant point of departure for a discussion of political obligation. Hobbes himself gave the lie to these critics—or at least attempted to do so—when he asserted in the seventeenth chapter of *Leviathan* that families had existed in the prepolitical world. To this position Thomas Tenison anonymously replied, "You rather overthrow than prove your supposed state of Nature."[7] Filmer had reasoned that if children were subjugated to their fathers, "there would have been little liberty in the subjects of the family to consent to [the] institution of government."[8]

Hobbes had gone even further than the remarks of Tenison and Filmer indicate; he had specifically identified familial and political rule, saying, "Cities and Kingdomes . . . are but greater Families."[9] In his own English translation of *De Cive*, he stated that "a family is a little city,"[10] later writing that "a great family is a kingdom, and a little kingdom a family."[11] Numerous similar and related comments are scattered throughout Hobbes' writings. Together they comprise a patriarchal element in his political philosophy that has not previously been recognized.[12] What follows is an examination of the familial aspects of the *Leviathan*, *De Cive*, and other works by Hobbes. While I have by no means attempted to reassess the whole of his political thought, I have, in several places, called attention to some of the problems that this patriarchalism raises for interpretations of other aspects of Hobbes' theory.

I

Political power, Hobbes said, arose either from acquisition or institution; the power of fatherhood—like that of conquest—was derived from acquisition:

The attaining to the Soveraigne Power, is by two wayes. One, by Naturall force; as when a man maketh his children, to submit themselves, and their children to his government, as by being able to destroy them if they refuse; or by Warre subdoeth his enemies to his will, giving them their lives on that condition. The other, is when men agree amongst themselves, to submit to some Man, or Assembly of men, voluntarily, on confidence to be protected by him against all others. This latter, may be called a Politicall Common-wealth, or Commonwealth by *Institution;* and the former, a Common-wealth by *Acquisition.*[13]

So far as Hobbes was concerned, there were no differences between instituted and acquired commonwealths once they were established, for "The Rights, and Consequences of Soveraignty, are the same in both."[14] In *De Corpore Politico* he wrote, in a

monarchy by acquisition . . . the sovereignty is in one man, as it is in a monarch made by *political institution.* So that whatsoever rights be in the one, the same also be in the other. And therefore I shall no more speak of them as distinct, but of monarchy in general.[15]

It therefore follows that acquisition provided no less valid a title than institution,[16] and it appears that Hobbes accepted patriarchal power and consent as equally valid though distinguishable sources of governance.

In fact, in his little known *Dialogue Between a Philosopher and a Student,* published in 1666, Hobbes implicitly adopted much of the patriarchal position of some of his critics and attributed to primitive fathers many of the characteristics of sovereignty:

And first, it is evident that dominion, government and laws, are far more ancient than history or any other writing, and that the beginning of all dominion amongst men was in families. In which, first, the father of the family by the law of nature was absolute lord of his wife and children: secondly, made what laws amongst them he pleased: thirdly, was judge of all their controversies: fourthly, was not obliged by any law of man to follow any counsel but his own: fifthly, what land soever the lord sat down upon and made use of for his own and his family's benefit, was his propriety by the law of first possession, in case it was void of inhabitants before, or by the law of war, in case they conquered it. In this conquest what enemies they took and saved, were their servants. Also such men as wanting possession of lands, but furnished with arts necessary for man's life, came to dwell in the family for protection, became their subjects, and submitted themselves to the laws of the family.[17]

In his debate with Bishop Bramhall Hobbes admitted, "*It is very likely to be true, that since the Creation there very likely never was a time when Mankind was totally without Society.*" Bramhall, Hobbes continued, "*saw there was Paternal Government in Adam, which he might do easily, as being no deep consideration.*"[18] But in *De Cive*, he dismissed as a justification for monarchy the argument "that paternal government, instituted by God himself at the creation, was monarchical" because, along with other similar notions, it made its case "by examples and testimonies, and not by solid reason."[19] In the *Leviathan* Hobbes asserted that an independent family was a small kingdom:

> a great Family if it be not part of some Common-wealth, is of it self, as to the Rights of Soveraignty, a little Monarchy; whether that Family consists of a man and his children; or of a man and his servants; or of a man, and his children, and servants together: wherein the Father or Master is the Soveraign. But yet a Family is not properly a Common-wealth; unlesse it be of that power by its own number, or by other opportunities, as not to be subdued without the hazard of war.[20]

Breaking sharply with the patriarchalism of Bramhall, Filmer, and Tenison, Hobbes insisted both that paternal power had existed in the state of nature and that it was not derived from fatherhood as such. If patriarchal sovereignty was a product of procreation, he reasoned, then the mother, who shares equally in the act of generation, should have an equal claim to dominion over the child. A sharing of authority was impossible, however, for it would have violated two axiomatic principles, that no man can serve two masters and that supreme power is indivisible.[21] Presumably, this judgment was applicable to the power of Adam, too, which, as has been shown, might well have been patriarchal for all Hobbes cared. Hobbes' denial of the generative origins of the governmental authority of fathers allowed him to rest his political doctrine on the proposition that no status among men was natural. The subordination of men was due to convention and human consent, not to nature.[22] The power of parents was a virtual reward for preserving the lives of their children when they had the ability and right to destroy them. For in their natural condition, because there was a potential danger from all equals, men were entitled to take steps to keep a subdued individual in a permanently weakened condition.[23] But a man who preserved someone whom he might have destroyed is entitled to obedience from the person he saved. Thus, in the state of nature, "if the mother shall think fit to abandon, or expose her child to death, whatsoever man or woman shall find the child so exposed, shall have the same right which the mother had before; and for this same reason, namely, for the power not of generating, but preserving."[24]

Power over a child initially belongs to the mother, according to Hobbes, "insomuch as she may rightly, and at her own will, either breed him up or adventure him to fortune."[25] The obligation of the child to obey a mother who does not destroy him is derived from his tacit or projected consent to her power over him. As Hobbes said in *De Cive*:

> If . . . [the mother] breed him, because the state of nature is the state of war, she is supposed to bring him up on this condition; that being grown to full age he become not her enemy; which is that he obey her. For since by natural necessity we all desire that which appears good unto us, it cannot be understood that any man hath on such terms afforded life to another, that he might both get strength by years, and at once become an enemy. But each man is an enemy to that other, whom he neither obeys nor commands.[26]

The point was more succinctly made in the *Leviathan* where Hobbes said that paternal authority "is not so derived from the Generation, as if therefore the Parent had Dominion over his Child because he begat him; but from the Childs Consent, either expresse, or by other sufficient arguments declared."[27] Ultimately, the future consent of the child was probably derived from Hobbes' fourth law of nature, the law of gratitude, which required *"That a man which receiveth Benefit from another of meer Grace, Endeavour that which giveth it, have no reasonable cause to repent him of his good will."* For if men fail to respond gratefully to such beneficence, "there will be no beginning of benevolence, or trust; nor consequently of mutuall help; nor of reconciliation of one man to another; and therefore they are to remain still in the condition of *War*."[28] Applied specifically to the relations of fathers and children in the state of nature, this aspect of Hobbes' theory of consent provided the means of legitimately transforming what was earlier termed "Naturall force" into sovereignty. The key to the process was the fact that the child did not resist his father's will. It will be seen that Hobbes apparently included this acquiescence within the category of consent "by other sufficient arguments declared" and could thus assert that paternal dominion was derived from the consent of the child. What was central to Hobbes' political thesis was, once again, a demonstration that men, not nature, were the authors of their own subjection.[29]

Howard Warrender, however, concludes that "the propriety on Hobbes's part of applying the notion of tacit covenant to the child-parent relationship is very doubtful."[30] This observation is based on Hobbes' having denied the ability of children to make covenants because they "have not the use of reason"[31] and on his later statement that

> Over naturall fooles, children, or mad-men there is no Law, no more than over brute beasts; nor are they capable of the title just, or unjust; because they had never power to make any covenant, or to understand the consequences thereof; and consequently never took upon them to authorise the actions of any Soveraign, as they must do that make themselves a Common-wealth.[32]

These notions, Professor Warrender suggests, "would seem to be more consistent with Hobbes's doctrine in general" than the "tacit covenant children are supposed to make with their parent(s) by whom they are preserved." He attributes Hobbes' derivation of parental authority from the consent of the child to a possible "anxiety to forestall at their inception . . . contemporary paternalistic theories of sovereignty."[33] Warrender seems to have missed, however, the full meaning of Hobbes' identification of political and familial authority in the state of nature; he therefore fails to appreciate the importance of Hobbes' notion that *all* sovereign power springs originally from voluntary human actions rather than from natural causes. The logical discrepancy would be removed if the tacit compacts of children were equivalent to the consents that would be forthcoming as soon as each child came of age and became master of his own reason. This is approximately the conclusion that Hobbes reached in his debate with Bishop Bramhall when he attempted to explain how children could be bound by the laws of their ancestors:

The Conquerour makes no Law over the Conquered by vertue of his power; but by vertue of their assent that promised obedience for the saving of their lives. But how then is the assent of Children obtained to the Laws of their Ancestors? This also is from their desire of preserving their lives, which first the Parents might take away, where the Parents be free from all subjection; and where they are not, there the Civil power might do the same, if they doubted of their obedience. The Children therefore when they be grown up to strength enough to do mischief, and to judgement to know that other men are kept from doing mischief to them, by fear of the Sword that protecteth them, in that very act of receiving that protection, and not renouncing it openly, do oblige themselves to obey the Lawes of their Protectors; to which, in receiving such protection they have assented.[34]

Functionally, authority over the child in the state of nature belonged to anyone who had the power to kill it. In the first instance this person was always the mother, and the patriarchal title originated in power over her, not in the inherent rights or superiority of either males or fathers. Fathers have this authority in society, Hobbes reasoned, "because for the most part Common-wealths have been erected by the Fathers, not by the Mothers of families."

In nature where there are no matrimonial regulations, without individual and specific contracts, children are under the dominion and subject to the disposition of their mothers. Without laws governing marriage, "it cannot be known who is the Father, unless it be declared by the Mother: and therefore the right of Dominion over the Child dependeth on her will, and is consequently hers." On the other hand, when the mother is subject to her husband, "the Child, is in the Fathers power,"[35] just as the child in society is the subject of his father's sovereign.[36]

II

It has been customary for modern commentators to draw sharp distinctions between two kinds of sovereignty in Hobbes' writings, that is, between the government that arises "when a man maketh his children, to submit themselves, and their children, to his government," and that which springs from the "Covenant of every man with every man."[37] The former is said to have been the true *historical* beginning[38] of society recognized by Hobbes, whereas the latter is supposed to represent the logical basis. An essential corollary to this view stresses the logical existence of the state of nature, falling back upon Hobbes' own words: "It may peradventure be thought, there was never such a time, nor condition or warre as this; and I believe it was never generally so, over all the world."[39]

G. C. Robertson was the first commentator to express this view. Despite the great attention Hobbes paid to the contract, Robertson said "that states had their natural beginning in families when not in conquest . . . is evidently the real opinion of Hobbes."[40] To the same end is the analysis of Leslie Stephen; he also sees an opposition between the two positions and goes even further than Robertson, claiming that the contract thesis is not only "absurd historically, but is also irrelevant to Hobbes."[41] Richard Peters, too, treats familial government as a form of rule apart from that instituted by men and calls attention to Hobbes' "lack of interest" in patriarchal authority, holding that "it was *institution* that appealed to his way of thinking."[42]

The most extreme member of this school is Leo Strauss, who says that Hobbes "maintained up to the end that paternal authority and consequently patrimonial monarchy is, if not the legal, nevertheless the historical, origin of all or the majority of the States." Professor Strauss further asserts that Hobbes always acknowledged "the precedence of the natural over the artificial State." According to Strauss, Hobbes "went beyond" the historical demonstration that society was originally patriarchal. Instead, he constructed "a completely defective state of mankind" from which even the most simple of human associations had been eliminated. This condition was "the war of every one against every one." Hobbes "derives this war from its origin in human nature," Professor Strauss continues, implying that even human nature and history are in opposition to the Hobbesian scheme. Finally, Strauss says, "Hobbes considered the philosophic grounding of the principles of all judgement on political subjects more fundamental, incomparably more important than the most thoroughly founded historical knowledge." Therefore, the state of nature is "not an historical fact, but a necessary condition."[43]

This interpretation is not altogether satisfactory, primarily because it omits two very important statements made by Hobbes: first, that there were no meaningful differences after inception between sovereignty by acquisition (which includes patriarchal power) and institution,[44] and, second, that patriarchal power was derived not from the right of the father but from the tacit or projected consent of the child to be bound by the governance of his parent(s) and from the fourth law of nature, the law of gratitude.[45] Further textual evidence—to say nothing of Warrender's persuasive reinterpretation of the status of obligation in the prepolitical situation—suggests that Hobbes conceived of the state of nature as something less than the "completely defective state of mankind" envisaged by Professor Strauss and not quite the total anarchy seen by his Stuart critics.

Professor Warrender is aware of the lack of significant differences between instituted and acquired sovereignty, but he, too, says, "In any event, when Hobbes turns to consider the general problem of men in the State of Nature and the erection of a sovereign authority, he is clearly interested in logical and not historical analysis." He does concede, however, that Hobbes "bases no important point" upon the distinctions between logic and history and argues that "it is more likely that he regarded the two types of sovereignty simply as different patterns determined by circumstance, without prejudice to where or how often each of them had been instanced historically."[46] Even this reading is incomplete, for there is yet a further interpretation possible, one that attempts to assert the similarities between the notions that political societies grew out of the family and, alternatively, that they sprang from the state of nature.

III

The difficulties of interpretation arise from Hobbes' imprecise use of the state of nature concept and his failure to distinguish at all times between two apparently different things he was doing in his political writings. In those works, Hobbes was both justifying a particular kind of political authority and discussing the historico-anthropological evolution of the state. To be sure, these are analytically separable operations that are carried out on different levels, and it is to the credit of previous commentators that they have drawn attention to these distinctions as they may be extracted from the political philosophy of Hobbes. In the seventeenth century, however, these activities were not always separate. For many political writers, historical origins provided a valid justification for authority,[47] and it is not at all apparent that Hobbes should be *totally* excluded from the authors who accepted this kind of reasoning. In fact, much of what Hobbes wrote might be rendered more intelligible if the moral significance that his age attached to origins is kept in mind. This is especially true of his theory of the state of nature, for the construct is appropriate to political and logical justification as well as to historical reconstruction. Hobbes clearly used the state of nature to serve both ends—and sometimes simultaneously. Seen in this light, Hobbes' two tasks are revealed as having been very much alike, and the differences between the historical and logical analyses in his writings need not be as great as Robertson, Stephen, Peters, Strauss, and Warrender suggest. If attention is directed primarily to the place of the family in the state of nature theory, it is possible to argue that there is no difference at all.

"A son," Hobbes declared in *De Cive*, "cannot be understood to be at any time in the state of nature, as being under the power and command of them to whom he owes his protection as soon as ever he is born, namely, either his father's or his mother's, or him that nourished him. . . ."[48] This statement was validly derived from the conception of the state of nature as the condition in which "there were no common Power to feare."[49] Removal of a son from the state of nature is doubly significant because, as the context reveals, it was part of an answer to a critic (whom Hobbes failed to identify) and not a possible confusion that had passed unnoticed. Moreover, this position had already been incorporated into the original text of *De Cive* when Hobbes declared that the equality of nature applied only to "all men of riper years."[50] It was as if the state of nature extended only to the door of the household but did not pass over the threshold, for Hobbes claimed that there was private property in the family but not in the state of nature. There can only be private ownership where there is sufficient security, a qualification that precluded the state of nature.[51] But a family, Hobbes wrote, "is a little city. For the sons of a family have a propriety of their goods granted them by their father, distinguished indeed from the rest of the sons of the same family, but not from the propriety of the father himself."[52] In the *Leviathan*, Hobbes said that the American Indians lived in a virtual state of nature and except for the internal organization of their families were without the benefits of order: "For the savage people in many places of *America*, except for the government of small Families, the concord whereof dependeth on naturall lust, have no government at all; and live at this day in that brutish manner, as I have said before."[53]

As has already been observed, Hobbes regarded a "great Family if it be not part of some Common-wealth," as itself a commonwealth so long as "it be of that power by its own number or by other opportunities, as not to be subdued without the hazard of war." A closer examination reveals that these family-commonwealths existed in a state of nature vis-à-vis other units, for they would have faced each other with "no common Power to feare." In the state of nature, independent fathers were "absolute Sovereigns in their own Families," and their rule was civil rule because they had authority over their children and servants, which "has no place but in a State Civill, because before such estate, there is no Dominion of Persons."[54] It is these fathers who, as the representatives of their families, were in the state of nature and engaged in the "warre of every man against every man." Thus, "every man" can certainly be understood as "every independent father" (or patriarch) without changing Hobbes' basic argument. The members of families were the subjects of their father-sovereigns who secured private belongings for them. "But fathers of divers families, *who are not subject to any common father nor lord*, have a common right in all things," Hobbes asserted in *De Cive*.[55]

All that was missing was a formal statement that it was the agreement of fathers rather than the consent of all persons that established commonwealths by institution. Hobbes said precisely this in two passages that have been overlooked by all of his commentators, both seventeenth-century and modern, who have perceived a fundamental conflict between the family and the state of nature. In justifying the authority over their offspring that fathers have in society, Hobbes said:

> [It must be remembered] that originally the Father of every man was also his Sovereign Lord, with power over him of Life and Death; and that *the Fathers of families, when by instituting a Common-wealth,* they resigned that absolute Power, yet it was never intended, they should lose the honour due unto them [from their children] for their education. For to relinquish such right, was not necessary to the Institution of Sovereign Power.[56]

Similarly, Hobbes wrote that "the Parent ought to have the honour of a Sovereign, (*though he have surrendered his Power to the Civill Law,*) because he had it originally by Nature."[57]

The importance of these statements can be grasped in part by contrasting them with Bishop Bramhall's insistence that Hobbes had erred in attributing the institution of civil society to the actions of naturally free men. He "builds upon a wrong foundation, that all Magistrates at first, were elective," the Bishop charged. "The first Governours were Fathers of Families; And when those petty Princes could not afford competent protection and security to their subjects, many of them did resign their severall and respective interests into the hands of one joint Father of the Country."[58] In the light of Hobbes' statements, there now appears to have been no disagreement between him and Bramhall on this matter. Sir Robert Filmer's criticism of Hobbes—that the subordination of children to their fathers left "little liberty in the subjects of the family to consent to [the] institution of government"—may also be qualified to the extent that dependents were not parties to the contract. On this reading, the Hobbesian doctrine is not far removed from Filmer's own statement in *Patriarcha* that "By the uniting of great families or petty Princedoms, we find the greater monarchies were at first erected. . . ."[59] Thus, both men had far more in common with their contemporaries than is generally acknowledged.[60]

IV

One of the most important results of this interpretation of Hobbes is that it invites a reassessment of certain aspects of his doctrine. In the first place, his state of nature no longer appears to have been altogether individualistic; rather it was composed of familial social units that faced each other as autonomous entities. As Thomas Tenison observed in his criticism of the *Leviathan*:

> It is further to be marked, that one Family, as it stands separated from another, is as one Kingdom divided from the Territories of a Neighbouring Monarch. If therefore the state of Nature remaineth in a Family not depending upon another Family, in places where there is no common Government; then all Kingdoms which have not made Leagues with one another, are, at this day, in the same state. . . . I know you esteem all distinct Kingdoms in a state of War in relation to each other, and therefore they have a right; if they have a Power of invading: but he that consult *Grotius*, in his Book *de jure belli & pacis* (designed chiefly to set forth the Rights, not of Domestick, but Forinsick War) will not be much of your opinion.[61]

Independent nations, according to Hobbes, did face one another as in a state of nature:

For as among masterless men, there is perpetuall war, of every man against his neighbour. . . . So in States, and Common-wealths, not dependent on one another, every Common-wealth, (not every man) has an absolute Libertie, to doe what it shall judge (that is to say, what that Man, or Assemblie that representeth it, shall judge) most conducing to their benefit. But withall, they live in the condition of a perpetuall war, and upon the confines of battel, with their frontiers armed, and canons planted against their neighbours round about.[62]

This description is no less applicable to families in the state of nature than to the relations of sovereign nations. Hobbes in fact did compare the activities of small, primitive families to cities and kingdoms of his own day.[63] The elemental social unit for Hobbes was not the individual but the family, and a characterization such as Bertrand de Jouvenel's that "Hobbes gives a picture of individuals living each man for himself,"[64] cannot be accepted without qualification.

Another consequence of this rereading is the possible revision of the modern estimate of Hobbes' status in relation both to his contemporaries and to traditional modes of thought. That Hobbes was an innovator is not open to serious question. Leo Strauss at one time regarded him as the "originator of modern political philosophy,"[65] and George Sabine has remarked that Hobbes' system was "the first wholehearted attempt to treat political philosophy as part of a mechanistic body of scientific knowledge."[66] The justification of absolute, undivided sovereignty with arguments "taken from general principles of psychology and ethics rather than from assertions about Divine Right" was also a new departure,[67] as was the use of consent along with natural freedom and equality as the source of an unlimited rather than a constitutional government. All of these Hobbesian innovations have long been known and are frequently commented upon. What has gone unnoticed, however, is the relation to traditional political patriarchalism of Hobbes' observations on the nature of familial power. In this instance, too, important new ground was broken. Although his identification of primitive paternal authority with political power was in keeping with the practices of many of his contemporaries who considered the question, Hobbes was altogether unique in attempting to derive the father's power over his children from their consent. Buttressing the arguments for original freedom and equality in this manner, he added greater consistency to his doctrine and was not confronted with the need to explain how men who were subjected to their fathers by nature could ever be sufficiently free to agree to a compact of government. And if it is remembered that the child's consent was projected into the future through the fourth law of nature, the law of gratitude, this thesis is no less plausible than anything else about the state of nature.

A more conventional way out of this dilemma was to insist that patriarchal subjugation was distinct from, and in no way prejudiced, man's natural political right. This argument had been used in the past[68] and would be employed again by Locke in his answer to Filmer.[69] Another solution was simply to accept the notion that political society indeed traced its origins to the primitive family and to build an argument on the nature of the familial society. Ultimately, of course, Hobbes did conform to this second pattern, but he avoided thoroughgoing patriarchalism by first validating the proposition that all status is conventional. To this extent, the alleged freedom of mankind was at least *theoretically* preserved. Since this freedom gave way to parental control as soon as the child was born—if only because its physical weakness made it dependent upon others at once[70]—the assertion that the family rather than the individual was the basic social unit for Hobbes is in no way qualified.

The historical reality of the state of nature is yet another question that might be re-examined in light of Hobbes' use of patriarchal political theories. It need not be argued that the condition of "meer Nature" *necessarily* corresponded to a genuine historical situation, but the showing that what recent commentators have regarded as Hobbes' history was potentially compatible with his state of nature does seem to place the entire matter in a new perspective. If the thesis of Leo Strauss and others is correct—that is, if Hobbes believed that actual states grew out of expanding families—and if independent sovereign familial commonwealths existed in the Hobbesian state of nature, it should follow that the state of nature was a representation of true history. Hobbes himself provided further evidence for this view in his very admission that the state of nature was a logical fiction. What is often overlooked about this admission, however—or allowed to stand without comment—is that Hobbes did not say that there had never been a state of nature. He said, "I believe it was never *generally so, over all the world:* but there are many places, where they live so now," and he immediately referred to the American Indians, who "except [for] the government of small Families . . . have no government at all."[71] What seems unmistakably clear is the complexity of the problem and the need for further analysis; an investigation of the relation of Hobbes' two historical works, the *Dialogue* and *Behemoth*, to the political philosophy of the *Leviathan*, *De Cive*, and *De Corpore Politico* would be especially valuable. At all events, prima facie dismissal of the issue is undoubtedly out of place, and it ought not be flatly asserted, to quote Professor de Jouvenel again, that Hobbes "was concerned to build not a historical reconstruction but a social mechanics."[72]

Notes

1. Thomas Hobbes, *Leviathan, or the Matter, Forme, & Power of a Common-Wealth Ecclesiasticall and Civill* (1651), ed. W. G. Pogson Smith (Oxford, 1909), 97, 94, 98.

2. John Bramhall, *A Defence of True Liberty from Antecedent and Extrinsicall Necessity* (London, 1655), 107.

3. Henry Sumner Maine, *Ancient Law: Its Connection with the Early History of Society and Its Relation to Modern Ideas*, ed. Frederick Pollock (4th American ed.; New York, 1906), 250.

4. G. P. Gooch, *Political Thought in England: Bacon to Halifax* (London, 1946), 34.

5. Sir Robert Filmer, *Observations Concerning the Originall of Government* (1652), reprinted in Peter Laslett (ed.), *Patriarcha and Other Political Works* (Oxford, 1949), 241.

6. See, for example, F. C. Hood, *The Divine Politics of Thomas Hobbes: An Interpretation of Leviathan* (Oxford, 1964), 74; C. B. Macpherson, *The Political Theory of Possessive Individualism: Hobbes to Locke* (Oxford, 1962), 20–22; John P. Plamenatz, *Man and Society: A Critical Examination of Some Important Social and Political Theories from Machiavelli to Marx* (London, 1963), I, 333; George H. Sabine, *A History of Political Theory* (3d ed.; New York, 1961), 464; Howard Warrender, *The Political Philosophy of Hobbes: His Theory of Obligation* (Oxford, 1957), 30, n. 1, 237–42; J. W. N. Watkins, *Hobbes' System of Ideas: A Study in the Political Significance of Philosophical Theories* (London, 1965), 72; and T. D. Weldon, *States and Morals: A Study in Political Conflicts* (London, 1946), 105. Some writers have challenged this view. See Stuart M. Brown Jr., "Hobbes: The Taylor Thesis," reprinted in K. C. Brown (ed.), *Hobbes Studies* (Oxford, 1965), 67 n. 25, and Isaiah Berlin, "Hobbes, Locke, and Professor Macpherson," *Political Quarterly*, XXXV (1964), 448–49.

7. [Thomas Tenison], *The Creed of Mr. Hobbes Examined in a Feigned Conference between Him and a Student in Divinity* (London, 1670), 134.

8. Filmer, 239; see, also, 241.

9. *Leviathan*, 129.

10. Thomas Hobbes, *De Cive* (1642), translated by Hobbes as *Philosophical Rudiments Concerning Government and Society* (1651), reprinted as volume II of Hobbes, *The English Works*, ed. William Molesworth (London, 1839–41), Chap. vi, Sect. 15, p. 84, note. This work will be cited throughout in accord with the established usage by the Latin title, *De Cive*, and the *English Works* will be cited as *E.W.*

11. *Ibid.*, viii, 1, *E.W.*, II, 108.

12. Since writing this article, I have read Keith Thomas' illuminating essay, "The Social Origins of Hobbes's Political Thought," in K. C. Brown, 185–236. Thomas has found "traces in [Hobbes'] writings of a patriarchalism which he did not succeed in justifying in wholly contractual terms" (p. 188). His treatment is very brief and differs from my analysis in its examination of Hobbes' use of this doctrine as a product of his times rather than logically and in terms of his own political philosophy.

13. *Leviathan*, 132. The same point was made in *De Cive*, v, 12, viii, 1, and ix, 10, *E.W.*, II, 70–71, 108, 121–22. But see viii, 1, *E.W.*, II, 109, and the earlier *De Corpore Politico*, where Hobbes made parenthood a distinct and therefore a third source of dominion in the state of nature. (*De Corpore Politico: or the Elements of Law* [1640], II, iii, 2, *E.W.*, IV, 149.)

14. *Leviathan*, 152; see, also, 154 and *De Cive*, ix, 10, *E.W.*, II, 121–22.

15. *De Corpore Politico*, II, iv, 10, *E.W.*, IV, 159.

16. *Ibid.*, II, iii, 1, *E.W.*, IV, 148–49.

17. Thomas Hobbes, *A Dialogue Between a Philosopher and a Student of the Common Laws of England* (1666), *E.W.*, VI, 147. See *Leviathan*, 133 ff., for a discussion of the nature of sovereign power. Hobbes' derivation of a father's authority over his family from the law of nature in the passage quoted above may perhaps be explained by reference to the fourth law of nature as discussed in the *Leviathan*. See below, n. 28.

18. Thomas Hobbes, *The Questions Concerning Liberty, Necessity, and Chance Clearly Stated and Debated* (London, 1656), 139.

19. *De Cive*, x, 3, *E.W.*, II, 129.

20. *Leviathan*, 157.

21. *Ibid.*, 154; *De Cive*, ix, 2, *E.W.*, II, 115.

22. See the statement quoted in n. 17, above, from the later and less philosophic *Dialogue*: "the father of the family *by the law of nature* was absolute lord of his wife and children" (emphasis added).

23. *De Corpore Politico*, I, i, 13, *E.W.*, IV, 85.

24. *Ibid.*, II, iv, 3, *E.W.*, IV, 155. See, also, *Leviathan*, 132.

25. *De Cive*, ix, 2, *E.W.*, II, 116.

26. *Ibid.*, ix, 3, *E.W.*, II, 116.

27. *Leviathan*, 153. See, also, *De Corpore Politico*, II, iv, 3, *E.W.*, IV, 156.

28. *Leviathan*, 116.

29. In *De Cive* Hobbes said that in their natural condition men are "without all kind of engagement to each other." He specifically limited to "three ways only" the procuring of "a dominion over the person of another." Those ways were contract, conquest, and generation. (*De Cive*, viii, 1, *E.W.*, II, 109.) In *Leviathan* it was asserted that there is "no Obligation to any man, which ariseth not from some Act of his own." (*Leviathan*, 166.)

30. Warrender, 124.

31. *Leviathan*, 125.

32. *Ibid.*, 208.

33. Warrender, 256, n. 1; 124.

34. Hobbes, *Liberty and Necessity*, 136–37.

35. *Leviathan*, 154–55. See, also, *De Cive*, ix, 6, 7, *E.W.*, II, 118–19.

36. *Leviathan*, 155; *De Cive*, ix, 6, *E.W.*, II, 118.

37. *Leviathan*, 132, 131.

38. Perhaps it should be indicated that by "history" I do not mean the recapturable pasts of specific states or peoples but the anthropologically real antecedents of human social and political organization in general. This definition has, I think, been at least implicit in the secondary literature and would not have to be mentioned were it not for Professor Warrender's having contrasted the explanation of the source of sovereign authority discussed here with "Hobbes's treatment of his subject where he is really concerned to give an historical survey, as when he traces the origins of some parts of the British Constitution to the customs of the Saxons, in his *Dialogue of the Common Laws*" (p. 239). Hobbes' interpretations of English history are not relevant here and seem to have very little to do with Warrender's argument. With the exception of J. G. A. Pocock, commentators have generally ignored Hobbes' views on specific or national history. (See Pocock's *The Ancient Constitution and the Feudal Law* [Cambridge, 1957], 162–70.) The only sustained attempt to relate this aspect of Hobbes to the more familiar components of his "political philosophy" of which I am aware is M. M. Goldsmith, *Hobbes's Science of Politics* (New York, 1966), 228–42.

39. *Leviathan*, 97.
40. G. C. Robertson, *Hobbes* (London, 1886), 146.
41. Leslie Stephen, *Hobbes* (London, 1904), 209–10.
42. Richard Peters, *Hobbes* (Baltimore, 1956), 211.
43. Leo Strauss, *The Political Philosophy of Hobbes: Its Basis and Genesis*, trans. Elsa M. Sinclair (Chicago, 1952), 60, 66, 104.
44. *Leviathan*, 152; *De Corpore Politico*, II, iii, 1, and II, iv, 10, *E.W.*, IV, 148–49, 159.
45. See above, nn. 26–28.
46. Warrender, 238–40.
47. This aspect of seventeenth-century English political thought and its historical antecedents have both escaped the attention of most commentators. However, see Sterling P. Lamprecht, *The Moral and Political Philosophy of John Locke* (New York, 1918), 41; Francis C. Haber, *The Age of the World: Moses to Darwin* (Baltimore, 1959), 72; and Guenter Lewy, *Constitutionalism and Statecraft during the Golden Age of Spain* (Geneva, 1960), 47.
48. *De Cive*, i, 10, note, *E.W.*, II, 10.
49. *Leviathan*, 97. In *De Corpore* Hobbes wrote, "The appetites of men, and the passions of their minds, are such, that, unless they be restrained by some power, they will always be making war upon one another." (*De Corpore* [1655], I, vi, 7, *E.W.*, I, 74.) These unbridled appetites and passions are recognizable as the state of nature of the *Leviathan* and *De Cive*.
50. *De Cive*, ix, 2, *E.W.*, II, 115. See, also, the discussion in the *Leviathan* of the inability of children to enter into covenants (p. 208).
51. *De Cive*, vi, 1, *E.W.*, II, 72.
52. Ibid., vi, 15, note, *E.W.*, II, 84. See, also, *De Corpore Politico*, II, iii, 4, *E.W.*, IV, 151.
53. *Leviathan*, 97.
54. Ibid., 157, 97, 180, 125.
55. *De Cive*, vi, 15, note, *E.W.*, II, 84 (emphasis added). A small problem arises in attempting to classify the relations among members of different families, none of whom were patriarchs or independent fathers. They, too, undoubtedly would have faced one another in a state of nature, for there would have been no authority above them. In this case, however, the state of nature would have been due to the individuals' having figuratively stepped out of their respective families. Patriarchs, on the other hand, were in the state of nature because of their very status and inherent condition. In arguing that independent nations faced each other in a state of nature, Hobbes clearly stated that the rights and liberties of that condition accrued to the commonwealths and their representatives and not to the individual residents.
56. *Leviathan*, 263 (emphasis added).
57. Ibid., 237 (emphasis added).
58. Bramhall, *Defence*, 100.
59. Sir Robert Filmer, *Patriarcha: A Defence of the Natural Power of Kings against the Unnatural Liberty of the People* (written ca. 1638, posthumously published in 1680), printed from a manuscript in *Political Works*, 61–62.
60. On one level, the notion that complex political communities grew out of the association of patriarchally ruled households is a recognizable part of the political philosophy of Aristotle. Separated from its teleological trappings, the anthropological doctrine was an important ingredient in English political thought from the Elizabethan period until well into the eighteenth century. What is more, it was employed by royalists as well as by their critics.
61. [Tenison], *The Creed of Hobbes*, 135.
62. *Leviathan*, 164–65.
63. Ibid., 128–29.
64. Bertrand de Jouvenel, *Sovereignty: An Inquiry into the Political Good*, trans. J. F. Huntington (Chicago, 1957), 232.

124   Gendered Politics

65. Strauss, xv.
66. Sabine, 460.
67. Peters, 27.
68. See, for example [Philip Hunton], A *Treatise of Monarchy* (London, 1643), 1.
69. See John Locke, *Two Treatises of Government* (1690), ed. Peter Laslett (Cambridge, 1960), II, 2, 71, 169, 173, 286.
70. ". . . to man by nature, or as man, that is, as soon as he is born, solitude is an enemy; for infants have need of others to help them to live, and those of riper years to help them to live well." (*De Cive*, i, 2, note, *E.W.*, II, 2.)
71. *Leviathan*, 97 (emphasis added).
72. de Jouvenel, 232.

6

Gordon Schochet on Hobbes, Gratitude, and Women

Nancy J. Hirschmann

It is oddly fitting that the first contemporary "feminist" essay on Thomas Hobbes was written by a man. Gordon Schochet's "Thomas Hobbes on the Family and the State of Nature," published in 1967—and reprinted with some modifications in *Patriarchalism in Political Thought: The Authoritarian Family and Political Attitudes in Seventeenth-Century England*, published by Basil Blackwell in 1975[1]—took up *the* central issue of feminist political thought before "feminist political thought" was really a term. His essay preceded by several years the very earliest feminist analyses of

---

An earlier version of this paper was originally presented at Gladly Learn and Gladly Teach: A Conference in Honor of Gordon Schochet, Rutgers University, May 5, 2009. Thanks to conference participants, particularly Lois Schworer and Gordon Schochet, for their comments.

historical canonical figures by such feminists as Susan Okin, Molly Shanley, and Julia Annas. Schochet was, in fact, an important resource for Carole Pateman's *The Problem of Political Obligation* even before her work on women, consent, and contract. And he has gone on to write several essays that explicitly take up feminist questions in early modern British political thought.[2]

As Quentin Skinner pointed out in the interview that opened this volume, Hobbes didn't really care whether the sovereign was a man or a woman; what he cared about was that the sovereign be obeyed. In this sense, Hobbes was blind to sex and would most likely maintain that it didn't matter whether a woman or a man wrote the "first" twentieth-century feminist interpretation of Thomas Hobbes. But Hobbes's "blindness" was not just to sex but to sexism as well, making him at best an ambiguous feminist idol, as various essays in the present volume attest. Schochet's essay, too, is an ambiguous model for feminist interpretations of Hobbes. I here take up a particular problem in Hobbes's text that Schochet has somewhat identified, and somewhat ignored. Specifically, he has identified the overtly patriarchal nature of the family in modern political thought and recognized that the state, as a result, takes a similarly patriarchal form. The family, accordingly, is inherently political in nature, and the apparent bifurcation of public and private that supposedly sits at the heart of liberalism is in fact illusory. This is radical and powerful stuff for feminist theorizing to make use of. But what Schochet has ignored is how women fit into this patriarchal family, and how they got there, as he acknowledged later.[3] It is as if Schochet gives us feminism without women. However, his work on the role of gratitude in Hobbes's theory of political obligation might provide a solution to the paradox that feminists have identified in Hobbes's construction of the family and the state: How is it that free and equal natural women are subordinated in the patriarchal family?

The Problem of Patriarchalism

On the face of it, this looks like a pointless question. Hobbes is writing in the seventeenth century—where else could women be *but* in a subordinated position in the patriarchal family?[4] Schochet indeed makes his case for patriarchalism as the foundation for Hobbes's political thought by noting Hobbes's infamous—at least to feminists—definition of a family as "a man and his children; or of a man and his servants; or of a man, and his children, and servants together" (*Leviathan*, ch. 20, 257).[5] This quote clearly shows that fathers are not just fathers but *rulers* of families in Hobbes's view—political sovereigns by virtue of being fathers. But even if we would expect this, the complete absence of mothers from this "family" looks odd: Why not say "a man, his wife, his children, and servants"? Wouldn't that reinforce, rather than weaken, the patriarch's position?

Schochet takes no notice of the mother's absence from Hobbes's definition. Yet on the very next page he rightly observes Hobbes's declaration that dominion over children normally lies with the mother, absent any contract to the contrary (including the social contract, which might establish matrimonial law).[6] And three pages later Schochet notes,

> Authority over the child in the state of nature belonged to anyone who had the power to kill it. In the first instance this person was always the mother. . . . In nature where there are no matrimonial regulations, without individual and specific contracts, children are under the dominion and subject to the disposition of their mothers. . . . On the other hand, when the mother is subject to her husband, "the Child, is in the Fathers power," just as the child in society is the subject of his father's sovereign."[7]

Aside from noting Hobbes's apparently radical idea regarding the mother's absolute dominion over the child, Schochet never asks *how* women become subject to men, except possibly through matrimonial law. But since matrimonial law does not exist in the state of nature, and yet the patriarchal family does, that does not help. Women's subjection must predate the social contract, on that view. Furthermore, Schochet indicates that a father's right over children must come by virtue of the mother's consent, or at least her subjection to the husband—which amounts to the same thing, given that dominion by institution and acquisition are equivalent for Hobbes. The question is: Why and how did she become subject to him in the first place?

Schochet rightly notes that patriarchy actually sometimes *includes* maternal dominion; mothers in the state of nature, Hobbes says, are their children's *lords*. So although one could argue that the need for a patriarchal form of authority is moral for Hobbes—because it is the only way to achieve security, which is the closest Hobbes comes to naming a *summum bonum*—the "fact" that the people who have assumed the role of patriarchs happened to be men much more commonly than women is what Schochet calls an "anthropological account" of the particular sexual content of patriarchy.[8] In this account, women *could be* patriarchs as easily as men, and in fact have been, in the case of queens. So one would have to argue that Hobbes does not care whether men rule women; he simply notes that they have happened to do so—the "just so" story that other contributors to this volume have noted.

Feminists, of course, tend to be concerned with *ideological* patriarchy, and with the ways in which apparently neutral descriptions of "what happened" and how social relations "happened" to be constructed through history often mask interpretive frameworks that encode moral, political, and ideological values of how social relations *ought to be* constructed. Such "anthropological" accounts also ignore the ways in which power and ideology shaped the events that "happened" to occur. That leads to the obvious question: *Why* didn't women generally become Hobbesian patriarchs?

What makes this question plausible is that Hobbes provides a view of women that is radically different from that of his contemporaries, such as Filmer, to whom Schochet compares and contrasts Hobbes. As all feminists who read Hobbes know, women start out perfectly free and equal in Hobbes's state of nature, just like men; just as the physical or mental inferiority of some men to others is evened out by the fact that no one can dominate another for long, so women, to the extent that they may be physically less strong than most men, are strong enough to make it an open question. Moreover, they have as much chance at being superior mentally as they do at being inferior physically: "There is not always that difference of strength or prudence between the man and the woman, as that the right [of "Dominion" over each other] can be determined without War" (*Leviathan*, ch. 20, 253). In *De Cive*, Hobbes puts it at once more strongly and more ambiguously: "The inequality of their natural forces is not so great, that the man could get the dominion over the woman without war" (9.3).[9] Women are free, like men, to do whatever they want, within the realm of whatever they can actually achieve. As Carole Pateman notes, "In Hobbes's state of nature female individuals can be victors in the war of all against all just as often as male individuals."[10]

Within the state of nature, because of women's overall equality with men in physical strength and "wit," women are not naturally under men's dominion and indeed seem to be on an equal par with men. Particularly significant to this equality is men's and women's "dominion" over children, the matter on which Hobbes devotes most of his attention to gender, and the matter on which Schochet bases his argument about the patriarchal foundation of political obligation. In the state of nature, as Schochet noted, there is no marriage, there being "no matrimonial law" (*Leviathan*, ch. 20, 254); but given "the naturall inclination of the Sexes, one to another, and to their children" (ch. 20, 253), men and women will have some occasion to negotiate with each other in relation to the children they produce. There thus may be marriage *covenants*, which Hobbes distinguishes from contract as relying on a promise of future action, though the problem with the state of nature is that covenants are virtually meaningless without a sovereign to enforce them. Nevertheless, some contract-like agreement would seem to operate within the family, because that is one foundation for men's dominion over children, and hence their position as patriarch. Accordingly, while dominion in civil society is generally granted to men because of custom (though Hobbes never speculates on how such customs arose), in the state of nature dominion over each child is to be determined by contract, which may grant dominion to the man or to the woman, or even divide the children between them—just as the Amazons supposedly contracted to keep female babies and sent males back to their fathers (ch. 20, 254). But given the difficulty, if not impossibility, of enforceable contracts in the state of nature, Hobbes notes that "if there be no Contract, the Dominion is in the Mother." Once this dominion is established, mothers gain an even firmer foothold by "nourishing" the child, rather than "exposing" it and leaving it to die; hence children owe obedience to her, and her claim to "natural" dominion is stronger than the man's (ch. 20, 254).

Schochet has noted all of this. He maintains that the state of nature is not static, but dynamic; patriarchal families eventually emerge in the state of nature, even if they were not there from the beginning. This is what I find troubling. For Hobbes goes on in this vein to say that if one member of a couple is subject to the other prior to a child's birth, the child is under the latter's dominion, and this can refer to men or women, "as when a Sovereign Queen marrieth one of her subjects" (*Leviathan*, ch. 20, 254), again raising the specter of the female patriarchal sovereign. Additionally, when two monarchs of different kingdoms produce a child, dominion is determined again by contract, or in the absence of contract, by residence. Furthermore, bucking a common tactic in the seventeenth century, Hobbes nowhere uses the Bible to justify wives' subservience to husbands, even in his references to Adam and Eve, and even though he cites scripture to justify the subservience of sons, daughters, and "maid servants" (ch. 20, 258–60).[11] In *The Elements of Law*, Hobbes similarly refers to queens to illustrate the point that "because sometimes the government may belong to the wife only, sometimes also the dominion over the children shall be in her only" (2.4.7), since all children are under the dominion of the sovereign, by virtue of the fact that their parents are under her dominion.[12]

Thus, Pateman is not entirely correct when she says that Hobbes "remains silent . . . about the status of any men who come under women's power."[13] But her broader point—that Hobbes defines the family in ways that presuppose men's dominion—is a fundamental notion of Schochet's theory of the patriarchal family as well. For despite the fact that Hobbes allows that "universally, if the society of the male and the female be such an union, as the one have subjected himself to the other, the children belong to him *or her* [my emphasis] that commands,"[14] it seems doubtful, from his writings, that Hobbes thinks women would gain consistent dominion over men (*De Cive* 9.5). Indeed, in *De Cive* and *Leviathan*, Hobbes uses queens to serve as the exception that proves the rule of men's dominion. Further, he seems to drop the claim that women who are not queens might hold dominion in marriage.

I thus disagree with Jane Jaquette's claim that all women in the state of nature are not members of families at all.[15] Such an argument would require women to be either sexless, in which case no children would be produced, or completely hapless in preventing men from stealing their children. It further denies the possibility that female babies would be born; just because they grow into women, they are not exempted from their continued obligations of obedience to their parent. It is therefore more likely that women become included in families as "servants." Historically, the Roman term *familia* refers to "the total number of slaves belonging to one man," so it would make sense for Hobbes to consider women within that category.[16] The conceptual question, however, of how women *became* servants is itself a problem. For it is their status as servants—people who consent to the dominion of another and who agree to obey and abide by that other's decisions—that constitutes the crux of feminist debate over the status of women in Hobbes's theory.

Certainly, at least in Hobbes's civil society, women seem to become invisible in that infamous definition of a family (*Leviathan*, ch. 20, 257).

Similarly, in *De Cive*, Hobbes says, "A *father* with his *sons* and *servants*, grown into a civil person by virtue of his paternal jurisdiction, is called a *family*" (9.10). But in *The Elements of Law*, women *are* mentioned in the definition of the family: "The whole consisting of the father or the mother, or both, and of the children, and of the servants, is called a FAMILY." Even here, however, he immediately follows with the phrase "wherein the father or master of the family is sovereign of the same; and the rest (both children and servants equally) subjects" (2.4.10), once again raising the question: Are women subject or not? This leaves servants as the only remaining possibility, and it seems to be the one that Schochet favors.

Could Hobbes again be given an out by declaring that women can be "masters"? He is quite slippery on that question; in this quoted passage, he designates "the father *or* the mother, *or* both" as the "sovereign." The use of "or" here indicates that women could be "masters." But in *De Cive*, shortly after he says that "every woman that bears children, becomes both a *mother* and a *lord*" (9.3), Hobbes adds that "the preserved oweth all to the preserver, whether in regard of his education as to a *mother*, or of his service as to a *lord*" (9.4). With that "or," he introduces a decided differentiation between the two categories of "mother" and "lord" (though it is possible that one person could occupy two distinct roles).

Certainly, despite his rather unexpected declarations of women's equality in nature, there are many places in which Hobbes seems to express a considerable degree of gender inequality, perhaps even discrimination, in his theory. For instance, on the topic of succession, he says that "a Child of his own, Male, or Female, be preferred before any other, because men are presumed to be more inclined by nature, to advance their own children, than the children of other men; and of their own, rather a Male than a Female; because men, are naturally fitter than women, for actions of labour and danger" (*Leviathan*, ch. 19, 250). And in *De Cive* he explains that sons are preferred "because for the most part, although not always, they are fitter for the administration of greater matters, but specially of wars" (9.16). Similarly, in *The Elements of Law* Hobbes notes that "generally men are endued with greater parts of wisdom and courage, by which all monarchies are kept from dissolution, than women are; it is to be presumed, where no express will is extant to the contrary, he preferreth his male children before the female. Not but that women may govern, and have in divers ages and places governed wisely, but are not so apt thereto in general as men" (2.4.14). And, of course, he refers to women as "helpers" to men whom "God hath ordained" (*Leviathan*, ch. 20, 253). As Sharon Lloyd suggests in the present volume, "small differences" may have greater weight in civil society, though of course Hobbes does not actually say that.

Thus, Hobbes's gender discrimination may be subtle, but it is no less effective than that of other, more overt sexists, such as Rousseau. This subtlety leads to sometimes conflicting readings of Hobbes on the major issue that concerns feminist interpreters, namely, women's status in the family. Most feminist commentators agree with Schochet that marriage exists in the state of nature and that it takes a patriarchal form in that state. But although Hobbes makes offhand references to the ways in which laws commonly determine father-right over mother-right, and seems to accept marriage as a given in civil society, he leaves open, without any direct explanation, the larger and prior question of why marriage is necessary in the first place.

Like his arguments regarding marriage, Hobbes's arguments about contracts for dominion over children contain a certain circularity that goes beyond the paradoxical character of contracts in the state of nature. That is, contracts over children are not only unenforceable without a sovereign, just like other contracts; they are virtually unimaginable. That is, prior to matrimonial law, men and women would have absolutely no cause—or even opportunity—to enter into contracts over children, since a woman would be long gone before she knew she was pregnant, making it impossible for a man to know that he fathered a given child, or even to be able to draw the logical association between copulation and birth. As Hobbes says, "In the condition of meer Nature, where there are no matrimonial laws, it cannot be known who is the Father, unlesse it be declared by the Mother" (*Leviathan*, ch. 20, 254). But unless the woman is already subordinate to the man, she has no reason to let him know about his paternity, since that provides him with a motive to seek dominion over the child as well as over her. This is something that most commentators have overlooked.

The fact that Hobbes does postulate such contracts, however, indicates that he must believe that marriage, or something resembling it, exists naturally, even despite the absence of matrimonial law, as Schochet indicates. But if Schochet is correct that such families are patriarchal, then Hobbes has defined away women's contracting abilities before even declaring them in his text. One of the great strengths of Schochet's argument is that he challenges the common understanding of Hobbes as an abstract individualist; Hobbes says that "no man can hope by his own strength, or wit, to defend himselfe from destruction, without the help of Confederates" (*Leviathan*, ch. 15, 204), and offers this as the major reason why people might want to keep covenants in the state of nature, because those who do not keep them will be unable to form such alliances. But it also suggests why people might want to establish marriage contracts.

Or rather, it suggests why *men* would want such contracts. Since a woman has natural dominion over her child in the absence of contracts to the contrary, due to the care she takes in preserving the child's life, a natural "confederacy" is built into the relationship between mother and child. This could be utilized to overcome particular men, who have no such natural confederacy and must, if they have them at all, depend on less reliable ones with peers. That is, whereas the consent of infants must be inferred "by other sufficient arguments declared" (*Leviathan*, ch. 20, 253), since they cannot speak, by the time the child reaches the age of speech she is already deeply indebted to her caretaker; in Hobbes's view, consent has already been given.

Recognizing the power women have over children and the advantage that such confederacy gives them, men would presumably want to get in on the act. But how? A marriage contract is the answer; but since such contracts must logically violate women's best interests—a woman would have to give up her natural dominion over both herself and her children unless men agreed to be subservient—patriarchal marriage contracts would not likely be made by "institution" in the state of nature. Women would have no reason to seek out such contracts or to subordinate themselves to men if they could negotiate different terms.

That leaves "acquisition," specifically conquest. Hobbes maintains that when someone is vanquished, he or she will contract to be a servant in order to avoid death, so the victor "shall have the use" of "his life, and the liberty of his body" (*Leviathan*, ch. 20, 255). In this, of course, it is not the conquest itself that produces the right of dominion, Hobbes says, but the covenants that the victor is able to exact from the vanquished under duress. It is in this specific way—not the simple fact of a patriarchal head—that the family is "a little Monarchy" (ch. 20, 257), as Schochet points out. In Hobbes's description of a family, the invisible wife is a "servant," which Hobbes defines as anyone "who is obliged to obey the commands of any man before he knows what he will command him" (*De Cive* 8.1). This description could easily cover wives in patriarchal marriage.[17] As Schochet maintains, in the state of nature, men's "patriarchal title" over children "originated in power over [the mother], not in the inherent rights or superiority of either males or fathers."[18] That is, even though patriarchy is "rule by the father," this rule is accessed through ruling the mother: that is *how* he gains dominion over children. This might seem to contradict Hobbes's earlier egalitarian views on the ability of women and men to contract equally for dominion over their children, but as Hobbes has just indicated, conquest and contract are not mutually exclusive. Indeed, contract is what gives meaning to conquest.

So Schochet seems to believe that women will always make such contracts from the position of the vanquished, not the victor. Indeed, in an article published thirty years after "Thomas Hobbes on the Family," he argues that most women were conquered in the state of nature after giving birth, when they were weakest.[19] This is a position with which many feminist commentators agree, in different ways. Carole Pateman, for instance, attributes women's submission—or the fact that supposedly free and equal women always seem to lose to men the battles for conquest—to the fact that they are mothers. She explains, "When a woman becomes a mother and decides to become a lord and raise her child, her position changes; she is put at a slight disadvantage against men, since now she has her infant to attend to. Conversely, a man obtains a slight advantage over her and is then able to defeat the woman he had initially to treat with as an equal. . . . Mother-right can never be more than fleeting." It is because of this prior subjection, she maintains, that the sexual contract precedes and indeed founds the social contract, which is formed specifically and exclusively by men: "If free and equal women could enter the original contract there is no reason whatsoever why they would agree to create a civil law that secures their permanent subjection as wives. Matrimonial law takes a patriarchal form because *men* have made the original contract."[20] Most other feminist commentators agree that women's subordination occurs in the state of nature prior to the social contract, for similar reasons: pregnancy makes women vulnerable to attack; having infants makes women even more vulnerable to attack; women want to care for their children even though it makes them vulnerable; women are simply less strong than men, regardless of reproductive status; women are less hostile and atomistic than men and thus are not as aggressive as men.[21]

A Challenge to Feminist Orthodoxy

If that is the case, however, then Hobbes's comments suggesting women's equality, and their natural superiority in terms of dominion over children, need to be reevaluated. For rather than being equal partners to a reciprocal contract, it would seem that women are either vanquished, and hence contract with men to be servants, or are not vanquished and do not enter into contracts at all.

Such treatment of women would cohere with Hobbes's other references to women in several passages where he seems to liken women to property. For instance, in "Quarrells of competition" in the state of nature, men "use violence, to make themselves masters of other men's persons, wives, children, and cattell" (*Leviathan*, ch. 13, 185). He goes on to write, "Of things held in propriety, those that are dearest to a man are his own life, & limbs; and in the next degree, (in most men,) those that concern conjugall affection; and after them riches and means of living" (ch. 30, 382). Hobbes also notes in several places that rape is a means for men to attain honor, as it is one way to attain dominion over another man's property; thus, "the ancient Heathen did not thinke they Dishonoured, but greatly Honoured the Gods, when they introduced them in their Poems, committing Rapes, Thefts, and other great, but unjust, or unclean acts" (ch. 10, 156). He further maintains that "forcible rapine, and fraudulent surreption of one anothers goods" are among the acts to which natural man is prone, and which the sovereign must outlaw (ch. 30, 383). Such statements have prompted Karen Green to remark that women are "treated as booty, rather than enemies, in war."[22]

Though Schochet takes note of none of these remarks about women in either "Thomas Hobbes on the Family" or *Patriarchalism in Political Thought*,[23] this popular feminist reading lends strong support to Schochet's interpretation; women exist in the state of nature not in the free and equal status that Hobbes originally describes, but rather in families where they are "property," or at least "servants." And, of course, Schochet cites other passages in which Hobbes writes explicitly about men *as* the parties to the original contract. Indeed, Schochet maintains that Hobbes is asserting that parties to the original contract are not just men, but male heads of families explicitly, and not merely implicitly as Pateman holds. Women would seem to be obliterated from the social contract except via the consent of their "lords" (or husbands); for in consenting to the authority of my lord, I automatically authorize his consent to a superior lord—that is, the sovereign.

Why, however, would Hobbes be so ambiguous on the issue of women's freedom and equality with men? After all, as Schochet has more recently said, "People had to be the authors of whatever statuses they occupied, which required the engagement, in some sense, of their wills." This "made each person the sovereign lord over his—and pointedly *her*—own movements and actions."[24] That indicates strongly that if women are subordinate in the family, it must be attributable in some way to their own choices. The question is, then, why women choose subordination.

In contrast to the dominant feminist view, and Schochet's as well, I maintain that mother-right is *not* a disadvantage in Hobbes's state of nature, but a power. Indeed, it is *because* it is a power that men are compelled to conquer women. There is no reason to assume, as Pateman and others do, that caring for a child makes a woman less able to defend herself unless we radically alter Hobbesian assumptions, according to which a woman would abandon (or kill) an infant if she found that it jeopardized her security. The idea proffered by Pateman and others that a woman's decision to raise a child is irrevocable is simply unsupported by Hobbes's text. Indeed, Hobbes says that the parent who raises the child and thereby gains dominion over it "may alienate them, that is, assign his or her dominion, by selling or giving them in adoption or servitude to others; or may pawn them for hostages, kill them for rebellion, or sacrifice them for peace, by the law of nature, when he or she, in his or her conscience, think it to be necessary" (*Elements of Law* 2.4.8). This is hardly the vision of nurturance that seems to be assumed by most feminists. If Schochet is correct that the family is the foundation for the state, then children must be seen by men and women alike as assets enabling confederacy; if children owe obedience to parents out of obligations of gratitude for keeping them alive, as Schochet notes, such obligations are a rich source of power.

Gratitude, as Schochet notes, is the linchpin of Hobbes's theory, and it may offer a solution to this dilemma. But it is important to note here that children owe gratitude to *mothers*, assuming that these mothers have nourished them, rather than to fathers in the state of nature. Generation in and of itself is meaningless to obligation, and hence fathers are owed nothing if they contribute nothing to the child's security and welfare. Accordingly, the more likely scenario than a woman's abandoning or killing the child is that, under the power of confederacy, the mother and child would work together to defeat the *man*. Children would not need to be very old to serve as useful confederates, after all; a two-year-old could distract an adult, a five-year-old could steal unobtrusively. The view that infants are burdens, placing women at such a disadvantage that cannot be overcome, coheres with romantic visions of childhood and motherhood that did not pertain in Hobbes's day but rather developed in the eighteenth and nineteenth centuries.[25] In Hobbes's formula, rather than being a liability, motherhood provides a natural source of power that would give women a strategic advantage over men. Accordingly, motherhood cannot be the cause of woman's downfall in the way that Pateman and other feminists maintain.

As I have already argued, however, motherhood does provide men with greater motivation to conquer women, because they thereby gain dominion over children at the same time. Yet understanding men's *motivation* to conquer women still does not explain how men come to be *successful* in their conquests to the point that patriarchy is established as a general practice. One cannot even use the argument that women are "servants" very fruitfully; Hobbes distinguishes between a slave and a servant in that the latter agrees not to kill her master if he releases her from physical bondage, whereas the slave must remain bound (*De Cive* 9.9; *Leviathan*, ch. 20, 255). But the logic of this statement is unclear due to Hobbes's claim—a claim which founds the entire idea of the social contract—that contracts are unenforceable in the state of nature. The fact that a man has agreed not to kill a woman—or any master his servant—does not mean that she can trust him not to do so; and though servitude and even enslavement are preferable to death on Hobbes's formula, a woman has every reason to kill her male captor when she can and reclaim her children. After all, once a man can claim dominion over a woman's child, its advantage to her diminishes, and she has little self-interest in keeping it alive. So what motive would she have to be a good mother, or even an adequate one? As long as she is under a man's dominion, her children belong to him, not her. She should only care about keeping them alive if she thinks that eventually she can reclaim them, or if their lives serve her interests in some other capacity. So the question of how men as a group are uniformly successful in subjugating women as a group is still left unanswered.

This realization leads to a second, related, and perhaps more important point on which I disagree with Schochet and the apparent feminist consensus. Namely, *marriage does not precede the social contract, but follows from it.* When we consent to the social contract, we consent to everything the sovereign decides and do not have a say about what laws the sovereign passes. We have no idea ahead of time whether she or he will decree mother-right or father-right, monogamy or polygamy, or even any family structure at all.[26] All we know is that, as individuals in the state of nature, we are miserable and desperate for relief—a relief that can only come through a "confederacy" that is seemingly impossible to maintain without a common authority over us. Even women's "natural" confederacy with children must have a certain degree of uncertainty; despite the law of gratitude, children can always be ungrateful and turn on their caregiver, as wrong as this might be in Hobbes's view. Given this, it makes sense within Hobbes's theory for women to consent to the social contract. Only then would women's subjugation come into play. That is, it is logical for a sovereign concerned with order and security to command an authoritarian family structure, for in this way the sovereign channels men's and women's natural desire for dominion into a formal structure that feeds the sovereign's interests: specifically, the sovereign need not control everyone directly, but only heads of families, who in turn keep their respective family members in line. As Schochet indicates, without an authoritarian family structure, the danger of people's interactions in daily commerce and the like degenerating into civil chaos is much greater. Families, as he suggests, provide a structure of discipline; they habituate men and women to obedience and curb their natural hostility and distrust. Thus, rather than predating the social contract, I maintain that the family is a by-product of the social contract, created by the sovereign to maintain order.

However, why a *patriarchal* authoritarian family structure? This makes less logical sense from the perspective of order, though perhaps it is logical enough. Given men's envy of women's natural dominion over children and given their continued desire for "honor"—which includes dominion over other people, particularly over children but also over women through means that include rape and adultery—it would make sense for the sovereign to write laws establishing father-right in order to secure peace among men. As Joanne Wright suggests, Hobbes is "interested in families, and hence gender relations, only insofar as they reveal something important about the nature of political relationships."[27] In particular, I believe that Hobbes's defining the family without reference to women, and under a patriarchal authority, serves a purpose of eliminating, or more likely suppressing, its most dangerous and disruptive element. Children are much less of a threat to the rule of the father than wives are to the rule of husbands. This is especially so when women stop having babies, for even if motherhood puts women at a disadvantage, when children grow up women are back on an equal footing with men, and there is no clear reason why they cannot change the terms of the contract if their families are still in the state of nature. Women would seem to have nothing to gain by sticking to a contract of servitude unless it was backed by the sword of Leviathan.

Patriarchal matrimonial law would thus help secure peace by establishing territorial or property rights over women—and perhaps even more importantly, over the products of women's bodies, namely children—which the sword of Leviathan now upholds.[28] The feminist objection that women would not consent to such subordination—such an obvious problem in the state of nature—dissolves in civil society, for such consent would not have to be "given" in any express way; it would automatically follow from women's original consent to the sovereign. In this, the family does for women what the social contract does for men: it takes away their ultimate natural powers. That the social contract alone is insufficient to tame women's powers is the only relevant difference between the sexes; for rather than being inferior in the state of nature, women are potentially superior.

Indeed, it is puzzling why Hobbes did not recommend matriarchy from the start, because that would remove men's motive for dominion over women (as they would have to obey and submit to them) and hence a major source of conflict in the state of nature. Indeed, men competing over women are more likely to kill *one another*, thereby leaving women in a superior position to then force the remaining men to submit. Hobbes's reference to the minor disadvantages women supposedly have in comparison to men, such as weeping, demonstrate the weakness of his argument when it comes to differentiating among citizens in terms of gender. While Hobbes can claim that men consent to the sovereign because the state of war unconditionally threatens all, women's consent to men's dominion cannot be rationally deduced in the state of nature because reproduction does not threaten women. Or, to be more precise, to the degree that reproduction does threaten women, the family cannot protect them. Thus, although the picture Hobbes seems to draw indicates that the family predates the social contract as Schochet and some feminists argue, the logical tenets of his theory suggest instead that the social contract must predate the family.

Hobbes's explanation in *De Cive* of how "dominion passes from mothers to others" further supports my argument. There are four ways in which this can occur: if the mother "exposes" the infant and abandons its care; if the mother is taken prisoner; if the mother becomes "a subject under what government soever," because the sovereign has dominion over her child, as he or she does over everyone living in the relevant territory covered by the sovereignty; and "if a woman *for society's sake* [my emphasis] give herself to a man on this condition, that he shall bear the sway" (9.5). The first three situations are covered by Schochet, as I have already discussed. The last one, however, suggests that women recognize that their reproductive and sexual capacities are a source of conflict among men, who can only be civilized through gaining patriarchal dominion. But, more significantly, it suggests that women can give up their individual good for the good of the whole. This could possibly serve as evidence of the "altruism" that some feminists suggest, but it is more likely evidence of the social contract predating patriarchy. For there is no "society" prior to the contract, and hence no "good" of society. Thus, submission to patriarchal marriage "for society's sake" could happen *only* after a social contract was formed; or at best, it could happen concurrently with the social contract's formation. Since Hobbes rejects the idea of *summum bonum*, the good of this society has to be order and peace, the first law of nature; but without the surety of a superior power, which the sovereign ensures, it would be irrational and contrary to self-interest for women to give over such powers to men without more of a guarantee than a simple reassurance from a single man.[29] As Hobbes notes, "The mutual aid of two or three men is of very little security. For the odds on the other side, of a man or two, giveth sufficient encouragement to an assault. And therefore before men have sufficient security in the help of one another, their number must be so great, that the odds of a few which the enemy may have, be no certain and sensible advantage" (*Elements of Law* 1.19.3). Without such force, the Hobbesian woman does not strike one as the type to be beguiled by such a trade with a single man, because she could probably do a better job of protecting herself. Or, even if she could not, objectively, she would *believe* that she could, for people in the state of nature suffer from the fault of "Vainglory, a foolish over-rating of their own worth" (*Leviathan*, ch. 27, 341).

If we claim that women are limitedly altruistic because of their propensity to care for children, even when that entails servitude to a man, then we completely upend Hobbes's depiction of the state of nature. Women's voluntary subordination is much more acceptable, however, if we assume that the social contract is already in place; since they have consented to the sovereign's authority, they have authorized, or "chosen," their own subordination, just as men "consent" to their own imprisonment when they break the law. In theory, of course, Hobbes has to allow the possibility that the sovereign could just as readily legislate matriarchal families in which women have power and dominion over men; men, after all, seem to be the troublemakers who need controlling. It is this possibility that I think Hobbes is responding to when he says that "for the most part Common-wealths have been erected by the Fathers, not by the Mothers of families" (*Leviathan*, ch. 20, 253), and I thus derive a somewhat different meaning from this statement than Schochet does.[30] In this, however, Hobbes is not *recommending* father-right and patriarchy as much as *observing* it. But, of course, such "explanation" is made possible only by virtue of Hobbes's normative framework, wherein he clearly endorses women's subjugation as more conducive to social order and peace.

The Role of Gratitude

There is a final objection to my reading, which feminists have failed to note but which Schochet supplies and does not develop—namely, gratitude. In a 1990 article, Schochet argued that gratitude plays an important role in Hobbes's theory. Hobbes is centrally engaged in constituting the social contract as "the mutuall relation between Protection and Obedience."[31] If Schochet is correct in "Thomas Hobbes on the Family and the State of Nature" that the family exists in the state of nature, and if Carole Pateman is correct in *The Sexual Contract*—like many of the other feminists I have discussed above—that it exists because men conquered women in the state of nature, then prior to the institution of the social contract, women must have obligations of gratitude to men for not killing them. Schochet points out that "sovereigns of acquisition . . . in effect enter into reciprocal agreements with their subjects—to spare their lives in return for obedience." But this "resultant obligation is directly conditional."[32] In other words, the obligation is ongoing, and my life is spared just so long as my obedience persists: that is, when I am conquered, I am in a position of vulnerability, and the position of servitude into which I contract continues that vulnerability in various ways. Once conquered, it is unlikely (though not impossible) that I will gain back the individual independent force that I had when I first fought you. Thus, my obedience is consensual—or rather consent is read back into my behavior under the umbrella of gratitude—because the threat of death is ongoing. This, of course, is the same logic that underlies the Leviathan's authority writ large.

What I like about this solution is that it explains a lot. Gratitude answers the question that Carole Pateman asks but claims there is no coherent answer for: Why should free and equal women consent to a position of subordination in the family? She says they simply would never consent, but rather are conquered and actively kept in a subordinate position. This dovetails with the not uncommon reading of Hobbes's sovereign as ruling successfully only insofar as he can keep all of his citizens in fear and awe. By contrast, Schochet could offer a more reasonable and plausible answer: gratitude provides Hobbes's foundation for women's *consent*. Women consent because of gratitude, and they are grateful because their lives were spared despite having been conquered.

The problem, of course, as I pointed out earlier, is that Hobbes maintains that although men are, on the whole, stronger than women, they are not so much stronger as to be able to hold women continually in thrall: "There is not always that difference of strength or prudence between the man and the woman, as that the right [of "Dominion" over each other] can be determined without War" (*Leviathan*, ch. 20, 253). We would have to assume—as most feminists do and as Schochet seems to suggest—that women always lose in war, but that doesn't follow from the starting point of his sentence. So the assumption that women, once they have become servants, are even more vulnerable and therefore in need of protection is a significant leap. Moreover, as I noted earlier, and as Schochet remarked in a later essay, gratitude should lead to matriarchy rather than patriarchy.[33] Similarly, much of the argument depends on how one constructs the sexual division of labor in the family, *how* weak one thinks Hobbes thinks women are compared to men, and how much of a disadvantage pregnancy puts women at. All of these factors will affect both the reasons for gratitude (i.e., what women should be grateful for: whether just not being killed, or more ongoing protection and provision) and its extent (that an individual man did not kill a woman in a particular conflict creates situational gratitude; but if women's weakness is endemic to femaleness, their gratitude for protection is more systemic).

Finally, it suggests that the fourth law of nature holds a kind of sway over people in the state of nature that the other laws of nature do not (excepting the second half of the first law: defend yourself when peace isn't possible). Peace, justice (or the keeping of covenants), and all the rest of the laws of nature would make life much better for people than war does, but these things are not obtainable without a sovereign. That is why we enter the social contract in the first place, and why, as Schochet correctly argues, acquisition (rather than institution) is the primary form of "consent" that we give. Gratitude makes sense under acquisition if there is a full-blown state mechanism to keep you in line; but the family, despite being "a little city," or even analogized to a state, is in fact not one, in that it lacks the sort of regularizing and policing mechanisms on which states are founded. It thus seems to me that gratitude is not an adequate motivation for women's continued obedience in the family, and for their continued "consent" to an ongoing relation of servitude. The puzzles concerning Hobbes on women and the family thus—perhaps fortuitously—remain for feminists to debate.

Notes

1. Reissued by Transaction Books in 1988 as *The Authoritarian Family in Seventeenth-Century England: Patriarchalism in Political Thought*.

2. See, for instance, Gordon Schochet's "De l'idée de sujétion naturelle à l'indifférenciation par convention: Les femmes dans la pensée politique de Sir Robert Filmer, Thomas Hobbes, et John Locke," in *Encyclopédie politique et historique des femmes: Europe, Amérique du Nord*, ed. Christine Fauré (Paris: Presses Universitaires de France, 1997), 73–93; "The Significant Sounds of Silence: The Absence of Women from the Political Thought of Sir Robert Filmer and John Locke (or 'Why Can't a Woman Be More Like a Man?')," in *Women Writers and the Early Modern British Political Tradition*, ed. Hilda L. Smith (Cambridge: Cambridge University Press, 1998), 220–42; and "Models of Politics and the Place of Women in Locke's Political Thought," in *Feminist Interpretations of John Locke*, ed. Nancy J. Hirschmann and Kirstie M. McClure (University Park: Pennsylvania State University Press, 2007), 131–54.

3. Schochet, "Models of Politics," 133.

4. Schochet suggests as much in "Models of Politics" and "De l'idée de sujétion naturelle," arguing that Hobbes and Locke needed to be read against the historical framework of patriarchy, which extended back two thousand years from Hobbes's time to Plato and Aristotle. As Schochet noted, that context made the challenge of social contract theory deeply radical did not seem to carry over into the contract theorists' view of women in the family; "there are very few seventeenth-century conceptions of women outside the household: they were wives and daughters" ("Models of Politics," 134).

5. Thomas Hobbes, *Leviathan*, ed. C. B. Macpherson (New York: Penguin, 1985). Citations to *Leviathan* are from this edition and given parenthetically by chapter and page number.

6. See Gordon Schochet, "Thomas Hobbes on the Family and the State of Nature," 000. Page numbers for Schochet's essay refer to its reprinting in chapter 5 of this volume.

7. Ibid., 000.

8. Schochet, *Patriarchalism in Political Thought*.

9. *Thomas Hobbes, De Cive*, in *Man and Citizen: "De Homine" and "De Cive,"* ed. Bernard Gert (Indianapolis: Hackett, 1991). Citations to *De Cive* are from this edition and given parenthetically by chapter and paragraph number. Of course, this latter quote could be interpreted in two ways. The obvious way is that, if there is a war, men and women have an equal chance of winning. The less obvious is to take it as a warning: in order to gain dominion, men must wage war on women, even though men would probably win. In that case, women need to decide whether the risk of war is worth the chance that they will beat the men. Presumably, however, women are as vainglorious as men, and so will not hear such a warning.

10. Carole Pateman and Teresa Brennan, "Afterword: Mere Auxiliaries of the Commonwealth in an Age of Globalization," in Hirschmann and McClure, *Feminist Interpretations of John Locke*, 79.

11. See Joanne H. Wright, *Origin Stories in Political Thought: Discourses on Gender, Power, and Citizenship* (Toronto: University of Toronto Press, 2004), 88.

12. Thomas Hobbes, *The Elements of Law, Natural and Politic*, ed. Ferdinand Tönnies (London: Frank Cass, 1969). Citations to *The Elements of Law* are from this edition and given parenthetically by part, chapter, and paragraph.

13. Pateman and Brennan, "Afterword," 79.

14. Why Hobbes follows "himself" with "him or her" once again illustrates the ambiguous treatment of gender in his texts, but at least it indicates the possibility that the man may be subjected to the woman.

15. Jane S. Jaquette, "Contract and Coercion: Power and Gender in *Leviathan*," in Smith, *Women Writers and the Early Modern British Political Tradition*, 200–219.

16. Friedrich Engels, *The Origin of Family, Private Property, and the State*, ed. Eleanor Burke Leacock (New York: International Publishers, 1972), 121.

17. Nancy A. Stanlick makes a similar point in "Lords and Mothers: Silent Subjects in Hobbes's Political Theory," *International Journal of Politics and Ethics* 1, no. 3 (2001): 171–82. So does Pateman in "'God Hath Ordained to Man a Helper': Hobbes, Patriarchy, and Conjugal Right," in *Feminist Interpretations and Political Theory*, ed. Mary Lyndon Shanley and Carole Pateman (University Park: Pennsylvania State University Press, 1991), 64.

18. Schochet, "Thomas Hobbes on the Family and the State of Nature," 000.

19. Schochet, "De l'idée de sujétion naturelle." However, the source he cites for this—*Leviathan*, ch. 20—contains nothing about childbirth except that it gives mothers dominion. Hobbes never claims that pregnancy or childbirth weakens women.

20. Pateman, "'God Hath Ordained to Man a Helper,'" 65, 67.

21. Stanlick, "Lords and Mothers"; Pateman and Brennan, "Afterword"; Christine Di Stefano, "Masculinity as Ideology in Political Theory: Hobbesian Man Considered," *Hypatia* 1 (1983): 633–44.

22. Karen Green, "Christine de Pisan and Thomas Hobbes," *Philosophical Quarterly* 44, no. 177 (1994): 460.

23. He does so in "De l'idée de sujétion naturelle" and "The Significant Sounds of Silence," but the problem I pose is resolved in neither of those essays.

24. Gordon J. Schochet, "Intending (Political) Obligation: Hobbes and the Voluntary Basis of Society," in *Thomas Hobbes and Political Theory*, ed. Mary G. Dietz (Lawrence: University Press of Kansas, 1990), 60.

25. Judith A. Plotz, *Romanticism and the Vocation of Childhood* (New York: Palgrave, 2001).

26. See esp. Hobbes, *Leviathan*, ch. 21, 271.

27. Wright, *Origin Stories*, 78.

28. Nancy J. Hirschmann, *Rethinking Obligation: A Feminist Method for Political Theory* (Ithaca, N.Y.: Cornell University Press, 1992), 42–44.

29. "For society's sake" could also mean that women give dominion to a man for the sake of *forming* a society—perhaps Hobbes thinks that women are more desirous of social relations and grant

dominion to men in order to have that. But this entails an extremely conventional twentieth-century understanding of gender that Hobbes does not advocate; aside from women's "weeping," they don't seem to be any more sociable or emotional than men.
30. Schochet, "Thomas Hobbes on the Family and the State of Nature," 000.
31. Schochet, "Intending (Political) Obligation," 61.
32. Ibid.
33. Schochet, "De l'idée de sujétion naturelle."

Part Three

Hobbes and His(torical) Women

7
Margaret Cavendish and Thomas Hobbes on Freedom, Education, and Women

Karen Detlefsen

Thomas Hobbes exerted one of the most significant contemporary influences on the thought of Margaret Cavendish. Hobbes's influence was both positive and negative. Cavendish shares many important doctrines with him, some of which put them in a very small minority in the seventeenth century. Both are materialists with respect to the natural world.[1]

I am grateful for criticisms and suggestions from audience members at the Works in Progress Seminar (Alice Paul Center for Research on Women, Gender, and Sexuality, University of Pennsylvania, 2011); Women, Philosophy, and History: A Conference in Celebration of Eileen O'Neill and Her Work (Barnard College, 2009); and the Philadelphia Political Theory Workshop (Political Science, University of Pennsylvania, 2007). Many thanks for helpful comments from two anonymous referees of this book. I owe an enormous debt of gratitude to Nancy Hirschmann and Joanne Wright for insightful comments and help at many stages of writing this chapter.

Both explicitly distinguish between the sphere of inquiry concerned with the natural and human (moral and civic) world on the one hand, and the sphere of inquiry concerned with God on the other hand.[2] Both take the maintenance of peace and stability, and concomitantly the avoidance of civil war, to be the primary civic goal, and both assert that a government based in absolute sovereignty is required to achieve the maintenance of peace. But to a significant degree, Cavendish's own philosophy emerges from her rejection of various doctrines of a number of her contemporaries, and Hobbes is among her principal targets. In this chapter, I focus on their divergent accounts of freedom, the social conditions in which freedom can be exercised, and the role of education and well-developed rationality in the exercise of freedom, to show that Cavendish provides a view of women's freedom that escapes some of the less advantageous aspects of Hobbes's own view.

Cavendish on Women, Education, and Freedom

In her nonfiction work, Cavendish notes with regularity that her own lack of superior education is the source of her own intellectual limitation, and she extends this to women in general.[3] But the point emerges even more forcefully and fully in her fictional work, specifically in many of her plays, where she also connects education and reason with freedom. Indeed, given that she explicitly (even if disingenuously) claims in her theoretical works to avoid political topics since they are the proper province of men, not women,[4] it is paramount that we look at her fiction, for it is there that we often see her delving extensively into precisely these sorts of topics, including what sort of society will best enable women's freedom. Here, I will focus on three of her plays as especially important to her theory of education and education's relation to women's freedom. These are *Youths Glory, and Deaths Banquet* (hereafter *Youths Glory*), *The Female Academy*, and *The Convent of Pleasure*.

There are two loosely related plot lines in *Youths Glory*. The one relevant for my concerns runs roughly as follows. Lady Sanspareille, daughter to Mother and Father Love, wants to pursue a life of education and oration and believes that she must forego marriage and having children in order to satisfy her life goals. Her mother would rather she pursue a more traditional female education, marry, and have children. Father Love encourages his daughter's choices and aids her in realizing her ambitions.

Lady Sanspareille gains a superior education, becomes a well-regarded orator—the only female among many wise men—but tragically dies young after contracting a terrible disease. In *The Female Academy*, a number of women have retreated to a women-only educational institution under the tutelage of an older matron. There, they converse among themselves "wittily and rationally,"[5] with men outside the walls furious at their unwillingness to make themselves available for marriage and procreation. The women's seclusion is not complete, however, for there is a large open grate where the women and men are able to converse. Eventually, the men contact the matron and help convert her from leader of women into marriage broker, and the women inside the gates are married off to the men after the matron rewrites the academy's purpose as that of teaching women to be better wives. In *The Convent of Pleasure*, Lady Happy is the mentor of a group of women enclosed in a women-only educational institution, this one with no opening to the outside world; the men outside contemplate removing bricks in order to see what goes on within.[6] Partway through the play, a princess arrives at the convent, and she and Lady Happy fall in love. Lady Happy openly contemplates pursuing what feels fully right and good to her—a lesbian relationship. In the end, the princess's identity is exposed; "she" is a prince, and the two enter into a heterosexual marriage.

Together, these plays present a strong voice in favor of a feminist line of argument. This argument pushes the conclusion that any actual connection found between sex and degree of intellect is the result of socialization and is therefore arbitrary and not natural. The cure for women's actual lesser degree of intellectual development is allowing women superior education typically afforded men alone. With such an education, women will find themselves freer both because they will have increased ability to pursue interesting projects and because they will have a wider range of projects to choose from. And given the realties of women's true social conditions, the way to attain such education and life chances is often through separation from debilitating social conditions such as having children, marrying men, and even being among men. This last point indicates a sensitivity to how relations enable or disable the development of capacities required for increased freedom, including a sensitivity to the power of women-only communities to enable women and to the fact that men have, in actual fact, often held women in relations that are disenabling. At the same time, Cavendish (herself the beneficiary of productive relations with men such as her husband, William, and brother-in-law,

Charles) recognizes that men (e.g., Father Love) can be the source of very productive relations for women, just as women (e.g., Mother Love) can be the source of detrimental relations for other women. This only serves to underscore the general gist of these three plays: if people are equal regardless of their gender, then a woman socialized according to unhelpful gender norms (Mother Love) would be less likely to recognize her daughter's equality with men than would a man (Father Love) who was socialized differently.

The idea that any connection between sex and intellect is conventional and not natural is voiced most clearly in *Youths Glory*. It is true that Mother Love thinks a male style of education for her daughter would "change a womans *nature* and disposition" (*Playes*, 124; emphasis added). But the more strongly developed argument—as opposed to assertion—comes from Father Love: "Let me tell you, Wife, that is the reason all women are fools; for women breeding up women, one fool breeding up another, and as long as that *custom* lasts there is no hope of amendment, and ancient customs being a second nature, makes folly hereditary in that Sex, by reason their education is effeminate, and their times spent in pins, points and laces, their study only vain fashions, which breeds prodigality, pride and envie" (123–24; emphasis added). Father Love's argument that custom shapes what women are, including the custom of women educating one another in nonintellectual pursuits of vanity, is joined by the strongest argument in favor of dissociating sex and intellect, namely, the fact that Lady Sanspareille decides to become a philosopher and orator-educator, gains the requisite education, and actually becomes highly respected for her intellect. She, like her father, believes that there is no *natural* connection between lack of intellect and sex, expressing surprise at the other opinion: "as if it were . . . against nature, for Women to have wit" (131). Mother Love's claim that a man's education would change her daughter's nature indicates that she, too, must take such a "nature" to be malleable and thus nonessential to women, even if she does not see this.

All three plays point to the necessity of good education for women as a crucial social change that will help develop women's intellectual abilities. "Good" education is not the rearing of girls to be concerned with fashion, nor is it (as Father Love emphasizes) the rearing of girls in less favorable forms of education often pursued by men who are "bred up to swear, swagger, gaming, drinking, Whoring" (*Playes*, 124). Good education for both women and men is education in the sciences, literature, and music

(123–24), a point echoed in *The Female Academy*, in which the matron educates the young women to be able to rationally discuss the nature of wisdom, truth, rhetoric, and friendship (passim).

Cavendish also connects increased intellectual ability through greater access to good education with women's increased freedom. Again, Father Love's arguments posed against Mother Love's beliefs spell this out clearly. Mother Love's fear is that the education envisioned for Lady Sanspareille by her father will "give her no time for recreation, nor no *liberty* for company, nor *freedom* for conversation, but keeps her as a *Prisoner*, and makes her a *slave* to her book" (*Playes*, 123; emphasis added). Father Love counters by asking rhetorically, "Can she have *freer* conversation, than with wit . . . ?" (123; emphasis added), thus indicating the freeing power of a developed intellect. Once again, Lady Sanspareille's choosing to live out such a life, and making herself into the person she envisions, speaks volumes for Cavendish's own recognition of (and quite possibly approval of) the increase of women's power and therefore freedom through education. Indeed, it is a position echoed by Lady Happy in *The Convent of Pleasure*: "My Cloister shall not be a Cloister of restraint, but a place for freedom" (*Convent*, 220).

Cavendish shows herself to be amply aware of how relations can both enable and constrain an individual's abilities and freedom, and she shows herself to be attune to the actual social fact that women have been routinely constrained by their relations with men, while men have been routinely unable to acknowledge the subjectivity of women. She furthermore demonstrates that she is alert to the possibilities for women (and threats to men) should women place themselves in more equitable, caring relations. The strong message found in all three plays is that such relations *cannot* come from most men as they have been socialized (again with notable exceptions such as Father Love)—neither intimate relations such as marriage, nor relations in broader communities—but they can often better come from women pursuing the individual, single life with the help of caring individuals, or from women cloistering themselves in female-only, closed communities. Thus, we find Lady Sanspareille eschewing marriage: "If I marry, although I should have time for my thoughts and contemplations, yet perchance my Husband will not approve of my works. . . . I am of opinion, that some men are so inconsiderately wise, gravely foolish and lowly base, as they had rather be thought Cuckolds, than their wives be thought wits, for fear the world should think their wives the wiser of the two" (*Playes*, 131). The theme of the marital relation often being a harmful one for women is echoed in *The Convent of Pleasure* when, for example, the women of the convent perform masques in which there are fully ten scenes depicting women suffering in various ways in the marital bond. It is no wonder that Lady Happy believes that the "best of men, if any best there be . . . [brings] more crosses and sorrows than pleasure, freedom or happiness," and that men "make the Female sex their slaves" (*Convent*, 218 and 220). An obvious solution to this problem—one presented in both *The Female Academy* and *The Convent of Pleasure*—is for women to provide themselves with the sorts of communities that offer healthy relations that enable women, develop their intellects, and thus make them more free. Not only will women in such circumstances find themselves with a greater measure of agency, but they will also find themselves able to take on a range of occupations not available to them in communities where men monopolize certain professions. In the convent, for example, there will be "Women-Physicians, Surgeons, and Apothecaries" (*Convent*, 223).

Even the apparently equivocal messages in each of the plays that seem to circumvent their feminist promise are either innocuous or actually underscore the feminist message. For the failure of the women to fully realize their freedom through great education is due in one case to natural causes (disease) and, tellingly, in the other two cases, to the intrusion into productive female communities by men who wish to dismantle those communities. That is, in the latter two cases, deleterious social relations thwart the women. Finally, Cavendish makes clever—and subversive— use of a convent, typically a place where women can enjoy the female pleasures of life,[7] for not only does she use a large portion of this play to present the dangers of marriage for women, but she also notes that in such a setting, women will need to take on pursuits that require considerable intellectual engagement, such as doctoring.

Cavendish, writing the century before Mary Wollstonecraft, already presents in these three plays the then-radical view that women are entitled to the same first-rate education and consequent careers as men, and in two of these plays, she champions the yet more radical view of single-sex education as the best way to realize women's full potential. This alone proposes a feminist alternative to any vision of women and education we see in Hobbes, but when we turn to the theory that grounds Cavendish's approach in her drama, her striking feminist alternative to Hobbes emerges with full force.

Human Nature, Civil Society, and Freedom

To understand the theoretical grounding of Cavendish's theory of women's freedom, it is helpful to explicate a few features of her theory of individuals, including human individuals. In her *Philosophical Letters*, she takes issue with what she sees as Hobbes's view of freedom, according to which the human will is not free. According to Hobbes, the will is assimilated to fully determined appetites—"the will is appetite; [man can no more] determine his will than any other appetite, that is, more than he can determine when he will be hungry and when not"[8]—and the will is simply the last appetite before action. It is thus a contradiction to speak of a "free will," even while it makes perfect sense to speak of a free human (*Leviathan*, ch. 21, 262). Deliberation is the alternating of desires (or appetites and aversions, including emotions such as hope and fear) to either perform or not perform a given action, before the final appetite (will) determines an action (ch. 6, 127). Similarly, human action is necessitated because human action follows from a necessitated human will. As a result, Hobbes must define liberty or freedom in such a way that it is consistent with necessity:

> *Liberty* and *Necessity* are Consistent . . . in the Actions which men voluntarily doe; which (because they proceed from their will) proceed from *liberty*; and yet because every act of mans will, and every desire, and inclination proceedeth from some cause, and that from another cause, which causes in a continuall chaine (whose first link in the hand of God the first of all causes) proceed from *necessity*. So that to him that could see the connexion of those causes, the *necessity* of all mens voluntary actions, would appear manifest. (ch. 21, 263)

In contrast, Cavendish disputes Hobbes's claim that voluntary motions "depend upon a precedent thought": "It doth imply a contradiction, to call them Voluntary Motions, and yet to say they are caused and depend upon our Imagination. . . . How can they be voluntary motions, being in a manner forced and necessitated to move according to Fancy or Imagination?" (*Philosophical Letters*, 45–46).[9] Cavendish disagrees with Hobbes on this point, and her disagreement is grounded in her divergent view of the human's essence. She believes that humans, along with every other individual, are comprised of inanimate matter thoroughly blended together with matter that is self-active or internally moved, as well as sensitive and rational. Accordingly, there are three types of matter for Cavendish: inanimate, animate sensitive, and animate rational, but because all three are thoroughly blended, no part of matter lacks any of these three types. Cavendish has good reasons for holding this seemingly strange view.[10] For my current purposes, I simply state Cavendish's belief on this issue, in order to explain the relation between her metaphysics of matter and the question of human freedom.

Matter's self-motion permits that any material thing—a human will, for example—can be the free and undetermined source of its own movement and does not need to be causally moved by something outside of itself—a prior desire in the human brain, for example. Cavendish explains, "By voluntary actions I understand self actions; that is, such actions whose principle of motion is within themselves, and doth not proceed from such an exterior agent."[11] If something material (such as the will) is moved due to the fact that other material "parts do drive or press upon" it, then "those are forced and constraint actions; whenas [sic] natural self-motions are free and voluntary."[12] In her *Philosophical Letters*, she explicitly notes that human wills can be entirely free from determination by everything outside themselves (*Philosophical Letters*, 95 and 225), and this includes a prior state of the human mind—a thought, desire, or emotion, for example.[13] The fact that the human will, like all material bodies in nature, is rational means that it can provide itself with its own reasons for acting in the way that it does. Therefore, human free will does not result in chaotic action; human actions following from our radical freedom are entirely meaningful and rational. Cavendish explicitly contrasts her position with that of Hobbes. Hobbes's materialism, according to which motion is externally imposed upon matter and is not intrinsic to matter itself, can only result in actions of matter that are extrinsically and antecedently determined, and so cannot allow freedom of the (material) will as in Cavendish's model.

Cavendish thus believes that all parts of the natural world share the same essence, namely, in being rational, sensing, and limited in their reasoning and sensing capacities. At the same time, humans are all alike—and unlike other individuals—in that we exhibit a specific, uniquely human form of rationality.[14] Consequently, here is an essential human nature, which we all share by virtue of our being human, and this is defined in terms of human rationality. Our essential rationality is crucial in underwriting our radical freedom, which includes our freedom from both internal constraints, such as passions like fear, and external constraints, such as other individuals attempting to exercise some sort of determining influence over one's will. Relatedly, our degree of freedom from internal and external constraints will depend upon the degree to which we have developed our rationality, and upon our ability to insulate a well-developed rational capacity from the influences of our sensitive nature, including our passions. Finally, Cavendish places a strong emphasis on the preservation of the unconstrained (both internally and externally) free will—indeed, it is prescriptively good to cultivate such a will—because to manipulate a human through fear or some external constraint is to misuse her rational capacity, thus violating that aspect of her essential nature and robbing her of her fullest possible freedom (e.g., *Grounds*, 248–49).

Given this background on pivotal aspects of Cavendish's theory of human nature, her advocacy of female education, to develop women's *natural* rational capacities as essential for women's freedom, makes perfect sense. Her theoretical philosophy grounds the powerful articulation in her plays of her feminist view on women, education, and freedom. This vision alerts us to one of a number of departures from Hobbes's account of freedom—departures that allow us to see Cavendish as presenting a recognizably feminist alternative to Hobbes. Hobbes has often been portrayed as the quintessential theorist of negative liberty. That is, as Quentin Skinner puts it, "[Hobbes] is claimed . . . to hold the view that an individual is unfree if and only if his doing of some particular action has been rendered impossible."[15] But Skinner and others[16] dissent from this characterization in numerous ways. Skinner disagrees on two fronts, but only one is key for my purposes. This reason, according to Skinner, is that many negative liberty theorists often equate the powerlessness to act with a lack of freedom. This equation does indeed hold for Hobbes when the lack of power comes about as a result of an agent's intrinsic power being thwarted in its attempt to act by an external, physical force. But the equation does not hold for Hobbes (*pace* typical negative liberty theorists) when the lack of power is due to an intrinsic physical (or psychological) impairment, such as in the case of a sick man unable to move from his bed (*Leviathan*, ch. 21, 262). So, "even if no one is rendering it impossible for an agent to act in a given way, it still does not necessarily follow for Hobbes that the agent is free to perform the action concerned. This is because . . . the action in question may still be beyond the agent's powers. . . . [In this case] what is certain is that, for Hobbes, the question of whether the action is one that the agent is or is not free to perform *simply does not arise*."[17] Nancy Hirschmann draws attention to this feature of Hobbes's thought in a way that is enlightening for a feminist analysis of him. For, according to a Hobbesian line of thought, a woman who, for example, stays with an abusive husband due to a lack of internal power to leave (due to fear of poverty, for example) does not thereby lack the freedom to leave.[18] Cavendish conversely recognizes that women may have more restrictive internalized constraints by virtue of their unique social experiences. Where there is a difference between the sorts of power or ability possessed by men (as men) and those enjoyed by women (as women), and where these differences allow for a narrower range of abilities that women can undertake, Cavendish's account of freedom can take note of these differences while Hobbes's cannot. That is, Cavendish's account is able to say that women are *less* free than are men, should women have less power or ability to act due to socially developed, internal constraints. So for Hobbes, one does not lack freedom should one happen to lack the power to act. For Cavendish, one *does* lack freedom when one lacks power, and in her plays she clearly articulates the degree to which women have *less power* and thus less freedom than do men for unnatural, wholly conventional reasons, due to their diminished rationality, due to their poor education.

Cavendish's view of human nature—humans are essentially rational and can enjoy radical freedom—is also the source of an important departure from Hobbes on civic freedom. While this divergence is not necessarily grounded in feminist concerns for Cavendish, it nonetheless underscores her emphasis on the importance of individual freedom, even from a sovereign's control, an emphasis that does ground her feminist vision. Given Cavendish's usual devotion to an absolute sovereignty, it would seem that she should agree with Hobbes that the sovereign determines laws which then exercise control over citizens (e.g., *Leviathan*, ch. 21, 263–64), binding their wills, even if through an internal constraint such as fear, and thereby aiming to prevent them from acting in the way they do in a natural state. As Hobbes famously writes, "Feare and Liberty are consistent. . . . And generally all actions which men doe in Commonwealths, for *feare* of the law, are actions, which the doers had *liberty* to omit" (ch. 21, 262–63). But in fact there is no such symmetry between her view and Hobbes's on civic freedom. Suppose that the sovereign did impose laws that exercised their power through fear, and this fear effectively directed the will. This would be a case of a lack of individual freedom for Cavendish (in contrast with Hobbes), for the will would be acting in accordance with something other than its own rational motivation. It would be forced into its actions through something that Cavendish considers external to the will itself—prior, fearful thoughts, for example. Fear and liberty are inconsistent for Cavendish. As a result, the realm of unfreedom is considerably wider for Cavendish than it is for Hobbes.

It is true that both Cavendish and Hobbes agree that the attempt to control citizens directly through laws and the fear they invoke will not always work reliably (*Philosophical Letters*, 47–48; *Leviathan*, ch. 21, 263–64). But the *normative* lesson each draws from her or his particular account of fear and law is crucial. For Cavendish, even if it were possible for a sovereign to fully control citizens through fear, the sovereign still *ought not* to try to do so precisely because in trying to control human volitions through the exercise of fear, he who governs thus violates the individual's capacity for *self*-governance, which arises from well-developed rationality as free as possible from passions such as fear. Cavendish clearly stresses the moral importance of respecting human freedom (as she conceives it) even in the face of potential discord brought about by the exercise of freedom (e.g., *Grounds*, 248–49). From the perspective of the human's nature, Cavendish has a principled way of securing radical freedom of thought and of the will against all determinants—internal or external—that may exercise influence over thought or will, while Hobbes must admit that all thoughts are fully determined by antecedent conditions—conditions which, if changed, will alter the thoughts of the person. And so the picture suggesting that an absolute sovereign enacts laws, which bind citizens through fear to act in accordance with those laws, cannot be Cavendish's considered view of how the polity *ought* to be managed (supposing that it could, in fact, be thus managed): "But when governmental laws were devised by some usurping men, who were the greatest thieves and robbers, (for they robbed the rest of mankind of their natural liberties and inheritances, which is to be equal possessor of the world), these grand original thieves and robbers, which are called moral philosophers or commonwealth makers, were not only thieves and tyrants to the generality of mankind, but they were rebels against Nature, imprisoning Nature within the jail of restraint."[19] Particularly interesting in this passage is Cavendish's reference to the *natural* state of the world, and the suggestion that civil laws can be a violation of nature itself—indeed, a violation, which is, in some important sense, to be avoided. I turn to this point now as crucial to another way in which we can read Cavendish as providing a feminist account of freedom as an alternative to Hobbes.

The State of Nature and Civil Society

Above, I argued that for Cavendish, our higher, rational selves will simply recognize what it is best to do without being manipulated by nonrational forces such as fear embodied in sanctions for not following civil law, and that the best thing to do, therefore, may not necessarily be to follow such law. What, then, is the source of normatively right action for Cavendish if *not* civil law? Answering this question alerts us to another way of seeing how Cavendish's theory of freedom offers a feminist alternative to Hobbes's theory. To show this, I now consider her view of the natural world writ large, including humanity's place within the whole of nature, focusing especially on the relations that we naturally, essentially bear to one another.

Cavendish believes that the natural world as a whole is intrinsically lawful, peaceful, and stable (*Philosophical Letters*, 146). This follows from the essence of matter as self-moving, sensitive, and (especially) rational. Because in its essence the world is imbued with reason, and does not consist merely of bits of matter moving and coming into contact with one another, the world is in itself governed by prescriptive laws, and not merely by descriptive laws. Nature as a whole is infinite, and so infinitely wise, and it prescribes, from the top down, norms and standards of orderly and harmonious behavior. As a result of this top-down prescribed order, all parts within nature must be understood as being naturally interrelated. That is, all parts are bound together by the various roles they play in the overarching, harmonious order.[20] Parts within the whole (human individuals, for example) can violate the peace because of their radical freedom to act against their prescribed roles, or because their finite share of reason leaves them ignorant of what the overall law requires of them (*Grounds*, 19–20).[21] Such violations are the source of, for example, civil war. So, because of nature's thoroughgoing peaceable order, which is *good*, an individual acting as if it were an individual isolated from all others and bound by no overarching norms would lead to disorder in its immediate environs at least. Since this violation of norms and standards of order would be bad, one ought not to behave as if one were such a hyperindividualistic being, even though our freedom permits exactly this sort of disorderly behavior, which is harmful to others.

Crucial to this picture is the fact that what is violated by disorderly conduct is not artificial civil law, but rather the normative lawful order of the whole of nature. Moreover, all parts of nature—for example, humans in what Hobbes would call a state of nature—are essentially interrelated, such that our actions impact both positively and negatively others and their abilities to act toward their ends. Reason must be cultivated so that we can understand as well as possible the good, overarching order of nature, and can be motivated to maintain that order by freely adopting our proper roles. The basic law of nature, according to a Cavendishean picture, would include no right to self-defense (as it does for Hobbes) because it would not need to; rather, humans with well-developed reason would simply freely keep the peace. It is not surprising, then, that Cavendish condemns (*pace* Hobbes) the artificial, civil realm to the extent that it departs from nature, and that she glorifies nature itself, entreating humans to live in accordance with the peacefulness of the natural world as a whole.[22]

This aspect of Cavendish's theory of freedom holds enormous promise from a feminist point of view, and, indeed, her account presages some recent sophisticated positions on freedom developed by contemporary feminists. As is clear from the above discussion, Cavendish extols the exercise of free will, even to the point of suggesting that a free will directed toward incorrect thought or action is better than one constrained to behave in the correct fashion. But, further, she extols a will that freely chooses to pursue actions conceived of in terms of how the agent relates to others, close and distant. This requires that we modulate our actions in accordance with our understanding of how they impact others, as well as how they impact the overall peace of the natural world. Cavendish's theory of freedom implicitly prescribes our being mindful of the fact that we are embedded in relations with others, that these relations make possible and impossible certain powers and abilities in ourselves and others, and that we should regulate our behavior accordingly. This requires that all individuals—men and women alike—recognize the needs and plans of others. Cavendish proves herself to be attuned to the specifically feminist potential of this approach in her belief that men have not, in fact, permitted women to develop themselves but have routinely "usurped" power for themselves, leaving women in "slavish" condition.[23] Similarly, and more forcefully, this point is driven home by her characterization of women's relations with men and with other women in the plays discussed above.

It is important to underscore how remarkably *modern*, from a feminist perspective, this aspect of Cavendish's theory of freedom or autonomy is—for in presenting it, she anticipates an approach to autonomy we see extolled by some feminists today. Lately, a number of feminist theorists, including Marilyn Friedman, Nancy Hirschmann, Diana Tietjens Meyers, and Natalie Stoljar,[24] to name a few, have argued forcefully that we should recognize the critical importance of freedom for feminist ends. Without women and men being free or autonomous agents, it is unclear how we can engage in the project of pushing against and overcoming oppression of women. Yet these theorists are still mindful of the important feminist criticisms levied against the ideal of hyperindividualistic autonomy that arguably grounds Hobbes's own theory. And so, recent theorists suggest that we "refigure" the concept of the autonomous or free individual. Central to one such refiguring is the acknowledgment that we simply do find ourselves in social relations, and that these relations are crucial to how we understand our freedom because of the range of human actions that our relations can permit or disallow. The kind and quality of our relations are important in understanding freedom or autonomy, according to these thinkers, insofar as agents are "intrinsically relational because their identities or self-conceptions are constituted by elements of the social context in which they are embedded," and insofar as social relations shape the range of options open to people.[25] Taking into account our relations with others allows us to take into account the different ways in which men and women have been socialized, such that men and women often have very different intrinsic abilities and very different ranges of options open to them. This feminist account of freedom or autonomy—dubbed "relational autonomy" by many—"reflects a sense of self . . . as both differentiated from and related to others, and a sense of others as subjects with whom one shares enough to allow for a recognition of their independent interests and feelings—in short for a recognition of them as subjects."[26]

Cavendish's general approach to freedom holds the promise of being strikingly in stride with recent relational autonomy theorists on some points at least. Her stress on rationality over emotions, however, might make her seem less in tune with contemporary feminists. Yet she believes that to be deprived of the capacity to act from a rationally governed will—even to act in a way that is socially detrimental—is to be deprived of a capacity that is essential to our freedom, as it is crucial to our resisting negative influences that might rob us of the power to act. But she also clearly wants to acknowledge the importance of our being mindful of our relations with other individuals, including our social relations with our fellow humans. Rationality is crucial to both features of her theory of freedom. The more rational the will, the freer it will be from the determining influence of the passions or other individuals who might influence one to act against one's own rationally determined course of action. Moreover, better-developed rationality will allow one to better apprehend the proper peaceable order that ought to attain among all individuals; that is, better-developed rationality will allow one to better apprehend how one ought to modulate one's own free behavior in order to sensitively respect the rationally based subjectivity of one's fellows. Because this is a *self*-modulation or *self*-determination, based in one's *rational* comprehension of her natural and social interrelations, one who acts thus is free. Once again, the message brought home by Cavendish's plays stresses the fact that she strongly presages many themes in contemporary relational autonomy theory. Her anticipation of such themes also grounds yet more points of divergence from Hobbes. Recent feminist readings of Hobbes offer numerous ways of thinking about Hobbes's state of nature and his understanding of the transition from a state of nature to civil society; but on any of these readings of the state of nature, Cavendish's philosophy as presented above offers a more promising alternative.

On one reading of Hobbes's state of nature, isolated individuals act independently of one another to maximize their power and chances of survival. This hyperindividualism would certainly provide fodder for a feminist critique to the extent that feminism takes specific issue with the view of the human as isolated from others. Still, such a critique could be defused by recognizing Hobbes's own belief that, in a state of nature, women can be victors no less than can men (*Leviathan*, ch. 21, 253). Cavendish's own relational account of humans, which would presumably hold in a Hobbesian state of nature given that the natural world is the source of such relations, offers a feminist critique against any version of this hyperindividualism, regardless of whether women or men are the victors. For Cavendish, one ought not to behave in a hyperindividualistic fashion at all, most especially not to vanquish one's fellows, for this would be a violation of their essential freedom.

A second way of reading the state of nature arises because Hobbes acknowledges the human's natural tendency to seek human relation,[27] thus calling into question the interpretation that humans are naturally atomistic individuals. Drawing on such texts, Gordon Schochet has therefore argued against the hyperindividualistic reading of humans in a state of nature and in favor of a more relational reading of the state of nature. Nonetheless, Schochet's reading resurrects feminist concerns, for he believes that the relational unit in the state of nature is patriarchal families, in which the authoritarian power of the patriarch both provides the family with stability and provides the model for the authoritarian sovereign.[28] Once again, Cavendish's very different relational account based on equal human rationality and equal right to freedom offers a heartening feminist alternative to the state of nature in this interpretation.

Hirschmann offers yet a third interpretation of the state of nature as well as an interpretation of what, according to Hobbes, must happen in the transition to civil society precisely because of the relations that hold in nature. To set the backdrop for Hirschmann's interpretation, consider Hobbes's contrast between natural liberty and the liberty of subjects:

> But as men, for the atteyning of peace, and conservation of themselves thereby, have made an Artificiall Man, which we call a Common-wealth; so also have they made Artificall Chains, called *Civill Lawes*, which they themselves, by mutuall covenants, have fastned at one end, to the lips of that Man, or Assembly, to whom they have given the Soveraigne Power; and at the other end to their own Ears. These Bonds in their own nature but weak, may neverthelesse be made to hold, by the danger, though not by the difficulty of breaking them. In relation to these Bonds only it is, that I am to speak now, of the *Liberty of Subjects*. (*Leviathan*, ch. 21, 263–64)

Civil laws act as "a coercive Power to tye their [men's] hands from rapine, and revenge" (*Leviathan*, ch. 18, 238; cf. ch. 30, 388, and ch. 46, 701). The actions of a subject in a civil society are constrained by what seem to be external impediments, namely laws, and so the subject in civil society would seem to lack freedom to the degree that civil laws keep one from acting in accordance with the determination of his own will. Relatedly, Hobbes contrasts the state of nature, where there is "a full and absolute Libertie in every Particular man" (ch. 21, 266), with civil society, where "*Civill Law* is an *Obligation*; and takes from us the Liberty which the Law of Nature gave us" (ch. 27, 334–35; cf. ch. 14, 189). In order to reconcile Hobbes's account of freedom in a state of nature with his account of freedom in civil society, Hirschmann offers the following interpretation:

> Consent is the only way to preserve . . . natural freedom. In a social contract, all agree to alienate certain of their liberties to a sovereign who will in turn oversee everyone's behavior. What makes this legitimate is that people *choose* to enter into this contract; the limitation of their liberty that the contract imposes is thus also an expression of their liberty—even, perhaps, its ultimate expression. . . . [But] we are compelled to consent to the social contract because we have no practical choice in the matter; it is the only choice we can rationally make.[29]

While freedom is that which brings about the social contract on this reading, freedom "is not an end in itself, but rather a means to other things that are of greater importance, such as security."[30] Moreover, since for Hobbes fear is not always adequate to compel consent, he turns to mechanisms such as education "to guide and shape people's desires" such that they will consent to the social contract.[31] Hirschmann further develops the argument that women's desires must be shaped very differently from men's in order to maintain patriarchal families in civil society, which provide the model for authoritarian governments.[32] Key to this last point is Hirschmann's belief (*pace* Schochet as characterized above) that women in a state of nature are not under men's power in patriarchal families, are thus a threat to men, and so need to be shaped to take on their proper role in the patriarchal family in *civil* society (rather than in a state of nature). Hirschmann's interpretation of Hobbes's state of nature thus maintains that humans are indeed in relations, but that these are instrumental relations entered into only insofar as they increase our natural power over potential threats (e.g., children are useful to women in helping them maintain their power over men);[33] they are not relations based primarily on nurture and care. Assuming this third interpretation of the state of nature, women need to be shaped through, for example, education to freely consent to their subordinate status in civil society for the sake of social stability.

Once again, Cavendish's understanding of productive human relations would not tolerate instrumental relations as we find in Hobbes on this third interpretation of his state of nature. Cavendish's theory requires that we acknowledge the rationality, and the freedom from internal and external constraints, proper to each human as subject. Such relations require seeing others as subjects with projects of their own, and not as instruments for one's own use. Finally, while education for Hobbes according to Hirschmann's interpretation must shape individuals to take on very specific and gendered social roles, Cavendish holds that women need to be educated to their full natural potential in order to be relieved of the submission in which they find themselves. This will allow women to understand clearly the ways in which they can naturally, equally with men, and productively contribute to the order and stability that follow from what is central, crucial, and never to be compromised: human freedom to act from well-developed abilities and powers, mindful of others and their freedoms.

Still, at least one commentator, Sharon Lloyd, believes that Hobbes's educational theory is not a form of indoctrination or "objectionable intellectual coercion,"[34] but rather is meant to lead citizens to a state of rational self-governance. For the sake of argument, let me suppose that this is an accurate interpretation of Hobbes's educational theory. His theory would still compare negatively to Cavendish's theory of education from a feminist point of view. For Hobbes's drive to have citizens well-educated (granting the belief that he endorses true education, not indoctrination) is a drive to educate *citizens*, not individuals considered in and of themselves. His aim with education is to achieve stability of a certain type of polity, with the benefit that will accrue to individuals (peaceful coexistence, for example) following derivatively upon this. This is in contrast with Cavendish's primary aim, which is to develop the capacities and abilities of individuals to their fullest. But, on Hobbes's view, education will therefore teach people to take on whatever social roles are necessary for the stability and longevity of the polity, and this opens up the threat, as Hirschmann notes, that men and women will be differentially educated to take on different, gendered roles. Differential education for men and women is blocked *in principle* on Cavendish's account, while it is not blocked in principle on Hobbes's account.

Regardless of which interpretation of Hobbes's state of nature is favored, Cavendish presents a promising feminist alternative to any of them in presaging the relational autonomy, grounded in the natural equality of men and women, that we find in contemporary philosophy. And she offers a theory of education in the social-civic world that promotes human rationality and freedom, both for the human's own sake and so that she or he can better understand how to enter into productive, caring, and equal relations with other humans, no matter their gender. These points, together with her recognition that women may have greater internal constraints due to their having been so socialized, and that these constraints represent a state of lesser freedom, indicate that Cavendish offers a refreshingly feminist alternative to Hobbes's theory of freedom.

Notes

1. On Cavendish's materialism and the argument for it, see, for example, Margaret Cavendish, *Observations upon Experimental Philosophy*, 2nd ed., ed. Eileen O'Neill (Cambridge: Cambridge University Press, 2001), 137. On Hobbes's materialism and a similar argument for it, see, for example, Thomas Hobbes, *Leviathan*, ed. C. B. Macpherson (New York: Penguin, 1985), ch. 34, 428–29. Subsequent references are given in the text by chapter and page number.

2. See, for example, Thomas Hobbes, *The English Works of Thomas Hobbes of Malmesbury*, ed. Sir William Molesworth, 11 vols. (London: J. Bohn, 1839–45), 1:412; Cavendish, *Observations* (2001 ed.), 17; and Margaret Cavendish, *Philosophical Letters, or Modest Reflections upon Some Opinions in Natural Philosophy* (London, 1664), 139, 142. Subsequent references to *Philosophical Letters* are given in the text. For complications associated with this view of Cavendish, see Karen Detlefsen, "Margaret Cavendish on the Relation Between God and World," *Philosophy Compass* 4, no. 3 (2009): 421–38.

3. See, for example, Margaret Cavendish, "An Epistle to the Reader," in *Philosophical and Physical Opinions*, 2nd ed. (London: William Wilson, 1663); Margaret Cavendish, "Birth, Breeding, and Life of Margaret, Duchess of Newcastle," in *The Life of William Cavendish, Duke of Newcastle*, ed. C. H. Firth, 2nd ed. (London: George Routledge and Sons, 1906), 157–58 and 175; Margaret Cavendish, *Orations of a Divers Sort*, in *Political Writings*, ed. Susan James (Cambridge: Cambridge University Press, 2003), 118 and 249; and Margaret Cavendish, "Preface to the Reader," in *The World's Olio* (London: printed for J. Martin and J. Allestree, 1655).

4. See, for example, Cavendish, *Philosophical Letters*, 47–48.

5. Margaret Cavendish, *Playes* (London: A. Warren, 1662), 653. Subsequent references are given in the text.

6. Margaret Cavendish, *The Convent of Pleasure and Other Plays*, ed. Anne Shaver (Baltimore: Johns Hopkins University Press, 1999), 227. Subsequent references are given in the text.

7. Thanks to Joanne Wright for drawing my attention to the purpose of seventeenth-century convents.

8. Hobbes, *English Works*, 5:34.

9. Here, she cites Hobbes's *Leviathan*, ch. 6, 127–28.

10. For an account of why Cavendish would hold such a peculiar view of the natural world, see Karen Detlefsen, "Reason and Freedom: Margaret Cavendish on the Order and Disorder of Nature," *Archiv für Geschichte der Philosophie* 89, no. 2 (2007): 157–89.

11. Cavendish, *Observations* (2001 ed.), 19.

12. Ibid., 127.

13. Margaret Cavendish, *Observations upon Experimental Philosophy* (London: A. Maxwell, 1666), 49, 54–55.

14. See, for example, Margaret Cavendish, *Grounds of Natural Philosophy* (London: A. Maxwell, 1668; facsimile repr., West Cornwall, Conn.: Locust Hill Press, 1996), 15. Subsequent references are given in the text.

15. Quentin Skinner, "Thomas Hobbes on the Proper Signification of Liberty: The Prothero Lecture," *Transactions of the Royal Historical Society*, 5th ser., 40 (1990): 127.

16. Including Nancy J. Hirschmann in her recognition that there are elements of positive liberty to be found in Hobbes. See Hirschmann, *Gender, Class, and Freedom in Modern Political Theory* (Princeton, N.J.: Princeton University Press, 2008), 63–70.

17. Skinner, "Thomas Hobbes," 127–28; emphasis added.

18. Hirschmann, *Gender*, 35.

19. Cavendish, *Orations*, 176.

20. For an account of this feature in Cavendish, including its broader implications in her philosophy, see Karen Detlefsen, "Atomism, Monism, and Causation in the Natural Philosophy of Margaret Cavendish," *Oxford Studies in Early Modern Philosophy*, ed. Steven Nadler and Daniel Garber, vol. 3 (Oxford: Oxford University Press, 2006), 199–240.

21. For a development of this, see Detlefsen, "Relation."

22. See, for example, Cavendish, *Observations* (1666 ed.), 4.

23. Cavendish, "Preface to the Reader."

24. For example, see papers in Catriona Mackenzie and Natalie Stoljar, eds., *Relational Autonomy: Feminist Perspectives on Autonomy, Agency, and the Social Self* (New York: Oxford University Press, 2000).

25. Mackenzie and Stoljar, introduction to *Relational Autonomy*, 22.

26. Evelyn Fox Keller, *Reflections on Gender and Science* (New Haven, Conn.: Yale University Press, 1985), 99.

27. See, for example, Thomas Hobbes, *De Cive*, in *Man and Citizen: Thomas Hobbes's "De Homine" and "De Cive,"* ed. Bernard Gert (Garden City, N.Y.: Anchor Books, 1972), 1.2.

28. Gordon J. Schochet, *The Authoritarian Family and Political Attitudes in Seventeenth-Century England: Patriarchalism in Political Thought* (New Brunswick: Transaction Books, 1988), 225–43. See also Schochet's "Thomas Hobbes on the Family and the State of Nature" in chapter 5 of this volume.

29. Hirschmann, *Gender*, 39–40.

30. Ibid., 62.

31. Ibid., 78. This social construction of the individual is the basis of Hirschmann's attributing elements of positive liberty to Hobbes, as mentioned above in note 16.

32. Ibid., 72–74.

33. Ibid., 54–57.

34. S. A. Lloyd, "Coercion, Ideology, and Education in Hobbes's *Leviathan*," in *Reclaiming the History of Ethics: Essays for John Rawls*, ed. Andrews Reath, Barbara Herman, and Christine M. Korsgaard (Cambridge: Cambridge University Press, 1996), 36–65. Cf. S. A. Lloyd, *Ideals as Interests in Hobbes's "Leviathan": The Power of Mind over Matter* (Cambridge: Cambridge University Press, 1992), 159–66.

8

When Is a Contract Theorist Not a Contract Theorist?

Mary Astell and Catharine Macaulay as Critics of Thomas Hobbes

Karen Green

Thomas Hobbes's version of social contract theory has played an important part in twentieth-century feminist critiques of liberalism. Despite the clear historical roots of contemporary feminism in eighteenth-century republicanism, and in those tendencies that led to the rise of liberal democratic institutions, feminist philosophers, since the 1980s, have developed a critique of liberalism based on a reading of its origins that accepts that commitment to social contract theory implies commitment to a Hobbesian, egoistic, instrumental rationality. Alison Jaggar, for instance, asserted in her influential overview of feminist political theory, published in 1983, that "liberal theorists assume that all individuals tend towards egoism, even though they may be capable of a greater or lesser degree of limited altruism."[1] The first strand of the feminist critique of liberalism rejects this psychological egoism, which, it is assumed, grounds contract theory.

Slightly earlier, Carole Pateman and the late Teresa Brennan had also criticized liberal social contract theory, basing their arguments on a close reading of Hobbes.[2] Pateman subsequently argued that the social contract is in reality a "fraternal social contract" forged between men for the sake of sexual access to women.[3] It cannot, therefore, provide the basis for a coherent feminist politics. The importance of Hobbes for these feminist critics is that his arguments both ground contract theory, as it is usually characterized, and demonstrate that actual contractual relationships may be no better than relationships of submission and domination. Taking off from Marxist critiques of the employment contract as establishing wage slavery, Pateman argues that other contracts, such as marriage or prostitution, which are represented by contract theorists as entered into by free individuals, are in fact mechanisms for masking relations of domination and subordination and are "tainted by the odor of slavery."[4]

In this chapter, I raise some doubts about the general validity of these feminist critiques of liberalism by questioning the centrality of Hobbes's philosophy for historical women writing in the liberal democratic tradition. When we turn to read the texts written by actual women with republican leanings during the eighteenth century, we find both reference to the social contract and a clear rejection of Hobbes's theory of human nature. This is particularly true of Catharine Macaulay, whose political thought will be the subject of the second half of this chapter. This raises the question of whether the standard account of the origins of liberal social contract theory is accurate. It suggests, at least, that this critique is grounded in, at best, a partial account of historical liberal traditions. In fact, early liberal feminists shared with their illiberal sisters a rejection of psychological egoism and a belief in a God who has made us by nature sociable creatures, who are at least potentially disposed to act virtuously.[5] The most influential eighteenth-century female democrat, and ancestress of the liberal feminist tradition, Catharine Macaulay was a severe critic of Hobbes.[6] Her multivolume republican history of England was popular in England and the American colonies prior to the American Revolution, and it was translated into French during the first years of the French Revolution. Since she exerted a direct influence on Mary Wollstonecraft, an appreciation of her philosophical views is important for understanding the historical roots of liberal feminism.

Macaulay was not the only eighteenth-century female political thinker who rejected Hobbesian assumptions. More than fifty years earlier, Mary Astell had also made disparaging remarks about his views and about social contract theory in general, which, according to two recent commentators, anticipate modern feminist critiques.[7] Yet, although Astell has been called a feminist, even her defenders acknowledge that her conservatism makes it difficult for modern feminists to identify with her.[8] Macaulay more clearly anticipates modern feminism, for while she shares a good deal of Astell's general outlook and has similar assumptions about God and humanity, she also manages to erect a democratic edifice on these foundations. Thus, she bases her social contract theory on assumptions quite different from the problematic egoism of Hobbes.[9] An unalloyed defense of feminist contract theory won't emerge from the political theory built up on this basis, for atheistic liberals will find Macaulay's outlook hard to swallow, and her feminism is largely implied rather than explicit. Nevertheless, her "contract theory" bears a striking resemblance to Pateman's anti-contractarian views and demonstrates that, if we fail to carefully read the works of earlier female political writers, we are in danger of misrepresenting the eighteenth-century foundations of republicanism and liberal feminism.

In order to make good this case, I will first say a little more about the feminist critique of contract theory. I will then briefly discuss Astell's reaction to Hobbes and her rejection of contract theory. This will provide part of the intellectual background to Macaulay's ethical and political views. While Astell's critique of Hobbes involves the rejection of contract theory, Macaulay, by contrast, develops a non-Hobbesian contract theory. Of course, one might question whether this is a contract theory at all, but I will argue that it clearly is a version of contract theory with a non-Hobbesian foundation. I will conclude with some reflections on the strengths and weaknesses of this version of contract theory from a contemporary feminist point of view.

The Feminist Critique of Contract Theory

According to Hobbes, the state of nature is a state of war. Individuals are sufficiently equal in strength and intelligence that none can rely on their capacity to dominate all others, and each is free to pursue their own self-interest. But the desire for self-preservation implies a love of peace, which can only be attained when the free and equal individuals contract to be governed by some sovereign power. Feminists have pointed out that there is an ambiguity, in this account, concerning the sexual status of the "free and equal" individuals. Do they come in two sexes? Or are they implicitly male? Hobbes explicitly accepts that the state of nature contains individuals of both sexes. But according to Hobbes, women, despite being the natural lords of their offspring, have in most societies been made subjects of the male heads of patriarchal families, and it is these heads of households who contract to set up commonwealths. So Hobbes's account equivocates. People are allegedly free and equal, but women are historically subordinated. Feminists have also pointed out that this account flies in the face of the obvious fact that humans are born weak and dependent, and that without the care and protection of their mothers, or others who are happy to act as surrogate mothers, they would not survive.[10]

As already mentioned, one strand of the feminist critique of contract theory emphasizes women's tendency to care for others and rejects Hobbes's claim that individuals are psychological egoists.[11] Christine Di Stefano in particular discusses Hobbes's suggestion that we consider men as sprung out of the earth like mushrooms, commenting that it denies "sexuality, reproduction and maternal nurturance."[12] The other, more devastating strand of the feminist critique depends on exposing the equivocation in Hobbes's theory.[13] Hobbes claims that humans are free and equal in the state of nature, yet also says that in most commonwealths it is men who have dominion over their children, "because for the most part Commonwealths have been erected by the fathers, not by the mothers of families."[14] In his classic paper on the family in Hobbes's theory, Gordon Schochet argued that Hobbes was closer to traditional patriarchalists than previous commentators had allowed and that he accepted that the historical state of nature had existed between patriarchal families.[15] Schochet did not consider why it is that the Hobbesian family is patriarchal rather than matriarchal. But Hobbes's comment that "there is not always that difference of strength or prudence between the man and the woman as that the right [of dominion] can be determined without war" suggests he is assuming that men have acquired dominion over women (like other servants of the family) through conquest.[16] So, in slightly different ways, the situation of both women and children shows that individuals are not actually equal in the state of nature. Furthermore, the situation of women serves as a striking example of the fact that Hobbes's "equal natural freedom" is compatible with the rationality and justice of consent to coercive political domination. Women are, in general, politically subordinate in commonwealths because they have been historically subordinated within patriarchal families, which are, according to Hobbes, little commonwealths.

Hobbes's own conclusions, arising from his understanding of the nature of the social contract, were not in fact liberal and imply allegiance to an absolute sovereign whose domination is limited only in those circumstances in which the subject is required to sacrifice their life. So, if we follow through the implications of Hobbes's contract theory for women's position within marriage, he can be read as having, in fact, offered a patriarchal justification for wifely submission, based on women's relative physical disadvantage in the battle for domination.[17]

One advantage of Hobbes's account, from a feminist point of view, is that it makes women's subordination within the family clearly political and based on the same kinds of circumstance of relative power that result in the sovereignty of some men or women over others in the public sphere. Perhaps sensing the radical potential of deeming women's subordination political, theorists such as John Locke and Jean-Jacques Rousseau part company with Hobbes on this issue and explicitly distinguish the political realm of the state from the private realm of the family, making women's subordination within the family "natural." They give up, to some degree, on the natural freedom and equality of women. Hobbes, by contrast, consistently, but implausibly, sees society as involving contracts all the way down. He even accepts consent as underpinning the unequal relations between parent and child. He thus obscures the distinction between coercion and free consent, undermining the claim that consent can, by itself, underpin legitimate political obligation.

Astell's Critique of Hobbes

Mary Astell's critique of Hobbes's assumptions, and her opposition to social contract theory in general, has been read as anticipating the contemporary critique by liberal feminists.[18] Ruth Perry and Patricia Springborg have both made it a virtue of Astell's politics that she rejected Hobbes's notion of a state of nature and anticipated modern feminist critiques of the idea that political legitimacy can be grounded in consent. Perry suggests that Astell's writing shows that "from the beginning, women were suspicious of the modern democratic state and their place within it."[19] Springborg points out that Astell anticipates Pateman's argument that contract theorists cannot distinguish legitimate authority from consent under duress.[20] Yet, while it is true that the nature of Astell's suspicions are of a sort as to completely undermine contract theory, her outlook is also incompatible with all the notions of political equality that are central to modern feminism.[21]

Astell argues that women are men's equals in virtue and reason, and her *Serious Proposal to the Ladies* envisages a college for women in which they can pursue higher learning, live in an unmarried state, and develop themselves as virtuous subjects.[22] But she also believes that reason enjoins obedience and that the education of women would not lead them to usurp men's legitimate authority as husbands.[23] According to her,

> nothing can assure Obedience, and render it what it ought to be, but the Conscience of Duty, the paying it for GOD's sake. Superiors don't rightly understand their own Interest when they attempt to put out their Subjects Eyes to keep them Obedient. A Blind Obedience is what a Rational Creature shou'd never Pay, nor wou'd such an one receive it did he rightly understand its Nature. For Human Actions are no otherwise valuable than as they are conformable to Reason, but blind Obedience is an Obeying *without Reason*, for ought we know *against it*. GOD himself does not require our Obedience at this rate, he lays before us the goodness and reasonableness of his Laws, and were there any thing in them whose Equity we could not readily comprehend, yet we have this clear and sufficient Reason on which to found our Obedience, that nothing but what's Just and Fit, can be enjoyn'd by a Just, a Wise and Gracious GOD.[24]

For Astell, our God-given reason shows the need for political subjection, and obedience to legitimate power, which she identifies with that enjoined by God.

In a famous passage, Astell charges the contract theorists with inconsistency, exclaiming, "*If* all Men are born free, *how is it that all Women are born Slaves? as they must be if the being subjected to the* inconstant, uncertain, unknown, arbitrary Will *of Men, be the* perfect Condition of Slavery? *and if the Essence of Freedom consist, as our Masters say it does, in having a standing Rule to live by? And why is Slavery so much condemn'd and strove against in one Case, and so highly applauded, and held so necessary and so sacred in another?*"[25] But her point is not to include women among those born free, but rather to deny that there is any prepolitical state of natural, equal freedom.[26] This denial may be compatible with feminism, if it is the denial of the historical existence of a natural state in which men and women are equally free. But it is incompatible with all those forms of feminism that interpret the desired political equality of women and men as deriving from general egalitarian principles. Astell does not subscribe to the normative principle that, since people are equal in value, they ought to enjoy equal political freedom.

According to Astell, Hobbes's conception of liberty is mere license, while true liberty is rational submission to the moral law and is quite compatible with political subjection.[27] As she notes in *The Christian Religion, as Profess'd by a Daughter of The Church of England*, "True liberty . . . consists in making a right use of our Reason, in preserving our Judgments free, and our integrity unspotted, (which sets us out of the reach of the most Absolute Tyrant) not in a bare power to do what we Will."[28] What Astell promises men and women is equality in subjection and obedience to established powers.[29] The conclusions that she draws from her rejection of contract theory, and of the related idea that we are born free and equal, are thoroughly monarchist, as is clear when one turns to her comments on Hobbes.

Astell's most explicit reference to Hobbes occurs in the preface to her *Moderation Truly Stated*. There, anticipating Di Stefano's comments, she mocks the idea that there was ever a state of nature in which "*Men sprung up like so many Mushrooms or* Terræ Filii, *without Father or Mother or any sort of dependency!*"—an idea that she suggests was "*a meer figment of Hobbs's Brain*" or borrowed from the fable of Cadmus, who sowed dragon's teeth and reaped a full-grown army.[30] She continues this passage by chiding the author she is discussing (Charles Davenant, 1656–1714) for having endorsed a doctrine that she believes undermines the authority of the monarch (at this juncture Queen Anne). For, as she sees it, it is an open invitation to rebellion and instability. Quoting Davenant against himself (in roman type), she says,

> *And truly who can blame a Man who finds himself not at* Ease, *or so well as he would be, if he reassumes a Fundamental Right, a Privilege of which no Man can divest himself, and so soon as he can get more Men of his Mind to make his Party strong enough, declares the* Contract broken *and that those who are* no wiser (*this a Man always supposes*) *and by this time no stronger, than he is, have no Right to Command*

him; *but* that he is return'd into the full Liberty his Progenitors enjoy'd in the Free State of Nature, and that he may Act for himself, and take all the ways of Consulting and Compassing his own Safety. *Most admirable Doctrine, equally true and Loyal! and is not her Majesty infinitely oblig'd to you Sir, for spreading it?*[31]

According to Astell, legitimate monarchs derive their authority from God, and the way in which faction and rebellion is to be avoided *"is to plant in our own Minds, and as much as we can, in the Minds of our Fellow Subjects, a Reverence for Authority."*[32] She is suspicious of contract theory, it is true, but this is because she believes in the legitimacy of monarchy, and her doctrine—that one should reverence God-given authority—leads her to the conclusion that a wife should accept being governed by her husband.[33] She justifies the general subjection of women in marriage, based on the scriptural injunction to obey, in the following way: *"Now unless this Supremacy be fix'd somewhere, there will be a perpetual Contention about it, such is the love of Dominion, and let Reason of things be what it may, those who have least Force, or Cunning to supply it, will have the Disadvantage. So that since Women are acknowledg'd to have least Bodily strength, their being commanded to obey is in pure kindness to them, and for their Quiet and Security, as well as for the Exercise of their Vertue."*[34] So, the origins of women's subordination within the family derive from men's superior strength, an explanation which we earlier saw was implicit in Hobbes's theory. Like Hobbes, Astell also insists that women's subordination is not universal and that men will be legitimately subject to a woman whenever there is a reigning queen.[35] But, more consistently than Hobbes, Astell takes the historically existing inequalities in power between men and women as evidence that there is no state of natural equality.

Although Astell is, in some sense, a defender of her sex, her doctrines are so bound up with a defense of monarchism that they offer little that is positive to modern feminism, apart from their historical interest. For Astell, Queen Elizabeth I is a model of what a monarch should be. Once again she uses Davenant's own words to argue that Elizabeth's reign shows

that when a Queen makes it "evident to the whole World that it can never enter into her Thoughts to make any step that shall hurt *England;* when she is known to have such Right Inclinations to the Realm, that she will make no ill use of her Authority; when she keeps the Ballance of Power even, never engaging in Wars, but what are unavoidable and manag'd with Frugality, Acts of Power should not be murmur'd at in her, nor her Proceedings oppos'd"; *but the more (I will not say Arbitrarily but) Sovereignly she Acts, so much the better, so much more is her Subjects Good consulted and her own Honour.*[36]

Astell clearly wishes Queen Anne to follow Elizabeth's example of exercising strong authority. And she argues that *"Absolute or Unaccountable Power, or which is the same thing, a last Appeal, must be lodg'd some where; otherwise there is, there can be, no Government, whatever Men may talk, but all is in Confusion: Therefore the only way is for the Supreme Power wherever it is Lodg'd to Govern it self, and to take all its Measures according to the Directions of the Laws; which tho' they may not be Infallible, are yet the Supreme Wisdom of the State."*[37] Like Hobbes, she accepts that the sovereign's power must be absolute. Like him, she thinks this demonstrates that it is not true that all women are subject to men, since men may be subjects of a queen. Yet Astell's desire to justify political subjection to the queen forces her to accept the polemical stance that women who are married should no more rebel against their husbands than the queen's subjects should rebel against her.[38] Despite some intimations of the possibility of marriage based on friendship, which warrant deeper exploration, Astell's rejection of contract theory is not so much an anticipation of late twentieth-century critiques of liberal theory as it is the last flourish in an established tradition of female, Christian defenders of their sex that reaches back to Christine de Pizan. While such "feminists" or "protofeminists" are committed to women's equal reason, capacity for virtue, and right to rule as queens, their conception of virtue as comprising submission to God's biblical injunctions precludes them from proposing any radical overthrow of husbandly authority and results, typically, in the defense of celibacy or widowhood as the only state in which a woman can legitimately exercise the same degree of liberty as a man.[39]

Catharine Macaulay's Contract Theory

While Astell's critique of Hobbes completely rejected accounts of political legitimacy based in a social contract, Catharine Macaulay was both a republican, who saw government as a compact between the people and their rulers, and a critic of Hobbes. In her discussion of the execution of Charles I, Macaulay cites Locke to justify the execution and clearly demonstrates her commitment to the idea that government is grounded in a compact between the people and their rulers.[40] She sets out her ideas for a republican government in a letter to Signor Paoli, appended to her early critique of Hobbes.[41] Astell blasted the civil war as demonstrating that people who question the necessary power of princes *"become in a little time mere Slaves to the Arbitrary Rule of some of the worst of their Fellow Subjects."*[42] Macaulay, by contrast, concludes her discussion of the events leading to the execution of Charles I by saying, "That the government is the ordinance of man; that, being the mere creature of human invention, it may be changed or altered according to the dictates of experience, and the better judgment of men; that it was instituted for the protection of the people, for the end of securing, not overthrowing the rights of nature; that it is a trust either formally admitted or supposed; and that the magistracy is consequently accountable; will meet with little contradiction in a country enlightened with the unobstructed ray of rational learning."[43]

Like Hobbes, then, Macaulay represents government as a human invention intended to secure the rights of the people. But she objects to his version of contract theory on at least three important grounds. First, she rejects his claim that people are not naturally social.[44] She accepts what was, at the time, the traditional view—that it is part of our God-given nature to have the capacity to develop into sociable and ethically responsible beings.[45] Second, she objects to his particular version of contract theory, according to which the people hand over absolute power to a sovereign.[46] And third, she objects more generally to the doctrine of psychological egoism, according to which "self-love is not only the governing principle, but the only principle which actuates the conduct of the human character," and she sets out to refute the conclusion, drawn from this doctrine, that justice and morality are just a matter of rational self-interest.[47] The first two lines of argument are developed in the relatively early *Loose Remarks on Certain Positions to Be Found in Mr. Hobbes's "Philosophical Rudiments of Government and Society."*[48]

Against Hobbes's claim that people are not sociable by nature, Macaulay argues in effect that Hobbes contradicts himself. Since he accepts that there is a law of nature, which can be recognized by reason, he ought to accept that our rationality makes us sociable. Macaulay implicitly assumes that recognizing the truth of the moral law is sufficient for us to have some motivation to obey it. She argues that while humans may not be born with the capacity to reason, just as they are not born with the capacity to walk, they are born with the means to acquire that capacity. She concludes, "Therefore man, by being born with the necessary means, is born a creature apt for reason; and a creature apt for reason is a creature fit for society."[49] This may at first seem to fail to come to grips with Hobbes's assumption that we need some external motivation—such as self-interest, fear, or the desire for peace—to impel us to obey the rationally recognizable truths of the law of nature, but, as we shall see, Macaulay's more general response to psychological egoism fills this gap.

In objecting to Hobbes's strange idea of a social contract, which establishes a sovereign power that upholds contracts but is not itself an ordinary agreement between two agents, Macaulay falls back on our ordinary, reasonable understanding of what a contract requires and argues that if one party to a contract were to dissolve or disappear, the contract would be void. Thus, if the people contract with a monarch or assembly to be governed for the greater good, this is an agreement that is always rescindable if the terms of the contract are not fulfilled.[50] Macaulay's third argument is spelled out at length in her *Treatise on the Immutability of Moral Truth*. Analyzing the position developed in this later work will enable us to see both the similarities between Macaulay's ethics and Astell's and the different conclusions they draw from their similar starting points.

Like Astell, Macaulay believes that we are endowed with a God-given reason that enables us to recognize the moral truth, and that true liberty is not merely the capacity to do what we will but involves being guided by reason. Both are intellectuals who accept that God's goodness conforms to immutable moral principles, which can in theory be discovered by reason, and they oppose the voluntarists who claim that moral truth depends on God's will alone.[51] Astell's intellectualism is more rationalist and innatist than Macaulay's, and while the first argues that a quietist commitment to passive obedience follows from innately known principles, the second deduces democratic consequences from our capacity to reason about our experience and to discover the fundamental nature of things. Macaulay argues that "if there is any such difference as constitutes the opposite essences of good and evil, there must be an abstract fitness and unfitness, in moral entities to this difference. There must be such a proportion and disproportion in the nature of things, as square with the idea of an eternal rule of right, and form the direct oppositions of a right and a wrong."[52] And she combines this belief in moral truth with a fundamentally Lockean account of the way in which we discover abstract truths—by means of a "power of combining and generalizing" ideas, which allows us "to apprehend truths of the most abstract nature."[53] She therefore allows herself to draw on empirical evidence in order to deduce the most rational form of government. By contrast, Astell's more Cartesian and Malebranchian inheritance inclines her to equate virtue with spiritual achievement and love of God.[54]

The overall aim of Macaulay's *Treatise on the Immutability of Moral Truth* is to argue for an intellectualist account of God, according to which his actions are governed by immutable moral principles discoverable by reason, and to defend the position on freedom of the will that she calls "moral necessity," according to which the will is determined by motives and achieves freedom when the motives that determine it are completely rational and, hence, fully moral.[55] It is this doctrine that grounds her belief in the perfectibility of humanity and society. She argues that our genuine self-interest, as rational moral beings, is to perfect ourselves as moral agents who act out of a sense of duty in obeying the rational moral law. Like Kant, who argued in his *Groundwork for a Metaphysics of Morals*, first published two years after Macaulay's *Treatise*, that we only act morally when we act out of a sense of moral duty, Macaulay argues that our true rational interest lies in "the conformity of action to the duties enjoined by [a] rational principle," where the rational principle that she intends allows us to judge exactly what is right and wrong.[56]

Macaulay argues that one cannot explain how people could be motivated to be virtuous if, as Hobbes and Lord Bolingbroke (one of her targets in this pamphlet) argue, all our motivations are selfish and we are moral only because this is the most rational means to secure our narrow interests. Her argument is that it is simply implausible to suppose that a purely avaricious, ambitious, or lustful person will be swayed by moral injunctions in the many cases in which they can satisfy their avaricious, ambitious, or lustful desires without suffering any immediate harm.[57] And, while there may be some people who have a natural desire to be moral (a moral taste), even they could have no reason to sacrifice themselves for the moral good.[58] It is only the belief in an "invariable rule of right" that can provide a secure moral standard to direct our conduct.[59] Her claim could be summed up as the assertion that if there were no motivation internal to the recognition that reason requires us to act morally, we would have no reason to do so.

Arguing in a fashion that may seem rather circular, but once again anticipating Kant, she insists that "if we had no other rule to walk by but the law of nature, traced by the idea that the corrupt mind of man forms of self-happiness, this rule would be of as variable a nature as are the different constitutions and the dispositions of the different characters of the species."[60] Either morality is contingent and depends on what humans desire, and what forces prevail in the conflict over the satisfaction of desire, or there is an invariable rule of right that can be recognized by means of reason and that enables us to criticize some established conventions as unjust. Not long after making this point, Macaulay makes one of her most clearly feminist statements and can be interpreted as anticipating that strand of the feminist critique of Hobbesian contract theory that maintains it is incapable of distinguishing consent from oppression.

Discussing the doctrine that might is right, associated with Hobbes's contractarianism, she points out that it authorizes the oppression of women and children and the "grievous servitude" that they have suffered in places such as China.[61] She continues,

> Nor is it any wonder that justice, in its more abstract or general sense, should be little considered, or little understood, by those who can believe that it is agreeable to the wisdom and goodness of an all-perfect Being to form two species of creatures of equal intelligence and similar feelings, and consequently capable of an equal degree of suffering under injuries, and should consign one of these species as a kind of property to a different species of their fellow-creatures, not endowed with any qualities of mind sufficient to prevent the enormous abuse of such a power.[62]

The fact that Macaulay can recognize the injustice of what was then, in many places, the actual situation of women rests on a capacity to judge the justice of what is actually the case in the light of what ought to be. She attributes this capacity to recognize how things might be improved to the existence of an all-perfect Being. Like Astell, she believes that God "lays before us the goodness and reasonableness of his Laws" and allows us to judge what is good and just. Unlike Astell, she makes it absolutely explicit that it is clear to reason that the actual subjection women suffer, because of their relative lack of strength, is unjust.

So, like Astell, Macaulay can be read as anticipating the later feminist critique of Hobbesian contract theory. "Consent" in circumstances where unequal might enforces subjection is insufficient for justice. But this does not prevent Macaulay's political philosophy from being a form of contract theory. She assumes that there is a standard of justice that can be perceived by reason and that rests on the assumption that individuals are free and equal, not in the empirical sense of having equal power and strength but rather in the normative sense of being equally capable of both suffering harm and exercising moral freedom, and of therefore being equal in value. She does not attempt to ground justice in consent, but having assumed an immutable principle of justice, she argues that the most secure way of guaranteeing the liberty of subjects, and protecting the rights they can be seen to deserve, is to put in place a republican system of government that enshrines consent in its processes, thus guarding against corruption and securing political liberty.

The kind of contract theory adopted by Macaulay does not ground legitimacy in consent, but rather in the fulfillment of the terms of the contract. For Macaulay, political power "is a trust either formally admitted or supposed." The citizens entrust their sovereign with the power necessary to protect their interests. Our sense of justice allows us to recognize that if one party to such a contract fails to fulfill its part of the bargain, the contract is void.[63] But if a government is fulfilling its purpose and upholding the terms of the contract with the people, then it is a legitimate government.

From this standpoint, the point of democracy and republicanism is to put in place safeguards against the observed corruptibility of mankind, in order to ensure that government performs the function for which it is intended, securing the rights and liberties of the governed. A citizen, Macaulay argues, cannot give an absolute prince advice without incurring the danger of giving offense, and so, since princes may be bad, ignorant, or foolish, we can see that this is a bad form of government.[64] In a democracy, the corruption of those in power can be guarded against by the rotation of all positions of trust and by "fixing the Agrarian on a proper balance," which is a means to prevent any citizens from becoming so rich as to be able to corrupt the political process through monetary means.[65]

For Macaulay, political liberty is only a means. The ultimate end is moral liberty. She argues that "it is only the democratical system, rightly balanced, which can secure the virtue, liberty and happiness of society," for "the very nature of slavish dependence and proud superiority are equally baneful to the virtues inherent in mankind."[66] Although Macaulay does not draw the consequence, Mary Wollstonecraft will elaborate the significance of this doctrine for women in her *Vindication of the Rights of Women*. For, in the first sections of her tract, Wollstonecraft argues at length that if women are to develop themselves as rational moral agents, they must be freed of "slavish dependence."[67] Thus, she makes explicit the implicit feminism in Macaulay's claim that we cannot genuinely exercise the virtues if we are victims of unjust subjection. According to these later feminists, virtue is not, as Astell claimed, something that we can exercise in a state of submission. In her response to Burke's *Reflections on the Revolution in France*, Macaulay considers and rejects the position, adopted by Astell and others, that we can be virtuous while offering a passive obedience even to a faulty government: "Though a false opinion of the rights and powers of citizens may *enslave* the ductile mind into a state of passive obedience, and thus secure the peace of government; yet in the same degree does it inflate the *pride* and *arrogance* of princes, until all considerations of *rectitude* give way to *will*, the barriers of personal security are flung down, and thence arises that *tremendous necessity* which must be followed by a state of *violence* and *anarchy*, which Mr. Burke so *justly* dreads."[68]

Since our passive obedience gives license to the vices of a bad prince, as virtuous beings we should put in place a government that reason tells us is likely to promote virtue and good government, thus enabling our progress toward moral perfection. Once again, Macaulay does not draw the consequences of this comment for marriage, but it implies that men are in danger of being corrupted by their arbitrary rule within marriage. It will be left to Wollstonecraft to make this point explicitly.[69] Nevertheless, Macaulay does assert the corollary that, as men come to recognize and pursue justice, they will renounce the privilege of enslaving their wives.

Macaulay's faith that we are beings capable of moral perfection ultimately rests on her belief in a good, all-powerful God who must have made it possible for us to comprehend what morality requires. For those feminists who are less certain than Macaulay was that there exists a good, all-powerful God whose existence underpins an immutable moral truth, her perfectionist path to contract theory may seem shaky. Nevertheless, it should be recognized that the actual growth of contract theory and feminism is entwined in these religious roots.[70] Mary Wollstonecraft admired Macaulay, briefly corresponded with her, and reviewed her *Letters on Education* in November 1790.[71] These letters set out the coeducational and egalitarian education that Macaulay believed was necessary in order for children to develop as free moral beings, and the volume also reprints much of the *Treatise on the Immutability of Moral Truth*. Wollstonecraft commended Macaulay's work and commented in her review on Macaulay's chapter "No Characteristic Difference in Sex" that "the observations on this subject might have been carried much farther."[72] Her own

Vindication of the Rights of Women does exactly that, and it owes much to Macaulay's arguments for an eternal foundation of moral truth and her dismissal, as absurd, of Rousseau's idea that the couple makes up a moral individual.[73]

A letter written to Macaulay from Boston in 1769 by "Sophronia" (actually Sarah Prince Gill) demonstrates that in the United States, also, the defense of liberty was taken to have a religious foundation.[74] Having praised Macaulay, whose history was popular in America, Sophronia agrees with her disappointment that many women lead licentious lives of pleasure, but insists that

> Principles so Opposite to the Genius of our Holy Religion, so repugnant to the design of the Gospel, which is a System of Universal Benevolence, must be detested by those who have partaken of its Spirit, unless through Ignorance or Misapprehension they have been led into Error.—Our Ancestors wisely took care to instill the principles of Liberty into the minds of their children, to this provident care it is owing that America hath made such a Noble stand against the inroads of Despotism, and produced such Noble Defenders of her Rights.[75]

Like Macaulay, Sophronia identifies true morality with a system of universal benevolence and gives it a religious foundation.[76] The defense of liberty, and of government that is limited by the consent of the people, is intended to promote this universal benevolence. There is no attempt here to ground justice simply in consent. Rather, it is proposed that only those governments that uphold their side of the compact with their people, and protect their moral as well as physical freedoms, are legitimate.

Hobbes has played an important role in feminist critiques of contract theory, first because his account of human nature is one that most feminists reject, and second because he narrows the distinction between consent and subjection. If liberalism is grounded in a contract theory committed to Hobbes's assumptions, then it is problematic from a feminist point of view. A reading of Macaulay reveals, however, an influential early feminist who is both committed to the idea that government is grounded in a contract, and firmly opposed to Hobbes. She rejects his account of human nature, arguing that reason by itself endows us with virtuous inclinations. And she rejects the idea that morality could be merely enlightened self-interest. Her political philosophy was profoundly influenced by the "neo-Roman" or "republican" writers, against whose democratic and anti-monarchical tracts Hobbes had directed his arguments.[77] As Quentin Skinner has ably demonstrated, Hobbes's reformulation of the concept of liberty, as merely absence of constraint, was specifically designed to rebut those who claimed that civil liberty was only exercised by those who were governed by laws to which they had consented, and was impossible where subjects were dependent on the arbitrary will of an individual.[78] Macaulay rejected Hobbes's concept of liberty as mere freedom from external constraint, arguing instead for "moral necessity," the claim that free acts are those that are determined by our rational judgement of what it is best to do. She recognized that it is only under certain social circumstances that one can secure this freedom. This underpins her emphasis on the need for appropriate education. It also underpins her belief that representative government is a necessary means to the abolition of the complementary vices of servility and arrogance. The result is a contract theory that shares a great deal with Pateman's anti-contractarian position. Certain social conditions are necessary in order for genuine freedom to be exercised. Consent under duress is insufficient for justice.

Since many modern social contract theorists do begin from Hobbesian premises, the feminist critique of Hobbes continues to operate as an important challenge to these strands of contractualism. But it is, I believe, worth acknowledging that it was a different species of contract theory that actually inspired eighteenth-century women. This contract theory is not a "contract theory" in the Hobbesian sense. Arguably, despite its religious origins, it offers as yet unexploited potential for the development of non-Hobbesian grounds for contemporary liberal feminism. At the very least, it remains significant that the actual inspiration of Catharine Macaulay and Mary Wollstonecraft rested on a critical rejection of Hobbes.

Notes

1. Alison M. Jaggar, *Feminist Politics and Human Nature* (Brighton, Sussex: Harvester Press, 1983), 45. See also Christine Di Stefano, "Masculinity as Ideology in Political Theory: Hobbesian Man Considered," *Women's Studies International Forum* 6, no. 6 (1983): 633–44.
2. Teresa Brennan and Carole Pateman, "'Mere Auxiliaries to the Commonwealth': Women and the Origins of Liberalism," *Political Studies* 27, no. 2 (1979): 183–200.
3. Carole Pateman, *The Sexual Contract* (Cambridge: Polity Press, 1988).
4. Ibid., 230.

5. See Sarah Hutton, "Liberty, Equality, and God: The Religious Roots of Catharine Macaulay's Feminism," in *Women, Gender, and Enlightenment*, ed. Sarah Knott and Barbara Taylor (Houndsmills, Basingstoke: Palgrave Macmillan, 2005), 538–50; Sarah Hutton, "Virtue, God, and Stoicism in the Thought of Elizabeth Carter and Catharine Macaulay," in *Virtue, Liberty, and Toleration: Political Ideas of European Women, 1400–1800*, ed. Jacqueline Broad and Karen Green (Dordrecht, Netherlands: Springer, 2007), 137–48.

6. For her biography, see Bridget Hill, *The Republican Virago: The Life and Times of Catharine Macaulay, Historian* (Oxford: Clarendon Press, 1992). For her political theory, see Karen O'Brien, "Catharine Macaulay's Histories of England: A Female Perspective on the History of Liberty," in Knott and Taylor, *Women, Gender, and Enlightenment*, 523–37; Susan Wiseman, "Catharine Macaulay: History, Republicanism, and the Public Sphere," in *Women, Writing, and the Public Sphere, 1700–1830*, ed. Elizabeth Eger et al. (Cambridge: Cambridge University Press, 2001), 181–99.

7. Ruth Perry, "Mary Astell and the Feminist Critique of Possessive Individualism," *Eighteenth-Century Studies* 23, no. 4 (1990): 444–57; Patricia Springborg, *Mary Astell: Theorist of Freedom from Domination* (Cambridge: Cambridge University Press, 2005), 127–30.

8. Ruth Perry, *The Celebrated Mary Astell: An Early English Feminist* (Chicago: Chicago University Press, 1986), 13. Joan K. Kinnaird thinks that the "paradox" of Astell's conservatism plus feminism "disappears" when she is properly understood; see Kinnaird, "Mary Astell and the Conservative Contribution to English Feminism," *Journal of British Studies* 19, no. 1 (1979): 53–75. Penny A. Weiss, who finds similarities between Hobbes and Astell, has argued for her relevance for feminists, claiming that like Hobbes, she "exposed the lineaments of power"; see Weiss, "Mary Astell: Including Women's Voices in Political Theory," *Hypatia* 19, no. 3 (2004): 67, and Weiss, *Canon Fodder: Historical Women Political Thinkers* (University Park: Pennsylvania State University Press, 2009), 144.

9. I have argued elsewhere that in an earlier period, as well, an early form of contract theory coexisted with non-egoistic moral psychology. See Karen Green, "Christine De Pisan and Thomas Hobbes," *Philosophical Quarterly* 44, no. 177 (1994): 456–75.

10. Sarah Hrdy, *Mother Nature: Maternal Instincts and How They Shape the Human Species* (London: Vintage, 2000).

11. See Carol Gilligan, *In a Different Voice: Psychological Theory and Women's Development* (Cambridge, Mass.: Harvard University Press, 1980). This work, in particular, spawned a large literature devoted to women's tendency to see moral problems in terms of care rather than contractual justice.

12. Di Stefano, "Masculinity as Ideology," 638.

13. See, in particular, Nancy J. Hirschmann, *Rethinking Obligation: A Feminist Method for Political Theory* (Ithaca, N.Y.: Cornell University Press, 1992), 35–44; Karen Green, *The Woman of Reason: Feminism, Humanism, and Political Thought* (Cambridge: Polity Press, 1995), 44–64; Carole Pateman, "'God Hath Ordained to Man a Helper': Hobbes, Patriarchy, and Conjugal Right," in *Feminist Interpretations and Political Theory*, ed. Mary Lyndon Shanley and Carole Pateman (University Park: Pennsylvania State University Press, 1991), 53–73; Brennan and Pateman, "'Mere Auxiliaries to the Commonwealth.'"

14. Thomas Hobbes, *Leviathan*, ed. A. P. Martinich and Brian Battiste (Peterborough, Canada: Broadview Press, 2010), 181.

15. Gordon J. Schochet, "Thomas Hobbes on the Family and the State of Nature," *Political Science Quarterly* 82, no. 3 (1967): 427–45. Reprinted as chapter 5 of this volume.

16. Hobbes, *Leviathan*, 181.

17. This is the way that I read him in *The Woman of Reason*, but it is not the only possible interpretation. See also Sharon Lloyd in chapter 2 of this volume.

18. Perry, "Mary Astell and the Feminist Critique."

19. Ibid., 445.

20. Springborg, *Mary Astell*, 127–30.

21. Sharon Achinstein points out that she denies natural liberty because of our dependence on God. See Achinstein, "Mary Astell, Religion, and Feminism: Texts in Motion," in *Mary Astell:*

Reason, Gender, Faith, ed. William Kolbrener and Michal Michelson (Aldershot: Ashgate, 2007), 22.

22. Mary Astell, *A Serious Proposal to the Ladies: Parts I and II,* ed. Patricia Springborg (London: Pickering and Chatto, 1997).

23. Mary Astell, *Reflections upon Marriage,* 3rd ed. (London: R. Wilkin, 1706), 91–92.

24. Ibid., 83–84.

25. Astell, *Reflections upon Marriage,* preface. Passages in Roman type are quotes from Locke's *Two Treatises.*

26. Melinda Zook, "Religious Nonconformity and the Problem of Dissent in the Works of Aphra Behn and Mary Astell," in Kolbrener and Michelson, *Mary Astell,* 112; Achinstein, "Mary Astell, Religion, and Feminism," 22.

27. Here Astell is applying a well-established concept of liberty that Hobbes had notoriously challenged. Quentin Skinner, *Hobbes and Republican Liberty* (Cambridge: Cambridge University Press, 2008), 20–34.

28. Mary Astell, *The Christian Religion, as Profess'd by a Daughter of The Church of England. In a Letter to the Right Honourable, T. L. C. I.* (London: R. Wilkin, 1705), 278.

29. Jacqueline Broad and Karen Green, *A History of Women's Political Thought in Europe, 1400–1700* (Cambridge: Cambridge University Press, 2009), 290.

30. Mary Astell, *Moderation Truly Stated: or, A Review of a Late Pamphlet, Entitul'd, Moderation a Vertue. With a Prefatory Discourse to Dr. D'Aveanant, Concerning His Late Essays on Peace and War* (London: R. Wilken, 1704), xxxv.

31. Ibid., xxxv–xxxvi.

32. Ibid., xxxviii.

33. This is the tenor of her *Reflections upon Marriage,* as well as the conclusion drawn in Broad and Green, *History of Women's Political Thought,* 281, and backed up by Ann Jessie Van Sant, "'Tis Better That I Endure': Mary Astell's Exclusion of Equity," in Kolbrener and Michelson, *Mary Astell,* 142. Nevertheless, in some circumstances—for instance, when a woman is a queen—the woman's husband may be a subject and therefore should defer to her authority. This was a possibility envisaged by Hobbes (*Leviathan,* 182) and was sufficiently disturbing to Jean Bodin that he took it to be a reason for refusing to accept reigning queens. Jean Bodin, *Les six livres de la République* (Paris: Librairie iuré, à la Samaritaine, 1583; repr., Aalen: Scientia Aalen, 1961), 1002.

34. Astell, *Reflections upon Marriage,* preface.

35. Hobbes, *Leviathan,* 182; Astell, *Moderation Truly Stated,* liv–lv. This is rightly taken by Joanne Wright as evidence that Hobbes's views are rather more sympathetic to women than those of some of his contemporaries. Joanne H. Wright, "Going Against the Grain: Hobbes's Case for Original Maternal Domination," *Journal of Women's History* 14, no. 1 (2002): 123–48.

36. Astell, *Moderation Truly Stated,* xxiii–xxiv.

37. Ibid., xxxviii.

38. Astell, *Reflections upon Marriage,* 91–92.

39. This tradition is explored at length in Broad and Green, *History of Women's Political Thought.*

40. Catharine Macaulay, *History of England, from the Accession of James I to the Elevation of the House of Hanover,* 5 vols. (London: Edward and Charles Dilly, 1769–72), 4:400–404.

41. Catharine Macaulay, *Loose Remarks on Certain Positions to Be Found in Mr. Hobbes's "Philosophical Rudiments of Government and Society," with a Short Sketch of a Democratical Form of Government, in a Letter to Signor Paoli* (London: T. Davies, in Russell-street, Covent Garden; Robinson and Roberts, in Pater-noster Row; and T. Cadell, in the Strand, 1767).

42. Astell, *Moderation Truly Stated,* xxxviii.

43. Macaulay, *History of England,* 4:403–4.

44. Macaulay, *Loose Remarks,* 3–4.

45. Hobbes's theory that the state of nature is a state of war explicitly contradicts this more traditional claim, which goes back at least as far as Aristotle. Skinner, *Hobbes and Republican Liberty*, 41.

46. Macaulay, *Loose Remarks*, 6–9.

47. Catharine Macaulay, *A Treatise on the Immutability of Moral Truth* (London: A. Hamilton, 1783), 128.

48. See also Wendy Gunther-Canada, "Catharine Macaulay on the Paradox of Paternal Authority in Hobbesian Politics," *Hypatia* 21, no. 2 (2006): 150–73. Reprinted as chapter 9 of this volume.

49. Macaulay, *Loose Remarks*, 3.

50. Ibid., 6–7.

51. Jacqueline Broad, *Women Philosophers of the Seventeenth Century* (Cambridge: Cambridge University Press, 2002), 103; Springborg, *Mary Astell*, 216–17; Karen O'Brien, *Women and Enlightenment in Eighteenth-Century Britain* (Cambridge: Cambridge University Press, 2009), 166–67.

52. Macaulay, *Treatise on the Immutability of Moral Truth*, 95.

53. Ibid., 98.

54. For the influence of Malebranche on Astell, see Broad, *Women Philosophers of the Seventeenth Century*, 90–113; Springborg, *Mary Astell*, 48–80.

55. Much more could be said about Macaulay's doctrine of the will, which is not entirely clear in its details. See Martina Reuter, "Catharine Macaulay and Mary Wollstonecraft on the Will," in Broad and Green, *Virtue, Liberty, and Toleration*, 149–69.

56. Macaulay, *Treatise on the Immutability of Moral Truth*, 129.

57. Ibid., 135–38.

58. Thus, she is implicitly criticizing Shaftsbury's doctrine of moral sense. O'Brien, *Women and Enlightenment in Eighteenth-Century Britain*, 46–48.

59. Macaulay, *Treatise on the Immutability of Moral Truth*, 139.

60. Ibid., 140.

61. Ibid., 155.

62. Ibid., 158.

63. Macaulay, *Loose Remarks*, 6–7.

64. Ibid., 25.

65. Ibid., 33.

66. Ibid., 29–30.

67. Mary Wollstonecraft, *The Works of Mary Wollstonecraft*, ed. Jane Todd and Marilyn Butler, 7 vols. (London: Pickering, 1989), 5:86–87, 92–93, 102–6.

68. Catharine Macaulay, *Observations on the Reflections of the Right Hon. Edmund Burke, on the Revolution in France, in a Letter for the Right Hon. The Earl of Stanhope* (London: C. Dilly, 1790), 16–17.

69. Wollstonecraft, *Works of Mary Wollstonecraft*, 5:93.

70. Hutton, "Liberty, Equality, and God" and "Virtue, God, and Stoicism."

71. Wollstonecraft, *Works of Mary Wollstonecraft*, 7:309–22; Bridget Hill, "The Links Between Mary Wollstonecraft and Catharine Macaulay: New Evidence," *Women's History Review* 4, no. 2 (1995):177–92.

72. Wollstonecraft, *Works of Mary Wollstonecraft*, 7:314.

73. See, in particular, ibid., 5:81.

74. Monica Letzring, "Sarah Prince Gill and the John Adams–Catharine Macaulay Correspondence," *Proceedings of the Massachusetts Historical Society* 88 (1976): 107–11.

75. "Sophronia" to Catharine Macaulay, Boston, December 8, 1769. The letter is available online through the Gilder Lehrman Institute of American History at http://gilderlehrman.pastperfect-online.com/,collection no. GLC01797.02.

76. See, for instance, Macaulay, *Treatise on the Immutability of Moral Truth*, 95.

77. For an extended discussion of this distinction, see Quentin Skinner, *Liberty Before Liberalism* (Cambridge: Cambridge University Press, 1998); Skinner, *Hobbes and Republican Liberty*; Philip Pettit, *Republicanism: A Theory of Freedom and Government* (Oxford: Clarendon Press, 1997), 23.

78. Skinner, *Hobbes and Republican Liberty*, 124–77.

9

Catharine Macaulay's "Loose Remarks" on Hobbesian Politics

Wendy Gunther-Canada

That the universe is governed by one God we will not dispute; and will also add, that God has an undoubted right to govern what he has himself created, and that it is beneficial to the creature to be governed by the Father of all things; but that this should be an argument for a man to govern what he has not created, and with whom a nation can have no such paternal connexion is a paradox which Mr. Hobbes has left unsolved.

—Catharine Macaulay, *Loose Remarks*

Revisions of the canon of political philosophy by feminist theorists such as Susan Moller Okin, Carole Pateman, and Nancy Hirschmann have drawn attention to a paradox in the political thought of Thomas Hobbes: while Hobbes rejected paternal power in his challenge to the theory of the divine right of kings, he promoted patriarchy in forming a social compact that excluded women from political subjectivity.[1] Yet there was a much earlier challenge to Hobbesian patriarchal politics found in a pamphlet by eighteenth-century England's most famous female historian, Catharine Macaulay. *Loose Remarks on Certain Positions to Be Found in Mr. Hobbes's "Philosophical Rudiments of Government and Society" with a Short Sketch of a Democratical Form of Government in a Letter to Signior Paoli* (hereafter, *Loose Remarks*) was published in London in 1769.[2] By this time, Macaulay had already published, to great acclaim, four of eight volumes of the *History of England from the Accession of James I to That of the Brunswick Line*. Her account of Stuart politics, the Civil War, and the Glorious Revolution became a best-selling Whig interpretation of seventeenth-century English politics. Macaulay's volumes competed with David Hume's rival Tory account *History of England from Julius Caesar to the Glorious Revolution*. Her international audience included George Washington, John Adams, and the Comte de Mirabeau.

Catharine Sawbridge Macaulay Graham (1731–1791) is the subject of Bridget Hill's groundbreaking biography *The Republican Virago: The Life and Times of Catharine Macaulay, Historian* and Kate Davies's more recent *Catharine Macaulay and Mercy Otis Warren: The Revolutionary Atlantic and the Politics of Gender*, as well as a handful of articles and book chapters.[3] Macaulay responded to patriarchalism in the political thought of seventeenth-century England and to patriarchal politics in the partisan debates among eighteenth-century Whigs throughout her writings. Her criticism of Hobbesian political philosophy reveals her to be a forceful opponent of patriarchy and a sophisticated analyst of gender politics. *Loose Remarks*, written in answer to *De Cive*, offered some of Macaulay's strongest criticism of absolutist monarchs and despotic regimes, concluding with an outline of a republican government for the island of Corsica. By examining at length the argument against paternal right in this pamphlet, I shall highlight how Macaulay's reading of *De Cive* weakened (and continues to weaken) key assumptions of patriarchal thought. The antipatriarchal dynamic that emerges from her argument with Hobbes suggests the makings of an early feminist, one who anticipated concerns about women, consent, and the social contract that are important to feminist theorists today. *Loose Remarks* provides contemporary readers with a vivid example of her challenge to the metanarrative of patriarchy in early modern political thought. Close attention to the argument in her first political pamphlet also gives us the chance to explore the limitations and possibilities of an emergent feminist theory. Further, a brief survey of Macaulay's writings provides proof of her antipathy to Hobbesian political principles, as the *Leviathan* provided the philosophical justification for the legitimacy of the Lord Protector, Oliver Cromwell, who is the villain of her eight-volume *History of England*. While Hobbes first appears as a target in *Loose Remarks*, he would be the focus of a lifelong animus, finding his way into many of Macaulay's writings as her philosophical bête noir. The issues addressed in her pamphlet, such as the

Hobbesian depiction of a selfish and solitary human nature requiring an artificial political strongman to keep us in our place and enforce peace, were returned to repeatedly and repudiated entirely in later publications. Thomas Hobbes's arguments in support of the godlike human Leviathan were completely at odds with Catharine Macaulay's stated belief that no man could or should rule us all.

The Paradox of Patriarchy in Hobbes

If Mr. Hobbes could prove that paternal power instituted by God was monarchical, he cannot from this conclude that the monarchical government is preferable to all others, without falling into his usual absurdities.

—Catharine Macaulay, *Loose Remarks*

In the introduction to the now-classic *The Authoritarian Family and Political Attitudes in Seventeenth-Century England: Patriarchalism in Political Thought*, Gordon Schochet noted that prior to his writing scholars had dismissed as ridiculous Sir Robert Filmer's identification of father-right and political right in *Patriarcha*. According to Schochet, "The word that has most frequently been used to describe both Filmer and patriarchalism is 'absurd.'" This derision of Filmer's thesis led to wholesale dismissal of patriarchalism as "a meaningful justification of political obligation."[4] Yet Schochet's historical exploration of the idea of patriarchy in political thought, rather than documenting the insignificance of patriarchal explanations of legitimate governance, demonstrated that by the end of the seventeenth century the "Filmerian position very nearly became the official state ideology."[5] One of the key contributions of Schochet's study was a detailed examination of patriarchalism in Thomas Hobbes's account of the state of nature. Traditional commentaries on the *Leviathan* have denied the presence of the family in man's original condition. Schochet, however, drew on a variety of sources to make a convincing case for a "patriarchal element"[6] in Hobbes's writing that expands our understanding of the role of consent in establishing legitimate authority in the social compact.[7]

There is, of course, a major distinction to be drawn between Filmer's patriarchal politics and the patriarchal element discernable in Hobbes's political thought. Schochet observed that while Hobbes likened familial and governmental authority, he did not base patriarchal authority on the generative power of fathers: "Breaking sharply with the patriarchalism of the mid-seventeenth century, Hobbes insisted that paternal power in the state of nature was not derived from fatherhood as such. If patriarchal sovereignty was a product of procreation, he reasoned, then the mother, who is a full partner in the act of generation, should have an equal claim to dominion over the child."[8] It is the first principle of patriarchal political thought that men are not naturally free and equal, since each man is born subject to the authority of his father. Hobbes, however, began with an assumption of the equality of all men in the state of nature, and so had to find a way to reconcile paternal authority with consent. Schochet argued that Hobbesian patriarchalism was consistent with natural equality because "paternal dominion is derived from the consent of the child," given in gratitude to the parent for preserving their life in the state of nature.[9] The notion of the tacit consent of infants has distinguished Hobbes from other patriarchal writers. But what really makes Hobbes unique among contract theorists is that he assumes the natural equality of both men and women. In the state of nature, women hold their own in the war of all against all, and as mothers they are the first sovereigns because a woman's decision to care for the child she has borne creates the original bond of obligation. Yet women enter the Hobbesian social contract as wives. Schochet's examination of patriarchy has informed much feminist scholarship. Carole Pateman, for instance, has suggested that modern readings of Hobbes's political writing have ignored a theoretical conundrum: "Hobbes is a patriarchal theorist but the possibility that is considered by neither conventional political theorists nor feminists is that he is a patriarchalist who rejects paternal right."[10]

Interestingly, Macaulay noted this paradox of paternal authority in Hobbesian politics more than two centuries ago. In *Loose Remarks*, she contested Hobbes's assumptions about paternal right to undermine his argument about the power of absolutist monarchs.[11] She asked what type of father would behave like a Stuart king and, in turn, what form of power a father might legitimately exercise in his own household. This questioning set up an even greater challenge to the subject position of women as wives within the Hobbesian social contract. Macaulay developed a theory of civic obligation between infants and adults, women and men, based on mutual support that secures the lives of the most vulnerable in society by limiting the political rights of fathers, husbands, and kings.

Macaulay began *Loose Remarks* by tackling the first principles of Hobbes's account of human nature: "Mr. Hobbes in his Philosophical

Elements of a True Citizen, sets out with an intention to confute this received opinion, That man is a creature born fit for society."[12] In *De Cive*, Hobbes asserted that men enter society out of fear of their mutual destruction, not for love of their fellow man. Since the decision to live together requires a rational calculation of survival, man must be "trained" for social interaction. Macaulay summarized this argument in the following manner: "Mr. Hobbes says that infants are born incapable of reason, and all men are born infants; therefore man is not born a creature fit for society." She employed an analogy to show that although newborns cannot walk, they are born with the physical attributes that will enable them to take their first steps: "New-born infants are incapable of walking; Therefore man, being born an infant, is not born a creature fit for walking; But infants are born with two legs, and the power of motion, which are the means for that action when it becomes necessary to their state. Therefore man, by being born with the necessary means, cannot be said to be born unfit for walking."[13]

Likewise, infants born with the capacity for rational thought will grow to reason for themselves: "And infants, though born incapable of reason, by being born with human attributes, are born with the means necessary for attaining it; Therefore man, by being born with the necessary means, is born a creature apt for reason; and a creature apt for reason is a creature apt for society."[14] Macaulay faulted the Hobbesian discussion of infancy because she recognized that some form of society is essential for the survival of a baby and equally necessary if a child is to grow into adulthood: "In his infant state, society is the only means of preserving his being; this makes him love it."[15] She contended that since God gives human beings the capacity to reason, each is therefore born fit for society.

The real debate between Macaulay and Hobbes concerned the question of what kind of society would enable humans to live well together, and Macaulay immediately turned to Hobbes's discussion of the rights of the sovereign. The Hobbesian sovereign was an absolute monarch, a law unto himself, for the "civil laws are no other than the commands of him who hath the supreme authority; and this supreme governor is not to be bound to the civil law, for that would to be bound to himself."[16] The radical moment in Hobbesian political thought was his assertion that the supreme commander is invested with the power to rule by the consent of the people, not divine right. Once the people form the social compact, they transfer their natural rights to the sovereign. Schochet remarked that for Hobbes political power "arose from acquisition or institution."[17]

While paternal power is a form of acquisition, Hobbes did not consider it significant how power was acquired. For Macaulay, these distinctions were critical in assessing the legitimacy of governance, and she took Hobbes to task for not differentiating limited and absolute power. She asked, "Who sees not that the assembly who prescribed these things had an absolute power?"[18] If the assembly has the power to raise one man above them as sovereign, this power to designate their leader limits the authority of the new monarch. She would make a similar argument regarding the authority of Parliament in placing William and Mary on the throne in her last pamphlet, responding to Edmund Burke's *Reflections on the Revolution in France* (1790).[19] "It is evident from this jumble, that Mr. Hobbes either willfully or ignorantly, here confounds absolute with limited power," she objected. "If there are regal privileges annexed to this executive power, we call it a limited power, because restrained by the aforesaid laws."[20]

In *De Cive*, however, the power of a monarch is absolute and cannot be limited by the people in consenting to form the social compact.[21] As Macaulay summarized, "A monarchy, says Mr. Hobbes, is derived from the power of the people transferring their right to one man. The whole right of the people conveyed on him, he can then do whatsoever the people could do before he was elected; and the people is no longer one person but a rude multitude, as being only one before by virtue of the supreme command, now conveyed from themselves on this one man." After the people transfer their rights to the sovereign, "the elector monarch can do his subjects no injury, because they have subjected their right and will to defend themselves to him." Once elected, the sovereign is under no obligation to any person to receive the people's command, since the person "ceaseth to be a person as soon as that act is done, and the person vanishing, all obligations to the person vanisheth."[22]

Macaulay countered that such a vanishing act voided the Hobbesian contract at the moment of its inception: "A contract made by two contracting parties must be equally binding; therefore Mr. Hobbes's figure of the dissolution of the person does not serve his argument a whit; for if the person, namely the people, dissolves, the obligation, if voided on one side, is so on the other." To her mind, the people could not make themselves void or transfer their sovereign power[23] without nullifying the contract. We cannot negotiate away our rights without negating our very being: "The people, in transferring their right to the monarch, look upon themselves as dissolved as a body, and return to so many individuals, yet if that monarch refuse to perform those stipulated articles previous to his being vested with that right, he by his non-performance forfeits that right: that right forfeited returns again to the people, and he himself is no more than one of the multitude."[24]

Macaulay's objections raised critical questions about gender politics, particularly regarding women's status within the marriage contract. Once a woman consented to wed and vowed to obey a husband, her civil existence was voided: since man and wife were one in the law, the woman vanished into the man as her husband became her sovereign. According to the logic of contract developed in *Loose Remarks*, a woman could not rationally enter into a contract that nullified her rights as an individual. While Macaulay did not explicate this argument there, in *Letters on Education* she criticized the terms of the marriage contract for exactly these reasons, noting the "total and absolute exclusion of every political right to the sex in general," and the fact that "married women . . . have hardly a civil right to save them from the grossest injuries."[25] Refuting Hobbes, she argued in *Loose Remarks* that a contract is lawful and binding if and when the exchange of rights is to the advantage of all the parties to the contract: "For the will of the contractor is necessary in making a lawful contract, and no rational person can will so absurdly as to give up his natural right to another, without the proposing to himself more advantages than he could otherwise have enjoyed, had he not divested himself of that right."[26] A woman, therefore, should accept a proposal of marriage only if the bonds of matrimony extend and protect her rights. Macaulay's challenge to patriarchy in this brief pamphlet laid the groundwork for later feminist analysis of the sexual injustices of the early modern social contract.

In ridiculing as "absurd" the arguments in *De Cive* about the origin of paternal power, Macaulay sounds just like the critics of Filmer mentioned earlier in this chapter. She agreed with Hobbes that procreation itself is not the basis of parental authority over children: "Parents can claim no dominion over their children from the act of generation, says Mr. Hobbes; that right belongs to the mother only, not from that act but because she may rightly, and at her own will, breed him up, or adventure him to fortune: if she breed him up, it is supposed to be on the condition that he is her servant."[27] For Schochet, who cited this same quotation from chapter 9 of *De Cive*, "Of the Right of Parents over Their Children and on Hereditary Government," this was an admission of the tacit consent of the child to parental rule.[28] Feminist theorists such as Nancy Hirschmann have used this claim to make a case for matriarchal sovereignty and to ask why women who are queens in the state of nature have no civil status under the social contract that creates the Leviathan.[29] In a more recent study, Hirschmann answers the question by suggesting that the confederacy of women and children threatens men in the state of nature, and thus their submission to patriarchs within the family is a necessary condition of sovereign authority.[30]

In fact, in chapter 9, Hobbes made the remarkable statement that it was natural that the "offspring goes with the womb" and claimed that the condition of the parent determined their relationship to the infant under the social contract, whether one be a wife or husband, slave or free, a queen or an Amazon.[31] He used the provocative example of the Amazons to demonstrate that fathers do not necessarily have a paternal right to their children. It was the practice of these ancient women warriors to mate with neighbors, choosing to raise their daughters themselves and returning sons to their paternal tribe according to the terms of their treaty. Hobbes noted that a child born of a queen belonged to her regardless of the traditional assumption that a child was the sole property of the father. The child of a married woman who by custom was treated as the property of her husband was by civil law part of the paternal estate. Macaulay did not respond to these arguments about the potential for women and men to form alternative households, to live separate lives except for occasional procreative activity, or to select consorts who had no power over them or their offspring.

Rather than championing the sovereignty of mothers over their children, Macaulay questioned the assumptions behind the Hobbesian matriarchy: "We know that the right of parents to expose their children has been the civil law of many countries; but that they have a natural right so to do is a bold assertion of Mr. Hobbes, which nature and reason contradict." Macaulay offered a different account of a mother's duty to her child: "The mother's care for the preservation of her young is an invariable dictate of nature through all her works."[32] Hobbes's claim that a parent can abandon an infant at will was, she believed, against the laws of nature. She argued, "The human species are more strongly bound of this obligation than brute animals: reason and morality strongly urges the care and preservation of an existence by themselves occasioned as a duty never to be omitted; by the law of justice, therefore, they, being thus bound to act, cannot have it in their option whether they will do it or not."[33] For Macaulay, the notion of willful maternal abandonment of a child was additional proof that "Mr. Hobbes will rather advance any absurdity, than own that power has its rights from reasonable causes."[34]

Hobbesian parents establish their right over a child by protecting its life in the state of nature. This right is not exclusive to the biological parent of the child but to anyone who would preserve a helpless infant from certain death. Hobbes wrote that the "person who raises the abandoned child will have the same Dominion as the mother had."[35] Macaulay concurred that care is the basis of parental right: "We are of Mr. Hobbes's opinion that it is very absurd to derive the right of parents over their children from the act of generation: their right proceeds only from the tender feelings which are inseparable from the quality of parents." That said, she completely disagreed with his assertion that a parent has a right to dispose of their child. Echoing John Locke's *First Treatise on Government*, Macaulay claimed that tender care is the "first natural obligation" that parents owe their children.[36] Since parents are obligated by nature to nurture their offspring, it is only reasonable that children be governed by caring guardians until they are able to think for themselves, as it "is more advantageous for them to be under the commands of their parents, than under any government."[37] The "helpless state of infancy" rightly obligates adults to care for their young, but once the child reaches maturity, "these obligations have force enough to make it the duty of the child to obey his parents in all things."[38]

Macaulay immediately qualified this obedience by stating that a child's duty is owed to the parents "if their commands are not opposite to the laws of his country, or the dictates of reason: but, as this authority has only its right from supposed benefits bestowed, it must be greater or lesser in proportion to the degree of those benefits."[39] The right to rule is commensurate with the benefit bestowed on an individual. Simply put, children owe obedience to their parents only if they were well cared for in childhood. Here Macaulay was reiterating her position that a contract must be advantageous to both parties in order for it to be valid—but in what sense do children contract with their parents? She made the terms of this contract between parent and child explicit: "Parents who are enemies, instead of benefactors, forfeit their right, which alone has its foundation from the obligation of received benefits."[40] Throughout *Loose Remarks*, Macaulay's message is that authority (right) is derived from benefit. Yet it is worth noting that she never detailed the standards by which a child is to evaluate whether a parent has been a benefactor or an enemy, and this complicates the consideration of the relationship of the subject to the sovereign that follows in the pamphlet.

Macaulay highlighted Hobbes's statement that "the grievance of subjects does not arise from the ill institution or ordination of government, (because in all manner of governments subjects may be oppressed) but from the ill administration of a well established government."[41] For her, this comment revealed that the philosopher did not have an adequate understanding of political science: "If Mr. Hobbes was as well acquainted with the science of policy as he is adept in the art of confounding things, he would know that the peculiar excellence of a government properly constituted, is to raise those to the administration whose virtues and abilities render them capable of this arduous task; and to deprive those of that office who upon trial are found at all defective."[42] This is a rhetorical slap at Hobbes's own involvement, as a member of the House of Commons, in the impeachment trial of Thomas Wentworth, Duke of Strafford, in 1640. To Macaulay, the basis of the good polity is the selection and promotion of virtuous men to positions of power and the removal of corrupt individuals from government. In the second volume of the *History of England*, Macaulay, approvingly quoting John Pym's speech to the House of Lords during Strafford's trial, declared that the "end of government was that virtue should be cherished, vice suppressed, but where arbitrary power was set up, a way was open for the advancement of evil."[43] In *Loose Remarks*, she contended that if a government is constituted so that it promotes the excellence of its administrators, it "can never be so long ill administered as to become a grievance to the subject."[44] Macaulay continued to develop her theme that government must benefit the people for the social compact to be legitimate. Thus, her argument with Hobbes in *Loose Remarks* encapsulated the central thesis of her historical project in the multivolume *History of England*: the prerogative of an absolute monarch is incompatible with the practice of good government.

In the remainder of the pamphlet, Macaulay's task was to discuss how to create the best polity. With these principles in mind, it is no surprise that she targeted Hobbes's political philosophy for his "praise of monarchy" and sought to answer his argument that monarchy is the best form of government.[45] Once again, her response specifically denied the legitimacy of patriarchal rule. In chapter 10 of *De Cive*, entitled "Comparison of the Disadvantages of Each of the Three Kinds of Commonwealth," Hobbes argued that the support of monarchy could be reduced to four fundamental premises. Macaulay paraphrased this section in *Loose Remarks:* "First, that the whole universe is governed by one God: secondly, that the ancients preferred the monarchical state beyond all others: thirdly, that the paternal government instituted by God himself, was monarchical: and, lastly, that other governments were compacted by men on the ruins of monarchy."[46] Hobbes dismissed the four premises in short order in the 1647 edition of *De Cive*, choosing, in his words, to "ignore" these arguments, "which present Monarchy to us as the preferred form, because they work not by reason but by example and testimony."[47] In *Loose Remarks*, however, Macaulay incorrectly assumed that Hobbes had based his own argument for monarchical government on exactly these premises. Her misreading was the result of an error in the 1651 unauthorized Royston edition of the text, which she used as her primary source.[48] Thus, as she systematically rejected each of these claims, her misdirected remarks amounted to a powerful refutation of the central tenets of a patriarchal political thought that she wrongly attributed to Hobbes.

In the quotation that serves as the epigraph to this chapter, Macaulay claimed that God alone has the right to govern what he has created, and that the Divine being did not transfer this right to any man: "That the universe is governed by one God we will not dispute; and will also add, that God has an undoubted right to govern what he has himself created, and that it is beneficial to the creature to be governed by the Father in all things; but that this should be an argument for a man to govern what he has not created, and with whom a nation can have no such paternal connexion, is a paradox which Mr. Hobbes has left unsolved."[49] Throughout *Loose Remarks*, she juxtaposed the image of a loving heavenly father who gave life to mankind with that of a man-made sovereign who threatens us with death. She objected to the impiety of a monarch appropriating the illegitimate title of father of his people for the same reason that she opposed equating God and man later in the pamphlet.

Macaulay used her extensive knowledge of ancient history to dispute the second claim—that monarchy was the best political regime. She retorted, "This assertion [is] contradicted by the only civilized societies in ancient history, namely the Greeks, from whom alone we can learn ancient prudence. They disdained this government, and called all pretenders to it tyrants and usurpers."[50] Hobbes had prefaced *De Cive* by quoting a popular saying among the Romans attributed to Cato the Censor: "Kings should be classed as predatory animals." He then pointedly asked, "What kind of animal were the Roman People?"[51] Ancient history proved to him that monarchy was the best form of government, because man can obey only one master and a hereditary monarch stood the greatest chance of maintaining order among self-interested men. Hobbes would later warn in *Behemoth* that neoclassicism had led to false notions of liberty among his countrymen and fanned the flames of the Civil War.[52] This dangerous perspective on freedom set the stage for Macaulay's Whig history of seventeenth-century English politics, and it provides a poignant segue to the third premise about paternal government. Macaulay contended, "The third argument, that the paternal government instituted by God was monarchical, is an assertion which is contradicted by many examples in the only history through which we know of this institution. The power Adam had over his children is not mentioned as of the monarchical kind. We find him no where exercising this power or claiming it as his due; and yet there could not have been a more equitable occasion for exercising it, than the perfidious murder of Abel presented."[53]

The absolutist monarchical regimes of James I and his son Charles I were based on the divine right of kings to rule as fathers of their country. In claiming the title of *pater patria*, these sovereigns were usurping the authority of God.[54] Here we directly confront what Macaulay took to be the paradox of paternal authority in Hobbesian politics: it is easy for an absolute monarch to destroy what he did not create. The pages of her *History of England* are a tragic chronicle of the torture and death of Englishmen at the behest of Stuart monarchs and their courtiers. James I may have fancied himself the "father" of his people, but his use of royal prerogative to dissolve parliaments demonstrated that he did not love his "children" enough to secure their property or their lives. His son and successor, Charles I, raised the standard of Civil War when Parliament refused to obey him as its sovereign lord. Macaulay noted in *Loose Remarks*, "But, if Mr. Hobbes could prove that paternal power instituted by God was monarchical, he cannot from this conclude that the monarchical government is preferable to all others, without falling into his usual absurdities, viz. that a man ought to have a right of governing creatures whom he has not generated, because God has given him the right of governing creatures whom he has generated."[55] For Macaulay, paternal power only extended to one's offspring, and in her sketch of a government for the island of Corsica, she further limited the extent of paternal power over adult children to a strictly advisory role.

The fourth and final argument in support of monarchy is that all other forms of government rise from the ruins of monarchical regimes: "If absolute monarchies were instituted in the earliest times, before the invention of mankind was improved by experience, those other governments built on its ruins, which have both experience and invention for their founders, should be infinitely more excellent from these superior advantages."[56] Macaulay, rather than arguing from prescription that the origins of institutions are indicative of their ends, was on the side of change as a champion of human reason and a devout believer in a providential God. She reiterated again and again in her writing a belief in the right of enlightened people to rule, culminating in a discussion of the millennial significance of the French Revolution.

In a version of this chapter published earlier, I argued that the significance of Macaulay's commentary on *De Cive* was to be found in her opposition to patriarchalism and monarchical government, which, given her reliance on the unauthorized edition, could only "loosely" be related to Hobbesian political theory.[57] Yet, when *Loose Remarks* is placed within the larger context of her historical survey and later writing, it becomes the first salvo in a sustained attack on Hobbes's arguments justifying Stuart absolutism and Cromwell's Protectorate. It is Cromwell whom she casts as the usurper of Parliament's authority and the people's legitimate claims for constitutional reform. And it is Cromwell whom she suggests popularized Hobbes's *Leviathan* while threatening her favorite James Harrington with prosecution for the publication of *Oceana* (1656), a text he indeed tried to suppress. She notes in volume 5 of the *History of England* that the Lord Protector favored Hobbes's *Leviathan* and even offered its author a secretarial position. A decade later, in the preface to the *Treatise on the Immutability of Moral Truth* (1783), Macaulay lashes out at Hobbes as one of a "tribe of misanthrophical writers" whose arguments about the "incurable depravity of man" had done lasting harm by popularizing a hateful doctrine of the "irreclaimable principle of vice in man" among the nation.[58]

Thomas Hobbes wrote *De Cive* during the English Civil War, an era marked by parliamentary challenge to the authority of the Stuart monarchy, which signified the historical transformation of political justification of the right to rule from paternal right to govern one's children to a contractual right to govern consenting adults. The vocabulary changed from philosophical arguments about paternal authority to political analysis of self-interest and the constitutional limits on monarchical power. For Hobbes, the transfer of power from a sovereign invested with a divine right to rule to a man raised to sovereignty by the consent of the people had the potential to create new political problems. He argued that men become discontented with monarchical regimes as they come to envy the man who is king: "There are those who object to a Government of *one* man precisely because it is by one man; as if it were unfair, among so many, that any *one* man should be so preeminent in power that he can determine the fate of all the rest at his own discretion. Evidently, they would like, if they could, to sneak away from the government of the *one* God."[59] This same envious disposition found in human nature also undermines regimes governed by a few men. Differences among men, while the subject of envy, could not be for Hobbes the source of discontent with their king, because in forming the social compact they agreed to raise him above themselves as sovereign. Macaulay reasoned, "Because, says Mr. Hobbes, we have shewn that the state of equality is a state of war, and that therefore inequality was introduced by a general consent; this inequality, whereby he, whom we have voluntarily given more to, enjoys more, is no longer to be accounted an unreasonable thing." Then she lashed out, "By this dogmatic assertion, that the state of equality is the state of war, it is plain that the poor philosopher is entirely ignorant of the following truth, that political equality, and the laws of good government, are so far from incompatible, that one never can exist to perfection without the other."[60]

Ultimately, what was at issue was Hobbes's depiction of selfish human nature. Just as Macaulay began *Loose Remarks* by criticizing his assertion that such a disposition in man makes him unfit for society, she concluded the pamphlet by challenging his assertion that some men might not willingly submit to a superior being, even God himself. She found this argument to be the epitome of absurdity:

> But, as if Mr. Hobbes intended to shew, that there was no absurdity, however extreme, that he could not fall into, he farther observes, that sure those men who think it an unreasonable thing, that one man should so far excel in power, as to be able to dispose of all the rest, if they could, would withdraw their allegiance from God. As there are few men, but the ingenious author of this observation, would be absurd and wicked enough to put such an equality between God and man, I think it no farther necessary to answer this blasphemy than the order of controversial argument requires.[61]

Macaulay believed that the basis of Hobbesian politics was his atheism. Referring to his political theory in her reply to Burke's *Reflections on the*

Revolution in France twenty years later, she again dismissed the ideas of *De Cive*'s author as those of a "fanatic atheist."[62] In *Loose Remarks*, she summarized the mistaken relationship of the deity to human creation, with references full of meaning for the analysis of paternal authority. She repeated for the third time—within three pages—Hobbes's assertion that some men would challenge the authority of God over their lives:

> Because men will not submit to be absolutely at the mercy of a weak brother, these men, would if they could, withdraw their allegiance from God. What is this but putting the creature upon an equality with the Creator? If not, where lies the comparison?
>
> For the same men, who would not be in the power of a creature, as weak, and perhaps weaker, than themselves, might bless the fate which only subjected them to the merciful, unerring jurisdiction of God.[63]

Returning to Hobbes's argument that envy undermines the rule of one man "in possession of what all desire," Macaulay retorted, "Is it not a very unreasonable thing, that one man, without pretension to superior virtue, should be alone in possession of what all men desire? and that every other individual in the whole nation, however fruitful that nation is of worthy eminent men, should be thus deprived of their share in government? Which must be esteemed the most consummate reward of virtue, if the possession of it is what all men desire."[64] Absolute monarchs by definition do not share the powers of government with their subjects. Of course, Hobbes claimed that personal security, not a personal share in government, is the possession that all men desire. Such a share was, however, what Macaulay desired most, for without political equality there can be no reward for virtue. The vices of absolutist regimes demonstrate that the exclusive privileges of monarchy do not lend themselves to good government.

The remainder of *Loose Remarks* consists of a cost-benefit analysis of monarchy and democracy. The sovereign in any form of regime requires money for the public ministries and the military. In a monarchy, the sovereign also needs financial resources to maintain the royal household. Thus, Hobbes wrote that a king may "exact monies at his pleasure to enrich his *children, relatives, favourites,* and even *flatterers.*" He admitted "that this is a kind of disadvantage, but it is the type of disadvantage found in every kind of commonwealth, and is more tolerable in a *Monarchy* than a *Democracy*. For if a *Monarch* does choose to enrich them, there are not many of them, because they depend on one man."[65] For Hobbes, monarchy was a more cost-effective form of government because the financial burdens associated with one-man rule are necessarily cheaper than those generated by a democracy consisting of numerous demagogues, each with many men to satisfy.

If the assumptions that Hobbes had made about paternal authority seemed absurd, his arguments about the financial restraint of monarchical rule appeared ridiculous. Macaulay had recorded the appetites of kings and courtiers throughout the *History of England*. Its pages offered an account of how James I enriched George Villiers, later the Duke of Buckingham, and of the wealth that his son, Charles I, afforded to Thomas Wentworth, the ill-fated Duke of Strafford. She knowingly remarked that "the common pomp of a court is a heavy burthen to society; and a man who has but few kindred and favorites, may lavish on them few the spoils of a whole nation." For Macaulay, the absolutist practice of impoverishing the people to enrich the court transcended time and place: "That this, in more or less degrees, has been the constant practice of every absolute monarch, the present situation of the greater number of inhabitants of France, Spain, and all other countries where this detestable government has taken place, fully evinces." Her historical research provided ample evidence "that the lust of one man is sufficient to dissipate all the riches that the industry and frugality of a whole nation can collect."[66]

In *De Cive*, however, Hobbes argued that "in a democracy where there are many to gratify and always new ones coming along, it cannot be done without exploiting the citizens."[67] Macaulay retorted that in democratic regimes, virtuous men had been awarded "honours of little costs" such as the Roman laurel wreath or the memorial statue "to perpetuate the memory of their worthiness." She added, "Few, if any, are the instances which Mr. Hobbes could have produced, where democracies ever impoverished the commonwealth, to enrich their favorites, however worthy they esteem them." This distinction between deserved merit and undeserved reward was a fundamental difference between democracy and monarchy for Macaulay: "If by chance any unworthy persons were promoted to high offices, they were never continued long in them; and though monarchs may do otherwise, it is almost always their practice to employ the most unworthy men they can find; and, indeed, the designs of a general assembly and an individual being commonly very different, the same sort of persons cannot be proper to execute both."[68] The choice of officers is indicative of the regime itself, with democrats promoting stewards of the public purse and monarchs designating deputies to prey on the people.

For Thomas Hobbes, it is rational for men to submit to the sovereign because he has the power to save lives. Consent to the social compact is given in exchange for personal protection. Yet Macaulay read his defense of absolutism as a perversion of power—the sovereign we created now threatens to use his power to destroy us. Subjects have every right to fear for their lives under such mismanaged government. Hobbes wrote that a man must live in "constant fear of death . . . when he reflects that the holder of sovereign power may not only set any penalty he pleases for any offense he wishes, but may also, from anger and greed, put innocent citizens to death who have done nothing against the laws."[69] For him, this is a danger of all commonwealths, one that is indicative of a problem with an individual ruler, not a specific type of regime. Macaulay responded that she did not understand this "absurd paradoxical distinction that a tyrant's having it in his power to slaughter his innocent subjects, is the fault of the ruler, not the government." She declared, "Though a ruler be malicious or sensual enough to desire the slaughter of innocent people for the gratification of his vices, yet, if the nature of the government does not allow him that power, his inclinations alone will not give it to him; therefore his capability of committing these injuries must proceed from the vicious nature of the government, and the sufferings of innocent subjects from the fault of the ruler is a consequence of that viciousness."[70] At least in the natural world a beast only kills out of hunger. Why leave behind the state of nature to be killed by the man-made sovereign?

In the final pages of *Loose Remarks*, Macaulay questioned what Hobbes could have intended by his problematic defense of royal government: "One would think, by our author's following arguments, that he had thrown off his usual gravity, and intended to ridicule the subject of his declared veneration." Taking Hobbes's argument that a king will only punish those who have something he desires, she asked, "Could the most inveterate enemy to absolute monarchy urge stronger arguments against it, than this man has unwittingly done?"[71] In his attempts to make men "love kingly power," Hobbes revealed a simple truth. Macaulay concluded, "This is Mr. Hobbes's description of a regal government, which he has made more intolerable than his state of nature, viz. every man at war with every man; for in this state, strength, prudence, and fortitude, may support one; flight and obscurity is the last resource; but Mr. Hobbes cannot prove, that even flight and obscurity will save a whole society from the evils of his regal government."[72]

Macaulay closed her pamphlet with a "short sketch of democratical government" addressed to the Corsican rebel Signior Paoli, who was in London to drum up support for the cause of Corsican liberty. She outlined a constitutional framework for maintaining the civic virtue of a republic through frequent rotation of office and the establishment of an agrarian law for the dispersion of landed property, much like Harrington's *Oceana*. Macaulay called for yearly elections and strict term limits to disperse political power widely. Senators were to be elected by the popular assembly for three-year terms in annual elections, so that the entire body would rotate every three years. Members of the senate could not be reelected until they had been out of office for another three years. Military leaders and civil magistrates would be appointed from among the senators with the same limitations on terms in office. All who shared in government would be accountable to the people.

Published with *Loose Remarks* is a letter from an unnamed American colonist who took Macaulay to task for allowing military men to have a place in her senate. Macaulay responded that measures for rotating office would restrain returning soldiers from exercising undue power, and she offered an intriguing comment on the appropriate role of senators in governing a just republic: "I should not have suffered generals, admirals, and such dangerous officers, to have a vote in the senate of my republic, if I had not thought I had sufficiently guarded against the selfish evils of such an assembly, or individuals of such an assembly, by only allowing them (like the fathers of adults, the society being of age to judge for themselves) the privilege of giving their advice."[73] Like Locke, Macaulay limited fathers to an advisory role after a child has reached the age of reason. Unlike the author of the *Two Treatises on Government*, however, she referred to grown children in gender-neutral terms, as adults rather than sons. This opened up new possibilities for imagining who would participate in the ideal republic. The intellectual equality of the sexes was a fundamental premise of all Macaulay's political writing. Here, as in other places, she subtly changed the political vocabulary in ways that further undermined patriarchal limitations on women's civic participation and went so far as to formulate a plan to secure women's property rights in an egalitarian republic. Given her concern that hereditary aristocracy was antithetical to republican government, Macaulay did not allow females to inherit land in her Corsican model. Instead she required that widows be provided an annuity upon the death of their husbands and that fathers settle income on their daughters to support their education rather than provide a dower payment to a spouse. Her reforms would empower future generations of republican women.

Just in case Macaulay's American correspondent missed the point, she reiterated her antipatriarchal position: "The senate I have placed in the character of fathers of the people, and invested them with the only rational authority which belongs to the father of an adult, the privilege of advising, but not that of coercing their advice."[74] What is particularly telling given her concerns about Hobbes's absolute sovereign is that there is no executive branch within her model republic. She argued against empowering any man to govern the republic except in times of extreme crisis, and even this authority she would limit to a single term of thirty days. There would be no Charles I or Oliver Cromwell. Her anxiety about the potential for founding fathers to abuse their power by contracting their children into servitude explains the extraordinary limits she placed upon all political leaders. In *Observations on the Reflections of the Right Honorable Edmund Burke,* she would condemn the paternalism of Hobbes's founding generation, who would bind posterity to the Leviathan: "*For he supposes an original right in the people to choose their governors:* but, in exerting this right, the citizen and his posterity for ever lose their native privileges, and become bound through a series of generations to the service of a master's will."[75] For Macaulay, this onetime contractual negotiation gave unacceptable and illegitimate authority to the founding fathers to settle all political questions in perpetuity, leaving their descendants no means to justly seek political reform. Only a bad father would consent to make a perpetual sacrifice of his child's natural equality and freedom for the dubious and dangerous protections of the Hobbesian sovereign.

The Lessons of *Loose Remarks*

Hobbesian patriarchalism allows for patriarchs in the state of nature, yet it does not negate the natural equality of all men. Macaulay agreed with Hobbes that all men are born equal and free. She also claimed that the relationship between parents and children is not founded in the generative power of adults but rather on the consent of children to the guardianship of their elders. However, she disputed his notion that a child owes allegiance to a parent simply because the adult did not leave it to die. Macaulay contended that parents do not have the right to make decisions regarding the life or death of their child, since the infant is a creature of divine origin. Throughout the pamphlet, she used the argument that we cannot destroy what we did not create to limit the rights of parents and to dispute the power of absolutist monarchs. If the mother or father of a child does not have the right to destroy it, neither does the reputed "father of a country" have the right to destroy his subjects. For Macaulay, a child consents to its parent's guardianship in response to the "tender affections" the parent has shown the child. These important differences between Hobbes's and Macaulay's accounts of the relationships of parents and children have great significance for their respective arguments concerning the legitimacy of the social contract. Macaulay argued that it is only rational to transfer our rights if we receive a greater benefit in return. A child owes obedience to the parent only to the extent that he or she has received benefits—a hateful parent is owed nothing. The same argument applies to what she termed the "irrationality" of loyalty to an absolute monarch. The *History of England from the Accession of James I to That of the Brunswick Line* depicts how kings exercising absolute authority savaged rather than secured the lives and liberty of their people. It is just as absurd, argued Macaulay, for a man to consent to be ruled by a tyrant as it is for a son or daughter to remain obedient to a parent who had abused them in childhood.

Hobbes based the social contract on a calculus of force. Will we live longer if we consent to live under another's dominion? Macaulay based the social contract on a calculation of care. Will we live better if we consent to live with one another in a society where no one is dominated by another? Her formula requires a rational choice analysis of benefits for a legitimate contract. We must decide that the terms of the contract are beneficial to us for the contract to be valid. Macaulay's analysis suggests that for the contract to be just, it must validate us as political subjects. It is irrational for us to give up our natural rights without securing greater civil rights. Macaulay's argument for children takes on an even greater analytical power when applied to women. If a reasonable people cannot enter a social contract that voids their natural rights, how could a rational woman consent to a marriage contract that denies her a civil existence?

For Hobbes, the act of transferring our natural rights to the man-made Leviathan transforms our being, as we become one with the body politic represented by the sovereign. We can have no separate identity from our sovereign because we continue to exist only by virtue of his authority. A similar civic transformation is accomplished through consent to the marriage contract. Hobbesian equity is such that a man is subject to the monarch no less than a wife is subject to her husband . . . except that a woman who consents to the marriage contract is subject to both husband and king. Why should women, equal in the state of nature, become doubly subjugated in civil society? Hobbes does not explain the need for a separate compact between the sexes. As we have seen, Macaulay questioned the terms of the Hobbesian social contract by ridiculing the promise of protection from the sovereign. What are the additional risks faced by women upon entering the social contract that require the further security of a marriage contract to protect them from the brutality of civil man?

I believe we can find further clues to Macaulay's understanding of women's status in the social contract in her most explicitly proto-feminist tract, *Letters on Education with Observations on Religious and Metaphysical Subjects* (1790). In this didactic work, Macaulay developed a "primal scene" that anticipated Carole Pateman's arguments about the subjection of women to the social contract. In the midst of a discussion of the sexual politics of Jean-Jacques Rousseau's *Emile; or, On Education* (1762), Macaulay remarked that differences in corporeal strength are the real basis of sexual inequality: "But whatever might be the wise purpose intended by Providence in such a disposition of things, certain it is, that some degree of inferiority, in point of corporeal strength, seems always to have existed between the two sexes; and this advantage, in the barbarous ages of mankind, was abused to such a degree, as to destroy all the natural rights of the female species, and reduce them to a state of abject slavery."[76] In this rendition of the battle of the sexes, Macaulay relied on brute force to explain the subjection of women to men in the war of all against all in the state of nature. Thus, as Pateman later observed, "mother-right is overturned and the state of nature becomes filled with patriarchal 'families.' All the women in the natural condition are forcibly incorporated (which for Hobbes, is to say contract themselves) into 'families' and become the permanent servants of male masters."[77] Macaulay's vision of women's subjugation in the state of nature and their subject position as "slaves" in the social contract predated by almost two hundred years Pateman's observations on the sexual contract.

Curiously, Macaulay overlooks the fact that Hobbes explicitly disqualified brute force as the basis of paternal authority in chapter 9 of *De Cive*, explaining that fathers rule households not because man conquered woman in the state of nature, but because men as a group constituted the original commonwealth. It is the contractual nature of the social compact among men and not physical force that is the foundation of paternal government in the state. What is unusual about Hobbesian reasoning is that he does not endorse such a division of society as best or exclusive. He reminds us that the Amazons choose to live separately from men and that the sexes can engage in intimacy without the sanctity of marriage and remain unattached even with the subsequent birth of a child; and he further notes that a sovereign queen is not governed by her consort, and the children born of her body are hers alone. Macaulay ignores these unconventional examples, which she might have used to further contest the traditional patriarchal relationship between men and women in the commonwealth. It is paradoxical indeed that she is the one who takes for granted a paternal social contract that denies women's subjectivity and reduces them to little more than domestic servants in the master's household.

Feminist readers can learn much from Catharine Macaulay's *Loose Remarks* about Thomas Hobbes's attempts to decouple paternal authority from patriarchy in *De Cive*. Her pamphlet reveals an alternative tale about the origins of the commonwealth set against the historical backdrop of seventeenth-century England. For Macaulay, patriarchal politics is the foundation of monarchical absolutism, and she reasoned that once you start to question the fundamental assumptions of patriarchy the edifice of absolute sovereignty begins to collapse. Her efforts to qualify parental authority and her criticism of the divine right of kings as an illegitimate form of father-rule underscored her republican principles. Macaulay takes a dim view of Hobbes's notion of a selfish human nature because it justifies his defense of monarchical politics. Closer attention to *De Cive*, however, makes us wonder whether her partisanship prevents her from seeing different subjective possibilities for her sex. Macaulay's self-described "loose" reading on "certain positions" misses critical commentary on gender equality and the limitations of brute force. In her pamphlet she fails to recognize the potentially emancipatory moments for women that Hobbes tantalizingly hinted at but never fully developed in *De Cive*. Their lopsided debate on the troubled relationship between parent and child exposes the philosophical tensions between authority and consent, with significant implications for men and women within the social contract, and it presages several modern efforts to fully explain the "sexual contract." Revisiting Hobbes's ideas through Macaulay's flawed but valuable interpretative lens provides a remarkably fresh perspective on the disputed role of paternal authority in his political philosophy.

Notes

1. Susan Moller Okin, *Women in Western Political Theory* (Princeton, N.J.: Princeton University Press, 1979); Carol Pateman, *The Sexual Contract* (Stanford: Stanford University Press, 1988); Nancy Hirschmann, *Rethinking Obligation: A Feminist Method for Political Theory* (Ithaca, N.Y.: Cornell University Press, 1992); *Gender, Class, and Freedom in Modern Political Theory* (Princeton, N.J.: Princeton University Press, 2008).

2. Catharine Macaulay, *Loose Remarks on Certain Positions Found in Mr. Hobbes' "Philosophical Rudiments of Government and Society" with a Short Sketch of a Democratical Form of Government in a Letter to Signior Paoli* (London: W. Johnson, in Ludgate-Street, 1769).

3. See Bridget Hill, *The Republican Virago: The Life and Times of Catharine Macaulay, Historian* (Oxford: Clarendon Press, 1992); Kate Davies, *Catharine Macaulay and Mercy Otis Warren: The Revolutionary Atlantic and the Politics of Gender* (Oxford: Oxford University Press, 2005); Barbara Brandon Schnorrenberg, "The Brood Hen of Faction: Mrs. Macaulay and Radical Politics, 1765–1775," *Albion* 11, no. 1 (1979): 33–45; Susan Staves, "The Liberty of a She-Subject of England: Rights Rhetoric and the Female Thucydides," *Cardoza Studies in Law and Literature* 1, no. 2 (1989): 161–83; Barbara Brandon Schnorrenberg, "An Opportunity Missed: Catharine Macaulay on the Revolution of 1688," *Studies in Eighteenth-Century Culture* 20 (1990): 231–40; Wendy Gunther-Canada, "The Politics of Sense and Sensibility: Catharine Macaulay and Mary Wollstonecraft on Edmund Burke's *Reflections on the Revolution in France*," in *Women Writers and the Early Modern British Political Tradition*, ed. Hilda L. Smith (Cambridge: Cambridge University Press 1998), 126–47; J. G. A. Pocock, "Catharine Macaulay: Patriot Historian," in Smith, *Women Writers and the Early Modern British Political Tradition*, 243–58; Phillip Hicks, "Catharine Macaulay's Civil War: Gender, History, and Republicanism in Georgian Britain," *Journal of British Studies* 41 (April 2002): 170–98.

4. Gordon J. Schochet, *The Authoritarian Family and Political Attitudes in Seventeenth-Century England: Patriarchalism in Political Thought* (New Brunswick: Transaction Books, 1988), 2.

5. Ibid., 193.

6. Ibid., 226.

7. "What has gone largely unnoticed, however, is the relationship of Hobbes's observations on the nature of familial power to the traditional patriarchal political theory. In this instance, too, important new ground was broken." Ibid., 241.

8. Ibid., 229.

9. Ibid., 231.

10. Pateman, *Sexual Contract*, 54.

11. The very title of Macaulay's 1769 pamphlet indicates that she was working from an early English translation of *De Cive*. Richard Tuck tells us that a volume entitled *Philosphicall Rudiments of Government and Society* was published in London by Richard Royston in 1651. Tuck and Michael Silverthorne, who issued a new translation from the Latin, argue in their introduction that the 1651 English translation was unauthorized by Hobbes. Thomas Hobbes, *On the Citizen [De Cive]*, ed. and trans. Richard Tuck and Michael Silverthorne (Cambridge: Cambridge University Press, 1998), xxxiv–xxxvii. Subsequent citations to *De Cive* are from this edition.

12. Macaulay, *Loose Remarks*, 1.
13. Ibid., 2.
14. Ibid.
15. Ibid., 3.
16. Ibid.
17. Schochet, *Authoritarian Family*, 227.
18. Macaulay, *Loose Remarks*, 4.
19. "The liberty that was taken in the year 1688, by a convention of Lords and Commons, to depose King James the reigning sovereign from the throne, and to vest the sovereignty of the realm in his daughter Mary, and her husband the prince of Orange . . . are indeed facts, which might warrant a plain thinking man in the opinion, that the present reigning family owe their succession to the choice or assent of the people." Catharine Macaulay, *Observations on the Reflections of the Right Honorable Edmund Burke on the Revolution in France* (London: C. Dilly, 1790), 9–10.
20. Macaulay, *Loose Remarks*, 4.
21. "The greatest power that men can transfer to man we call ABSOLUTE power. For anyone who has subjected his will to the will of the commonwealth on the terms that it may *do with impunity* whatever it chooses—*make laws, judge disputes, inflict penalties*, and make use of everyone's *strength and wealth* at its own discretion—and may do all this by right, has surely given him the greatest power that he could give." Hobbes, *De Cive* 6.12. References are to chapter and section number.
22. Macaulay, *Loose Remarks*, 5.
23. Ibid.
24. Ibid.
25. Catherine Macaulay, *Letters on Education with Observations on Religious and Metaphysical Subjects* (1790; repr., Oxford: Woodstock Books, 1994), 210.
26. Macaulay, *Loose Remarks*, 6.
27. Ibid., 7.
28. Schochet, *Authoritarian Family*, 231.
29. "Hobbes did not even try to construct an argument that women consent to the family. To do so would violate the logic of his argument, so he merely passes over the issue, knowing that none of his contemporaries—and probably not posterity either—would note the contradiction." Hirschmann, *Rethinking Obligation*, 43–44.
30. In her later study, Hirschmann provides a compelling and nuanced treatment of women's power derived from motherhood in the state of nature. Positing that a mother in confederation with her daughter or son could threaten the lives of the various men who could be their father, she theorizes a new narrative of why women must enter the social contract as wives, counter to Pateman's argument about the subjection of women by male conquest: "That women have more natural liberty than men, in the power of reproduction and the power of confederacy it affords them, makes them that much a greater threat to civil order." To ensure the order and peace that are the true political ends of the Leviathan, women, like men, must consent to be subject to the sword. The patriarchal family becomes the model of the proper relationship of the subject to the sovereign: "Within the family, children and servants—including wives—are subjected and bound to their master without qualification. And it is this aspect of the family that provides the strongest model for civil society." Hirschmann, *Gender, Class, and Freedom*, 77, 75.
31. Hobbes, *De Cive* 9.6.
32. Macaulay, *Loose Remarks*, 7.
33. Ibid., 7.
34. Ibid., 8.
35. Hobbes, *De Cive* 9.4.
36. Macaulay, *Loose Remarks*, 8. Locke argued, "For children being by the course of Nature, born weak, and unable to provide for themselves, they have by appointment of God himself, who hath

thus ordered the course of nature, a Right to be nourish'd and maintained by their Parents, nay a right not only to a bare Subsistence, but to the conveniences and comforts of Life, as far as the conditions of their Parents can afford it." John Locke, *First Treatise*, in *Two Treatises of Government*, ed. Peter Laslett (Cambridge: Cambridge University Press, 1988), 207.

37. Macaulay, *Loose Remarks*, 8. According to Pateman, "Hobbes did not merely leave no room for nurture or argue that the family was conventional, a political rather than a natural social form. For Hobbes a 'family' was solely composed of a master and servants of various kinds and had its origins in conquest." Carole Pateman, " 'God Hath Ordained to Man a Helper': Hobbes, Patriarchy, and Conjugal Right," in *Feminist Interpretations and Political Theory*, ed. Mary Lyndon Shanley and Carole Pateman (University Park: Pennsylvania State University Press, 1991), 56.

38. Macaulay, *Loose Remarks*, 8.
39. Ibid.
40. Ibid.
41. Ibid.
42. Ibid., 9.
43. Catharine Macaulay, *History of England from the Accession of James I to That of the Brunswick Line*, vol. 2 (London: J. Nourse, 1766), 440.
44. Macaulay, *Loose Remarks*, 9.
45. Ibid.
46. Ibid.
47. Hobbes, *De Cive* 10.3.
48. The section should read as follows: "*Monarchy* is the best of the listed kinds of commonwealth, *Democracy*, *Aristocracy*, and *Monarchy*. This is to be shown by a comparison of their advantages and disadvantages in detail. We will therefore ignore certain arguments which present *Monarchy* to us as the preferred form, because they work not by reason but by example and testimony: namely, that the *universe* is governed by *one God*; that the *Ancients* preferred the *Monarchical* form to the others, ascribing the government of the Gods to Jupiter alone; that in the early stages of affairs and of nations the decisions of princes were the law; that the *Paternal* government instituted by God at the Creation was *Monarchical*; that the other regimes have been cobbled together by human artifice from the rubble of *Monarchy* after it had been destroyed by sedition; and that the people of God lived under Kings" (Hobbes, *De Cive* 10.3). The Royston edition omits the critical sentence indicating Hobbes's dismissal of these arguments. See Thomas Hobbes, *Philosophicall Rudiments Concerning Government and Society*, trans. anon. (London: J. G. for R. Royston at Angel in Ivie-Lane, 1651), available at http://etext.lib.virginia.edu/toc/modeng/public/HobDeci.html (accessed March 22, 2004).
49. Macaulay, *Loose Remarks*, 9–10.
50. Ibid., 10.
51. Hobbes, *De Cive*, preface.
52. Thomas Hobbes, *Behemoth, or The Long Parliament*, ed. Ferdinand Tönnies (Chicago: University of Chicago Press, 1990).
53. Macaulay, *Loose Remarks*, 10.
54. In a 1628 speech delivered to the House of Lords on behalf of Charles I, the attorney general stated, "It is a maxim of our law that the King can do no wrong. . . . The reason is, as the King is supreme governor of his people, so he is *pater patria*, therefore he cannot want the affection of a father towards his children." Catharine Macaulay, *History of England from the Accession of James I to That of the Brunswick Line*, 3rd ed., vol. 1 (London: E. and C. Dilly, 1770), 384–85.
55. Macaulay, *Loose Remarks*, 10.
56. Ibid., 11.
57. "Catharine Macaulay on the Paradox of Paternal Authority in Hobbesian Politics," *Hypatia* 21, no. 2 (2006): 150–73.

58. "It is too derogatory to the character of the Divine Being, to allow that such observations on the nature of man have been advanced by Hobbes and Mandeville, and other writers of this class, have any authority, in fact; therefore, diminishing such opinions as are founded in error or malignity, we shall look for the causes of the steady depravity in human manners, and the continued prevalence of moral evil . . . in circumstances altogether independent of any such fixed and irreclaimable principle of vice in man, as has been dogmatically asserted by the tribe of misanthropical writers." Catharine Macaulay, *Treatise on the Immutability of Moral Truth* (London: C. Dilly, 1783), 16.

59. Hobbes, *De Cive* 10.4.

60. Macaulay, *Loose Remarks*, 12.

61. Ibid.

62. Writing of the succession of William and Mary, Macaulay criticized the notion of a founding generation to bind all future generations to the terms of an unalterable social compact: "Should we once admit of *a power so incompatible with the conditions of humanity*, and only reserved for the dictates of *divine wisdom*, we have not, in these enlightened days, improved on the politics of the fanatic atheist Hobbes[.]" Macaulay, *Observations on the Reflections*, 13–14.

63. Macaulay, *Loose Remarks*, 13.

64. Ibid.

65. Hobbes, *De Cive* 10.6.

66. Macaulay, *Loose Remarks*, 14.

67. Hobbes, *De Cive* 10.6.

68. Macaulay, *Loose Remarks*, 15. She went on to write, "The design of a general assembly must ever be the good of the commonwealth, as conducive to their own general and particular good: this leads them to pitch on those persons, whose virtues and abilities are most capable of serving the public. Now, the designs of an individual being commonly to gratify his own lusts and private advantages, and those lusts and private advantages being ever incompatible with the good of the public, it leads him to employ those villains, whose abilities are equal only to cunning, and proper only to the destruction of the commonwealth" (15–16).

69. Hobbes, *De Cive* 10.7.

70. Macaulay, *Loose Remarks*, 16–17.

71. Ibid., 18.

72. Ibid., 20.

73. Ibid., 33.

74. Ibid., 34.

75. Macaulay, *Observations on the Reflections*, 14.

76. Macaulay, *Letters on Education*, 206.

77. Gordon J. Schochet, "Intending (Political) Obligation: Hobbes and the Voluntary Basis of Society," in *Thomas Hobbes and Political Theory*, ed. Mary G. Dietz (Lawrence: University Press of Kansas, 1990), 65.

Part Four

Hobbes in the Twenty-First Century, or What Has Hobbes Done for You Lately?

10

Thomas Hobbes and the Problem of Fetal Personhood

Joanne Boucher

Introduction

Abortion has been central to feminist aspirations and campaigns to win full reproductive rights for women since the earliest days of the Second Wave of the women's movement of the 1960s in North America. Abortion offers a dramatic illustration of the feminist insight that the "personal is political," given that women require access to safe, legal, affordable (and/or state-funded) abortion to fully control their bodies and the trajectory of their lives. Moreover, the criminalization or unavailability of abortion often forces women to resort to illegal abortions, frequently resulting in medical complications or even death. Further, abortion has been overwhelmingly understood by feminists as but one component (albeit a central one) of a broad array of conditions required to ensure women deep and meaningful control of their reproductive destinies. These would include, for example, safe, readily available contraception, free access to sex education, good-quality prenatal and obstetric care, child-care options, no enforced abortion or sterilization, and freedom from discrimination, violence, and coercion.[1]

However, since the women's movement placed abortion on the political agenda, this demand has been met with unrelenting opposition from an anti-abortion movement whose objective is to criminalize all abortion. Anti-abortion activists have used all manner of tactics to achieve this goal, including demonstrations, legislative battles, lobbying, media campaigns, and even the bombings of abortion clinics and murders of abortion providers. Abortion, as a consequence, has significantly framed contemporary debates concerning reproductive rights, though far too often on the terms set by the anti-abortion movement, which depicts opponents of abortion as "pro-life" and those who support the availability of this medical procedure as "anti-life."[2]

In what follows I contend that aspects of Hobbes's political philosophy offer rich, albeit unexpected, resources for feminists as they think through this seemingly intractable debate. I suggest that Hobbes's epistemological and ontological premises offer positive promise in helping us grapple with the politics of abortion. His insights allow us to deepen arguments that bring women's right to bodily integrity and autonomy to the fore. The suggestion that Hobbes's political philosophy be utilized for feminist purposes might strike many readers as counterintuitive. After all, Hobbes's notorious authoritarian politics, which imbue the mighty Leviathan with awesome powers, would, at first blush, seem most likely to militate against the rights of citizens generally and perhaps of women in particular. Further, Hobbes's work has been carefully and critically analyzed by feminist scholars who have rightly found many aspects of it problematic as a framework from which to conceptualize women's full social and political liberty. Thus, in making the case for feminist promise embedded in Hobbes's political philosophy, I position this work as part of an emerging trend within feminism to read Hobbes as favorable to a feminist political project. Viewing Hobbes through feminist eyes, I also hope to emphasize his contemporary relevance and demonstrate that a consideration of abortion politics through the prism of Hobbes's political philosophy is but one indication of this emerging trend, which appreciates its radical potentialities.

In this chapter, I read Hobbes in conjunction with the groundbreaking arguments developed by Judith Jarvis Thomson and Eileen McDonagh to defend women's right to abortion on the basis of consent to pregnancy and a right to self-defense. I attempt to illustrate the ways in which Hobbes's work, particularly his conception of the right of nature—that is, self-preservation—neatly intersects with and may be seen as deepening these scholars' arguments in favor of abortion rights.[3]

In her seminal article "A Defense of Abortion," Judith Jarvis Thomson constructs an ethical defense of abortion rights from the vantage point of women's right to self-defense. Most notably, Thomson builds her powerful case accepting the premise of fetal personhood, which is usually the intellectual preserve of the anti-abortion movement. She offers an imaginary scenario in which an individual awakens from sleep to find that they have been plugged into the circulatory system of a world-renowned violinist in order to maintain the violinist's kidney function. Thomson draws an analogy between the moral responsibilities of the person hooked up to the violinist and that of a pregnant woman in relation to her fetus. She concludes that "you are not morally required to spend nine months in bed, sustaining the life of that violinist," and that to deny women access to abortion forces them unreasonably into the position of a Good Samaritan.[4]

Eileen McDonagh's book *Breaking the Abortion Deadlock* builds on Thomson's insights and develops the self-defense perspective on abortion rights; it similarly adopts, as she phrases it, "pro-life premises to get to pro-choice conclusions."[5] That is to say, McDonagh takes the fetus to be an unborn person possessing rights equivalent to those of a born person. McDonagh's admission of pro-life premises refocuses the abortion debate on women's bodies and their experiences of pregnancy.[6] Specifically, her case is that any woman's right "to kill a fetus is based on her primary right to privacy to be free from intrusions of her body and liberty by other private parties."[7] McDonagh forcefully carries the logic of the right of self-defense against those who might intrude upon a woman's bodily integrity and safety throughout her analysis of abortion. She argues that if the fetus is deemed a person with rights equivalent to those of a born person, it must not be allowed to intrude unreasonably upon the body of another. As she puts it, "Recasting abortion rights in terms of a woman's right to consent to what the fetus does to her body [shows] that the fundamental liberty at stake in the abortion debate is not merely women's right to choose what to do with their own bodies, but, more important, their right to consent to what another private party, the fetus, does to their bodies and their liberty when it makes them pregnant."[8]

Central to the case she makes is an account of the massive transformations to which women's bodies are subject when pregnant. For instance, "the fertilized ovum reroutes a woman's circulatory system so that her blood is available for its own needs and uses. As a result, blood plasma volume increases 40 percent, cardiac volume increases 40 percent, heart rate increases 15 percent, stroke volume increases 30 percent, peripheral resistance increases 25 percent, and diastolic blood pressure increases 15 percent." These dramatic changes are also exemplified in the growth of the pregnancy-specific placenta: "It is a new tissue structure, more complicated than a lung. . . . It grows the entire time a woman is pregnant, eventually attaining a size approximately 15 centimeters in diameter and 2 centimeters in thickness. At birth, the placenta may weigh 300 to 1200 grams."[9] Therefore, she argues, enforced pregnancy, entailed in a ban on abortion, places a woman in a position that is equivalent not so much to that of a *Good Samaritan* who selflessly allows the fetus to develop in her body for a full term despite her wishes, as posited by Thomson, as to that of a *Captive Samaritan* who allows the fetus to develop in her body for a full term under duress.

If one agrees that the fetus is a person, then its rights will be recognized as being as extensive and as restricted as those of born persons. So, McDonagh argues, "from the perspective of a woman's right to terminate a nonconsensual pregnancy, the key comparison is to the position of the state if a born person imposed such physical transformations on another born person's body. Such impositions would not be viewed as merely an inconvenience. No born person has such a right to impose such physically invasive processes on the body of another person, nor does any preborn potential person."[10] Thomson's and McDonagh's arguments are very powerful because they meet the anti-abortion movement on its own rhetorical terrain—as the claim of fetal personhood and the fetus's consequent right to life is the movement's political linchpin—and pursue so carefully the logical consequences of granting the fetus a status of personhood equivalent to that of a born individual.[11] It is my argument that Thomson and McDonagh's discursive shift to the question of individual women's right to consent to pregnancy and right to self-defense against the fetus coincides with Hobbes's premise of the right of nature, the inviolable right to self-preservation. It is on this seemingly unpromising ground that I contend we may build and sustain feminist insights.[12]

In what follows, I argue that despite the ostensibly dismal terrain of Hobbes's political absolutism, concentrating on Hobbes's materialist epistemology and his foundational political tenet of the right to self-preservation opens up a subtle but competing theoretical thread in his thought that, if unraveled and drawn out, might make it possible to read Hobbes as a potential defender of the need for protection of bodily autonomy. On this basis, a credible rationale for women's right to abortion on the grounds of self-defense (as framed by Thomson and McDonagh) may be constructed. While Hobbes is generally understood to offer subjects only the prospect of absolute obedience as the corollary of absolute sovereignty, by interrogating the concept of self-preservation and firmly allying it with Hobbes's corporealist epistemology, we may uncover a potentially mitigating counterpoint that could be exploited to feminist ends. That is to say, in Hobbes's political philosophy there is an immanent tension between the pervasive imperatives of sovereignty and the right to individual self-preservation. In my view, reading Hobbes with an eye to this inviolable right allows for the detection of currents in his thought that provide a counterpoint to the loud claims of political absolutism. Indeed, there is ample textual evidence that, for Hobbes, the health and well-being of subjects' individual physical bodies are of paramount import for the commonwealth. Furthermore, as has been noted by many feminist scholars, Hobbes begins his dissection of civil society in *Leviathan* on a radical note, as he initially grants a thoroughgoing natural equality to men and women in his state of nature. So, as I will explore in what follows, placing a concerted accent on these aspects of Hobbes's thought opens up theoretical space (though just how far this is the case is highly debatable) to destabilize the total political supremacy of the sovereign. On this basis, I contend that sufficient scope is available to accommodate women's reproductive rights and specifically the right to abortion.

"Every Part of the Universe Is Body": Hobbes's Biopolitics

According to Hobbes, "The World . . . is Corporeall, that is to say, Body; and hath the dimensions of Magnitude, namely Length, Bredth, and Depth: also every part of Body is likewise Body, and hath the like dimensions; and consequently every part of the Universe, is Body, and that which is not Body, is no part of the Universe."[13] Sensation, originating in the external motions of physical things, is the foundation of all human experience.[14] Every human feeling and action is the result of appetites and aversions, all of which originate in the body. There is little distinction between high and low appetite—from the slaking of our thirst and hunger to the will to perform grand deeds—since all flow from the same source, the body. Originally, what is good, true, right, or wrong are merely those things that satisfy or impede our desires. Human bodies, then, are the basis of what we are and are able to be in this world. The body is the great leveling "fact" that all humans confront. The basis of human equality lies in the paradoxical characteristics shared by human beings, who are at once fragile and powerful. Humans' frailty is manifest in their mortality, while humans' power is evident in their equal ability to kill one another. As Hobbes frames the issue, any person can kill another, no matter how "weak" or "strong" they are imagined to be.[15] This physicality and its consequences fundamentally link all human beings, and a main thrust of Hobbes's philosophy is to demonstrate to the reader that this is so.[16] For Hobbes, natural human equality is acknowledged as a law of nature, which must be recognized in positive law. On this score, he posits that the ninth law of nature calls for every person to "*acknowledge other for his Equall by Nature*," and the tenth ensures that no one "*require to reserve to himselfe any Right, which he is not content should be reserved to every one of the rest.*"[17] To breach the former law is to display pride and the latter, arrogance.[18] And, of course, the conquest of pride and arrogance is indispensable to Hobbes's political project. To recognize our sameness is the beginning of political wisdom. We are all equally powerful and so need one sovereign, one "King of the Proud," to serve as a bulwark against chaos.

This determinedly corporeal conception of humanity and the innate value of the individual body allows feminists to find common intellectual terrain with Hobbes's political philosophy. The possibility of flexible social relations between men and women, then, is premised on the equal powers of their bodies. As regards men and women, they are equal precisely because they find themselves in the same human bodies whose chief characteristic is immutable—mortality. Men, for Hobbes, are the same as women in the sense that they are both fully and equally human and therefore frail, mortal beings. Further, our human bodies do indeed make us frail vessels, but they simultaneously confer a power that is shared by all. That is to say, the notion that men are innately physically stronger than women has no immanent significance. Hobbes renders this timeworn explanation for women's oppression an empty abstraction.

Even if the cliché that "men are stronger than women" were true, in Hobbes's hands this matters not at all.[19] Unlike contract theorists such as Locke and Rousseau, Hobbes follows the implications of natural equality as comprising explicitly all men and all women. In the state of nature, physical differences between people are leveled, in that "nature hath made men so equall, in the faculties of body, and mind; as that though there bee found one man sometimes manifestly stronger in body, or of quicker mind then another; yet when all is reckoned together, the difference between man, and man, is not so considerable. . . . For as to the strength of body, the weakest has strength enough to kill the strongest, either by secret machination, or by confederacy with others, that are in the same danger with himselfe."[20] Moreover, as to intellectual differences, Hobbes finds "a greater equality amongst men, than that of strength. For Prudence, is but Experience: which equall time, equally bestowes on all men, in those things they equally apply themselves unto."[21]

Hobbes, in these formulations, removes commonplace sexist arguments that take women's secondary social status to be a consequence of physical and intellectual weakness. Indeed, he makes the point unambiguously in his discussion of the character and origins of parental power, stating, "Whereas some have attributed the Dominion to the Man onely, as being of the more excellent Sex; they misreckon in it. For there is not always that difference of strength, or prudence between the man and the woman, as that the right can be determined without War."[22] Hobbes does not allow that sex differences necessarily translate into sexual inequality. Moreover, he contends that in the state of nature there is no preordained family structure, maternal role, or sexual hierarchy. Human beings may construct the ways in which gender relations will be made manifest.

It is the political promise connected to this pervasive social constructiveness that has captured the imagination of many feminist scholars. Radical sexual equality, original maternal power, and familial forms that are merely conventional are remarkable features of Hobbes's state of nature. Preeminent power in the family does not naturally adhere to either sex. Nevertheless, Hobbes does posit original maternal dominion over children, stating, "If there be no Contract, the Dominion is in the Mother," and further explaining, "Where there are no Matrimoniall lawes, it cannot be known who is the Father, unlesse it be declared by the Mother: and therefore the right of Dominion over the Child dependeth on her will, and is consequently hers. Again, seeing the Infant is first in the power of the Mother, so as she may either nourish, or expose it; if she nourish it, it oweth its life to the Mother; and is therefore obliged to obey her, rather than any other; and by consequence the Dominion over it is hers."[23] However, this original dominion may shift depending on subsequent contractual arrangements. Happenstance, it seems, explains the predominance of male-ruled households, as "for the most part (but not always) the sentence is in favour of the Father; because for the most part Common-wealths have been erected by the Fathers, not by the Mothers of families."[24] For good disruptive measure, Hobbes mentions the Amazons as a case in which children are systematically governed by mothers.[25]

Given such theoretical premises, Joanne Wright reckons Hobbes to be a theorist who "effectively disrupted gender norms, opening a space in which gender relations could be dramatically—if briefly—reconceived."[26] According to Wright, Hobbes's sexual politics are at the heart of his larger political/philosophic project, which is to explicate the rational-scientific basis of state theory and political practice. She writes, "His highly contentious reconfiguration of gender should be understood as centrally important to the justification of his political theory, for it is this argument that allows him to combat the theory that all political power is derived from Adam, and that both fatherly and kingly rule are natural and God-given. . . . In the end, Hobbes posits the consensual nature of familial and political relations, and in the process presents a provocative account of original political right."[27] Thus, his positing of the equality of men and women in the state of nature "disrupts the conventional view that women are the lesser sex as dictated by nature [and] implies that the power relationship of dominance and submission between men and women is one that must be decided by battle, which . . . bears the marks of convention rather than nature."[28] And "positing maternal dominion is the final step to *rationalizing every human relationship,* making every relationship the product of artifice not nature."[29]

The groundwork for Hobbes's systematization of all human relations is laid with his individualist, rationalist ontology. Self-actualizing, calculating persons have the capacity to grasp the need for political order as Hobbes envisages it. This ontological stance has been carefully criticized by some feminist thinkers. For example, Christine Di Stefano and Diana Coole argue that Hobbes constructs a "masculine" individual to represent humanity as a whole and that his atomistic individualism may be seen as inaugurating the reign of the self-actualized, isolated, competitive, and asocial modern person. This perspective emphasizes the deleterious effects of abstract individualism on women, as it elevates the male experience to universal experience, which then becomes the basis of human subjectivity, and the possible gendered grounds of that experience are masked or suppressed.[30]

However, in contrast, Ingrid Makus locates feminist possibilities here. She argues that an ontologically consistent Hobbesian position necessarily entails a radical position *in favor* of women's full bodily autonomy and reproductive rights and provides a strong rationale for the state to aid (in ways that wholly benefit women rather than through paternalistic interventions masked as aid) in the process of child rearing.[31] Makus (while attending to the many limitations in Hobbes's work), offers the following summary evaluation:

> In Hobbes' model we find the grounds for extending to women radical rights over all stages of the reproductive process. They would be extended on the assumption that women are rational, self-interested, and without a natural predilection for caring or a natural maternal instinct. To prevent the chaos of a return to the state of nature, the state would have to provide the support and inducements for women (and men as well) to have and care for children in appropriate ways. Since women have first access to a new life and no natural predilection for caring, the need for positive inducements is amplified if women are to wield their reproductive powers to care for children and perpetuate the community.[32]

In a similar vein, Jane Jaquette defends Hobbes's contractualism on account of the fact that its initially egalitarian view of the state of nature challenges conventional views of women as irrational, excessively emotional, and consequently unfit to engage in contractual relations. She argues, "Hobbes aligns his theory of contract to a theory of individualism that is radically egalitarian, challenging all claims of 'natural' dominance. . . . The hypocrisy of actual contracts only serves to make the ideal of contract that much more compelling." This radical promise is retrievable precisely because Hobbes takes women to be rational, autonomous subjects.[33]

Our individual embodied humanity, then, renders us equal beings. It is also our most essential and precious possession, as Hobbes claims: "Of things held in propriety, those that are dearest to a man are his own life, & limbs."[34] The preservation of the body is never secure in the natural condition because it allows that "every man has a Right to every thing; even to one anothers body."[35] The social contract requires the revocation of the right to all things and bodies and so establishes personal physical safety on a sound basis. This is one of the prime attractions of and the raison d'être of the commonwealth. Consequently, Hobbes unrelentingly insists upon the inviolability of self-preservation. That is to say, the body is the terrain of the self, and other parties may not disturb it without the consent of the individual. It is as if Hobbes draws an invisible shield around each singular body through which no one (including the sovereign) may pass without the individual's consent. This perspective brings into focus a politics potentially amenable to feminist concerns for women's bodily integrity. This is certainly not to deny that Hobbes's unrelenting focus is to persuade all persons that politics must adhere to the principle of indivisible sovereignty if there are ever to be peaceful and stable commonwealths. Rather, it is to indicate the potentially fruitful fissures (for feminist purposes) that might surface from Hobbes's materialist account of human mind and body.

In this regard, for Hobbes, self-preservation is the right of nature; it is "the Liberty each man hath to use his own power, as he will for himselfe, for the preservation of his own Nature; that is to say, of his own Life; and consequently, of doing any thing, which in his own Judgement, and Reason, hee shall conceive to be the aptest means thereunto." What drives people into civil society is precisely the need to ensure their self-preservation from the harrowing consequences of the state of nature in which "every man has a Right to every thing; even to one anothers body."[36] Hence, "the motive, and end for which this renouncing and transferring of Right is introduced, is nothing else but the security of mans person, in his life, and in the means of so preserving life, as not to be weary of it."[37] Self-preservation provides both an individual and collective rationale for the introduction of the state and for sovereign power. That is, they are not ends in themselves but only the means to the fundamental end—individual self-preservation. Sovereign power is rational in that it aims to produce peace. The underlying purpose of peace is at base individual self-preservation. As Samantha Frost notes, Hobbes "rearticulates the natural impulse to self-preservation as the social or political desire for peace."[38] Moreover, while Hobbes's social contract depends on the transfer and renunciation of the original right to everything, he nonetheless insists that self-preservation is inviolable. He elaborates this principle in considerable detail, explaining,

> There be some Rights, which no man can be understood by any words, or other signes, to have abandoned, or transferred. As first a man cannot lay down the right of resisting them, that assault him by force, to take away his life; because he cannot be understood to ayme thereby, at any Good to himself. The same may be sayd of Wounds, and Chayns, and Imprisonment; both because there is not benefit consequent to such patience; as there is to the patience of suffering another to be wounded or imprisoned: as also because a man cannot tell, when he seeth men proceed against him by violence, whether they intend his death or not. And lastly the motive, and end for which this renouncing and transferring of Right is introduced, is nothing else but the security of a mans person, in his life and in the means of so preserving life, as not to be weary of it. And therefore if a man by words, or other signes, seem to despoyle himselfe of the Ende, for which those signes were intended; he is not to be understood as if he meant it, or that it was his will; but that he was ignorant of how such words and actions were to be interpreted.[39]

Consequently, Hobbes contends that "a covenant not to defend my selfe from force, by force, is always voyd." And he continues, "For (as I have shewed before) no man can transferre, or lay down his Right to save himselfe from Death, Wounds, and Imprisonment, (the avoiding whereof is the onely End of laying down any Right,) and therefore the promise of not resisting force, in no Covenant transferreth any right; nor is obliging."[40] Thus, Hobbes demonstrates that his political philosophy is keenly concerned to protect our bodies, lives, and limbs from physical harm by others in both the state of nature and civil society.

This view is also evident if we approach the question of the liberty Hobbes grants to subjects with an eye to the concept of self-preservation, whereby a physically secure body may be read as a litmus test for determining the possible parameters of legitimate human action in political society. Hobbes writes, "If wee take Liberty in the proper sense, for corporall Liberty; that is to say, freedome from chains, and prison, it were very absurd for men to clamor as they doe, for the Liberty they so manifestly enjoy."[41] Hobbes is generally and correctly understood with such statements to advance his limited and negative conception of liberty, which "lyeth . . . only in those things, which in regulating their actions, the Soveraign hath praetermitted."[42] However, it is also the case that regardless of what the sovereign legally permits, subjects never cede the right to resist incursions on their physical well-being. Certainly in regard to other subjects this is unsurprising. But the consequence of this insistence seems to be that subjects may also defend against attempts by the sovereign and its political officers to harm them.[43] That is to say, individual political resistance is one possible course of action for subjects. In this regard, Hobbes catalogues some of the political effects of the inviolability of the body when he delineates "the particulars of the true Liberty of a Subject," particularly "what are the things, which though commanded by the Soveraign, he may neverthelesse, without Injustice, refuse to do."[44] Hobbes elaborates that this encompasses the liberty to disobey the sovereign (which must extend to the sovereign's officers, who enforce the law) and to resist any punishment that entails direct physical harm as well as the denial of any of the necessities of life: "If the Soveraign command a man (though justly condemned) to kill, wound, or mayme himselfe; or not to resist those that assault him; or to abstain from the use of food, ayre, medicine, or any other thing, without which he cannot live; yet hath that man the Liberty to disobey." Hobbes summarily comments, "When therefore our refusal to obey, frustrates the End for which the Soveraignty was ordained; then there is no Liberty to refuse: otherwise there is."[45] This is a curious formulation if sovereign power is understood as an end in itself, insofar as refusal to obey any of the sovereign's orders should *by definition* be deleterious to the commonwealth. If subjects are only expected to obey the sovereign, then any refusal to do so is rebellious. However, Hobbes's statement is clearer if understood to encompass the subject's right to refuse an order from the sovereign or state official if it threatens to cause them physical harm. Indeed, Hobbes further allows that even breaking a law may be completely excused if the person acted in self-defense, commenting, "If a man by the terrour of present death, be compelled to doe a fact against the Law, he is totally Excused; because no Law can oblige a man to abandon his own preservation."[46] Furthermore, Hobbes excuses the theft of food if it is necessary for one's physical survival, as well as the theft of another's sword on similar grounds.[47] However, the lessening of culpability for a crime on the grounds of self-defense is acceptable only to the extent that one individual is involved and seeks only physical safety. Hobbes does not accept disobedience if it springs from a position of individual strength (rather than fear). An individual or groups of individuals who resist the law on the basis of their strength, their riches, or alliances can make no appeal to a claim of self-defense. According to Hobbes, their disobedience originates in arrogance. Their motive arises from an assumption of their right to challenge sovereign authority. This sense of entitlement marks such people as potential conspirators against state power. As Hobbes remarks, "For Presumption of impunity by force, is a Root, from whence springeth, at all times, and upon all temptations, a contempt of all Lawes; whereas in the later case [the individual resisting on the grounds of self-defense], the apprehension of danger, that makes a man fly, renders him more obedient for the future."[48] So, a person's singular concern to protect his or her own body is acceptable grounds for a crime or resistance to authority, but the assumption of a right to rebel against authority is a grave crime against power. Thus, Hobbes allows theoretically for the physical defense of an individual's body but does not countenance any extension of this principle beyond these bounds. The right to rebellion is foreclosed, but the protection of a singular person's corporeal being is acceptable.

To underscore this body-centrism of Hobbes's politics, the litmus test for the legitimacy of the sovereign is the guarantee of the physical safety of subjects of the commonwealth. Individual persons rightly expect physical protection from the sovereign. As Hobbes writes, "The Office of the Soveraign . . . consisteth in the end, for which he was trusted with the Soveraign Power, namely the procuration of *the safety of the people*."[49] At the moment the sovereign can no longer guarantee the protection of the people, the sovereign dies, since "the Obligation of Subjects to the Soveraign, is understood to last as long, and no longer, than the power lasteth, by which he is able to protect them."[50] Thus, Hobbes accepts both consent (the social contract) and conquest (foreign invasion or usurpation of sovereign power) as grounds for the political legitimacy of a regime. However, conquest is *not* valid if the conquered individual *or* conquered sovereign is not physically free. Conquest becomes "consent" only on condition that the subject "hath his life and corporall Libertie given him." Bodily autonomy and integrity are the mark of "consent" to conquest, as Hobbes states, "If a man be held in prison, or bonds, *or is not trusted with the libertie of his bodie;* he cannot be understood to be bound by Covenant to subjection."[51] The freedom to use one's body as one wishes, so as to avoid privation and harm, impinges here on the very existence of the commonwealth.

Moreover, arguably, the sovereign's assurance of the people's safety is not to be understood narrowly. As Hobbes indicates, "By Safety here, is not meant bare Preservation, but also all other Contentments of life, which every man hath by lawfull Industry, without danger, or hurt to the Common-wealth, shall acquire to himselfe."[52] Thus, on a generous reading of Hobbes's political objectives, we may interpret him as endorsing a vision of the felicitous life as one enjoyed as far as possible in health, physical freedom, and self-direction. That is to say, it is life lived so "as not to be weary of it." For instance, Hobbes says that we lay down our right to everything in the state of nature, but it is nonetheless necessary for us to retain something, such as the "right to governe their owne bodies; enjoy aire, water, motion, waies to go from place to place; and all things else, without which a man cannot live, or not live well."[53] The sentiment expressed here is that we aim to "live well" and that physical freedom and well-being are paramount to fulfilling this endeavor. Such a life would be filled with all of the richness that the state of nature lacks: trade, agriculture, technology, arts, letters, architecture, culture, and so on.[54]

Self-Preservation and the Right to Abortion

As regards abortion, then, granting Thomson and McDonagh's premise of the fetus as a person competing for the bodily resources of the pregnant woman, it is entirely feasible to depict the fetus as a threat to her physical well-being that she cannot control. This point may be pressed even further. There is arguably, in each and every pregnancy, no matter how distant, the threat of maternal mortality. Certainly in Hobbes's time this danger was omnipresent, as it is estimated that about one woman died in every forty childbirths.[55] Risks for contemporary women are dramatically lower—at least in the developed world. Yet it remains the case that about five hundred thousand women worldwide die each year as a result of pregnancy or childbirth. Ninety-nine percent of deaths in childbirth occur in lesser-developed countries. It has been calculated that one woman dies every seven minutes from postpartum hemorrhage, the most common cause of maternal death.[56] Thus, on Hobbes's terms, the pregnant woman, or Captive Samaritan, faces "wounds and imprisonment" in each pregnancy and the prospect, however faint, of death. Therefore, she must be able to choose whether to take this risk—to both her bodily health and life itself. That is to say, she must have the right to abortion available to ensure her physical security if she deems such a risk too great.

On this score, it is notable that while Hobbes does grant original maternal dominion to women over their born children in the state of nature, he effectively ignores the long months of gestation in which the mother's reproductive labor creates a being in her womb, and the political implications thereof. Hobbes's postpartum focus is radical insofar as it does direct our gaze at the embodiment of pregnancy and the logical conclusion that the child is initially under the mother's power in the state of nature. But, recalling McDonagh's insistence on the dramatic transformations the fetus produces in a pregnant woman's body, this focus significantly diminishes the importance of the gestational period. The physical labor entailed in any pregnancy is given less significance as Hobbes concentrates on the shared and more obviously social labor of creating contracts and relationships to determine dominion. Moreover, Hobbes's formulation mitigates the extent to which the pregnancy and the subsequent birth represent concerted acts of will on the part of the mother. Specifically, the woman makes an ongoing commitment to preserve the life of the child *in utero*. In this sense, while Hobbes has politicized the mother's power postpartum, he has concomitantly obfuscated the political implications of the gestational period. The extent to which the pregnancy is an act of volition by the pregnant woman is obscured, and so are all of the political dilemmas that accompany her decisions during pregnancy. Women make innumerable choices in very specific social and political contexts and in the face of the numerous limitations and possibilities available to them concerning reproduction. Should a woman attempt to become pregnant? Should she use contraceptive measures to avoid pregnancy? When should she announce herself to be pregnant? Should she declare the identity of the father? Should she continue a pregnancy? Such decisions obtain in every woman's term of pregnancy.

Indeed, since time out of mind, women have attempted to control their fertility with the resources available to them, and the seventeenth century was not exceptional in this regard. There is ample evidence that contraceptive as well as abortion aids and techniques were known to exist and were used by women. Exact information concerning their efficacy, and the extent to which women were aware and availed themselves of these technologies, is difficult if not impossible to ascertain. Nonetheless, countless herbal guides, midwifery manuals, apothecaries' and physicians' tracts, and books for housewives attest to widespread interest in recipes for contraceptive and abortifacient drinks, pills, teas, baths, and pessaries for rural and urban women. Most commonly presented as remedies to induce menstruation, concoctions based on the oils or juices of more than one hundred herbs and plants were available; parsley, Queen Anne's lace, mugwort, pennyroyal, savin, cyclamen, rue, and wild mint represent only a few of those cited in innumerable sources. Abortion via such abortifacient agents was thus presented as an option for women, albeit camouflaged as aids to regulate or induce the menses. The use of these herbal remedies and techniques would not necessarily have been spiritually or legally problematic for women, particularly given the long-standing belief that prior to "quickening" the fetus was not "alive." Knowledge of pregnancy, then, was the province of a woman herself. It was her testimony as to the transformations in her body that authenticated the pregnancy.[57] That is to say, "subtle alterations of moisture and motion, known only to the woman herself, announced the beginning of pregnancy."[58] Abortion only became a moral or criminal issue after "quickening," which was assumed to occur anywhere between the forty-fifth and ninetieth day of a pregnancy.[59] The moment of quickening was crucial given that "ensoulment" was thought to accompany it. The soul entering the fetus marked its entry into the human community as a moral being.[60] Thus, "if there was no quickening there could be no abortion and therefore no crime in ejecting an unwanted foetus."[61] For our purposes, early modern women's access to such techniques emphasizes the degree to which pregnancy was potentially a fluid and alterable condition and could be volitional on the part of the woman. Moreover, the ever-present threat of maternal mortality made access to contraception and abortion a matter of life and death for women. These characteristics of a woman's relationship to her fertility continue to hold true today, as each pregnancy entails countless choices for her.

Further, the existence of knowledge of contraceptive and abortive techniques overtly positions a woman as an active agent in a pregnancy. Her body nourishes the fetus and, granting the premise of fetal personhood, she is under no obligation—certainly in the state of nature, but I would also argue in civil society, even if it is patriarchal—to consider its needs over hers. If there are contraceptives or abortifacients available to her, there appears, within the logic of Hobbes's argument, to be no reason for her not to avail herself of these if she so chooses. Certainly, Hobbes would not be bound by concerns with "ensoulment," given his unyielding materialism. Thus, the woman's right to bodily integrity and self-preservation is so compelling as to supersede the rights of the "person" she carries in her womb.

In this sense, then, reading Hobbes through the prism of his preoccupation with the body and the inviolable right to individual self-defense and self-preservation leads to a pro-choice position on abortion. This is in no way to say that Hobbes's notorious political absolutism and his seeming indifference to the disastrous effects of patriarchal systems on women as such are not issues that might trouble this depiction of a Hobbesian "pro-choice" stance. He is in no sense a feminist. Indeed, as Joanne Wright reminds us, there is a strong element of opportunism in Hobbes's "feminist" gestures. She demonstrates that his foundational account of the state of nature "uses" women to make his broader case against political patriarchalism and for absolutism. I have attempted to illustrate the liberatory potential of a central tenet of his body politics, the right to self-preservation. Imagining the fetus as a person, as Thomson and McDonagh posit, allows one to envisage an unwanted pregnancy as akin to "Chayns, and Imprisonment." Hobbes's materialist epistemology and his commitment to the right to self-preservation as the essence of the social contract confront squarely the fact that the fetus is embodied in the confines of the body of another being—a woman whose physical autonomy and integrity she is charged, by virtue of her humanity, to preserve. Regardless of how the issue of abortion (and reproductive autonomy more generally) is framed in terms of the status of the fetus, whether the anxiety concerns "ensoulment" or the "right to life," Hobbes's materialist epistemology reminds us that it is inescapably a woman's body that is the site of the biopolitics of abortion. In the twenty-first century, we may be able to "see" the fetus with a vast assortment of visualizing technologies, but fundamentally this central fact of the embodied pregnancy remains. And, as I have attempted to argue, Hobbes is a (rather unexpected) ally for feminists in their endeavors to recall this linchpin of the politics of abortion.

Notes

1. Numerous organizations are dedicated to the fight for women's reproductive rights in North America and conceptualize them as requiring that interconnected technologies and services be made

available to women to fulfill this goal. See, for example, the mission statements of the Abortion Rights Coalition of Canada, the National Abortion Rights Action League, the Center for Reproductive Rights, and the Women's Global Network for Reproductive Rights. For a concise account of the dire consequences of the unavailability and/or criminalization of abortion, see Susan A. Cohen, "Facts and Consequences: Legality, Incidence, and Safety of Abortion Worldwide," *Guttmacher Policy Review* 12, no. 4 (2009): 2–6.

2. The National Abortion Federation reports that between 1997 and 2009, there were 8 murders and 17 attempted murders of abortion providers, as well as 17 bombings, 41 arson attacks, 391 invasions, and 763 blockades of abortion clinics. For a full account of violence and disruption targeted at abortion providers in Canada and the United States, see the "NAF Violence and Disruption Statistics," available at http://www.prochoice.org/pubs_research/publications/downloads/about_abortion/stats_table2009.pdf. It should also be noted that anti-abortion activists often embrace a "family values" approach to politics, which encompasses a broad range of socially conservative positions, such as exclusive support of "traditional" heterosexual, monogamous marriage and opposition to homosexuality as such; opposition to same-sex marriage and adoption rights; opposition to myriad forms of contraception; support of male dominance in the family, and so on.

3. Judith Jarvis Thomson, "A Defense of Abortion," *Philosophy and Public Affairs* 1, no. 1 (1971): 47–66; Eileen L. McDonagh, *Breaking the Abortion Deadlock: From Choice to Consent* (New York: Oxford University Press, 1996). Nancy J. Hirschmann drew my attention to the importance of these authors.

4. Thomson, "Defense," 66.

5. McDonagh, *Breaking the Abortion Deadlock*, 10. An extensive feminist literature directly engages with the impact of new medical imaging techniques on the construction of fetal personhood and anti-abortion politics. See, for example, Joanne Boucher, "A Window to the Womb? Obstetric Ultrasound and the Abortion Rights Debate," *Journal of Medical Humanities* 25, no. 1 (2004): 7–19; Celeste Michelle Condit, *Decoding Abortion Rhetoric: Communicating Social Change* (Urbana: University of Illinois Press, 1990); Barbara Duden, *Disembodying Women: Perspectives on Pregnancy and the Unborn*, trans. Lee Haoinacki (Cambridge, Mass.: Harvard University Press, 1993); Sarah Franklin, "Fetal Fascinations: New Dimensions to the Medical-Scientific Construction of Fetal Personhood," in *Off-Centre: Feminism and Cultural Studies*, ed. S. Franklin, C. Lury, and J. Stacey (London: HarperCollins, 1991), 190–203; Valerie Hartouni, "Fetal Exposures: Abortion Politics and Optics of Allusion," in *The Visible Woman: Imaging Technologies, Gender, and Science*, ed. Paula A. Treichler, Constance Penley, and Lisa Cartwright (New York: New York University Press, 1998), 198–217; E. Ann Kaplan, "Look Who's Talking Indeed: Fetal Images in Recent North American Visual Culture," in *Mothering: Ideology, Experience, and Agency*, ed. Evelyn Nakano Glenn, Grace Chang, and Linda Rennie Rocey (New York: Routledge, 1994), 121–37; Meredith W. Michaels, "Fetal Galaxies: Some Questions About What We See," in *Fetal Subjects, Feminist Positions*, ed. Lynne M. Morgan and Meredith W. Michaels (Philadelphia: University of Pennsylvania Press, 1999), 119–32; Lisa M. Mitchell, *Baby's First Picture: Ultrasound and the Politics of Fetal Subjects* (Toronto: University of Toronto Press, 2001); Karen Newman, *Fetal Positions: Individualism, Science, Visuality* (Stanford: Stanford University Press, 1996); Rosalind Pollack Petchesky, "Foetal Images: The Power of Visual Culture in the Politics of Reproduction," in *Reproductive Technologies: Gender, Motherhood, and Medicine*, ed. Michelle Stanworth (Cambridge: Polity Press, 1987), 57–80; Nathan Stormer, "Prenatal Space," *Signs: Journal of Women in Culture and Society* 26, no. 1 (2000): 109–44; Janelle S. Taylor, *The Public Life of the Fetal Sonogram: Technology, Consumption, and the Politics of Reproduction* (New Brunswick: Rutgers University Press, 2008).

6. McDonagh, *Breaking the Abortion Deadlock*, 17.

7. Ibid., 11.

8. Ibid., 39, see also 17.

9. Ibid., 70.

The Problem of Fetal Personhood   237

10. Ibid., 71.

11. On this point, see Emily Bazelon, "The Reincarnation of Pro-Life," *New York Times*, May 27, 2011; Jill Filipovic, "'Personhood' and the Pro-lifers' Long Game," *The Guardian*, November 14, 2011.

12. For an innovative example of the use of Thomson's and McDonagh's self-defense paradigm, see Nancy J. Hirschmann, "Stem Cells, Disability, and Abortion: A Feminist Approach to Equal Citizenship," in *Gender Equality: Dimensions of Women's Equal Citizenship*, ed. Linda C. McClain and Joanna L. Grossman (Cambridge: Cambridge University Press, 2009), 154–73. Hirschmann builds on Thomson's and McDonagh's insights but also deploys the concept of citizenship to construct a feminist and disability rights case in favor of stem cell research.

13. Thomas Hobbes, *Leviathan*, ed. Richard Tuck (Cambridge: Cambridge University Press, 2002), ch. 46, 463. References are to chapter and page number.

14. As he writes, "Sense in all cases, is nothing els but originall fancy, caused . . . by the pressure, that is, by the motion, of externall things upon our Eyes, Eares, and other organs thereunto ordained." Ibid., ch. 1, 14. And all thoughts, fantasies, desires, creative imaginings, science, and speech derive from sense, since "whatsoever we conceive, has been perceived first by sense . . . a man can have no thought representing anything, not subject to sense." Ibid., ch. 3, 23–24.

15. See ibid., ch. 13, 86–87.

16. *Read thyself*, Hobbes urges, and this essence of our humanity is revealed—"that for the similitude of the thoughts, and Passions of one man, to the thoughts, and Passions of another, whosoever looketh into himself, and considereth what he doth, when he does *think, opine, reason, hope, feare*, & c, and upon what ground; he shall thereby read and know, what are the thoughts and Passions of all other men, upon the like occasions." Ibid., introduction, 10.

17. Ibid., ch. 15, 107.

18. Ibid., ch. 15, 107–8.

19. This, of course, does not accord with Hobbes's assumption that most families will emerge from the state of nature with male heads of households.

20. Hobbes, *Leviathan*, ch. 13, 86–87.

21. Ibid., ch. 13, 87.

22. Ibid., ch. 20, 139.

23. Ibid., ch. 20, 140.

24. Ibid., ch. 20, 139–40.

25. Ibid., ch. 20, 140.

26. Joanne H. Wright, *Origin Stories in Political Thought: Discourses on Gender, Power, and Citizenship* (Toronto: University of Toronto Press, 2004), 77.

27. Ibid., 87.

28. Ibid., 88. Nancy J. Hirschmann argues that despite such "disruptive" strands of argument, Hobbes ultimately rationalizes patriarchalism in civil society. Women promote social instability insofar as they inspire men's lust, covetousness, and competition and are a constant reminder of social difference (and hence the endless possibility of interpersonal quarrels). Consequently, Hirschmann sees a (masculinist) logic to the founding of *patriarchal* families—even though Hobbes does not posit women as innately inferior to men. Further, she argues that the sovereign could sanction patriarchy in order, for instance, to put population growth ahead of women's individual preferences. This, I am arguing, would contradict Hobbes's assertion of the inviolable right of self-preservation. See Nancy J. Hirschmann, *Gender, Class, and Freedom in Modern Political Theory* (Princeton, N.J.: Princeton University Press, 2008), esp. ch. 1, and Nancy J. Hirschmann, *The Subject of Liberty: Toward a Feminist Theory of Freedom* (Princeton, N.J.: Princeton University Press, 2003), 72–73.

29. Wright, *Origin Stories*, 95.

30. According to Christine di Stefano, Hobbesian man "bears the tell-tale signs of a modern masculinity in extremis: identity through opposition, denial of reciprocity, repudiation of the

(m)other in oneself and in relation to oneself, a constitutional inability and/or refusal to recognize the ambivalence of identity in relation to others." Christine Di Stefano, *Configurations of Masculinity: A Feminist Perspective on Modern Political Theory* (Ithaca, N.Y.: Cornell University Press, 1991), 104. See also Diana Coole, who concludes that "although Hobbes's materialist logic is sexually neutral, we might ask whether the human nature that he describes is as universal as he believes. . . . [While his] ascription of a nature common to both sexes is an advance, what he accredits them with is a peculiarly male psyche: aggressive, competitive and egoistic." Diana Coole, *Women in Political Society* (Sussex: Wheatsheaf Books, 1988), 75.

31. Ingrid Makus, *Women, Politics, and Reproduction: The Liberal Legacy* (Toronto: University of Toronto Press, 1996), esp. chs. 1, 4, and 5.

32. Ibid., 195.

33. Jane S. Jaquette, "Contract and Coercion: Power and Gender in *Leviathan*," in *Women Writers in the Early Modern British Tradition*, ed. Hilda L. Smith (Cambridge: Cambridge University Press, 1998), 214–15. Jaquette further argues that it is other factors, such as social norms, prejudices, and lack of alternative strategies, that constitute unequal relations, rather than contract as such. Moreover, she comments that contract provides "a strong commitment to individual agency and a clear indication of what justice in a dynamic society requires: equality, choice, negotiation," and suggests that Hobbes's "stern gender egalitarianism . . . [has] proven foundationally critical to women's . . . claims to equal rights in all spheres" (218–19).

34. Hobbes, *Leviathan*, ch. 30, 235–36.

35. Ibid., ch. 14, 91.

36. Ibid.

37. Ibid., ch. 14, 93.

38. Samantha Frost, "Faking It: Hobbes's Thinking-Bodies and the Ethics of Dissimulation," *Political Theory* 29, no. 1 (2001): 37.

39. Hobbes, *Leviathan*, ch. 14, 93–94.

40. Ibid., ch. 14, 98.

41. Ibid., ch. 21, 147.

42. Ibid., ch. 21, 148.

43. For arguments that similarly place the right of self-preservation at the heart of Hobbes's politics, see George Kateb, "Hobbes and the Irrationality of Politics," *Political Theory* 17, no. 3 (1989): 355–91; James R. Martel, "The Radical Promise of Thomas Hobbes: The Road Not Taken in Liberal Theory," *Theory and Event* 4, no. 2 (2000); Susanne Sreedhar, "Defending the Hobbesian Right of Self-Defense," *Political Theory* 36, no. 6 (2008): 781–802; Susanne Sreedhar, *Hobbes on Resistance: Defying the Leviathan* (Cambridge: Cambridge University Press, 2010); Jeremy Waldron, "Self-Defense: Agent-Neutral and Agent-Relative Accounts," *California Law Review* 88, no. 3 (2000): 711–49.

44. Hobbes, *Leviathan*, ch. 21, 150.

45. Ibid., ch. 21, 151.

46. Ibid., ch. 27, 208.

47. Ibid.

48. Ibid., ch. 27, 209. The bracketed interpolation is my own.

49. Ibid., ch. 30, 231.

50. Ibid., ch. 21, 153.

51. Ibid., ch. 21, 154. My emphasis.

52. Ibid., ch. 30, 231.

53. Ibid., ch. 15, 107.

54. Certainly, though, the imperative of absolutism troubles this liberal and open account of Hobbes's political sentiments.

55. Louis Schwartz, "Seventeenth-Century Childbirth: 'Exquisite Torment and Infinite Grace.'" *The Lancet* 377, no. 9776 (2011): 1486–87.

56. Rafael Lozano et al., "Progress Towards Millennium Development Goals 4 and 5 on Maternal and Child Mortality: An Updated Systematic Analysis," *The Lancet* 378, no. 9797 (2011): 1139–65; "Moving Forward with Maternal Health and Human Rights," *The Lancet* 373, no. 9682 (2009): 2172.

57. On the topic of early modern reproductive technologies, see, for example, David Cressy, *Birth, Marriage, and Death: Ritual, Religion, and the Life-Cycle in Tudor and Stuart England* (Oxford: Oxford University Press, 1997), esp. ch. 2; Eve Keller, "Embryonic Individuals: The Rhetoric of Seventeenth-Century Embryology and the Construction of Early-Modern Identity," *Eighteenth-Century Studies* 33, no. 3 (2000): 321–48; Angus McLaren, "'Barrenness Against Nature': Recourse to Abortion in Pre-industrial England," *Journal of Sex Research* 17, no. 3 (1981): 224–37; John M. Riddle, *Eve's Herbs: A History of Contraception and Abortion in the West* (Cambridge, Mass: Harvard University Press, 1997); Rebecca Wilkin, "Descartes, Individualism, and the Fetal Subject," *Differences: A Journal of Feminist Studies* 19, no. 1 (2008): 96–126; E. A. Wrigley, "Family Limitation in Pre-industrial England," *Economic History Review* 19, no. 1 (1996): 82–109.

58. Cressy, *Birth, Marriage, and Death*, 42.

59. Ibid., 45.

60. Ibid.

61. Ibid., 48. For further exploration of the epistemological problems explored by early modern theorists in regard to embryological and fetal development, see Wilkin, "Descartes, Individualism," and Eve Keller, "Embryonic Individuals." Keller, for instance, argues that anxiety concerning its implications for male identity formation pervades early modern accounts of embryological development: "Its distinguishing features of autonomy and self-determination arise not so much as unencumbered achievements of human reason or human will, but rather as compensatory responses to perceived threats to the unique and privileged status of human, and particularly masculine identity. The more man in his physiology resembles a machine or the product of a machine—something 'stamped in a mould'—the more it becomes necessary to ensure that he is known to be something other than a machine, that he is a person, a human, a subject, from the first moment of his conception, or even before" (343).

11

Choice Talk, Breast Implants, and Feminist Consent Theory

Hobbes's Legacy in Choice Feminism

Joanne H. Wright

In an era of abundant "choice talk," the proliferation of individual choice is equated with freedom and liberation. A variety of feminist thinking that we might call "choice feminism" subscribes to the widely held societal perspective that the provision of more choices for women is feminism's primary goal and that, regardless of the circumstances in which a woman finds herself, if we can state "she chose it," then her consent to

---

Earlier versions of this chapter were presented at Scholarship, Teaching, and Learning in the Age of the Plastic Body at Kwantlen Polytechnic University, Surrey, British Columbia (2010), as well as in the Multi-disciplinary Gender Research Seminar at the University of Cambridge (2012). I wish to thank participants in each for their feedback and to acknowledge David Bedford, Christine Saulnier, Kate Bezanson, and Nancy Hirschmann for their valuable editorial suggestions, and Kerri Krawec for her excellent work as my research assistant.

her actions ought to be taken at face value. Underlying the rhetoric of choice is the presumption that consent is unproblematic, that a woman's consent to her own actions is implied in the fact of her engaging in the actions. The emphasis is on women as choosing subjects, and we need investigate no further the conditions in which a woman acts.

In this chapter, I argue that the contemporary enthusiasm about choice conceals a fraught relationship between consent and coercion, dangerously collapsing the two in what can be best described as a Hobbesian manner. In fact, an examination of Hobbes's political thought can be instructive for contemporary feminist attempts to rethink the politics of consent, for Hobbes understood better than most the power and the risks of consent-based political theories. In his own political theory, he acknowledges coercion only to mask it with the language of consent and the will. In what follows, I suggest that the contemporary acceptance of choice as the governing ethos of feminism fails to pay heed to the lessons that stem from Hobbes's theory, just as it elides decades of important feminist analysis of the problematic politics of consent and coercion. Certainly, from the beginning of the Second Wave, feminists have made issues surrounding consent and coercion a focal point of their efforts to understand women's behavior in patriarchal society. Indeed, such issues have been central to feminist debates about the workings of patriarchal social relations. Yet the present enthusiasm for choice as a signifier of women's freedom and liberation—the choice to opt out of the labor market, for example, or the choice to have elective breast augmentation—threatens to depoliticize and render unproblematic the issues of consent and coercion, and, ultimately, to hinder feminist efforts to improve the lives of women.

Hobbes, Consent, and the "Indifference to Coercion"

Hobbes is not one of the political theorists to whom feminists typically turn for analysis of concepts useful to feminism, and yet he has a great deal to offer the discussion of consent.[1] Even if we do not accept his conclusions, his rational unpacking of human relations can be instructive for its errors and especially for the political lacunae it points to. It will be useful, therefore, to examine briefly his consent theory and his political motivations for employing it, before looking at how it illuminates feminist debates.

Hobbes's theory of consent is intertwined with his definition of contract, and with the distinctions he makes between sovereignty by institution and sovereignty by acquisition. In *Leviathan*, Hobbes explains that "whensoever a man Transfereth his Right, or Renounceth it; it is either in consideration of some Right reciprocally transferred to himselfe; or for some good he hopeth for thereby."[2] A contract is a mutual transferring of right, which is voluntary and aimed at achieving "some *Good to himselfe*" (ch. 14, 92–93). Transferring right creates obligation, for in the transfer, "he is said to be Obliged, or Bound, not to hinder those, to whom such right is granted, or abandoned, from the benefit of it" (ch. 14, 92), and he has a duty to carry out his part of the arrangement. Significantly, Hobbes claims that fear does not play a role in our assessment of a contract's legitimacy; fear can only act as a hindrance to the performance of one's end of the bargain after a contract is made and as a result of some new fact. By the same logic, a contract made in the unstable state of nature is nevertheless obligatory, for, at base, it is a contract made "wherein one receiveth the benefit of life" or some other good (ch. 14, 97–98). Ordinary contracts, made with an eye to some mutual benefit to the contracting parties, cannot be considered void because there was a differential of power, or because one party was afraid of the consequences of not agreeing; fear or no fear, the agreement is consensual and thus legitimate.

If these principles lay the foundation for Hobbes's thinking about the creation of the social contract—sovereignty by institution—through which the inhabitants of the state of nature transfer their right to a sovereign, leaving the state of war behind, a surprisingly similar logic underlies Hobbes's discussion of conquest, or sovereignty by acquisition. In counterintuitive fashion, Hobbes describes sovereignty by acquisition as arising from an act of force by which the people "authorise all the actions of that Man, or Assembly, that hath their lives and liberty in his Power" (ch. 20, 138). Once again, and more importantly in this case, the presence of fear does not undermine the contract made, nor is the power derived from this act of force illegitimate because it was seized. What creates the obligation to obey is not conquest itself but consent of the conquered. Hobbes elaborates, "It is not therefore the Victory, that giveth the right of Dominion over the Vanquished, but his own Covenant. Nor is he obliged because he is conquered; that is to say, beaten, and taken, or put to flight; but because he commeth in, and Submitteth to the Victor" (ch. 20, 141).

While we might assume that conquest is inherently nonconsensual, Hobbes posits consent as the basis for political obligation even in this scenario. "For in the act of our Submission," Hobbes writes, "consisteth both our *Obligation*, and our *Liberty* . . . there being no Obligation on any man, which ariseth not from some Act of his own" (ch. 21, 150). Our actions reveal our intentions, and in submission, Hobbes sees a tacit consent: "When the Vanquished, to avoyd the present stroke of death, coventeth either in expresse words, or *by other sufficient signes of the will*, that so long as his life, and the liberty of his body is allowed him, the Victor shall have the use thereof, at his pleasure" (ch. 20, 141; italics mine). By Hobbes's estimation, all actions "proceedeth from the will" and are therefore free. Our actions reflect our will since the will is "the last Appetite, or Aversion, immediately adhering to the action" (ch. 6, 44). In "Of Liberty and Necessity," Hobbes states that the "will is the last act of our deliberation."[3] As Quentin Skinner explains, from Hobbes's perspective, "it makes no sense to speak of being coerced into acting against your will, since the will lying behind your action will always be revealed by your action itself."[4] Thus, you are coerced into choosing a particular path not *against* your will, as we would usually claim; rather, you are induced "to deliberate in such a way that you give up your will to disobey, acquire a will to obey, and thereafter act freely in the light of the will you have acquired."[5]

Hobbes's definition of the will and his use of the concept of gratitude work in tandem to sustain his argument about the consensual basis of conquest. The conquered are inclined to submit precisely because "of all Voluntary Acts, the Object is to every man his own Good" (ch. 15, 105). That is, they perceive some benefit to themselves. The recognition of benefits received—or gratitude—binds subjects to a conqueror in the same manner that it binds children to a parent. Similarly, when the people seek to "avoyd the present stroke of death," thereby preserving their lives and liberty, they are grateful for the sovereign's benevolence, and thus they owe him or her their obedience. Their submission, being an act of will, cannot then be called injurious or illegitimate (ch. 15, 104).

In the service of this argument, Hobbes makes a distinction between what it means to be forced and what it means to be compelled. To be forced is to be physically hindered or prevented from acting according to one's will. Only in this way can we lack freedom, since the concept of freedom cannot rightfully be "applyed to any thing but *Bodies* . . . for that which is not subject to Motion, is not subject to Impediment" (ch. 21, 146). Alternatively, if our will is coerced, we are compelled but still free as far as Hobbes is concerned.[6] Thus, as long as a person is not physically hindered, he or she is free to act according to his or her own will. In assuming such a narrow conception of freedom, as being thwarted only by material obstacles, Hobbes avoids consideration of the ways in which the will is shaped and manipulated, or even coerced into agreement with things that are not in the subject's objective or real interests.[7] Having closed this door, Hobbes can equate submission with consent without internal contradiction. Combining gratitude, tacit consent, and the will in this way served Hobbes's immediate political interests well, insofar as his stated aim in *Leviathan* is to demonstrate "the mutuall Relation between Protection and Obedience" (*Leviathan*, "A Review, and Conclusion," 491). Against his political opponents who were reluctant to endorse the new Commonwealth government, and who identified its origins with the worst kind of political coercion and military force, Hobbes claimed that their consent had essentially already been given and thus the issue of coercion was moot.[8]

To be sure, a number of these ideas are politically troublesome: the suggestion that the mere receipt of benefits is equivalent to consent, the collapsing of consent and coercion on the basis that we only act where we have a will to do so, and the idea of the will as free so long as the physical body is not impeded. In these passages, Hobbes demonstrates his comfort with a significant degree of coercion and his savvy in managing it as a political problem. Hobbes's interpreters raise concerns about this facet of his thinking. For example, Gordon Schochet points to the "number of traps" Hobbes "set for his readers, starting with his indifference to coercion."[9] Additionally, Nancy Hirschmann argues that "we are compelled to consent to the social contract because we have no practical choice in the matter; it is the only choice we can rationally make."[10] In a different vein, Deborah Baumgold describes Hobbes's theory of consent as "one of the more curious features of his theory," noting that he offers a "particularly expansive definition of consent, which extends the concept of voluntary action to include coerced acts, especially acts motivated by fear."[11] Certainly, Hobbes's indifference to the presence of both fear and coercion poses serious difficulties for a feminist analysis of meaningful consent. Here I suggest that Hobbes effectively depoliticizes the relationship between consent and coercion, carefully moving the problem of coercion out of political view. It is this specific aspect of Hobbes's analysis, and its effect on our own modern understanding of consent and choice, that is most relevant to the discussion of choice feminism.

While Hobbes's concerns were very different from our own, his methodical theorizing points to trouble spots in consent theory where feminist theory needs to shine a bright light. Not only from a feminist perspective, there are serious problems with the proposition that an individual's actions can, on the surface, convey all of the information we need about their choice, their intentions, and their consent. Hobbes is instructive because he is open and frank about his line of reasoning, and surprisingly forthright about the presence of coercion, even as he handily dismisses it as a problem. He acknowledges its presence in cases of submission only to take it off the table, ensuring that we will not focus unnecessarily on its political effects.

Making Consent Political: Feminist Analysis from the Second Wave to the Present

It is one of Hobbes's legacies, I am arguing, that we continue to accept, in some form, the idea that our will and our consent are revealed by our actions. For Hobbes, the fact that we *are* doing something is indication enough that the action is consensual and was freely chosen. Although vitally aware of the psychological drives that propel our actions—envy, vainglory, pride—he is unwilling to consider the ways in which our wills are shaped and coerced by a mix of external and internal pressures, and, consequently, unwilling to consider our choices illegitimate because they are coerced. Since the will is the last act of our deliberation, and we are free to the extent that we are not physically hindered, our actions reveal our choices in transparent fashion.[12] Significantly, Hobbes's legacy continues to be visible in contemporary choice feminism—a commonsense feminism that is culturally validated in the public discourse and the media. On this view, any action or behavior can be counted as consensual, even feminist, insofar as women themselves say they chose it. As Summer Wood describes, the language of "It's my choice" has "become synonymous with 'It's a feminist thing to do'—or, perhaps more precisely, 'It's antifeminist to criticize my decision.'"[13] I suggest that this thinking is not merely indicative of the general triumph of liberal discourse, but owes a debt to Hobbesian consent theory as well.

Linda Hirshman may have been responsible for coining the term "choice feminism" in a controversial 2005 article in *American Prospect*.[14] Stemming from the article, her provocative book *Get to Work . . . And Get a Life Before It's Too Late* charts a tendency among a relatively small but nevertheless noticeable demographic of educated women to depart from the career path to look after home and children.[15] Although the women who are "homeward bound" defend their decision as a viable choice, Hirshman argues that such a choice is not as straightforward as it might appear to be—that women making these choices are not fully aware of, or not willing to acknowledge, the powerful ideological pressures acting upon them from both left and right. Such pressure admits of degrees, as does coercion in general—obviously no one is forcing women to withdraw from the public world. Yet in perpetuating this uncritical discourse of choice, the opt-out revolution prevents us from seeing how both material and ideological factors are coming together to encourage women's acceptance of this pattern.

Certainly, from its inception, Second Wave feminism has sought actively to problematize the politics of consent and coercion and has worked against the simplistic assumption that choice can be taken at face value. Moreover, feminists of the Second Wave have identified the significant problems associated with tacit consent, or the Hobbesian belief that silence or submission can be equated with consent. However, the feminist efforts to show the complexity of consent and choice are at risk of being subsumed under the wholesale adoption of choice talk within feminism and the public discourse at large. Before considering the Hobbesian elements of choice feminism further, it will be useful to highlight briefly some of the ways in which feminists have sought to politicize consent and choice.

We might begin by reflecting on an early debate that has received little attention in the retelling of Second Wave history, but which illustrates some of the nuances in feminist thinking on choice. Early in the Second Wave, one of the driving questions that feminists addressed was how to understand women's apparent acceptance of traditional gender roles in patriarchal society. Then, as now, most feminists—liberal, radical, and socialist alike—accepted a version of the sex-role socialization theory. According to this thesis, women (and men) are taught from infancy how best to conform to society's ideas of proper gender behavior; these lessons are reaffirmed in the family and through the education system, popular culture, and the media. For example, early radical feminist Marlene

Dixon writes in her 1969 article "Why Women's Liberation?" that in order for women to be truly liberated, "it is necessary to destroy the ideology of male supremacy which asserts the biological and social inferiority of women in order to justify institutionalized oppression."[16] Dixon goes on to describe women as "trapped in their false consciousness," proving themselves to be obstacles in their own path to liberation: "From their earliest training to the grave, women are constrained and propagandized."[17]

Early on in the movement's development, some radical feminists began to challenge the widely accepted theory of socialization on the basis of its characterization of women and the nature of their oppression. The New York group Redstockings argued that socialization theory implied women's passive acceptance of, and even consent to, their own oppression. Redstockings took exception to this implication in its statement of group principles: "We also reject the idea that women consent to or are to blame for their own oppression. Women's submission is not the result of brainwashing, stupidity, or mental illness but of continual daily pressure from men."[18]

Indeed, soon after its formation in 1969, Redstockings articulated what came to be known as the pro-woman line—the view that feminists must "take the woman's side in everything,"[19] and especially that women must be credited with the capacity to see their own situation clearly. The pro-woman line set itself against the belief that male supremacy is a psychological problem from which women can be cured by freeing their minds. Its advocates argue that women "comply" with patriarchal social relations not because they have internalized their own oppression, or because "women oppress themselves," but because there are real material consequences for failing to comply: social marginalization and isolation, loneliness, poverty, violence, and so forth. Advocates of the pro-woman line took a distinctive stance, seeing women who marry or wear makeup neither as victims of patriarchal socialization nor as freely choosing agents, but as having made a pragmatic choice to survive in a patriarchal world that expects their conformity to gender roles and beauty standards. Taking a materialist approach, pro-womanists argue that a woman's "appearance is her work uniform"; if she wishes to secure employment, she must choose to conform to these standards or risk economic marginalization.[20] Most important, the decision to marry and stay at home to look after children or, pushing forward several decades, the choice to undergo elective cosmetic surgery, cannot simply be taken at face value, as choice feminists would now have it, nor can it be seen as a sign of false consciousness; rather, it must be understood as a response to the real conditions of patriarchy and women's need for economic security and social inclusion. From Redstockings' point of view, to argue otherwise was tantamount to suggesting that women are stupid, that they don't know their own situation, and that they cannot see the conditions of their lives clearly enough to act.

Advocates of the pro-woman line and advocates of the socialization thesis could not agree on the source and nature of women's oppression, a disagreement that caused the splintering and reforming of radical feminist groups but which ultimately spurred more theorizing on the problems of consent.[21] Had women internalized their female roles, or had they consciously adopted them in the name of survival? In answer to this question, both sides brought something important to the table. While pro-woman advocates warned against the assumption of women's complicity with their own oppression and politicized the context in which choices are made, socialization advocates held that women are socially conditioned, culturally shaped, into accepting social roles without the opportunity to make meaningful choices or exercise their real capacity for consent. When we examine the politics of breast implants in the following section, it will become clear that to overlook the ways in which women assimilate patriarchal values is to miss an important aspect of women's oppression, as many contemporary feminists have continued to analyze women's subjectivity as constituted through a myriad of power relations. The debate between these two perspectives remains important, however, for its illustration of the historicity of feminist struggles with consent, for pointing to a shared set of concerns about women's inability to exercise meaningful consent under patriarchy, and for demonstrating the feminist commitment to accounting for the political and coercive forces acting upon women.

Another area in which we see Hobbes's legacy and the fetishization of choice talk play out is sexual assault law. Here, too, many feminists have sought to politicize the issues of consent and coercion. While the law in Western nations has typically not viewed consent to sexual relations from the woman's point of view—Canadian law no longer allows the defense of implied consent, but still permits a defendant to claim a "false but mistaken belief in consent"—feminists have consistently attempted to draw attention to the absurdity of equating silence or acquiescence with meaningful consent. As Carole Pateman articulates in her formative article, "Women and Consent," on the question of women's consent and rape, "Popular opinion and the courts are Hobbesian; they identify submission, including forced submission, with consent."[22] In fact, popular opinion and the courts are Hobbesian in the other important sense as well, in equating a victim's actions with her true will.

This sort of Hobbesian logic is clearly evident in the infamous "No Means No" case in Canadian Supreme Court history. In this case, a host of familiar rape myths were brought out to justify the defendant's acquittal by the lower courts: coercion and consent were conflated, despite the complainant's repeated "No's"; her apparel was taken to signal her consent to sex; and, in a less familiar but uniquely Hobbesian vein, the complainant was judged a willing participant because she gave her attacker (a prospective employer) a back massage.[23] Although the court accepted her claim that she was afraid for her life, she was still found to have implied consent through her actions. The lower courts, and later the public, were "hung up" on the question of her consent, blinded by this one action that, for her, was a survival strategy. Here we might return to Hobbes's distinction between being forced and being compelled. That the woman was not physically forced to give her attacker a massage was taken as an indication that she was a free and willing participant, despite her own statements of fear. Using a Hobbesian logic, the lower courts and the public were unwilling to consider the ways in which she was compelled by fear to comply with his request. This notion that her actions revealed all that was needed to know about her will adds a new twist to the old rape myth that "she was there, therefore she was consenting," making it yet more difficult for women's perspectives on consent to be heard.

Despite decades of feminist attempts to politicize these issues, the apolitical, Hobbesian version of consent continues to hold appeal. Why should this be? Why do we continue to depoliticize choice, especially in situations that are so obviously underwritten by relations of power? As we employ the discourse of choice, we individualize the problem: the complainant must have done something to invite this, she asked for it, or she made poor choices. Operating on this terrain of choice, we never have to confront the fact that women are vulnerable to sexual assault even during a job interview, and we maintain what Deborah Rhode labels a "belief in a just world."[24] But to revert to rape myths and the language of choice is to adopt a posture of willful ignorance, a denial of the facts before us. It denies the attempts by feminists to render coercive sexual relations more visible, and, more than this, it suppresses the existence of gender inequality altogether.

Choice feminism operates on precisely this same terrain. It employs what Charles Mills calls an epistemology of ignorance, a kind of anti-knowledge about the state of political affairs that puts forth its own rosy view as the only publicly acceptable one and actively works to suppress any counterview that might draw our attention to the presence of racial, gender, or class oppression.[25] Starting with the denials of gender inequality put forward by popular writers of the 1990s, such as Katie Roiphe, Christina Hoff Summers, Naomi Wolf, and Camille Paglia, choice feminism holds appeal precisely because it is able to argue that feminism has essentially already won the battle for equality. All that remains is for women to seize the power now available to them. Any residual discussion of victimization—from sexual assault to harassment, to constraints on women in the labor market—figures as purely passé in this new political landscape, while talk of woman and girl power constitutes the new lingua franca.

Choice feminism fits the bill as a feminism that celebrates women's power to the exclusion of everything else, power to make choices in the ever-expanding marketplace of lifestyle and consumer options. Choice feminism "moves beyond" the discussion of the politics of choice and consent, of the language of women's oppression altogether, to the celebration of women as individuals with agency. As the discussion of the pro-woman line shows, feminists have long been concerned to assert women's agency, and the pro-woman perspective added its own corrective to socialization theory on the basis that it did not grant women the agency to see their own options and to act accordingly. Yet choice feminism *overcorrects for women's agency* by actively forgetting the various forms of coercion exercised upon women. This epistemology of ignorance comes from a place marked by racial and class privilege, where speaking of women as able to construct themselves and their own lives from a bank of desirable choices has at least some resonance. In actively forgetting that their realities do not resonate with the realities of many women in North America, choice feminists universalize their specific opportunities as possible for all women.[26] They also fail to see that their choices happen to coincide with the very patriarchal values and preferences rejected by many feminists earlier on in the Second Wave. Historically, the radical feminists who advanced the pro-woman line, along with liberal and socialist feminists, understood the context of coercion, a context in which patriarchal values and preferences shaped and made possible the range of acceptable options for women and laid out the parameters for their so-called choices. Presently, choice feminism fails to account for the political force field in which women make choices, and it thus risks taking our understanding of consent and choice back to the Hobbesian terrain where women's troubles began.

Hobbes's Legacy in Choice Feminism: The Case of Breast Augmentation

The ways in which women's choices are socially constructed, given social and political meaning in a broader context that molds and shapes their ideas about what it means to be a woman, are central to this discussion. What sorts of social and material pressures are acting upon women to foster their appetite for certain choices, such as the desire to undergo elective caesarian section? Such a preference could not have been expressed as recently as twenty-five years ago, yet it is now commonplace in North America and beyond. In a similar vein, how do women arrive at a place where looking after their bodies is equated with undergoing a range of surgical and nonsurgical cosmetic procedures, including elective breast augmentation surgery? Just as in the case of the opt-out revolution and the legal discourse surrounding sexual assault, the rhetoric surrounding breast implant surgery, when considered more closely, is permeated with the ideology of choice feminism and the fetishization of choice as an end in itself. In what follows, I consider briefly an example of the contemporary discourse surrounding breast augmentation as reflective of choice feminism, before turning to analyze how choice feminism and Hobbesian consent theory overlap in mutually illuminating ways.

Despite cautions offered by some segments of the medical community, breast implant surgery has been on the rise in Canada and the United States for the last decade or more. The British Columbia Centre of Excellence for Women's Health released a study in 2003 that found that women who had undergone breast implant surgery were four times more likely to seek medical attention or require hospitalization than the control group of women who had not had this surgery.[27] In an interview on CBC Radio, surveillance epidemiologist Dr. Aleina Tweed suggested that her study's findings point to the high rate of local complications associated with breast augmentation surgery and concluded that more research needs be done to show the safety of this surgery for women.[28] Asked for her response, one of Canada's leading users of silicone-filled implants and a lone woman practitioner in a sea of male cosmetic surgeons, Dr. Julie Khanna, did not address the study's key finding of higher use of medical and hospital services, although she did state that she informs her patients that they must be prepared for a repeat or follow-up surgery since, like any device, implants can be expected to fail or lose function over time. Carefully using the neutral term "medical device" to discuss breast implants, Dr. Khanna compared women's choice to undergo surgery in spite of the risks to the choice to take up downhill skiing.[29] We know that downhill skiing can be risky, but we do it because we enjoy the danger of it and feel exhilarated. Breast implants, she suggests, offer women a similar kind of exhilaration, and those who choose it are presented as thrill seekers who want to live a full and exciting life.

Dr. Khanna's comparison bears further consideration, as it illustrates the completely depoliticized language with which the rise in elective cosmetic surgery is frequently discussed. The more we think of breast implant surgery in these terms, the less we will really understand its cultural, political, and gendered meaning. In fact, there are very few similarities between downhill skiing—a long-standing sport that offers its participants the benefits of fresh air, exercise, and a healthy enjoyment of the body—and an elective cosmetic surgery that involves some known risks as well as the possibility of many that are as yet unknown. Elective breast implant surgery, like other elective cosmetic surgery, is by definition a medical procedure that is not "medically necessary, but is undertaken to change appearance rather than to improve health."[30] Such a comparison drains breast augmentation of its medical, political, and cultural baggage in a society that is already obsessed with the body, and makes an elective surgery appear as benign as the choice to take up a sport that, if one is healthy and able-bodied, will likely increase overall health, not diminish it. Dr. Khanna's comparison also distracts us from the material facts about the rise of these privately funded surgeries—that women across a broad economic spectrum are indebting themselves to lending agencies and cosmetic surgeons to obtain these procedures, while the lending agencies and cosmetic surgeons themselves accrue significant financial benefits.[31]

In being compared to downhill skiing, breast implant surgery is rendered politically neutral, no less and no more significant than the choice of any product or leisure activity. Still, the comparison is useful in that it allows us to see plainly the political work being done to sell the concept of cosmetic surgery, and, more than this, it allows us to see both choice feminism and Hobbes's legacy on consent more clearly. From a choice feminist perspective, this is one more option for women to choose, and if it is available and desired, they should be entirely free to select it. Such an analysis is thoroughly Hobbesian in that it assumes that consent can be taken at face value, that all consent is legitimate regardless of the political circumstances in which it is given. Also Hobbesian, I suggest, is the belief that if women *are* doing it, they must legitimately want it. Advertisers, surgeons, and women themselves confirm this view by stating that women "do it for themselves." Indeed, a woman choosing it is making a liberated choice, even a feminist one, because she is making it for herself—as the powerfully narcissistic advertisement for Botox puts it, "For me, myself, and I."

Choice feminism can offer no measure of whether such a practice is healthy or good for women; just the fact that women are choosing it is all the evidence we need that their actions are consensual. Recalling Skinner's summation of Hobbes—"the will lying behind your action will always be revealed by your action itself"—if women did not wish to be surgically altered, their will would have changed and they would have done otherwise. The idea that women's subjectivity is shaped and constrained in its formation by patriarchal social relations, or that there is a context of coercion at work that may be facilitating women's choices for nonessential, potentially risky surgical procedures, is simply not on the table for discussion.

As feminist anti-rape activists and consent theorists have long argued, patriarchal social relations cast women as consenting parties without regard to whether the choices they make reflect legitimate and meaningful consent. Take, for example, the complainant who "chooses" to give her attacker a back massage or the survivor of intimate partner violence who "chooses" to return to her abusive spouse.[32] Ostensibly these women are making choices, but do their choices reflect a meaningful consent? Must we not also acknowledge, as Nancy Hirschmann suggests, how "oppression decidedly creates conditions that undercut the innocence of individual choice"?[33]

While an in-depth discussion of body politics proper is beyond the scope of this chapter, it is nevertheless central to our understanding of the choice discourse surrounding cosmetic surgery that we acknowledge the influence of "makeover culture"[34] on women's subjectivity. Indeed, we have now reached a point of total obsession with the body, a cultural place in which "the body project"[35] has eclipsed hobbies, work, and most everything else. As Susie Orbach articulates in *Bodies*, modern individuals view the body as an object to be relentlessly "honed and worked on," as our modern "calling card." Judged for its conformity or its sloth, it is a key signifier of "one's membership in modernity."[36] Thus, conforming to beauty standards is not just about social inclusion and economic survival, as pro-woman advocates once argued, although it is that, too; it is tied in to our ideas of modern citizenship. To be ideal, modern citizens, women have little choice but to enlist in this project of self-improvement.[37]

In this context of bodily obsession, it is no longer possible to think of the male gaze as setting the standard for what will be deemed attractive. The male gaze has in effect been internalized, functioning as an internal panopticon.[38] Internal surveillance of one's own appearance precedes external assessments and happens both consciously and unconsciously, with this internal lens functioning at the deepest level of socialization, or through what Hirschmann calls "the discursive construction of social meaning."[39] If we think in Foucauldian terms of the self as constituted through discourses of power, such that we only know the body as an entity, only know our desires for the body, through the discursive practices and systems available to us, then it becomes much more difficult to speak about women choosing cosmetic procedures "for me, myself, and I," because the self is, as Hirschmann states, "'always, already' socially constructed."[40] Therefore, to argue that women freely choose procedures to feel confident and better about themselves—a recurring trope in the narratives from women and in the advertising of implants[41]—simply begs the question of what discourses are at work to direct women to this project of improvement, and to construct cosmetic surgery as an increasingly normal and reasonable option. The internal panopticon operates at a much deeper level than straightforward socialization, such that we cannot think of the subject apart from its constitutive discourses and the highly charged, bodily driven, political landscape that makes possible the discursive construction of breast implants as an essential correction to the late modern female body. If feminism is to move beyond Hobbes's legacy on consent, it must do so by identifying and examining the coercive impulses that affect women's ability to make choices, including the coercive elements in the arena of women's appearance; and it needs to transcend the simplistic discourse of choice to understand how women's subjectivity is itself constituted through and by this overdetermined bodily oriented context.

The fetishism of choice is the logical extension of a liberal individualist ethos in its emphasis on choosing life options like products in the marketplace. Still, as I have argued here, choice feminism is more Hobbesian than it might care to admit. It is Hobbesian in its canny ability to mask as options what are really imperatives. For women, and increasingly men, there is no place outside the discourses of power that discipline the late modern body, no place outside this body-citizenship discourse in which we are judged as acceptable or not based on our efforts at improvement. If the body is so problematized as in need of refiguring and improvement, serving as the grounds on which we are granted or refused social inclusion and proper citizenship, the stakes become that much higher for women, the costs of opting out of makeover culture that much greater.

Although the gulf between Hobbes's political interests and those of contemporary feminism is wide, Hobbes's thinking about consent can help us understand the choice feminist language that legitimizes breast augmentation, just as the problems inherent in choice feminism can, in turn, aid us in better understanding Hobbes's own thought. In a sense, choice feminism's choice talk does for elective breast augmentation surgery what Hobbes's language of consent does for the creation of sovereignty by acquisition. Hobbes's subjects submit because submission is really the only option; it is the only game in town. Choice talk is Hobbesian in yet another sense, for, like Hobbes, it accepts all choices as politically neutral and deems any choice as a legitimate reflection of an individual's will. Not only is the individual's consensual submission, if we can think of it in these terms, emptied of political meaning, but it takes place outside the realm of morality as well. By depoliticizing the relationship between coercion and consent and taking the moral judgment away from the event of submission, Hobbes removes the basis on which we can judge the conquest as coercive, a basis for judgment that many of Hobbes's contemporaries believed to be essential to assessing the government of Cromwell. Similarly, choice feminism empties breast augmentation surgery of any larger social or political meaning, just as it empties feminism itself of the potential to have any substantive political meaning as an analysis of patriarchal social relations. As Linda Hirshman argues, with choice feminism, "feminism switched from offering a clear blueprint for liberation to choosing from Column A and Column B"; it went from seeking to define what a "good life" or "good lives" might look like for women—as difficult a project as that might be—to stressing women's freedom to make choices. It is not the place of feminism to question or evaluate the meaning of a particular choice, only to validate it as a sign of women's empowerment to chart her own destiny in a sea of many options.[42] Seen in this light, downhill skiing and cosmetic surgery are on equal footing, with the appearance imperatives acting on women's subjectivity neatly removed from view. Both the choice feminist and the Hobbesian perspective operate on the belief that the individual's actions are an uncomplicated reflection of the individual's desires, and there remains no reason to question our actions any further.

As I have discussed, Hobbes's disregard of the forms of compulsion or coercion that influence an individual's choices is the result of his materialist understanding of the will. With his theory of the will and consent, Hobbes was able to get around the political problem of the coercive origins of Cromwell's rule and to argue that the English people had effectively already submitted to it. Hobbes effectively builds an epistemology of ignorance into his political theory of consent: how else can an act of overt coercion such as the conquering of a nation come to look like a consensual agreement? Hobbes's careful attempts to steer his readers away from the primary fact of conquest—that it is nonconsensual—and his desire to legitimate conquest in the will of the conquered are signs of an environment in which consent was already highly politicized. The fact that he rests his argument in the will of those who effectively had no choice signals an active forgetting of the real implications of both conquest and consent. It strips the politically fraught event of submission of all political and moral significance. Moreover, Hobbes's epistemology of ignorance in his consent theory carries forward into liberal thinking on consent. While liberal political thought is premised on a rejection of some aspects of Hobbesian consent theory, especially the idea that submission equals consent, it retains others. Hobbes's legacy is alive and well in a liberalism that believes consent can be taken at face value, that our choices reflect our will, and that context is not determinative of the legitimacy of consent. The Hobbesian refusal to engage the messy politics of consent and coercion is a problem inherited by, and still deeply embedded in, liberal political thought, as is evident in the present frenzy for choice.

And choice feminism, too, frames the politics of consent and choice simplistically, reducing the complexity and nuance that necessarily accompany questions of consent in a manner that signals its own epistemology of ignorance. This is not just a forgetful or accidental kind of ignorance, but rather a substantive ignorance that does important political work for choice feminism, notably suppressing knowledge of the framework of oppression in which women's choices are socially constructed and, presently, doing the political work of normalizing breast augmentation for women.

If feminism is to learn something from Hobbes's stark analysis of coercion in political relations, it might be to pay close attention to political arguments that profess to have solved the problem of consent. Consent is a necessarily fraught concept; indeed, it is much simpler to identify what should not qualify as meaningful consent than what should. Yet retaining such a distinction between apparent consent and meaningful consent is the cornerstone to a critical feminist politics. In paying attention to Hobbes's legacy, it becomes possible to identify how and why consent gets depoliticized and to observe the consequences of taking it off the table. While choice feminism is laudable for its desire to attribute agency to women, it does so at the cost of any analysis of existing patriarchal social relations, and therefore at the cost of the feminist project of affecting real change in the conditions of women's lives.

Notes

1. See Ingrid Makus, *Women, Politics, and Reproduction: The Liberal Legacy* (Toronto: University of Toronto Press, 1996), ch. 1. See also Jane S. Jaquette, "Contract and Coercion: Power and Gender in *Leviathan*," in *Women Writers and the Early Modern British Political Tradition*, ed. Hilda L. Smith (Cambridge: Cambridge University Press, 1998), 200–219.

2. Thomas Hobbes, *Leviathan*, ed. Richard Tuck (Cambridge: Cambridge University Press, 1994), ch. 14, 93. Citations to *Leviathan* refer to chapter and page number and are subsequently given in the text.

3. Thomas Hobbes, "Of Liberty and Necessity," in *Hobbes and Bramhall on Liberty and Necessity*, ed. Vere Chappell (Cambridge: Cambridge University Press, 1999), sect. 33, 39. References are to section and page number.

4. Quentin Skinner, *Liberty Before Liberalism* (Cambridge: Cambridge University Press, 1998), 7–8.

5. Ibid.

6. See Quentin Skinner, *Hobbes and Civil Science*, vol. 3 of *Visions of Politics* (Cambridge: Cambridge University Press, 2002), 212.

7. For discussion of internal barriers to liberty, see Nancy J. Hirschmann, *The Subject of Liberty: Toward a Feminist Theory of Freedom* (Princeton, N.J.: Princeton University Press, 2003), 11.

8. Skinner, *Hobbes and Civil Science*, 20 and 228–29. As to the extent of Hobbes's commitment and enthusiasm for the de facto theory of sovereignty, see Deborah Baumgold, *Hobbes's Political Theory* (Cambridge: Cambridge University Press, 1988); Skinner, *Hobbes and Civil Science*; Gordon J. Schochet, "Intending (Political) Obligation: Hobbes and the Voluntary Basis of Society," in *Thomas Hobbes and Political Theory*, ed. Mary G. Dietz (Lawrence: University Press of Kansas, 1990), 55–73; Glen Burgess, "Contexts for the Writing and Publication of Hobbes's *Leviathan*," *History of*

Political Thought 11, no. 4 (1990): 675–702; and Glen Burgess, "Usurpation, Obligation, and Obedience in the Thought of the Engagement Controversy," *Historical Journal* 29, no. 3 (1986): 515–36.

9. Schochet, "Intending (Political) Obligation," 67.

10. Nancy J. Hirschmann, *Gender, Class, and Freedom in Modern Political Theory* (Princeton, N.J.: Princeton University Press, 2008), 40.

11. Baumgold, *Hobbes's Political Theory*, 93.

12. Hobbes, "Of Liberty and Necessity," sect. 33, 39.

13. Summer Wood, "On Language: Choice," in *Bitchfest: Ten Years of Cultural Criticism from the Pages of "Bitch" Magazine*, ed. Lisa Jervis and Andi Zeisler (New York: Farrar, Straus, and Giroux, 2006), 146.

14. Linda Hirshman, "Homeward Bound," *American Prospect*, November 21, 2005.

15. Linda R. Hirshman, *Get to Work . . . And Get a Life Before It's Too Late* (Toronto: Penguin, 2006).

16. Marlene Dixon, "Why Women's Liberation?" *Ramparts* 8, no. 6 (1969): 57–63. Reprinted in Barbara Crow, *Radical Feminism: A Documentary Reader* (New York: New York University Press, 2000), 71–81, quote on 73.

17. Ibid., 73–74.

18. "Redstockings Manifesto" (1969). Reprinted in Crow, *Radical Feminism*, 223–25.

19. Redstockings of the Women's Liberation Movement, "Principles," mimeo., Printed Ephemera Collection on Organizations, PE.036, Tamiment Library, New York.

20. [Barbara Leon], "Brainwashing and Women: The Psychological Attack," Redstockings of the Women's Liberation Movement, mimeo., Printed Ephemera Collection on Organizations, PE.036, Tamiment Library, New York.

21. See Ellen Willis, *No More Nice Girls: Countercultural Essays* (Hanover: Wesleyan University Press, 1992), 125–31; Alice Echols, *Daring to Be Bad: Radical Feminism in America, 1967–1975* (Minneapolis: University of Minnesota, 1989); and Judith Hole and Ellen Levine, *Rebirth of Feminism* (New York: Quadrangle Books, 1971).

22. Carole Pateman, "Women and Consent," in *The Disorder of Women: Democracy, Feminism, and Political Theory* (Stanford: Stanford University Press, 1989), 78.

23. See Joanne H. Wright, "Consent and Sexual Violence in Canadian Public Discourse: Reflections on Ewanchuk," *Canadian Journal of Law and Society* 16, no. 2 (2001): 173–204.

24. Deborah L. Rhode, *Speaking of Sex: The Denial of Gender Inequality* (Cambridge, Mass.: Harvard University Press, 1997), 9.

25. Charles W. Mills, *The Racial Contract* (Ithaca, N.Y.: Cornell University Press, 1997). See also Shannon Sullivan and Nancy Tuana, eds., *Race and Epistemologies of Ignorance* (Albany: State University of New York Press, 2007).

26. This point is taken up by Jennet Kirkpatrick in "Introduction: Selling Out? Solidarity and Choice in the American Feminist Movement," *Perspectives on Politics* 8, no. 1 (2010): 241–45, esp. 243.

27. Aleina Tweed, *Health Care Utilization Among Women Who Have Undergone Breast Implant Surgery* (Vancouver: British Columbia Centre of Excellence for Women's Health, 2003), 36.

28. Aleina Tweed, surveillance epidemiologist, British Columbia, interview with Anna Maria Tramonte, *The Current*, CBC Radio, October 29, 2003.

29. Dr. Julie Khanna, cosmetic surgeon, Oakville, Ontario, interview with Anna Maria Tramonte, *The Current*, CBC Radio, October 29, 2003.

30. Catherine Baker-Pitts, "Symptom or Solution? The Relational Meaning of Cosmetic Surgery for Women" (Ph.D. diss., New York University, 2008), 1.

31. Medicard Finance is the lending agency in Canada that advertizes its ability to approve loans while patients wait in the doctor's office.

32. Hirschmann, *Subject of Liberty*, ch. 4.

33. Nancy Hirschmann, "Choosing Betrayal," *Perspectives on Politics* 8, no. 1 (2010): 271–78, quote on 272.

34. See Meredith Jones, *Skintight: An Anatomy of Cosmetic Surgery* (New York: Berg, 2008), 1.

35. Joan Jacobs Brumberg, *The Body Project: An Intimate History of American Girls* (New York: Vintage, 1997).

36. Susie Orbach, *Bodies* (New York: Picador, 2009), 2, 6, 13. For discussion of the way Western culture judges women's moral worth on the basis of body size, see Sharlene Nagy Hesse-Biber, *The Cult of Thinness* (New York: Oxford University Press, 2007), introduction and ch. 1; and Eve Ensler, *The Good Body* (New York: Villard Books, 2004).

37. Jones, *Skintight*, 58.

38. For discussion of this, see Barbara Brook, *Feminist Perspectives on the Body* (New York: Longman, 1999), ch. 4.

39. Hirschmann, *Subject of Liberty*, 81.

40. Ibid.

41. See Andi Zeisler, "Plastic Passion: Tori Spelling's Breasts and Other Results of Cosmetic Darwinism," in Jervis and Zeisler, *Bitchfest*, 259; Baker-Pitts, "Symptom or Solution?" ch. 4; and Kathy Davis, *Reshaping the Female Body: The Dilemma of Cosmetic Surgery* (New York: Routledge, 1995), 161.

42. Quoted in Patricia Cohen, "Today, Some Feminists Hate the Word 'Choice,'" *New York Times*, January 15, 2006. Michaele L. Ferguson argues that this refusal to judge stems from a fear or reticence to engage in politics itself within choice feminism. See Ferguson, "Choice Feminism and the Fear of Politics," *Perspectives on Politics* 8, no. 1 (2010): 247–53.

12

Toward a Hobbesian Theory of Sexuality

Susanne Sreedhar

The field of sexual ethics is a surprising place to encounter a discussion of Thomas Hobbes. After all, this field is concerned with debates about the moral status of various sexual desires, behaviors, relationships, and practices, and, at first glance, Hobbes appears to have little or nothing to say on these matters. He does not provide an explicit theory of human sexuality, and his writings contain very little discussion on the topic of sex. Yet his views are far from irrelevant to these debates. If we pay close attention to his broader philosophical commitments, to those few remarks that he does make about sexuality, and to what he does *not* say on the matter, what emerges is a position that is rich and complex, though at times apparently inconsistent. In this chapter, I (re)construct a Hobbesian theory of sexuality centered on the following three questions:

(1) Regarding sexuality, what follows from Hobbes's broader philosophical commitments? (2) What does he actually say on the matter, and how should we understand it? (3) What does he not say, and is there any significance to these omissions? I argue that if we look carefully at these three aspects of Hobbes's thought, a (largely) coherent and (largely) plausible picture emerges. This picture suggests a radical and indeed liberatory theory of sexuality. I argue that recognizing this position is fruitful for understanding Hobbes in his own right and in relation to debates in sexual ethics, both contemporary and historical.

My chapter proceeds in three stages. First, I develop a radical reading of Hobbes, taking as my starting point a detailed examination of his references to the sexual practices of Amazon women. Second, I consider two potential concerns about this reading: namely, the existence of various pieces of (apparently) countervailing textual evidence, and the potentially dangerous ambivalence of Hobbes's moral conventionalism and legal positivism. I respond to this latter concern in the final section, by turning to Hobbes's discussion of "ordinances concerning copulation." Ultimately, I argue that Hobbes's pragmatic guidance offered to sovereigns, combined with his unwillingness to offer anything like a theory of natural sexuality, makes him a better ally to contemporary progressives and sexual radicals than he is to the problematic regimes that they wish to alter.

Sex in the State of Nature

Hobbes is famous for claiming that life in the state of nature is "solitary, poore, nasty, brutish, and short." At first blush, one could plausibly think that sex in the state of nature—even if it was not "solitary"—was at least "poore, nasty, brutish, and short." After all, the state of nature is characterized by the constant threat of attack by others, sometimes motivated by a desire for goods, sometimes by a desire for dominance, and sometimes simply as a preemptive strike to eliminate a possible future threat. There is no mention of sex in the famous description of the state of nature in chapter 13 of *Leviathan*, though, in a puzzling remark, Hobbes includes "wives" in the list of things that people try to take from others when they "invade."[1] Hobbes also describes a more "advanced" state of nature, one in which people live in small kinship groups held together by "natural lust," but even this more detailed description does not give us a definitive picture of how, if at all, human sexuality is structured in what Hobbes calls the "natural condition of mankind."

The only time Hobbes explicitly takes up the topic of what sexual relations would look like in the state of nature is in his discussions of parental right. Here, he is concerned with the question of how "dominion" or right over children is established (a topic taken up by a number of essays in this volume). He includes a discussion of parental right in all three of his major political works, and though there are some minor differences between these discussions, all three make the same key points regarding natural maternal right and the various options for establishing child custody.[2] These discussions are highly suggestive. Most of the scholarship on this topic has focused on the claim that there is natural maternal right—that, in the absence of a prearranged agreement between mother and father, dominion over a child defaults to the child's mother.

I want to consider the other aspect of Hobbes's discussion, in which he canvasses a variety of options for child custody by providing a taxonomy of "covenants of copulation" (as he talks about them in *The Elements of Law*). First, there are covenants in which one parent is subjugated to the other. In this case, the child belongs to the dominant parent. He explains that when a woman has subjected herself to a particular man's control, he gains authority over their child. For Hobbes, mastery is a transitive relation. This covers not only mothers who are subjected to fathers but also fathers who are subjected to mothers, as he tells us happens when a queen has a child with one of her male subjects. The principle of transitive dominance applies in this case, and the child belongs to the dominant parent—the mother. If the parents are both subjects in a commonwealth, then the child goes to whichever parent is specified in the civil law. Hobbes posits that this will most often be the man, but he notes that it need not be.

The harder and more interesting cases arise when the parents are relative equals. If they live outside a commonwealth—that is, in the state of nature—then the child goes to whomever the two parents have agreed will get him or her (if they do not make an agreement, then it defaults to the mother, as covered above). Hobbes makes two further distinctions: these covenants of copulation can (1) be temporary ("for a time") or permanent ("for life"); and (2) involve domestic relations ("covenants of cohabitation") or not ("covenants of copulation only"). To illustrate this last category, he offers an example of Amazon women. While we now know them to be a historical fiction, Hobbes treats their existence and practices as a matter of historical fact, noting that "in the copulation of the Amazons with their neighbors, the fathers by covenant had the male children only, the mothers retaining the females."³ He describes their practices by saying, "We find in history that the *Amazons* contracted with the men of the neighboring countries, to whom they had recourse for issue, that the issue male should be sent back, but the female remain with themselves, so that the dominion of the females was in the mother."⁴ In Hobbes's taxonomy, the contract he references here would count as a *temporary* covenant of *copulation only*.

While Hobbes makes reference to the Amazons in all three of his major works, only the 1994 edition of the *Leviathan*, edited by Edwin Curley, remarks on their inclusion in a short footnote to the text.⁵ Curley maintains that Hobbes likely read about the Amazons in classical sources such as *History of Alexander* by Quintus Curtius. A close look at the original story is revealing. Curtius describes a meeting between the Amazon queen Thalestris and Alexander the Great. Thalestris, intent on procreating with Alexander, arrives at his camp surrounded by three hundred women dressed in armor and carrying spears. He agrees to her terms: she will give him the male offspring and take the female as her own. We can see what so deeply influenced Hobbes only when we consult the relevant passage in full.

> On the border of Hyrcania . . . lived a tribe of Amazons. They inhabited the plains of Themiscyra in the area of the river Thermodon, and their queen, Thalestris, held sway over all those between the Caucasus and the river Phasis. Passionately eager to meet Alexander, she journeyed from her realm and when she was not far off she sent messengers ahead to announce that a queen had come who was longing to see him and make his acquaintance. Granted an immediate audience, she ordered her company to halt while she went forward attended by 300 women: as soon as she caught sight of the king she leaped unaided from her horse, carrying two spears in her right hand. The dress of Amazons does not entirely cover the body: the left side is bare to the breast but clothed beyond that, while the skirt of the garment, which is gathered into a knot, stops above the knee. One breast is kept whole for feeding children of female sex and the right is cauterized to facilitate bending the bow and handling weapons. Thalestris looked at the king, no sign of fear on her face. Her eyes surveyed a physique that in no way matched

his illustrious record—for all barbarians have respect for physical presence, believing that only those on whom nature has thought fit to confer extraordinary appearance are capable of great achievements. When asked if she had a request to make she unhesitatingly declared that she had come in order to share children with the king, since she was a fitting person on whom to beget heirs for his empire. A child of the female sex she would keep, she said, but a male she would give to his father. Alexander asked if Thalestris wished to accompany him on his campaigns, but she declined on the grounds that she had left her kingdom unprotected, and she kept asking him not to let her leave disappointed in her hopes. The woman's enthusiasm for sex was keener than Alexander's and she pressed him to stop there for a few days. Thirteen days were devoted to serving her passion, after which Thalestris headed for her kingdom and Alexander for Pathiene.[6]

The extent to which Amazon women are portrayed as fierce, fearless, and the embodiment of sexual autonomy is striking. Thalestris not only initiates the encounter, but she is also described as more enthusiastic for sex than Alexander, and they spend thirteen days "serving her passion." In the end, she declines to accompany him on his campaigns "on the grounds that she had left her kingdom unprotected." The sexual independence and power attributed to the female Thalestris is reflected in the physical description of their encounter. She appears half-naked but armed, and even her breasts—so often seen as the physical manifestations of gentle, maternal femininity—have been repurposed for the strength of the female line. One is tasked for nurturing female children, and the other removed to facilitate warfare. The picture is completed by the two weapons she carries in her right hand, above her bared legs. Alexander is apparently astounded and smitten—Thalestris, less so. Instead, she faces "a physique that in no way matched his illustrious record." This is hardly a picture-plate of natural male sexual domination, or indeed prowess at all. Instead, it is a radically powerful depiction of female sexuality.

Hobbes's retelling of the story is revealing insofar as he shows no particular reaction to it. The image of women's power and sexuality conveyed by Curtius was deeply at odds with standard portrayals of female sexuality as dangerous or unclean. Hobbes takes an example that is clearly remarkable—even astounding—to his contemporary audience (and arguably to ours as well) and repeats it without a hint of surprise or even remarking upon it. Not only does Hobbes seem to find nothing strange or out of line in representations that would have been offensive or even sacrilegious in his culture, but he cites these autonomous, sexually liberated warrior women as evidence for his claims about both maternal right and the various plausible structures of relationships between men, women, and children.[7] This serves, in an important way, to legitimate the "experience" of the Amazon women; in using them as evidence, he is crediting them with a certain legitimacy that many of his contemporaries would not have granted.

Hobbes's reaction to this story is also revealing: he was sufficiently impressed with this literary encounter to make it the basis of his conclusions about the variation of child custody arrangements, and yet he apparently sees no need to comment on, or even repeat, the rather astounding physical details that contribute to its memorability. At the very least, it reveals how absolute his commitment to covenant is: none of the other details of the story are relevant. It also suggests that he firmly embraces a form of cultural relativism regarding sexuality. Insofar as individual covenants will emerge within and reflect the values of a particular culture or people, so too will the sexual and family practices these covenants enact and legitimize. This is not problematic or even remarkable in a Hobbesian picture: *all* social and moral norms function this way. I will return to this point shortly.

The rest of Hobbes's discussion of the origin of parental right in the state of nature is equally intriguing, and it provides further support for the picture of natural female sexuality as liberated and powerful that, I have argued, underlies Hobbes's use of the Amazon story. It is clear that there is natural female sexual independence and autonomy, and, furthermore, that casual, promiscuous, and perhaps even indiscriminate sex seems to be the norm. The prevalence of nonmonogamy is implied by remarks such as "In the state of nature, it cannot be known who is a *child's father* except by the *mother's* pointing him out."[8] "Force and fraud" might be cardinal virtues in the state of nature,[9] but virginity and sexual fidelity are not.

Taken as a whole, the picture of sexuality that starts to emerge from a close reading of Hobbes's repeated discussions of "copulation" in the state of nature would find a favorable reception in theories of sexual liberation. Historian James Turner takes this to the extreme, claiming that Hobbes's discussion of natural maternal right reveals libertine strains in his thought and qualifies him to be considered as a "feminist theorist," presumably of the sex-positive stripe.[10] Perhaps Turner goes a bit too far in this reading, suggesting that the picture of radically liberated female sexuality was what Hobbes thought *would* happen in the absence of the constraints of civil society. That strong claim does not follow from what Hobbes says, even at a maximal reading. Rather, all that can be inferred is that radically liberated and empowered female sexuality *could* happen. Even so, this is still a fairly innovative and contentious claim.

The Hobbesian Theory of Sexuality

A radical theory of sexuality also emerges from consideration of various other remarks that Hobbes makes as well as from consideration of the implications of his more general philosophical commitments. There are at least four pieces of text that deserve comment in this regard. First, consider Hobbes's statement that "in the natural state . . . all sexual unions were licit."[11] Second, he remarks upon male homosexuality in ancient Greece without excessive (or in fact any) judgment or condemnation, calling it merely the "use of the time."[12] Third, he insists that what constitutes adultery in one context could constitute marriage in another; what would be illicit under one set of laws could be entirely appropriate under another. In this context he suggests that indissolubility is not a necessary feature of marriage when he claims that "the pagans sexual relations [which were presumably temporary in nature] were by their laws legal marriages."[13] Finally, he recognizes the acceptability of social arrangements that grant the "liberty" to marry more than one person at a time. He remarks without comment that "in some places of the world men have the liberty of many wives; in other places such liberty is not allowed."[14] The first of these comments concerns the state of nature, while the other three remark on the different sexual mores of other cultures. These points are importantly connected: it is *because* nothing sexual is naturally forbidden that various contradictory sexual norms are acceptable within differing contexts. This permissive understanding of sexuality seems stable across his corpus: two of these claims are found in *De Cive*, one in *The Elements of Law*, and one in *Leviathan*. Notice that when these texts are taken together, we see Hobbes rejecting the naturalness and goodness of three of the structuring pillars of heteronormativity:

(1) heterosexuality, (2) monogamy, and (3) lifelong partnerships. Homosexuality, multiple partners, and temporary arrangements are equally as valid as heterosexual, monogamous, lifelong partnerships.

That Hobbes makes such apparently radical claims regarding sexuality, sexual unions, and sexual partnerships is not merely coincidental: his remarks are consistent with—and in fact entailed by—the philosophical underpinnings of his approach to law and morality. Hobbes is famous for insisting that natural right and natural law are reducible to an individualistic pursuit of self-preservation. Very briefly, in the absence of government, people are not required to follow any normal rules of morality, such as refraining from injuring one another or keeping their promises. They are only required to follow those rules once they live in civil society. Moreover, the content of morality is determined by the civil law; providing common standards, definitions, or "measures" is one of the main, if not *the* main, functions of the sovereign. The sovereign determines, for example, what counts as "mine" and "thine"—those things do not exist in nature; they do not have determinate content until given it by the civil law of a particular state. The sovereign determines proper religious worship in the same way. In a telling example, Hobbes considers what to say about deformed births—that is, whether they count as human. He concludes that, because there is no objectively true and knowable right answer, the sovereign must set the criteria and make the judgment.[15] It is not surprising, and in fact is to be expected, that he would treat issues of sexual morals in much the same way. It follows from his wholesale rejection of teleological or divinely ordained morality.[16]

Thus, Hobbes's metaethics serve to deny any claim to found sexual normativity in a conception of "nature," and his philosophy of law and political philosophy serve to legitimate the differing ways of structuring sexuality among cultures. His overriding commitment to moral conventionalism and legal positivism explains his insistence on the validity of polygamy in societies that authorize it, for example, despite the fact that he must have known this would be an unpopular view.[17]

This suggests a rather coherent picture: Hobbes says that people are required to "avoid intercourse forbidden by the [civil] laws";[18] but his point is to insist that it is entirely up to the civil laws to determine what kinds of intercourse should be forbidden or permitted! There is nothing *in nature* that can make those determinations. No independent, objectively knowable answers to questions about sexual ethics exist. To put the point strongly: according to Hobbes's moral conventionalism and legal positivism, the decision to permit one form of sexual union while prohibiting another is, in important ways, analogous to the decision to adopt the metric or the imperial system of measurement or even to the decision to drive on the right- or left-hand side of the road.

Furthermore, Hobbes's commitment to the primacy of covenants in establishing normativity—sexual or otherwise—distinguishes him from the natural law tradition that dominates discussions of sexuality in the history of philosophy. The tradition against which Hobbes argued took it for granted that norms governing human sexuality were somehow built into nature, either directly through the divine ordinance of God or from the (God-given) natural order of the universe. Aquinas and Augustine both had well-developed theories of human sexuality that gave strict guidance about which particular sexual acts were permissible and which were intrinsically evil.[19] Even Grotius (an important influence on Hobbes) purported to find evidence in natural law that women's virginity was not only morally salient but actually a virtue.[20] We can see the degree to which Hobbes stands in stark contrast to this tradition with his unconditional rejection of any notion that nature could provide such guidance.

The radical potential of Hobbes's scattered remarks on sexuality has been noted by other scholars, though for the most part only in passing.[21] A more extensive analysis of Hobbes on sexuality reveals two important insights, however. First, there is an underlying philosophical unity to these apparently unconnected comments; Hobbes's description of sexuality in the state of nature serves both to ground his approach to sex in other cultures and to reveal his philosophical commitments to moral conventionalism and legal positivism. At the same time, close attention to textual detail complicates the story of Hobbes as an undiscovered sexual radical.

Countervailing Textual Evidence

Unfortunately, Hobbes cannot so easily be read as a forerunner of sexual liberation and free love. The relatively small amount of text on the subject of sex cannot all be read as straightforwardly as I have presented it above. For example, there is a tension between Hobbes's explicit acknowledgment of male homosexuality in ancient Greece and the way that he (sometimes) defines "LUST" as the "indefinite desire of the different sex, as natural as hunger."[22] But Hobbes could not have thought that human lust was exclusively heterosexual, because then the acknowledged cases of homosexuality would be inexplicable. I suggest that the appearance of contradiction may emerge from the understandable influence of Hobbes's own cultural background. In fact, whatever the empirical observation he seems to be making about lust, it is clear that nothing normative follows from it. In short, Hobbes can make comments about "natural" heterosexual lust alongside tolerant remarks about Greek homosexuality because, for him, the "naturalness" of heterosexuality (as he apparently saw it) does not have the same normative overtones it would have for a sexual foundationalist or natural law theorist. In fact, "natural" heterosexual desire can have no normative overtones at all on Hobbes's account, because, as we will see below, Hobbes's metaethics deny such a possibility. When push comes to shove, Hobbes will always give absolute normative primacy to the conventions and laws of a given society.

It is less easy to explain the problematic view of women that underlies many of Hobbes's remarks in his discussion of marriage and elsewhere. For example, while he does deny that any sexual behavior is by nature illicit, his reasoning behind this claim deserves scrutiny. He explains that, in the state of nature, "first, nothing was another's (because nature gave all things to all men), and it was consequently not possible to encroach on what was another's; where, secondly, all things were in common, for which reason also all sexual unions were licit."[23] He reasons that all sexual unions are licit in the state of nature because everything is held in common, and it is apparent from the passage that he means *women* are held in common. The sexual unions that he means to pick out as "licit," then, seem to be the sexual unions of one man with another man's woman. There is no adultery in the state of nature for the same reason that there is no theft in the state of nature; as he says, "It was . . . not possible to encroach on what was another's." The implication is that it is women who were *the objects* of "encroachment" in the state of nature. There is a reference to the same effect in chapter 13 of *Leviathan*, where Hobbes makes reference to people (presumably men) in the state of nature invading one another for the purpose of stealing wives, as noted above.

The worrisome ambivalence toward women and female agency (sexual and otherwise) in these remarks has not gone unnoticed in the secondary literature on Hobbes. Canonical criticisms of Hobbes on this count are offered by Carole Pateman and Susan Moller Okin, and more (though not entirely) sympathetic readings are provided by Joanne Wright, Gabriella Slomp, Nancy Hirschmann, Karen Green, and others.[24] There are important differences between the criticisms of Hobbes in this regard, as well as between the various defenses or rereadings; but my concern is not to engage with this debate regarding Hobbes on gender. Given that my project is to develop a (reconstructed) Hobbesian theory of sexuality, I will only point out that while the troublesome nature of at least some of what Hobbes says about women is undeniable, his basic philosophical assumptions and claims about human nature are neither irredeemably nor even consistently misogynistic.

Conventionalism—A Double-Edged Sword?

I contend that these occasional, and even offensive, textual inconsistencies are not damning for a progressive theory of Hobbesian sexuality. But unfortunately a second and much stronger objection operates on the philosophical level. The same factors that make a Hobbesian theory of sexuality attractive to feminists and sex radicals also threaten to make it profoundly *un*attractive. Above, I distinguished Hobbes from the natural law tradition in sexual ethics on the grounds of his conventionalism and positivism, the view that moral norms are grounded in human law, not natural law. This position is a valuable weapon against attempts to enshrine heteronormative patriarchy in God and Nature, but this weapon is equally effective at guarding against attempts to ground universal rights to life, liberty, and sexual equality in the aforementioned God and Nature. In *Leviathan*, Hobbes refers to the right of nature as "a right to everything, even to one another's body."[25] It is generally understood from the text that this describes the right to kill, hurt, and enslave one another, but it could just as easily be extended to rape and sexual violence. On a natural reading of Hobbes's arguments, he seems to have no resources for grounding any claims that one form of sexuality is inherently better than another.

It is true that, on Hobbes's account, there is nothing inherently valuable about consent that would make sex without consent inherently objectionable. From a Hobbesian perspective, a law requiring that women who have sex outside of marriage (voluntarily or involuntarily) be stoned to death is unimpeachable and no different in kind from a law that requires people to pay income tax and specifies a penalty for failing to do so. If the law requires that sexual acts occur only in the context of monogamous, heterosexual marriage, then sexual acts between persons of the same sex or between persons of different sex who are not married are not just illegal but also immoral. Thus, the progressive potential of a Hobbesian theory of sexuality seems to be lost, as his positivism eliminates far too much; while Hobbes drains the force from arguments that purport to establish the inherent superiority of heterosexual monogamy, and arguments for the natural justification of "family values," this theory also undercuts arguments for sexual equality and diversity as well as a moral requirement that sex be consensual. Of course, theorists in contemporary sexual ethics have many resources available to them, besides those of the natural law tradition, for arguing that certain sexual behaviors and practices are immoral or unacceptable. The worry here is that those resources are not available to a Hobbesian, because, for Hobbes, what is right or good is simply *given* by the content of the civil law.

A Possible Way Out: The Hobbesian Basis for Public Policy

At this point, the sympathetic, progressive reader of Hobbes finds herself facing a dilemma. One the one hand, Hobbes is to be credited for denying any "natural" basis for normative sexuality, but, on the other, his reasons for denying a natural basis for normative sexuality are far from helpful and potentially dangerous—especially if the only candidate to fill the vacuum left by natural law is the contingent and arbitrary whim of the sovereign (or, in contemporary terms, the state). In this final section of this chapter, I wish to suggest that a modest solution to this dilemma can be found in Hobbes's public policy recommendations—that is, in his discussion of how a good (effective) sovereign would rule.

My solution emerges from an analysis of his rarely discussed recommendation in *The Elements of Law* that the sovereign ensure the "multitude" of the populace. In all three of his major political works, he includes a chapter on the duties of the sovereign. Even though the Hobbesian sovereign is not contractually bound to provide for his subjects or to enact reasonable and fair policy, he *is* bound to do so by the dictates of Hobbesian laws of nature,[26] and Hobbes spends a good amount of time explaining what this duty requires. In *The Elements of Law*,

Hobbes introduces the discussion of the duties of sovereigns by stating that he has just finished detailing the causes of the weakening and destruction of commonwealths, and he will now lay out what is necessary for their preservation. He states that the duty of the sovereign is to procure the temporal good of the people and stipulates that this good consists of four elements: "1. Multitude. 2. Commodity of living. 3. Peace amongst ourselves. 4. Defence against foreign power." It is in his discussion of the first, multitude, that we find the interesting and important material for our purposes. Let us look at the crucial passage in detail.

> Concerning multitude, it is the duty of them that are in sovereign authority, to increase the people, in as much as they are governors of mankind under God Almighty, who having created but one man, and one woman, declared that it was his will they should be multiplied and increased afterwards. And seeing this is to be done by ordinances concerning copulation: they are by the law of nature bound to make such ordinances concerning the same, as may tend to the increase of mankind. And hence it cometh, that in them who have sovereign authority: not to forbid such copulations as are against the use of nature; not to forbid the promiscuous use of women; not to forbid one woman to have many husbands; not to forbid marriages within certain degrees of kindred and affinity: are against the law of nature. For though it be not evident, that a private man living under the law of natural reason only, doth break the same, by doing any of these things aforesaid; yet it is manifestly apparent, that being so prejudicial as they are to the improvement of mankind, that not to forbid the same, is against the law of natural reason, in him that hath taken into his hands any portion of mankind to improve.[27]

Here, we see that Hobbes specifies that the sovereign should enact certain "ordinances concerning copulation," which, for example, forbid incest, "the promiscuous use of women," and women taking more than one husband at the same time (i.e., polyandry). He describes these as "copulations that are against the use of nature." However, his motivation and reasoning for making these claims are highly revealing. The goal is, as Hobbes says, to "increase the people." His first move is to say that it is not "evident" that "a private man living under the law of natural reason alone" (i.e., the state of nature) violates the law of nature by engaging in any of these practices (incest, promiscuity, and, presumably, being one man among others attached to the same woman). But, he reasons, because such practices are "prejudicial to the improvement of mankind" (by which he means increase in numbers), the sovereign is bound by the law of nature to forbid them.

The main steps in Hobbes's argument thus seem to be as follows. The good of the commonwealth depends on a healthy and growing population. The duty of the sovereign is to ensure the good of the commonwealth (he is bound by the law of nature to do so). So the duty of the sovereign is to promote population growth. Population growth is best achieved by enacting certain legislation that regulates sexual behavior in certain ways, specifically by prohibiting certain behaviors that might well have been acceptable in the state of nature. Therefore, the sovereign has a duty to enact that legislation. So, for Hobbes, the ultimate aim of population control via sexual regulation is the healthy, economic growth of the state. Adultery and polyandry are thus not seen as natural abominations; they are treated more like the wrong that you commit in not paying your taxes. Hence, Hobbes's discussion of possible "ordinances concerning copulation" confirms his distance from the natural law tradition discussed above; the only grounds for regulating and prohibiting sexual behaviors are to be found in the dictates of civil law, not in anything inherent in the behaviors themselves. Even the requirement that sex acts be procreative is contingent upon the demands of civil society, contra Aquinas and those in the natural law tradition.

This point disappears in Hobbes's later iterations of the same discussion. In *De Cive*, chronologically the next work, the four duties of sovereigns are "1) defence from external enemies; 2) preservation of internal peace; 3) acquisition of wealth, so far as that is consistent with public security; 4) full enjoyment of innocent liberty."[28] Population control and copulation have disappeared entirely. He mentions the commonwealth's (and so the sovereign's) interest in having a strong populace, fit to serve; and this is not unrelated to the point in *The Elements of Law*. But his first point of business in *De Cive* is to discuss the necessity of having "intelligence agents" or spies; then he talks about raising money for armies and the problems with the universities (though the last two were present in *The Elements of Law*, they were toward the end of the discussion). Fecundity is simply no longer a matter of concern in the mature statements of his political philosophy.

The concern with a strong populace (both in numbers and in health) was familiar to those of Hobbes's era. Historians have remarked that the significantly smaller populations of European countries often led to imperatives to increase fertility.[29] This broader context of concern offers a better explanation for Hobbes's interest in multitude than the rather puzzling biblical reference at the beginning of the passage in *The Elements of Law*. Given that population numbers were a matter of great concern in seventeenth-century England, it is more likely that Hobbes's pronatalism was an expression of that existing sentiment rather than a concern to take the words of Genesis seriously. After all, if he really had found the impetus to recommend multitude in the injunctions of the Bible, it does not make sense that this requirement drops out of his later discussions. Moreover, the logic of this passage as a whole is inconsistent with an appeal to scripture. If a country were overpopulated, by his own reasoning, Hobbes would have to recommend measures that would limit population growth.[30] So, though he appeals to scripture here, it is absolutely superfluous to the argument.

It is important to note that the justifications for these ordinances are entirely *pragmatic* and *consequentialist*. If population growth is not necessary for the "improvement of mankind," then it is not against reason for the sovereign to allow the behaviors Hobbes lists in the passage above. The common good is the only measure by which the sovereign's actions are to be guided and evaluated.

It is equally significant that Hobbes follows his discussion of multitude with the claim that the sovereign should not limit the "harmless liberties" of subjects any more than necessary for the common good. He does not explicitly connect the limit on harmless liberties to sexual behavior, but understanding the ramifications of his juxtaposition of the two points is crucial to understanding the Hobbesian view on sexual morality. He reiterates the point regarding harmless liberties in later works; if anything, it becomes more of a centerpiece in his discussion of the duties of sovereigns. Combined with the requirement that public policy be grounded in rational, empirically defensible analyses, we have very good reason to think that, when applied to sexuality, Hobbes would recommend policies that are devised to promote the common good (rather than to serve some particular moralistic camp at the expense of the liberty of other citizens).

How does this help answer the worry about the philosophical emptiness of his moral conventionalism and legal positivism? Recall the examples above: conventions regarding which side of the road to drive on and the imperial and metric systems of measurement. Both policies concern problems of coordination: it is better for the commonwealth that everyone drive on the same side of the road and that everyone use the same system of measurement. In some cases, it is an entirely arbitrary decision—it is no better or worse to drive on one side versus the other. The sovereign cannot go wrong in choosing one of these options, as a single enforced decision is all that is needed. But in other cases, there can be advantages and disadvantages to picking one option over the other (it is not merely a solution to a coordination problem). It is better for the commonwealth that everyone use either the imperial or the metric system than if there is general confusion in measurement, but there may also be grounds for recognizing one as more rationally defensible than the other. And it is reasonable to think that, at least in many cases, public policies regarding sexuality fall into the latter camp rather than the former (especially if the default is to allow harmless personal freedoms).

When we think of the decisions in sexual ethics that face us today, applying Hobbes's reasoning yields useful outcomes. For example, if we take seriously the idea that we should not limit people's "innocent" liberties any further than necessary to ensure a peaceful, prosperous commonwealth, then it seems that sodomy laws, for example, are unjustifiable. The judicious sovereign is unlikely to find a rational, empirically defensible analysis of how private, consensual acts of sodomy jeopardize the good of the state. The moralistic assumptions required to substantiate such policies are rendered bankrupt by Hobbes's analysis. Moreover, if we take seriously the idea that the sovereign (or state) should employ a rational basis for public policy, we get compelling grounds for critiquing, for example, Don't Ask Don't Tell (DADT), which most experts agree does not have a beneficial effect on the army's ability to do its job—in fact, quite the reverse, as it undermines morale, harms individual service people, and leads to significant numbers of discharges during times of war and need.[31] The presumption in favor of innocent liberty and the demand for rational, empirical evidence on which to base policy decisions will act (all other things being equal) to the benefit of sexual minorities and liberation. The point is that a well-functioning sovereign who follows the general principles of governing that Hobbes lays out is likely to have a relatively "good" sexual policy (or public policy on matters of sexuality).

One attractive feature of this argument is that it makes no appeal to contentious notions of "right" or "equality." The Hobbesian approach radically undercuts the moralistic basis for so much of what is offensive and unattractive in sexual ethics without replacing problematic concepts with equally controversial ones. In their place, Hobbes offers suggestions that start from a position of neutrality regarding the moral status of various practices and develop from there, using only appeals to rational evidence and the common goods of peace and safety.

Nevertheless, enthusiasm for this approach can only be moderate. Note that appeals to fairness and justice have no place in Hobbes's account. Specific recommendations will always depend on a consequentialist analysis. While I am confident in assuming that, in most cases, rational consequentialist thinking will result in good policy from the perspective of sexual liberation, this is by no means guaranteed across all societies. In the case of a stable but sexually repressive society, such as Victorian England (which severely limited the sexual rights of women and outlawed male homosexuality), a Hobbesian approach might very well not provide particularly useful resources for criticism. In part, this is because he denies the kinds of appeals to justice and fairness that would necessarily ground such criticism.

Conclusion

My aim in this chapter has been to (re)construct a Hobbesian theory of sexuality. In doing so, it has not been my intention to speculate regarding Hobbes's actual intentions in writing what he did about sex or sexuality, or *a fortiori*, to argue that such a theory is latent in the texts. The mark of a rich, significant body of philosophical writing is that it can go beyond what was intended by—or is even acceptable to—the philosopher himself.

I have argued that Hobbes can be distinguished from the majority of those who write about sexual ethics in the philosophical tradition, because of his staunch resistance to notions of natural or divinely ordained sexual prohibitions, his consistent commitment to moral conventionalism and legal positivism, and his willingness to entertain visions of diverse sexual practices and mores, marriage contracts, and relationships of dominance—not to mention his distinct lack of alarm at portrayals of strong, commanding female sexuality (as evidenced in his discussion of the Amazons). Moreover, the approach to public policy decisions that is articulated in Hobbes's ordinances concerning copulation offers an appealing alternative to the ways in which discourses of sexual policy are framed in contemporary debates. Someone hoping to argue that legal questions of sexual ethics should be determined by appeals to the common good, based on rationally defensible grounds, rather than the morality of a few at the expense of the rights of the many, will find in the writings of Hobbes—if not the man himself—a surprising ally. Given his aversion to political dissent and any actions that could result in civil unrest, however, the Hobbesian perspective will be a better friend to the progressive nation-builder than to the progressive reformer. Perhaps this explains why these particular aspects of Hobbes's corpus have received little or no attention in contemporary discussions of sexual ethics—we live in societies where we need reform. Nonetheless, even the reformer can draw inspiration from the rational, liberated form of sexuality Hobbes (or Hobbes reconstructed) seems to offer.

Notes

1. This is puzzling, as Nancy Hirschmann argues in this volume, because it is clearly a misnomer: there is no marriage in the state of nature (as Hobbes himself insists), so there cannot be "wives" in the state of nature. Presumably, Hobbes assumes the natural agents in question to be male and there to be womenfolk who are associated with or attached to them, much as a wife might attach herself to a husband.

2. These discussions are located in Hobbes, *The Elements of Law* 2.4.1–8, *De Cive* 9.1–8, and *Leviathan* 20.4–7. Hobbes's works are cited by part (if applicable), chapter, and paragraph number, using the following editions of his texts: Thomas Hobbes, *The Elements of Law, Natural and Politic*, ed. Ferdinand Tönnies (London: Frank Cass, 1969); Thomas Hobbes, *On the Citizen [De Cive]*, ed. and trans. Richard Tuck and Michael Silverthorne (Cambridge: Cambridge University Press, 1998); Thomas Hobbes, *Leviathan with Selected Variants from the Latin Edition of 1668*, ed. Edwin Curley (Indianapolis: Hackett, 1994); Thomas Hobbes, *Behemoth, or The Long Parliament*, ed. Ferdinand Tönnies (London: Frank Cass, 1969).

3. Hobbes, *Elements of Law* 2.4.5.

4. Hobbes, *Leviathan* 20.4.

5. Ibid., 129n7.

6. Quintus Curtius Rufus, *History of Alexander* 6.5.24–32, quoted in J. C. Yardley and Waldemar Heckel, *Alexander the Great: Historical Sources in Translation* (Oxford: Blackwell, 2004), 197.

7. One might worry that Hobbes's appeal to the Amazons could be read as a manifestation of the xenophobic racist and sexist attitudes that often underlie portrayals of women of other cultures, especially insofar as it hypersexualizes them. But I think we should hesitate before accepting this interpretation. As I see it, there is nothing at all in the text to suggest any kind of denigration (or moralistic judgment at all) of the Amazonian women. Notably, the other example he gives of these particular kinds of contracts (i.e., contracts between men and women in the state of nature that specify the status of the children ahead of time) is the contracts between kings and queens of

different nations. It is more plausible, then, to read Hobbes's appeal to the Amazons as a disinterested move in an effort to canvass logical space. What is notable about them is the unique contracts they made, not their status as "savages" or their "other" sexual expression.

8. Hobbes, *De Cive* 9.3.
9. Hobbes, *Leviathan* 13.13.
10. James Grantham Turner, *Libertines and Radicals in Early Modern London: Sexuality, Politics, and Literary Culture, 1630–1685* (Cambridge: Cambridge University Press, 2002), xv, 86–88. Joanne Wright expresses a more moderate version of this point, saying that "in this sustained argument about the Amazons, Hobbes creates a space in his political theory for an alternative conception of women, thereby disrupting conventional views"; Joanne H. Wright, *Origin Stories in Political Thought: Discourses on Gender, Power, and Citizenship* (Toronto: University of Toronto Press, 2004), 92. Wright, unlike Turner, does not want to read Hobbes as an undiscovered feminist radical; in fact, from a feminist perspective, she is often more critical of Hobbes than not.
11. Hobbes, *De Cive* 14.9.
12. Hobbes, *Elements of Law* 1.9.17.
13. Hobbes, *De Cive* 14.10.
14. Hobbes, *Leviathan* 21.18.
15. Hobbes, *Elements of Law* 2.10.8. The full paragraph expresses the philosophical point quite well. Hobbes says, "In the state of nature, where every man is his own judge, and differeth from other concerning the names and appellations of things, and from those differences arise quarrels, and breach of peace; it was necessary there should be a common measure of all things that might fall into controversy; as for example: of what is to be called right, what good, what virtue, what much, what little, what *meum* and *tuum*, what a pound, what a quart, &c. For in these things private judgments may differ, and beget controversy. This common measure, some say, is right reason: with whom I should consent, if there were any such thing to be found or known *in rerum naturâ*. But commonly they that call for right reason to decide any controversy, do mean their own. But this is certain, seeing right reason is not existent, the reason of some man, or men, must supply the place thereof; and that man, or men, is he or they, that have the sovereign power, as hath been already proved; and consequently the civil laws are to all subjects the measures of their actions, whereby to determine, whether they be right or wrong, profitable or unprofitable, virtuous or vicious; and by them the use and definition of all names not agreed upon, and tending to controversy, shall be established. As for example, upon the occasion of some strange and deformed birth, it shall not be decided by Aristotle, or the philosophers, whether the same be a man or no, but by the laws."
16. This is especially clear in Hobbes, *De Cive* 6.16.
17. In fact, Edward, Earl of Clarendon, very famously disparaged Hobbes on just this point.
18. Hobbes, *De Cive* 14.9.
19. For example, Augustine says in *De nuptiis et concupiscentia*, "A man turns to good use the evil of concupiscence . . . when he bridles and restrains its rage . . . and never relaxes his hold upon it except when intent on offspring, and then controls and applies it to the carnal generation of children . . . not to the subjection of the spirit to the flesh in a sordid servitude"; Augustine, *On Marriage and Concupiscence* [written 419–20], in *The Works of Aurelius Augustine, Bishop of Hippo*, ed. Marcus Dods, trans. Peter Holmes, vol. 12 (Edinburgh: T. and T. Clark, 1874), 107. Saint Thomas Aquinas wrote extensively on sexual ethics, arguing, for example, that all nonprocreative sex was morally forbidden because "when the act of its nature is incompatible with the purpose of the sex-act [procreation] . . . we have unnatural vice, which is any complete sex-act from which of its nature generation cannot follow." Moreover, for Aquinas, such procreative sex is only permissible within the context of heterosexual monogamous marriage: "It is evident that the bringing up of a human child requires the care of a mother who nurses him, and much more the care of a father, under whose guidance and guardianship his earthly needs are supplied and his character developed. Therefore indiscriminate intercourse is against human nature. The union of one man with one woman is postulated, and with

her he remains, not for a little while, but for a long period, or even for a whole lifetime"; St. Thomas Aquinas, *Summa theologiae*, vol. 43 (2a2ae.141–54), *Temperance* [written 1265–74], ed. Thomas Gilby (Cambridge: Cambridge University Press, 2006), 213.

20. For an interesting discussion of Grotius's views on sex and gender, see Helen M. Kinsella, "Gendering Grotius: Sex and Sex Difference in the Laws of War," *Political Theory* 34, no. 2 (2006): 161–91.

21. See, for example, Turner, *Libertines and Radicals*; Simon Blackburn, *Lust* (Oxford: Oxford University Press, 2004), esp. ch. 10, entitled "Hobbesian Unity"; and Richard Hillyer, "Hobbes on Sex," *Hobbes Studies* 22, no. 1 (2009): 29–48. Hillyer notes that Hobbes's views on lust are "significantly non-judgmental . . . by the standards of his time" and that Hobbes has "an essentially uncensorious view of human sexuality [and a] critique of sexual repression" (29), but he is concerned to discuss the literary, religious, and historical context of Hobbes's views on sex as well as how those views were received. So, while Hillyer's discussion is informative, it sheds little light on Hobbes's views on sex understood as part of his philosophical project.

22. Hobbes, *Elements of Law* 1.9.15. For a discussion of Hobbes's views on love, see Haig Patapan and Jeffrey Sikkenga, "Love and the Leviathan: Thomas Hobbes's Critique of Platonic Eros," *Political Theory* 36, no. 2 (2008): 803–26. Note that, although Patapan and Sikkenga do not call attention to this fact themselves, Hobbes's views on love are distinctly nongendered.

23. Hobbes, *De Cive* 14.9.

24. For representative examples, see Gabriella Slomp, "Hobbes and the Equality of Women," *Political Studies* 42, no. 3 (1994): 441–52; Joanne H. Wright, "Going Against the Grain: Hobbes's Case for Original Maternal Dominion," *Journal of Women's History* 14, no. 1 (2002): 123–32; Karen Green, "Christine de Pisan and Thomas Hobbes," *Philosophical Quarterly* 44, no. 177 (1994): 456–75; and Nancy J. Hirschmann, *Gender, Class, and Freedom in Modern Political Theory* (Princeton, N.J.: Princeton University Press, 2008).

25. Hobbes, *Leviathan* 14.4.

26. The similarity of phrasing here is, of course, unfortunate: it is important to keep in mind just how different natural law (understood normatively, as in the Thomistic tradition) is from the Hobbesian laws of nature, which bear closer resemblance to the laws of motion, for example.

27. Hobbes, *Elements of Law* 2.9.3.

28. Hobbes, *De Cive* 13.6.

29. See, for example, Angus McLaren, *Reproductive Rituals: The Perception of Fertility in England from the Sixteenth Century to the Nineteenth Century* (London: Methuen, 1984), esp. ch. 2, entitled "'To Remedy Barrenness and to Promote the Faculty of Generation': Promoting Fertility, 1500–1800."

30. Hobbes might very well have supported China's one-child policy, for example.

31. Every report commissioned by the Department of Defense and Congress has concluded that the presence of gays and lesbians in the military does not jeopardize national security or negatively affect military readiness; for more information, see "About 'Don't Ask, Don't Tell,'" Servicemembers Legal Defense Network, http://www.sldn.org/pages/about-dadt. In December 2009, congressman Jim Moran and ninety-six other representatives wrote an open letter to Secretary of Defense Robert Gates outlining some of the negative effects of DADT: "This discriminatory policy results in the Department of Defense losing tens of millions each year in unrecoverable recruiting and training costs. The 2006 Blue Ribbon Commission's report on DADT found that the Pentagon wasted over $360 million due to this policy from 1994 until 2003, the last year studied. Since its enactment in 1994, over 13,500 service members have been discharged under DADT, including 730 mission critical soldiers and over 65 Arabic and Farsi linguists vital to the war on terrorism"; the letter is available on the Palm Center website at http://www.palmcenter.org/letter_congressman_moran_and_96_other_representatives_pentagon.

Notes on Contributors

Joanne Boucher is Associate Professor in the Department of Politics at the University of Winnipeg. Her research focuses on early modern political thought, feminist theory, reproductive rights, and new reproductive technologies.

Karen Detlefsen is Associate Professor of Philosophy and Education at the University of Pennsylvania. Her research focuses on seventeenth-and eighteenth-century philosophy with emphases on natural philosophy, women philosophers, and philosophy of education. She is the editor of *Descartes' Meditations: A Critical Guide* (2012).

Karen Green is Associate Professor in the School of Philosophical, Historical, and International Studies at Monash University. She is the author, with Jacqueline Broad, of *A History of Women's Political Thought in Europe, 1400–1700* (2009) and editor, with Broad, of *Virtue, Liberty, and Toleration: Political Ideas of European Women, 1400–1800* (2007). With Constant Mews and Janice Pinder, she translated Christine de Pizan's *Book of Peace* (2008), and edited, with Mews, *Virtue Ethics for Women, 1250–1500* (2011). She is currently working on a follow-up volume to the *History of Women's Political Thought in Europe* covering the years 1700 to 1800.

Wendy Gunther-Canada is Professor of Government at the University of Alabama at Birmingham and is the current chairperson of that department. She is the author of *Rebel Writer: Mary Wollstonecraft and Enlightenment Politics* (2001) and co-author of the third, fourth, and fifth editions of *Women, Politics, and American Society* (2002, 2005, 2011). Gunther-Canada is completing a book-length manuscript on Catharine Macaulay's political thought. She received her Ph.D. from Rutgers University.

Nancy J. Hirschmann is Professor of Political Science at The University of Pennsylvania. Her most recent books include *Gender, Class, and Freedom in Modern Political Theory* (2008) and *The Subject of Liberty: Toward a Feminist Theory of Freedom* (2003), which won the 2004 Victoria Schuck Award for the best book on women and politics. She is also co-editor with Kirstie McClure of *Feminist Interpretations of John Locke* (2007) and with Beth Linker of *Civil Disabilities: Theory, Citizenship, and the Body* (forthcoming 2013).

Jane S. Jaquette is a teaching Emeritus Professor of Politics and Diplomacy and World Affairs at Occidental College and Adjunct Research Professor at Brown University's Watson Institute for International Studies. She is the editor of and a contributor to several books on women's political participation in Latin America and on women and development, most recently *Feminist Agendas and Democracy in Latin America* (2009). She contributed an essay to *Feminist Interpretations of Niccolò Machiavelli* (2004) and is currently working on a book on rethinking U.S.–Latin American relations with her husband, Abraham Lowenthal.

S. A. Lloyd is Professor of Philosophy, Law, and Political Science at the University of Southern California. She is the author of *Ideals as Interests in Hobbes's "Leviathan"* (1992) and *Morality in the Philosophy of Thomas Hobbes* (2009), editor of *Hobbes Today* (2012), and author of many articles in contemporary liberal feminism and Rawls studies.

Su Fang Ng is Associate Professor of English at the University of Oklahoma. She is the author of a book, *Literature and the Politics of Family in Seventeenth-Century England* (2007), and articles ranging from the medieval to the postcolonial periods. She is currently working on Alexander the Great, cross-cultural ideas of empire, and Anglo-Dutch-indigenous relations in the East Indies. Her work has been supported by long-term residential fellowships at the Radcliffe Institute for Advanced Study at Harvard University, at the National Humanities Center, and at the Harrington Faculty Fellows Program at the University of Texas at Austin.

Carole Pateman is Distinguished Professor Emeritus in the Department of Political Science at UCLA and Honorary Professor in the School of European Studies at Cardiff University (UK). She is the winner of the Johan Skytte Prize in Political Science for 2012 and is a former president of the American Political Science Association (2010–11) and the International Political Science Association (1991–94). Her publications include *Participation and Democratic Theory* (1970), *The Problem of Political Obligation* (1979; 2nd ed. 1985), *The Sexual Contract* (1988), and, with Charles Mills, *Contract and Domination* (2007). Her new book, edited with Matthew Murray, *Basic Income Worldwide: Horizons of Reform*, was published by Palgrave in 2012.

Gordon Schochet is Professor Emeritus of Political Science at Rutgers University, where he taught political and legal philosophy and the history of political thought for over forty years. He is one of the founding directors of the Center for the History of British Political Thought at the Folger Shakespeare Library, and the author of *Patriarchalism in Political Thought* (1975), numerous articles on the history of British political thought, and the forthcoming *Rights in Context*.

Quentin Skinner is the Barber Beaumont Professor of the Humanities at Queen Mary, University of London. He was at the Institute for Advanced Study at Princeton between 1974 and 1979 and was the Regius Professor of History at the University of Cambridge from 1996 to 2008. His publications on Hobbes include *Reason and Rhetoric in the Philosophy of Hobbes* (1996); *Hobbes and Civil Science* (2002), the third volume of *Visions of Politics*; and *Hobbes and Republican Liberty* (2008), all published by Cambridge University Press.

Susanne Sreedhar is Assistant Professor in the Philosophy Department at Boston University. She received her Ph.D. in philosophy from the University of North Carolina at

Chapel Hill and a graduate degree in women's studies from Duke University. Cambridge University Press published her book, *Hobbes on Resistance: Defying the Leviathan*, in 2010.

Joanne H. Wright is Associate Professor of Political Science at the University of New Brunswick. Her primary research area is early modern political thought. She is the author of *Origin Stories in Political Thought: Discourses on Gender, Power, and Citizenship* (2004) and is currently writing a monograph on the political thought of Margaret Cavendish.

Index

abortion
    Gonzalez v. Carhart, 14
    McDonagh on, 221–22
    right to, 219–20
    self-preservation and, 232–35
    Thomson on, 221
absolute sovereignty
    argument for, 1, 74–76
    Astell and, 177
    Cavendish and, 158–60
    description of, 50
    Macaulay and, 199
    as perversion of power, 206
    vices of, 204
acquisition
    paternal power as form of, 195
    power derived from, 108–9, 113–15, 133–34
    as primary form of "consent" given, 143
    sovereignty by, 242–44
action
    information given by, 245–51
    as proceeding from will, 243, 253, 255
Agamben, Giorgio, 89, 96, 97
Alexander the Great, 263–64
altruism, 140–41
Amazons
    children of, 129
    as commonwealth of women, 28, 261
    contracts of copulation of, 51, 262–65
    as matriarchal society, 58
    paternal right and, 197
American Indians. *See* Native Americans
animalization of body, 85–87, 88–89, 97
animals, views of, 68

Annas, Julia, 126
Anne (queen), 175, 177
anthropology
    account of patriarchy as, 128
    account of state of nature as, 30, 31, 122
    in account of state, 115
    cultural, interpretation compared to, 41
Aquinas, 268
Aristotle, 4, 72
Ashcraft, Richard, 87, 94
Astell, Mary
    The Christian Religion, 175
    on Civil War, 178
    critiques of Hobbes of, 171, 173–77
    Moderation Truly Stated, 175
    as political theorist, 39
    Serious Proposal to the Ladies, 174
    views of, compared to views of Macaulay, 179, 180, 181
    on virtue, 183
    on women's subordination to men, 29
Aubrey, John, 38
Augustine, 268
authority. *See also* mother-right; patriarchy/patriarchalism; sovereignty; state
    degendering of, 85, 86, 97
    derivation of in consent, 111–13
    of fathers, 110–12, 134
    laws of nature and, 73
    Macaulay on, 198–99
    of monarchs, 175–77
    over children, 127, 129
    rational-legal compared to compassionate, 65–66
authorization in civil philosophy, 40

Bacon, Francis, 67
Baumgold, Deborah, 74, 244
Behemoth (Hobbes), 70, 91, 201
Bérubé, Michael, x–xi
Bloch, Ruth, 10
body
  of Amazons, 263–64
  biopolitics, 223–32
  breast implants, 251–53
  effect of fetus on, 221–22, 233
  Hobbes's preoccupation with, 230, 235
  liberty and, 229–31
  mechanization and animalization of, 85–87, 88–89, 97
  obsession with, 253–54
  preservation of, 228–29, 235
  right to, in state of nature, 270–71
  of sovereign, gender of, 83–85
  as vulnerable to decay, 98
Bolingbroke, Lord, 180
Botox, advertisement for, 253
Boucher, Joanne, 77
Bramhall, John, 86–87, 94, 107, 110, 117–18
breast implants
  choice of, 252–53
  complications with surgery, 251–52
  politics of, 248, 255–56
  popularity of, 251
Brennan, Teresa
  critiques of social contract theory, 170
  "'Mere Auxiliaries to the Commonwealth,'" 2, 19
Brett, Annabel, 34
Bruce, Christian, 38
Burke, Edmund, *Reflections on the Revolution in France*, 183, 195, 203–4
Butler, Todd, 93

Cambridge school, 6, 7
canons of philosophy, ix–xi, 190
Captive Samaritan argument, 222, 233
Cartesian dualism, 67
Cato, 88, 89
Cavendish, Charles, 151–52
Cavendish, Margaret
  The Convent of Pleasure, 151, 153–54
  The Female Academy, 151, 153, 154
  Hobbes influence on, 149–50
  on human nature, civil society, and freedom, 155–60
  Philosophical Letters, 155–56
  plays of, 150–51
  as political theorist, 37–38, 39
  on state of nature and civil society, 160–67
  on women, education, and freedom, 150–54
  Youths Glory, 150, 152
Cavendish, William (1st Duke of Newcastle), 151–52
Cavendish, William (2nd Earl of Devonshire), 92
Charles I, 28, 177–78, 201, 205
childbirth, death from, 232–33
children
  ability of to make covenants, 112–13
  authority over, 127, 129
  confederacy with mothers, 133, 136–37, 138, 197
  consent of, 111–12, 114–15, 119–20, 193, 196
  dominion of mothers over, 29, 74, 131, 140, 225–26
  gratitude to mothers, 136–37
  obligation of, 111, 198–99
choice feminism
  breast augmentation and, 251–57
  description of, 240–41
  epistemology of ignorance in, 250–51, 256–57
  Linda Hirshman and, 246, 255
  as masking imperatives as options, 255
  political meaning and, 255–56
  view of actions in, 243, 245–51, 253, 255
The Christian Religion, as Profess'd by a Daughter of The Church of England (Astell), 175
citizens/subjects
  education of, 166
  ideal, 84–85
  liberty of, 164, 229
  relations among, 89
  right of rebellion, 81 nn. 76, 78, 230–31
civil society. *See also* commonwealth; state
  Bramhall on, 117–18
  dominion in, 129, 130
  equality in, 72
  human nature and freedom in, 155–60
  sons in, 131
  state of nature and, 87, 160–67
  transition to, 164–66
  women in formation of, 95
Civil War
  Astell on, 178

De Cive and, 202–3
Hobbes view of, 75, 201
Lloyd on, 75
Macaulay on, 178
social contract and, 70–71
Clark, Lorenne, 2
coercion. *See also* force
consent and, 242–45, 246, 255
cosmetic surgery and, 253
materialism and, 256–57
Coli, Daniela, 67–68
commonwealth. *See also* state
families in, 95, 116–17, 126, 133, 138–39, 143
men and establishment of, 28, 117–18
origins of, 172
relations among, 89
safety, security, and, 228–29, 231–32
concord of natural lust and Native Americans, 29, 30, 33
Configurations of Masculinity (Di Stefano), 2, 10
conflict
absolute sovereignty and, 74–75
causes of, 69–71, 139–40, 142
logic of, in state of nature, 59–60
conquest
political legitimacy of regimes after, 231
sovereignty by acquisition, 242–44
conquest of women
contracts and, 133–34
gratitude and, 141–43
motivation for, 137
consent. *See also* social contract
of child to authority, 111–12, 114–15, 119–20, 133, 193, 196
choice feminism and, 240–41
coercion and, 24, 143, 244–45, 246, 255
as concept, 31, 49, 126
conquest and, 242–44
epistemology of ignorance and, 256–57
to fetus effects on bodies, 221–22
Macaulay on, 181–82
to oppression, 247–48
under patriarchy, 248
to sovereign, 126, 130, 135–36, 138–39, 141–42
as revealed by actions, 245–51
to sex, 270–71
sexual assault law and, 248–50
theory of, 241–42

of women to husbands, 24–25, 127, 135–36, 139, 142
consequentialism, 276
Considerations (Hobbes), 26
contemporary problems. *See also* abortion; choice feminism; sexuality, theory of
application of philosophy to, 13–14, 31, 276
opposition to, 220
sexual ethics, 275–76
contraception, 233–34. *See also* abortion
Contract and Domination (Pateman and Mills), 30
contractarianism, 42. *See also* original contract
contracts. *See also* marriage contracts; original contract; social contract
conquest and, 133–34
in state of nature, 132–33
contract theory. *See* social contract theory
contributors to volume, 3–4
The Convent of Pleasure (Cavendish), 151, 153–54
Coole, Diana, 226
copulation
covenants of, 262–65
ordinances concerning, 272–73, 274
cosmetic surgery, elective. *See also* breast implants
growth of, 251–52
political work to sell concept of, 252–53
covenants
ability of children to make, 112–13
distinguished from contract, 129
of copulation, 262–65
in establishing normativity, 268
political, conceptions of, 26
in state of nature, 133, 143
Cromwell, Oliver, 37, 191, 202
Curley, Edwin, 263
Curtius, Quintus, *History of Alexander*, 263–64

Davenant, Charles, 175–77
Dawson, Hannah, 34
De Bry, 32
De Cive (Hobbes)
Civil War and, 202–3
dedicatory letter of, 88
on definition of family, 131
on democracy, 205
on dominion of mother, 74, 131, 140
on duties of sovereigns, 273

De Cive (continued)
- on equality of women, 128, 130
- on fathers, 117
- on families, 108
- frontispiece of, 32
- Hobbes translation of, 108
- on individualism, 107
- Macaulay response to, 191
- on obligations of children, 111, 116
- on obligation to mothers, 111
- on paternal government, 110
- on paternal power, 196
- on power of monarchy, 195
- on queens, 130
- on reasons for entering society, 194
- on Roman people, 200–201
- on safety and trust, 70
- on servants, 133, 137
- on sons, 116, 131
- on support of monarchy, 199–200
- on workings of state, 83

De Corpore Politico (Hobbes), 109
de Jouvenel, Bertrand, 119, 121
democracy, Macaulay on, 204–6
Derrida, Jacques, critique of project of recovering intended meaning, 20–21
Descartes, René, 67, 68
Dialogue Between a Philosopher and a Student (Hobbes), 109
Dietz, Mary, 72–73
diffidence, as cause of conflict, 69, 70
"A Discourse of Rome" (Hobbes), 93
discrimination and gender inequality, 131–32
Di Stefano, Christine, 2, 10, 49, 172, 226
Dixon, Marlene, "Why Women's Liberation?," 246–47
Don't Ask Don't Tell policy, 275

early feminist critiques of Hobbes
- by Elshtain, 64
- by Jones, 65–66
- by Merchant, 64–65
- by Pateman, 65

education
- Astell on, 174
- children's obligation to parents for, 117, 131
- Macaulay on, 183, 210
- women and, 150–54, 166

educational context of Hobbes, 21–22
egoism, psychological, 169–70, 171, 172, 178, 179–81

Eisenstein, Zillah, 2
The Elements of Law (Hobbes)
- on characteristics of men, 131
- on family, 40, 131
- on population growth, 271–73, 274
- on queens, 130

Elizabeth I, 71, 176–77
Elshtain, Jean Bethke, 2, 64, 68, 71
epistemology of ignorance, 249–51, 256–57
equality
- ambiguity on, 136
- characteristics shared by humans and, 224, 227–28
- in civil society, 72
- Hobbes and, 4, 52, 172–73
- Macaulay and, 207, 208
- between men and women, 6, 12, 19–20, 24, 42, 51–52, 54–57, 59–60, 63, 65, 128, 131, 134–36, 139, 142
- of parties to the social contract, 19–20, 48
- in state of nature, 24–25, 47–48, 51–53, 68–71, 126, 128–29, 131, 134, 135
- strength and, 128, 142, 224–25
- women's rights and, 76–77

family. *See also* children; fathers; mothers; patriarchal family
- authoritarian structure of, 138
- in civil society, 29
- as commonwealth, 116–17
- concept of, 71
- definitions of, 40–41, 126–27, 130–31
- Hobbes on, 1–2
- Native Americans and, 29, 94–95, 116
- relation to state, 90–91
- social contract as predating, 139–40
- in state of nature, 29, 107–8, 116–18, 118–19
- story of Romulus and Remus, 98
- women in, 5, 95, 130–31, 133–34, 165

fathers. *See also* paternity; patriarchal family; patriarchy/patriarchalism
- authority of, 110–12, 134
- caretaking, power of, 58–59
- establishment of commonwealth and, 117–18
- power of fatherhood, 108–11, 114–15, 119–20, 195, 196–97

fear
- acts motivated by, 244, 249

exercise of power through, 159
  as foundation for state power, 142
  legitimacy of contract based on, 242
The Female Academy (Cavendish), 151, 153, 154
feminism. *See also* choice feminism
  "Cambridge school" and, 7–8
  choice as governing ethos of, 240–41
  critiques of Hobbes from early feminists, 64–66
  effect of on reading Hobbes, 19–20, 23–26, 29–30, 42–43
  and the history of political thought, 25, 34–36, 39
  Hobbes and, 4–5
  political theory and, 7, 19–20, 23–25, 34–37
  Second Wave, 246, 250
  Skinner and, 125–26
fertility, control of, 233–34
fetal personhood and right to self-preservation, 221–22, 232–35
Filmer, Robert
  on father dominion, 108
  Patriarcha, 118, 192
  patriarchalism of, 94–95, 110
  on right of nature, 107
  view of women of, 128
Flathman, Richard, 68, 74, 76
force. *See also* coercion
  mastering others by, 54, 243–44
  in patriarchal family, 210–11
The Foundations of Modern Political Thought (Skinner), 21
freedom. *See also* liberty
  Cavendish theory of, 161–63
  civic, 158–60
  coercion and, 242–44
  education and, 150–54
  human nature and, 155–57
  in natural world, 160–61
  security and, 165
  of women, 42–43, 157–58
Friedman, Marilyn, 162
Frost, Samantha, 228

Geertz, Clifford, 41
gender. *See also* feminism, women
  Hobbes and, 2, 26, 98
  inequality based on, 131–32
  intellect and, 151–54
  of philosophers in canons of philosophy, ix–x
  role of in Hobbes interpretation, 7–8
  of sovereigns, 27–29, 83–86, 126, 129–30
gender analysis in history of political thought and history of philosophy, 34–37
gender ideologies and process of canonization, xi
Genovese, Elizabeth Fox, 10
Gill, Sarah Prince ("Sophronia"), 184
glory, as cause of conflict, 70–71
God, Hobbes view of, 80 n. 28
"'God Hath Ordained to Man a Helper'" (Pateman), 6, 19, 27
Gonzalez v. Carhart, 14
Gooch, G. P., 107
government. *See* commonwealth; sovereign; sovereignty; state
Graham, Catharine Sawbridge Macaulay. *See* Macaulay, Catharine
gratitude
  of children to mothers, 136–38
  as concern of moral philosophers and theologians, 106
  consent of child and, 111–12, 114–15
  equality and, 51
  as fourth law of nature, 11, 51, 72, 106,
  and political obligation, 126
  role of in subordination of women, 141–43
greed, 69, 72
Green, Felicity, 34
Green, Karen, 135, 270
Grotius, 268

Haraway, Donna, 89
Harrington, James, *Oceana*, 202, 207
Hill, Bridget, *The Republican Virago*, 191
Hill, Christopher, 20
Hirschmann, Nancy
  on agency, 68
  on consent and coercion, 244
  critiques of Hobbes, 270
  on freedom and transition to civil society, 164–66
  on freedom of women, 158, 162
  on Hobbes's theory of freedom, 158
  on matriarchal sovereignty, 196–97
  on oppression, 253
  on prudence, 54
  revision of canon by, 190

Hirschmann, Nancy (*continued*)
  on socialization, 254
  on women's status in seventeenth century England, 77
Hirshman, Linda, 246, 255
historical origins of state, 115–16
history, Schochet definition of, 122 n. 38
History of England from the Accession of James I to That of the Brunswick Line (Macaulay), 191, 199, 202, 205, 209
Hobbes, Thomas. *See also De Cive; The Elements of Law; Leviathan*
  Behemoth, 70, 91, 201
  biopolitics of, 223–32
  Cavendish and, 37–38
  Considerations, 26
  Dialogue Between a Philosopher and a Student, 109
  "A Discourse of Rome," 93
  early life of, 38–39
  educational context of, 21–22, 39
  Horae Subsecivae, 90, 92, 94
  impeachment trial of Strafford and, 199
  as innovator, 119–20
  as member of Virginia Company, 30
  role of women in life of, 25
  view of God, 80 n. 28
Hobbes and Civil Science (Skinner), 25–26
Hobbes and Republican Liberty (Skinner), 21
"Hobbes on Representation" (Skinner), 37
"Hobbes's *Leviathan*" (Skinner), 20
homosexuality, 268–69, 275
Horae Subsecivae (Hobbes), 90, 92, 94
humanism and Hobbes, 22
human nature
  Cavendish on, 155–60
  Hobbes on 63, 64, 68–70, 128, 131, 135, 138, 140, 170, 184, 192, 203, 211, 270
  Macaulay on, 178–79, 193–94, 203–4
Hume, David, *History of England from Julius Caesar to the Glorious Revolution*, 191

individualism
  abstract, 2, 3, 9, 33, 63, 64, 66, 133, 226–27, 267
  Cavendish on, 12, 155–57
  and hyperindividualism, 2, 162, 163–64
  methodological, 2, 66
  radical, 2, 13, 22, 23, 33, 42–43
institution, sovereignty by, 27, 49, 108–09, 113–15, 117–18, 127, 133, 141, 143, 241–42

instrumental power, 53, 54–55
intellect and gender, 12, 128, 142, 151–54
intellectualism of Astell and Macaulay, 179–80
interdisciplinarity of contributors to volume, 3–4
interpretation, future of
  Pateman on, 42–43
  Skinner on, 41–42

Jaggar, Alison, 169
James I, 201, 205
Jaquette, Jane, 130, 227
Johnston, David, 4
Jones, Kathleen, 65–66, 69, 71, 74, 75
"just so" theory of subordination of women, 55–57, 128

Kahn, Victoria, 70, 84–85
Kant, I., *Groundwork for a Metaphysics of Morals*, 180
Khanna, Julie, 252

Lange, Lynda, 2
language, holistic view of, 23
law, life without, 30, 32, 33
Laws of Nature. *See also* gratitude; obligation
  on achievement of justice, 75
  binding force of, 73, 76
  as civic attributes, 72–73
  civil association and, 71–72, 78
  compleasance (fifth), 72
  covenants, 51
  equality of sexes, 52, 224
  gratitude (fourth) 11, 51, 72, 106, 111, 115, 120, 142–43
  of justice (third), 75
  of liberty (first), 71–72
  on parental power, 59, 136, and positive law, 76
  against pride (ninth), 72
  on rights, 49, 224
  seek peace (first), 33–34, 49, 60, 140
  of self-preservation (first), 74
  as set of virtues and opposing vices, 72
Letters on Education (Macaulay), 183, 196, 210–11
Levellers, 77
Leviathan (Hobbes)
  avoidance of gender in, 26
  biblical injunctions and, 76
  Cromwell and, 191, 202

on families, 40–41, 71, 108, 110
frontispiece of, 28, 32–33, 84
on gender, 95
on gender of sovereign, 27
on human-animal opposition, 87
as humanist text, 22
on life of man in state of nature, 86
on methodology, 67
on Native Americans, 94–95
opening image of, 83
on paternal authority, 111–12
on political covenants, 26
on queens, 130
on right of nature, 270
on transfer of rights, 242
as treatise, 37
Tricaud on, 70
on wives, 130, 261, 269
liberalism
critiques of, and social contract theory, 169–70
feminist hostility to, 78
as fundamentally patriarchal, 63–66
ideals of, 77–78
individualism and, 66–71
liberty. *See also* freedom
Astell on, 175
choice and, 240
coercion and, 244
Hobbes's materialist conception of, 243–244
Macaulay on, 182–83, 184, 185
natural, compared to liberty of subjects, 164
necessity and, 155
negative liberty theory, 157, 230
presumption in favor of, 275–76
reformulation of concept of, 185
self-preservation and, 229–31
in state of nature, 32
theory of, 41–42
Lloyd, Sharon, 75–76, 132, 166
Locke, John
answer to Filmer, 120
First Treatise on Government, 198
Macaulay and, 178
on marriage, 77
on public and private realms, 173
social contract theory of, 60
Two Treatises on Government, 207
women, family, and, 1
Loose Remarks on Certain Positions to Be Found in Mr. Hobbes's "Philosophical Rudiments of Government and Society" (Macaulay), 178, 190–91, 208–12
Lucretia, rape of, 90, 91

Macaulay, Catharine
as anticipating modern feminism, 171
on children owing obedience, 198–99
contract theory of, 181–83, 185
on execution of Charles I, 177–78
History of England, 191, 199, 202, 205, 209
Hobbes as target of, 191–92, 202, 203–4
on human nature, 178–79, 193–94, 203–4
on legitimacy of social contract, 208–10
Letters on Education, 183, 196, 210–11
Loose Remarks, 178, 190–91, 208–12
on marriage contract, 196
on matriarchy, 197–98
on model republic, 207–8
on monarchy, 199–202, 206–7
Observations on the Reflections of the Right Hon. Edmund Burke, 183, 195, 203–4, 208
on origin of paternal power, 196–99
political philosophy of, 184–85
on power, 195
on psychological egoism, 179–81
publications and writings of, 170, 190–91
on religion, 183–84
on sovereignty, 194–96
Treatise on the Immutability of Moral Truth, 179, 180, 183, 202
on types of government, 204–6
on virtue and government, 183
Macpherson, C. B., 7, 20, 22, 23
Maine, Henry Sumner, 107
"makeover culture," 15, 253, 255
Makus, Ingrid, 227
Malcolm, Noel, 38
male gaze, as internalized, 254
Mansbridge, Jane, 75
marriage
Cavendish on, 153–54
as conventional, 20
Macauley on, 183
patriarchal, 139
social contract and, 137–38
in state of nature, 129, 132
marriage contracts
as covenants of cohabitation, 51–52
Macaulay on, 196, 210

marriage contracts (*continued*)
　Pateman on, 65, 84
　relationships of power and, 57
Martinich, A. P., 93
materialism, 67–68, 156, 235, 256–57
matriarchy, 139, 141, 142, 196–98
matrimony, laws of, 29
McDonagh, Eileen, *Breaking the Abortion Deadlock*, 221–22, 232, 233, 235
mechanism, 64–65
mechanization of body, 85–86, 97
men. *See also* fathers; patriarchal family; patriarchy/patriarchalism
　characteristics of, 131
　commonwealth and, 28, 117–18
　Pateman on, 130
　social contract as creation of, 23–25, 27–28, 96, 135
Merchant, Carolyn, 64–65
"'Mere Auxiliaries to the Commonwealth'" (Brennan and Pateman), 2, 19, 20, 30
methodology
　Pateman on, 22
　Skinner on, 20–21, 23
Meyers, Diana Tietjens, 162
military command and titles, 57–58
Mill, John Stuart, 39
Mills, Charles, 30, 250
Moderation Truly Stated (Astell), 175
modernity, concepts and ideas of, 4
monarchy. *See also* sovereign; sovereignty
　cost-benefit analysis of, 204–6
　Macaulay on, 199–202, 206–7
　queens, 28–29, 130
　Stuart, 202–3
　succession and gender, 131
moral truth, Macaulay on, 179–80, 183–84
mother-right. *See also* mothers: dominion over children
　claim of natural, 262
　female sexuality and, 265–66
　myth of she-wolf and, 85–86
　as power, 136–37
　as pre-civil sovereignty, 95–97
　in state of nature, 86, 93–94
mothers. *See also* mother-right; women
　caretaking, power of, 58–59
　choice of childrearing over career, 246
　confederacy with children, 133, 136–37, 138, 197
　in definition of family, 126–27
　dominion over children, 29, 74, 127, 129, 131, 140, 225–26
　during gestational period, 233
　gratitude of children to, 136–37
　in *Leviathan*, 41
　as lords in state of nature, 24
　nursing, stereotypes of, 92, 136
　obligation of children to, 111
　power of, 58–59
　Rousseau on, 77

Native Americans
　concord of natural lust and, 29, 30, 33
　families of, 116
　references to, 94–95
　state of nature and, 30–31, 33–34, 116, 120
natural power, 53–54, 55–57
Newcastle, Duke of, 38
"No Means No" Supreme Court case in Canada, 249
North, Thomas, *The Lives of the Noble Grecians and Romaines, Compared Together*, 91
nursing mothers, stereotypes of, 92
Nyquist, Mary, 95

Oakeshott, Michael, 74
obligation. *See also* gratitude
　of child to mother, 111, 130, 136
　equality and, 51
　instrumental view of, 73
　of obedience to sovereign, 141
　political, after conquest, 242–44
　in prepolitical situation, 115
　right and, 41
　of servants, 133
　transfer of rights and, 242
　of women to men, 141
Observations on the Reflections of the Right Hon. Edmund Burke, on the Revolution in France (Macaulay), 183, 195, 203–4, 208
Okin, Susan Moller, 2, 35, 126, 190, 270
ontological stance of Hobbes, 226–27
Orbach, Susie, *Bodies*, 254
original contract
　covenant contrasted with, 27–28
　gender equality and, 19–20
　Hobbes as theorist of, 42
　as justification for institutions of state, 31
　parties to, 135
　practice of contracting and, 33–34

Rawlsian theory contrasted to, 31–32
subordination of women and, 49
Oxford University, classical rhetoric at, 21–22

Paglia, Camille, 250
Paoli, Signior, 207
parents. *See* fathers; mothers
Pateman, Carole
  anti-contractarian views of, 171, 185
  on Astell, 29
  critiques of Hobbes, 65, 71, 193, 270
  critiques of social contract theory, 170
  dialogue with Skinner on democratic theory, 7–8
  on equality in state of nature, 128
  on fraternal social contract, 170
  "'God Hath Ordained to Man a Helper,'" 6, 19, 27
  importance and influence of, 5–6
  on interpretation, 42–43
  on marriage contracts, 65, 84
  on men under women's power, 130
  "'Mere Auxiliaries to the Commonwealth,'" 2, 19, 20, 30
  on methodology, 22
  on mother-right, 134, 210
  The Problem of Political Obligation, 10, 19, 31, 43, 126
  revision of canon by, 190
  on Rousseau, 65
  Schochet and, 126
  "The Settler Contract," 30, 34
  The Sexual Contract, 2, 6, 19, 22, 42, 141
  social contract theory and, 6
  Springborg on, 174
  on subordination of women, 24–25, 48, 134,
  Wollstonecraft and, 37
  "Women and Consent," 249
Patriarcha (Filmer), 118, 192
paternity
  and acquisition, 195
  and Amazons, 197
  in *De Cive*, 110, 196
  difficulty of determining in state of nature, 113, 132
  as source of dominion, 112, 119, 131, 136
  and form of government, 107, 110
  in *Leviathan*, 111–12
  Macauly on, 196–99
  in state of nature, 110–11

Strauss on, 114
Warrender on, 112
patriarchal family. *See also* family; subordination of women in patriarchal family
  argument for, 138–40
  based on consent, 119–20
  as foundation of social contract, 117–18
  founding of, 109–11, 237 n. 28
  liberalism and, 63–66
  Schochet theory of, 130
  Strauss on, 114
  Warrender on, 112, 115
  women's desires in, 165
Patriarchalism in Political Thought (Skinner), 10
patriarchy/patriarchalism. *See also* patriarchal family
  brute force as basis of, 210–11
  choice feminism and, 250–51, 253
  consent under, 248
  Filmer and, 118, 192
  as foundation for state, 108–112, 118–20
  gender roles within, 246–48
  Hobbes as theorist of, 108–112, 118–120
  Macaulay challenge to, 190–91, 199–202, 208
  origin of paternal power, 196–99
  paradox of, 192–93, 201
  political, and familial power, 119–20
  in political philosophy, 108–10
  problem of, 126–34
  revisionist reading of, 94, 97–98
  in social contract theory, 172–73
  in state of nature, 192–93
peace
  as law of nature, 33–34, 49, 60, 140
  self-preservation and, 228
Peleus's daughters, myth of, 98
Perry, Ruth, 10, 173–74
Peters, Richard, 114, 116
Philosophical Letters (Cavendish), 155–56
philosophy, history of, gender analysis within, 34–37. *See also* canons of philosophy
Pizan, Christine de, 177
Plato and status of women, 4
Plutarch, *Life of Romulus*, 91, 93
political obligation after conquest, 242–44
political theory
  feminist approaches to, 7, 19–20, 23–25
  feminist promise embedded in, 220
  gender analysis within, 34–37

political theory (*continued*)
  historical approaches to, 7–8, 20–22
  of Hobbes, paradox of, 190
  key concepts of, 8–10
  of logic in reading, 23–24
  patriarchy in, 108–10
  women and, 37–38, 39
Pollaiuolo, Antonio, 92
population growth, 271–74
power
  from acquisition, 108–9, 113–15, 133–34
  of caretaking parent, 58–59
  constitution of self and, 254
  definition of, 53
  differences between sexes in, 53–58
  familial, and political patriarchalism, 119–20
  of fatherhood, 108–11, 114–15, 119–20, 195, 196–99
  feminization of, 86
  gendering of, 94
  lack of, and freedom, 157–58
  limited and absolute, 195
  lupinization and mechanization of, 96–97
  mother-right as, 136–37
  political, 108–9
  through fear, 159
predatory acts, justification for, 88–89
pregnancy. *See also* abortion
  death from, 232–33
  fetal personhood and, 221–22
  as volitional, 233–34
  women as active agents in, 234–35
The Problem of Political Obligation (Pateman), 10, 19, 31, 43, 126
pro-woman line, 247–48, 250
prudence, 54
public policy, Hobbesian basis for, 271–76
Pym, John, 199

queens, 28–29, 130
Quine, 23

Racial Contract, The (Mills), 6
rape
  of Lucretia, 90, 91
  sexual assault law and, 248–50
  view of, 135
rationalist approach to science, 66–67
rationality, Cavendish on, 156–57, 163
Rawls, John, social contract theory of, 31–32, 35, 48, 60

Reason and Rhetoric in the Philosophy of Hobbes (Skinner), 21
rebellion, right of, 81 nn. 76, 78, 231
Redstockings, 247–48
Regarding Method (Skinner), 20
relational autonomy, 160–63
relevance, 41–42
religion and constraints on women, 53
representation, 26–28, 37, 40
republicanism, 177, 182
republican myth of founding of Rome, 87, 90, 92, 98
republican principles, 91, 207–8
Rhode, Deborah, 249
rights. *See also* mother-right
  abortion, 219–20
  to body, in state of nature, 270–71
  Laws of Nature on, 49, 224
  of nature, 107, 270
  rebellion, 81 nn. 76, 78, 231
  self-defense and self-preservation, 74, 221–22, 228–29
  transfer of, and obligation, 242
  of women, 76–77
Robertson, G. C., 114, 116
Roiphe, Katie, 250
Rome
  behavior of people of, 88
  "A Discourse of Rome" (Hobbes), 93
  foundational myth of, 87, 90–92, 98
  Tarquins of, 90
  visit to Capitoline Hill in, 92
Rousseau, Jean-Jacques
  Macaulay on, 210
  on morality, 184
  Pateman on, 65
  on public and private realms, 173
  sexism of, 132
  on women, sexuality, and family, 4
  on women's rights, 77

Sabine, George, 119
Sapiro, Virginia, 10
scarcity, as cause of conflict, 69
Schochet, Gordon
  on abstract individualism, 132–33
  The Authoritarian Family and Political Attitudes in Seventeenth-Century England, 125, 143 n. 1, 192–93
  on authority over children, 127

on consent and coercion, 244
on consent of child, 196
on gratitude, 136
on hyperindividualism, 164
Pateman and, 126
on patriarchalism, 126–27, 172
on political power, 194
on rule by fathers, 134
theory of patriarchal family, 130
"Thomas Hobbes on the Family and the State of Nature," 125–26, 141
on women in state of nature, 135
on women's rights, 77
works of, 106
Second Wave feminism, 246, 250
security
　commonwealths and, 228–29, 231–32
　consequences of, 76
　freedom and, 165
　lack of, and conflict, 69, 70
　private property and, 116
self-defense/self-preservation
　abortion rights and, 221–22, 232–35
　Cavendish on, 161
　contract as a means to, 9
　liberty and, 229–31
　right of, 74, 228–29
　by warfare, 88, 92
　women equal to men in, 128, 134, 142, 144 n. 9
senators, role of in governing republics, 207–8
Seneca, 89
sensation, as foundation of experience, 223–24
Serious Proposal to the Ladies (Astell), 174
servants, women as, 95, 130–31, 133–34
The Settler Contract (Pateman), 30, 34
sexism
　blindness to, 126
　of Hobbes, 131–32
　stowaway, 49
sex-role socialization theory, 246–47
sexual assault law, 248–50
The Sexual Contract (Pateman), 2, 6, 10, 16 n. 4, 19, 22, 42, 141
sexual contracts, 4
sexuality, theory of
　based on appeals to common good, 277
　conventionalism, positivism, and, 270–71, 274–76
　covenants in, 268
　cultural relativism in, 265, 266
　overview of, 260–61
　as permissive, 266
　pillars of heteronormativity and, 266–67
　population growth and, 271–74
　self-preservation and, 267–68
　state of nature and, 261–66
　textual evidence for, 268–70
Shanley, Mary Lyndon (Molly), 10, 126
she-wolf. *See* wolf
Skinner, Quentin
　on actions and will, 253
　on coercion, 243
　dialogue with Pateman, 7–8
　on family, 29
　The Foundations of Modern Political Thought, 21
　on gender of sovereigns, 84
　historical interpretation and, 7–8, 20–22, 41–42
　Hobbes and Civil Science, 25–26
　Hobbes and Republican Liberty, 21
　"Hobbes on Representation," 37
　"Hobbes's *Leviathan*," 20
　on Hobbes's conception of liberty, 185
　importance and influence of, 5, 6–7
　on Hobbes's conception of the will, 243, 253
　on methodology, 20–21, 23
　on negative liberty theory, 157
　Patriarchalism in Political Thought, 10
　Reason and Rhetoric in the Philosophy of Hobbes, 21
　Regarding Method, 20
　on sovereignty, 125
　view of Hobbes of, 4
Slomp, Gabriella, 270
Smith, Hilda, 37, 39
social contract. *See also* consent; original contract
　civil War and, 70–71
　as creation of men, 96
　freedom and, 165
　legitimacy of, 208–10
　Macaulay on, 13, 210–11
　marriage as following from, 11, 137–38
　sexual contract as preceding, 11, 134
　subordination of women and, 49, 138–41
social contract theory. *See also* family; liberalism; marriage contracts
　account of origins of, 170

social contract theory (*continued*)
  account of power and, 53–58
  Astell on, 173–77
  critiques of, 71–73, 169–73, 185
  gender inequality and, 51–53
  gendered dimenions of, 5–6
  of Hobbes, 171–72
  Law of Nature and, 49
  of Locke, 60
  of Macaulay, 177–85
  need for sovereign and, 59–60
  outcome of conflict and, 58–59
  Pateman on, 6
  of Rawls, 31–32, 35, 48, 60
  terms of consent in, 78
socialization theory, 246–48
social relations and freedom, 161–62
sodomy laws, 275
Sophronia (Sarah Prince Gill), 184
sovereign
  gender of, 27–29, 83–86, 126, 129–30
  ordinances of, 52, 73, 138, 267
  public policy recommendations for, 271–76
  religious doctrine and, 53
  as representative of One Person, 26–28
  right to refuse order from, 81 nn. 76, 78, 230–31
  as soul of commonwealth, 28
  as wolf, 89
sovereignty. *See also* absolute sovereignty
  by acquisition, 127, 133, 141, 143, 242–44
  embodiment of, 97
  as female in state of nature, 93
  by institution, 113–15, 127, 133, 241–42
  Jones on, 65–66
  Macaulay on, 194–96, 199–202
  myth of she-wolf and, 85–86
  pre-civil, 95–97
  transformation to, 111–12
  types of, 113–14
Springborg, Patricia, 173, 174
state. *See also* commonwealth
  embodiment of, 85–86
  family and, 40, 90–91
  historical evolution of, 115–16
  as indivisible, 98
  as legitimate only if beneficial, 199
  personal share in, 204
state of nature. *See also* original contract; family
  as anthropology, 30, 31, 33, 115, 128
  brutish conditions of, 86–87, 106, 116, 138
  Cavendish on, 160–61
  children in, 113, 129, 132, 136–37
  civil society and, 87, 160–67
  contracts in, 129, 132–33, 137
  critiques of views of, 107–8
  description of life in, 106–7
  equality in, 24–25, 47–48, 51–53, 68–71, 128–29
  family in, 107–8, 116–19, 127–30, 139,141
  father right in, 110–11, 113
  gendered power in, 94
  gratitude in, 142–43
  as history, 23, 28, 30, 33, 108, 116
  interpretations of, 163–66
  as logical device, 23, 24,28, 30–33, 108, 114, 116, 120–21
  logic of conflict in, 59–60
  marriage in, 128–29, 132–33
  mother-right in, 86, 111, 113, 128–29, 132, 136, 139
  Native America as, 30–31, 33–34, 116, 120
  paternal power in, 110–11
  patriarchalism in, 192–93
  as pre-civil sovereignty, 95–97
  real compared to logical, 33
  sex in, 261–66
  women in, 128–30, 132, 134–37, 139–40, 269–70
Staves, Susan, 39
Stephen, Leslie, 114, 116
Stoljar, Natalie, 162
stowaway sexism, 49
Strauss, Leo, 70, 114, 116, 119, 120
subjects. *See* citizens/subjects
subordination of women. *See also* subordination of women in patriarchal family
  Astell on, 176–77
  in civil society, 9, 11, 19, 20, 24
  as conventional, 4, 6
  doctrine that might is right and, 181
  "just so" theory of, 55–57, 128
  Laws of Nature and, 51–53
  Macaulay on, 210–11
  overview of, 48, 49–51
  Pateman on, 24–25
  as political, 173
  relationships of power and, 53–58
  social contract and, 49
  in state of nature, 24, 28, 42, 65, 134
subordination of women in patriarchal family
  consent to social contract and, 138–41

problem of, 126–34
  role of gratitude in, 141–43
succession and gender, 131
Summers, Christina Hoff, 250

Tarquins of Rome, 90
Tenison, Thomas, 108, 110, 118
Thalestris, 263–64
Thomas, Keith, 40
"Thomas Hobbes on the Family and the State of Nature" (Schochet), 125–26, 141
Thomson, Judith Jarvis, "A Defense of Abortion," 221, 222, 232, 235
Tickner, Ann, *Gendering World Politics*, 66
transition from state of nature, 84
transitive dominance, 262
Treatise on the Immutability of Moral Truth (Macaulay), 179, 180, 183, 202
Tricaud, Francois, 70
Tuck, Richard, 2–3, 4
Turner, James, 265–66
Tweed, Aleina, 251

uncertainty and conflict, 69

vainglory, 70, 140, 144 n. 9
value, human, definition of, 57
Villiers, George, 205
Vindication of the Rights of Women (Wollstonecraft), 182–84
virtue, Wollstonecraft on, 182–83
voting by women, 40

war
  causes of, 69–71
  in service of self-preservation, 88, 92
Warrender, Howard, 112, 115, 116
Wentworth, Thomas, Duke of Strafford, 199, 205
White, John, 32
widows, 29–30, 40, 177
will
  actions as proceeding from, 243, 249, 253, 255

Cavendish on, 156, 157, 159, 161
coercion of, 244
Hobbes on, 155
wit, mastering others by, 54
Wittgenstein, 23
wolf
  in foundational myth of Rome, 90–92, 93
  mother-right and, 95–97
  references to, 85
  significance of, 87
  sovereign as, 89
  statue of, 92, 93, 94
Wolf, Naomi, 250
Wollstonecraft, Mary
  critical rejection of Hobbes by, 185
  Macaulay influence on, 170, 183–84
  Pateman and, 37
  as political theorist, 39
  Vindication of the Rights of Women, 182–84
women. *See also* mother-right; mothers; subordination of women in patriarchal family; widows
  in canons of philosophy, ix
  education of, 150–54, 166
  equality of, 42–43
  in families, 95, 130–31, 133–34, 165
  in formation of civil society, 95
  freedom of, 42–43, 157–58
  Hobbes relationships with, 37–40
  liberty of, 177
  male gaze, as internalized in, 254
  references to, 135
  religion and constraints on, 53
  in state of nature, 269–70
Wood, Summer, 245
Wright, Joanne
  on a sympathetic reading of Hobbes, 270, 278 n. 10
  concerning Hobbes's instrumental use of gender, 76–77, 138, 235
  on Hobbes as reconfiguring gender, 99, 226

Youths Glory (Cavendish), 150, 152